THE FRAMEWORK
OF THE
NEW TESTAMENT STORIES

The Framework
of the
New Testament Stories

by

ARNOLD EHRHARDT

*Bishop Fraser Senior Lecturer in
Ecclesiastical History in the
University of Manchester*

HARVARD UNIVERSITY PRESS
CAMBRIDGE, MASSACHUSETTS
1964

PRINTED IN GREAT BRITAIN

PREFACE

THE papers which are published here have all appeared in print before, either in English or in German, in various Journals or Festschriften. In collecting and presenting them in book form, I follow an urge which Norman H. Baynes once described as the conviction of every author that his work was reasonably good and might deserve a little more attention than it had received originally. Whilst confessing to this natural desire, I am well aware that it cannot by itself justify such an attempt at gaining a second hearing. Neither is it enough to offer a selection of essays to the public only because they are representative of one side of the author's research during the last twenty years. Such a reason would be sufficient only for the publication of the collected essays of one of the few men who are to be counted as leaders of thought in their field of research during such a period; but I cannot claim to belong to this select circle.

The publication of my contributions to New Testament research in the form of a book is due firstly to the fact that members of the New Testament seminar, which my friend and colleague Professor F. F. Bruce and I hold together for post-graduate students of the Faculty of Theology in the University of Manchester, have used one or other of these essays repeatedly as starting points in our debates. It appeared that they were apt to provoke the members to try to formulate their views on the questions raised, and to lead them to pursuing them even further in matters connected with the points raised in these essays. It is my hope that they may exhibit this quality of stimulating debate by promoting unfamiliar questions and offering new solutions to fellow theologians outside Manchester as well; and that they may show that these questions and solutions have not been proposed irresponsibly, but also that they are open to further clarification and correction. Many of them aim at giving a new view rather than a final one.

My book has one even more important purpose. Although we are living at a time when reprints have become fashionable, and tend to become even more so, I want to stress that the collection of these essays has a scope beyond the renewal of each single one. To explain this I have to mention the man by whom I was introduced to New Testament research, the late Karl Ludwig Schmidt. It was after the end of the first world war that the new method of *Formgeschichte* was promoted by three young and highly talented German theologians, Martin Dibelius, Rudolf Bultmann, and Karl Ludwig Schmidt. In the nineteen-twenties the method raised so many objections, and at the same time proved so fruitful, that the significant differences between these three scholars were frequently passed over and perhaps not even recognized by the great majority of opponents and followers. Such an attitude was encouraged and fortified in the time of the Third Reich so-called, when each of them courageously withstood its onslaught upon the Christian Church (although it is my conviction that the fate of Schmidt was the hardest to endure, being expelled from the country which he loved with an unsurpassed affection). For almost three years I was allowed to share in Bâle his grief and sorrow as his pupil and—I hope—friend; and it is my belief that his premature death was due in the first instance to his exile, although to outsiders his situation may have seemed quite tolerable.

It is my conviction that Schmidt's theological principles, which have attracted the attention of the present generation of theologians far less than they deserve, were different from those of either Bultmann or Dibelius. In particular his conception of historical truth was different. The result of his *formgeschichtliche* criticism would never lead him to the conclusion that any event recorded in the New Testament did or did not happen. He considered any such statement as totally irrelevant to the theological point of view. The New Testament, he would teach his students, was not written to inform Christians that in the year 4 B.C. a young Jewish woman, called Mary, conceived a baby without male cohabitation. The New Testament is not there to teach gynaecology, but theology. And his approach to the miracle stories of the Gospels and Acts was essentially the same. From this axiom he came to the conclusion that a distinction has to be made between the 'frame' and the 'scope' of every story in the Gospels. Unless the intention with which an action or a saying of Jesus is recorded in the Gospels is clearly established, i.e. unless it is clearly understood that such a report adds a distinctive feature to the Good News that Jesus Christ is Lord and Saviour, and why, no valid interpretation of any Gospel passage can be made; but when this scope of a report has been clearly understood, then the method of its presentation becomes important as well. For this 'form' of the report makes us aware of the human limitations of the Evangelist, and it also warns the reader of the fact that his own understanding is limited, so that he can grasp the eternal truth only when it is stated against its background or *Sitz im Leben*.

With regard to the interpretation of this framework of the Gospel stories, Karl Ludwig Schmidt, who was a brilliant classical scholar, gave preference to their Hellenistic component. Having known him personally for several years, I believe that he knew the Old Testament so well that he would take it for granted that his students too would see the Old Testament roots of the Gospel records—especially with the help of the references in the Nestle edition of the Greek New Testament—without much further ado; for he was always inclined to believe the best, and even more, of his students. He was, however, deeply impressed by the linguistic discoveries of the generation which had produced in particular the great Dictionary by Moulton and Milligan. Thus more often than not, after the theological exegesis, he would begin his form criticism with the words, 'let's look for the Greek'.

I consciously refrain from a detailed comparison between this method of form criticism and those employed by Martin Dibelius and Rudolf Bultmann. Let it suffice to state that Dibelius differed rather by the stresses which he put or omitted than by the substance of his New Testament theology, whereas it seems to me that a comparison between Bultmann and Karl Ludwig Schmidt would reveal considerable discrepancies in substance. What I wish to stress is the fact that the following essays were all written in conscious consideration of my obligation to Karl Ludwig Schmidt. In a time such as ours, a time of bewilderment about the necessity of axioms, and in particular theological axioms, it should be made known that an approach to the New Testament similar to his is still capable of producing questions—and answers too—which offer to re-arm the naked Achilles with arms to be found not on the road from the frame to the centre, but on that from the theological centre to the frame. To the memory of the teacher and friend by whose advice I have been guided in this direction, I gratefully dedicate these studies.

My essays first appeared in the following publications: 'The Gospels in the Muratorian Fragment', in *Ostkirchliche Studien*, ii, 2, July 1953; 'Jesus Christ and Alexander the Great', in the *Journal of Theological Studies*, vol. xlvi, no. 181-2, Jan.–April 1945; 'Greek Proverbs in the Gospel', and 'Christianity before the Apostles' Creed', in the *Harvard Theological Review*, vol. xlvi, no. 2, April 1953, and vol. lv, no. 2, April 1962, respectively; 'The Construction and Purpose of the Acts of the Apostles', 'The Birth of the Synagogue and R. Akiba', and, 'Creatio ex Nihilo', in *Studia Theologica*, vol. xii, 1, pp. 45–79 and 86–111, 1958, and vol. iv, 1, pp. 13–43, 1950; 'Jewish and Christian Ordination', in the *Journal of Ecclesiastical History*, vol. v, no. 2; and 'Christian Baptism and Roman Law', in the *Festschrift Guido Kisch*, W. Kohlhammer Verlag, Stuttgart, 1955. 'The Theology of New Testament Criticism' and 'Holy Sacrament and Suffering' first appeared in German in *Evangelische Theologie*, nos. 12, pp. 553–63, 1955, and 3/6, 99–114, 1947, respectively, and 'Social Problems in the Early Church' was published, also in German, in the *Festschrift* for *Erik Wolf*. I am indebted to the editors and publishers of all these publications for kind permission to gather together my essays in the present volume.

I wish to thank Mrs. J. M. Sutcliffe, Assistant Secretary, Manchester University Press, for incessant and kindly help in the production of this book, and Dr. Robert A. Kraft for making the index.

ARNOLD EHRHARDT

Manchester University
1963

CONTENTS

THE THEOLOGY OF NEW TESTAMENT CRITICISM

I

A CHAPTER in *The Ministry of the Word*, by R. E. C. Browne, raised serious doubts with regard to the sanity of Christian theologians who indulge in the apparently dangerous enterprise of New Testament criticism. It was maintained that a Christian minister occupying his spare time during the week with critical research in the New Testament and going into the pulpit on Sunday to preach a biblical sermon must be suffering from an advanced state of schizophrenia. As I feel that I belong to the comparatively small group of clergy who may claim the doubtful distinction of doing the very thing which caused Mr. Browne to digress into the field of psychiatry, I decided to apply such tests as were known to me in order to ascertain whether my mental balance was really deranged to such an extent that some sort of medical treatment might be advisable.

The result of this examination has been, on the whole, reassuring. It is true that certain New Testament critics might be described as slightly schizophrenic or, to use a somewhat more old-fashioned term, suffering from pangs of a bad conscience at the results of their critical enterprise. It is, after all, not uncommon for Christian theologians to feel that the simplicity—or, as St. Paul calls it, the foolishness—of God has no chance against the cleverness of worldly-wise critics, unless it is supported by the shrewdness of pious theologians who manage to proclaim probabilities—and even improbabilities—as certainties. The conviction that the Fourth Gospel was written by St. John, the son of Zebedee, or the Epistle to the Hebrews by St. Paul, will however do just as little for the advancement of the kingdom of Christ as will their opposite effect its detriment. A bad conscience is not a prerequisite for successfully engaging in New Testament criticism.

There is yet another type of New Testament critic, who seems to rejoice in discovering 'mistakes'. It is reported of J. Wellhausen, the famous German Old Testament scholar, that he once —as a joke—remarked that, of course, Jesus of Nazareth was by no means an accomplished specialist in the field of Old Testament research. I believe this statement to be quite correct; but I feel that the conclusions drawn on account of our better knowledge of Jewish archaeology, history, Hebrew grammar, etc., do not compel us to assume that we are also of necessity more clever than Jesus of Nazareth, or St. Paul for that matter, and to reject such passages in the Gospels and Epistles as appear to contradict our more enlightened insight into the subject as untrue. Undoubtedly, certain New Testament critics seem to incline towards this megalomaniac approach to the New Testament, which maintains that what is clever is also true; but it has to be stated once and for all that the rejection of biblical passages by modern theologians is more frequently based upon sentimental and so-called ethical considerations than upon critical ones. It is the sentimentalist who takes exception to St. Paul's question, 1.Cor.9:9, 'is it for the oxen that God careth?'; and it is the moralistic teetotaller who maintains that Jesus made a mistake when, at the marriage feast at Cana, He changed water into wine. Megalomania, although it is undoubtedly found also among New Testament critics, does not, therefore, qualify as the professional disease of New Testament critics.

Paranoia—delusions, fixed ideas, occasional depressiveness—is yet another mental derangement which is frequent amongst scholars of all descriptions, and may claim a number of victims also in the field of New Testament criticism. It is well known, for instance, that M. R. James was not only a high authority on spook stories, but may at times even have inclined to the belief that he was in touch with supramundane beings. Such an attitude may be due to paranoiac delusions; but one would hesitate to ascribe his research in the field of New Testament apocryphal literature to any such disposition—or indisposition. Finally the description by Aldous Huxley of the effects of an intoxication with mescalin, does not suggest that New Testament critics have drawn very heavily on that particular source of inspiration.

To put the point I want to make more seriously: the psychological approach is useless for the discussion of the reason why research in a certain field is being made, however much light it may shed on the method by which such research is being made. That is correct in all cases of research, unless, of course, we deny the possibility that any truth can be stated about the subject under investigation. The reason why research is being carried out in any field, as for example in the field of New Testament criticism, is precisely that there is a question of truth and untruth involved. It does not help to denounce the work of scholars in this particular field as the ravings of lunatics, for in so doing we only reveal that we are not aware of the difference in quality between the true quest for truth and the hallucinations of madmen. I know full well that the delimitations between the one and the other are fluid; but they exist nevertheless, and it is futile to disregard them.

II

The problem with which every scholar is faced is therefore that of Pontius Pilate: 'what is truth?' and the special problem of the New Testament critic is that he in particular is called upon to find out the truth about Truth. What we are meant to understand here is this: Jesus Himself has said in John 17:17, the High Priestly prayer, 'sanctify them in the truth, thy word is truth'—or, as the New Testament critic would say: thy word is the truth, i.e. only thy word is truth. The Fourth Gospel, as you will know, is the Gospel in which the word ἀλήθεια, truth, plays a more prominent part than in any other Gospel. Together with 1.John and the two other Johannine Epistles it contains almost one half of all the occurences of ἀλήθεια in the New Testament, 42 out of 89, and therefore appears to set an especial store by the conception of truth. (Dare I add in parenthesis that the Revelation, by contrast, nowhere uses ἀλήθεια and thus appears to be far distant from the theological view of the other Johannine writings!)

Thus we hold that God's Word is the Truth, and by God's Word we understand three things, the incarnate Logos of God, Jesus Christ; the written record of the incarnation of God's Logos, the Bible; and finally the proclamation of His incarnation in the Divine Service of the Word and Sacrament by the Church. By criticising the text and content of the New Testament we therefore examine the Truth. For we do not believe that the Bible is only 'in a sense' the Word of God. We are deeply suspicious of such a qualified approach which, as we have reason to believe, is in most cases not the approach of misguided criticism, but an entirely uncritical one, and in any case is contrary to the express confession of the Church of England, art.vi, 'all the books of the New Testament, as they are commonly received, we do receive, and account them canonical'.

If, therefore, we state unreservedly that the New Testament is the Word of God, we have to align our conception of the Bible as the Word of God to the two other forms of the Word of God which are known to us, Jesus Christ, and the Word proclaimed in Divine Service. I have criticized the way in which critical research in the New Testament and preaching a biblical sermon were connected by means of a psychiatric examination in Mr. Browne's book, but I wish to state emphatically that a constant connection between the critical study of the Word and the preaching of the Word has to be established and maintained. It would be unscholarly to neglect the fact that the subject of research in New Testament criticism is at the same time the driving power in the Church, the greatest religious organization the world has ever seen. The truth can only be ascertained by taking all facts into account, and the tremendous spiritual power of the New Testament is one of the most important facts in the task of New Testament criticism. We would not be critically sound if we proceeded to treat the New Testament in the way in which magistrates' courts have of recent years treated the obscene literature of today.

As a matter of fact, New Testament criticism has always been keenly aware of the special character of its subject. So far as I can see, modern criticism in the New Testament has three distinctive roots. The first, which is particularly strong in Roman Catholicism, but is very often overlooked by non-Roman scholars, is the attempt to establish the authority of Church tradition over the New Testament. By proving how the New Testament canon was established in the course of the history of the Church, by the Church and for the Church, it is thought that the mastery of the Church even over the written Word of God can be established. This is a legitimate approach only when it is fully realized that the Church is the body of Christ, inspired by His Holy Spirit, taking part in His incarnation—and even here the matter of confusing the persons of the Trinity causes some hesitation; but it becomes a dangerous fallacy when it is used for the establishment of the infallibility of Councils and Popes. The second root is that of reason seeking faith. The marvellous blasphemy of *credo quia absurdum* is constantly challenged by reason testing our faith. This reasonable approach is sound when it starts from the fact that human cognition cannot grasp anything non-human. When St. Paul was 'caught up even to the third heaven', he 'heard unspeakable words which it is not lawful for a man to utter', 2.Cor.12:2,4. That means to say that the language of heaven is not for earthly man; our eyes cannot perceive God as He is. God's revelation to man had to take place by His being 'made in the likeness of men', Phil.2:7. The primitive theologian who discusses the incarnation of the Logos will insist upon the physiology of His body whereby conclusions are reached which, for example, in the discussions on the virginity of blessed Mary or the state of digestion of ordinary food at the fasting reception of the Sacrament, may become simply nauseating. The critical theologian will know that 'flesh' (Heb. *basār*) means the entirety of earthly life, and will find in the discovery of facts about biblical origins and tradition characteristic features of the incarnation of God's Word. The third root of New Testament criticism is that of honest, though often bitter, radical criticism of the truth of Jesus' assertion that He was the incarnate Word of God, an assertion so staggering that, if it were made to us by any of our contemporaries, it would be met by our derision. Men like Alfred Loisy in France and Bruno Bauer in Germany set out to detect and convict the age-old fraud which Voltaire had denounced already by his famous *écrasez l'infâme*.

This last approach is the one which rightly gets most of the limelight, for it is the only one which really tests the truth of Truth. The approach from the ground of the validity of Church tradition is, after all, no more than a pastime game, a race in which the horses are so handicapped that the favourite must win. The rationalist's approach is always ready to admit that reason after all is not the chief thing in religion, that emotion and contemplation, ethical resolve and patient suffering, are of much higher value in the sight of God—completely forgetting, of course, that it is the critic's business and duty before God to use his reason, however inadequate it may be, and not to indulge in pipe-dreams. Only the radical critic is in reality qualified to claim with the Psalmist 'the zeal of thy house has eaten me up', Ps.69:9; John 2:17.

III

What then is the position, theologically, of the New Testament critic? It is the position in which, according to our faith, all humanity finds itself at all times when it is faced with the cross of Christ. The New Testament critic takes his stand amongst the accusers of the incarnate Word of God. First of all, we criticize, i.e. call into judgment, the written Word of God with regard to its outward appearance. Referring back to Wellhausen's remark that Jesus of Nazareth was far from being an accomplished Old Testament scholar, we may translate this into biblical language by quoting John 8:57, 'Thou art not yet fifty years old, and hast thou seen Abraham?' This verse denotes exactly the position of the biblical critic who confronts his results about Old Testament conditions with the ideas expressed about them in the New Testament. It appears to us as an instructive quotation when we attempt to define the place taken by the New Testament critic. It is the place of the—not necessarily Jewish—scholar of all ages, who is faced with the claim of one particular historical person, this Jesus of Nazareth, to be the living Word of God, to be the revelation of infinite, eternal Truth.

The scholar—the real scholar—is of necessity a specialist, and the truth at which he can aim is of necessity a special truth, the truth about some special subject. Yet, if he is convinced that he aims at recognizing the truth, though it be only the truth about some special subject, he must assume that this special truth cannot be contradictory to universal Truth; otherwise either his results would be erroneous, or the assumed universal truth would be disproved. It is from considerations like this that the New Testament critic finds it so utterly unbelievable that people—and in particular ill-instructed theologians—should constantly accuse him of being at least un-Christian, if not anti-Christian. All that the New Testament critic attempts to do is to follow out the advice given by the Psalmist, 'and in thy light shall we see light', Ps.36:9. 'Thy light', that is the universal Truth of Him who has said 'I am the way and the truth and the light', John 14:6, and the light we shall see is the special truth about the one particular point which the New Testament scholar examines. He is fully aware that in each case such an examination is an experiment fraught with deadly danger, for if at any time his result would be that there are parts of the New Testament which are not true, the critic would have to say that they at least are not the Word of God, and he would realize that in view of the close connection which exists between all the various parts of the New Testament the whole edifice may come down and bury him, a conclusion which seems to be unknown to the uncritical theologian who joyfully rejects parts of the Bible because of their insufficient religious standard, as for example Ps.137, or the second half of the Venite, however important it may be for the understanding of the Epistle to the Hebrews.

What the New Testament critic is faced with, therefore, is first of all the incredibility of many of the New Testament reports. The average Christian seems to be calmly unconcerned about the disturbing discovery of D. F. Strauss that so many of Christ's miracles seem to be no more than repetitions of Old Testament miracles, as for example the raising of Jairus' daughter, Mark 5:22f., which is modelled upon the raising of the son of the Shunnamite by Elisha, 2.Kings 4:18f., and incidentally upon well-known magical practices of the Near East. Christian theologians coolly accept the innumerable parallels between New Testament and Talmudic sayings, which have been uncovered in Billerbeck's monumental work, without discussing their bearing upon the truthfulness of the New Testament reports. Most disturbing is the fact that the probably no less extensive borrowings of the New Testament from Hellenistic proverbial lore, to which, among others, I have recently drawn the attention of theological scholars, are just as coolly received. They ought to have been remembered and discussed all along, since Wettstein's great collection of Greek parallels to the New Testament has been available to those who can read Greek for more than 200 years. They prove that heathen material is incorporated in the Word of God and cry out for a theological explanation of such an unexpected feature in the chief document of our faith. If Christian theologians refuse to comment on these facts, others will do so, and have done so. Finally, if a survey were made of the extremely numerous variants in modern editions of the New Testament, as Souter or Nestle, it might prove, perhaps, that the ones which actually change the meaning of our accepted, 'authorized' version of the New Testament are less negligible than is generally assumed. Especially the cavalier treatment which is accorded to the use of the Greek particles has less to commend it than overworked chaplains, attempting in vain to wade through that wealth of evidence afforded by these—and still more so by larger editions, like Clarke's Acts—with their somewhat unwilling candidates for ordination, would be ready to admit. As a general statement, the New Testament critic would be inclined to answer the question of the Pharisees, John 9:40, put in a recent book, 'are we then also blind', in the affirmative, when the overall reaction of Christian ministers to the theological problem of New Testament criticism is contemplated.

IV

So far we have outlined the dangers which arise out of the situation that the clergy in general just fail to take notice of the true facts which New Testament criticism has uncovered. We will ask finally, what profit there may be gained by critical research in the New Testament for the Church of Christ. We would maintain that the critical research in the New Testament is indeed no less than a form of Christian worship, and in particular a form of fulfilling the Bishop's bidding at the Ordination Service (which now apparently is to be repeated in Synod by the Dean of the Cathedral, for what reason we know not):

Consider how studious you ought to be in reading and learning the Scriptures, and in framing the manners both of yourselves and of them that specially pertain unto you according to the rule of the same Scriptures: and for this self-same cause, how you ought to forsake and set aside (as much as you may) all worldly cares and studies.

This passage seems to enjoin biblical criticism to every priest as his foremost duty, for how else can we 'read and learn' the Scriptures? The mind of man in the modern world—and despite all evidence to the contrary we still regard priests of the Church as men in the modern world—is trained, for good or for ill, in critical reasoning, and the parrot-like repetition of the office-book at Matins and Evensong every day is a caricature of that 'reading and learning' of the Scriptures that is expected of us. Mystical contemplation of the sacred texts, on the other hand, sets at nought the principle of the incarnation, inasmuch as it puts these texts outside the context of time and makes them timeless. It thus dehumanizes the New Testament and makes it inhuman. Ordinary, reasonable folk will find it hard to follow us to the regions of mystical theology, whereas those who are prepared to do so, theosophists and the like, will soon find that the mystic wisdom of the East, the Hermetic literature and Neo-Platonism, the Ghinza, the Bundahish, the Bhuddist literature, the Bhagavat-Ghita, etc., satisfy their demands much better than the New Testament. For they were written with the express claim—a claim which is as false as it is sincere—to be timeless. The New Testament, however, claims no more than to contain historical, Apostolic documents.

It is from this correct appreciation of the theological import-ance of New Testament criticism that the modern demand for demythologizing has started, a demand that theologians should face and discuss the facts—in so far as they are facts—with regard to the New Testament. This demythologizing is by no means a purely German sport, but was put clearly to all who were willing to hear by the late Dr. Barnes of Birmingham. It may be true to say that his *History of the Early Church* does not come up to very high standards of critical scholarship; but that does not do away with the fact that he has clearly put the correct questions, especially: 'What do we mean when we say the virgin birth and the resurrection of Jesus Christ are true? in what sense —if any—do we recite the Apostles' Creed every day? How can we align its statements to that type of truth that first predicts the fact that the atom contains energy, and then goes on to prove it by killing 100,000 Japanese at Hiroshima and Nagasaki?' This last question in particular has its equivalent already in the Fourth Gospel, 'what then doest thou for a sign, that we may see, and believe thee? What workest thou?' John 6:30.

Do not expect me to give an answer to these questions. I am only outlining an attempt at analysing the theological position of New Testament criticism, and criticism is no more than the negative approach to Holy Scripture which, however, is a necessary prerequisite to its preaching. Without it you will never be able to give an honest answer to the one question which is involved in all political and economic discussions about security, the question how Jesus Christ, the God of life, can truthfully claim to be the Truth in a world of death and destruction.

THE GOSPELS IN THE MURATORIAN FRAGMENT

I

THE document which we call the Muratorian Fragment is an annotated list of the canonical books of the New Testament, i.e. of such books as were deemed worthy, according to certain standards, to be used in Church Services. The only manuscript is written in a barbarous Latin by a monk of the Irish monastery at Bobbio in Northern Italy. The original was probably written in Latin, not in Greek, though in a better style.[1] This means that the Muratorian Fragment is of western origin. It can also be stated that it is of an early date. It treats the Apocalypse of Peter as a canonical book, and we can say for certain that such a view was no longer tenable after about A.D. 240. As to the *terminus a quo* we have, on the one hand, to consider the character of the document, and on the other the positions both of the Church universal and of that of its origin as reflected in the Muratorian Fragment. Regarding the latter it is generally assumed that the Muratorian Fragment was produced at Rome, and in its analysis I shall show reasons to substantiate this view. If my analysis is correct, the Muratorian Fragment will appear as a product of the Catholic Church at Rome, probably under Pope Zephyrinus (A.D. 197–217), the successor of Victor I. Regarding the first it will appear

---

[1] Attempts at proving a Greek original were made by Th. Zahn, *Geschichte des Kanons*, 1890, part II, vol.1, p.1f., and in particular by J. B. Lightfoot, *Clement of Rome*, 2nd ed., p.405f. Lightfoot's attempt was countered by H. Achelis, *Nachrichten der Gesellschaft der Wissenschaften*, 1890, p.272f., who has shown that the reading of the inscription on Hippolytus' statue, upon which Lightfoot's theory rests, is inadmissible. A. Harnack, *Geschichte der altchristlichen Literatur*, vol.1, p.647, and especially *Z.N.W.*, 24, 1925, p.1f., has given good reasons why the original of the Muratorian document should have been Latin.

as a milestone on the way to the formation of the canon of the New Testament marking the occasion when the four Gospel canon was established in the Church at Rome.

When dealing with the Muratorian Fragment the barbarisms, in so far as they do not interfere with the meaning of the document, will be quietly corrected. The mutilated beginning of the Fragment, however, needs closer attention. In its present state it begins with a defective sentence:

1. quibus tamen interfuit et ita posuit.

This line undoubtedly refers to our Second Gospel, and in particular to its author, St. Mark. For we find in the next line that the Gospel according to St. Luke is called the Third Gospel, and shortly afterwards the Gospel according to St. John the Fourth. There have been changes in the sequence of the four Gospels. The Gospel according to St. John has taken in several instances the second place, and even the first; but never was the first place claimed by the Gospel according to St. Mark, and most frequently by the Gospel according to St. Matthew.[1] Thus the words 'quibus tamen interfuit et ita posuit' refer to St. Mark. What is their meaning? The dominant view, introduced by Th. Zahn,[2] suggests the reading 'ali-/quibus', assuming that St. Mark had been present at some events of Jesus' earthly ministry and faithfully recorded them. This I find hard to believe. There is no reputable tradition that St. Mark had been a personal disciple of Jesus. In fact, the fairly frequent change of the position of the Gospel according to St. John was due to our Second and Third Gospels not being Apostolic in the strict sense. The words, however, recall strongly a remark of Papias of Hierapolis about St. Mark,[3] which I shall place beside them:

'Quibus tamen interfuit et ita posuit' ὅσα ἐμνημόνευσεν ἀκριβῶς ἔγραψεν. 'Quibus interfuit' and ὅσα ἐμνημόνευσεν seem to express the same idea, and so do 'et ita posuit' and ἀκριβῶς

---

[1] Cf. E. Nestle, *Einführung in das Griechische Neue Testament*, 4th ed. E. v. Dobschütz, 1923, p.9f.

[2] Cf. Harnack, *Z.N.W.*, 24, 1925, p.9, n.3.

[3] Eusebius, *H. E.*, book III, ch.39, §15.

ἔγραψεν, for it has always been assumed that 'posuit' in this context means 'he put in writing'. The construction of the sentence too is identical, and thus the conclusion is at hand that we have here a trace of the use of Papias' work.[1]

This impression is strengthened when we analyse the remark about St. Luke which follows shortly afterwards, ll.6–7, 'Dominum tamen nec ipse vidit in carne'. It seems that 'nec ipse' demands the translation 'he too' did not see the Lord in the flesh. This implies that another Evangelist did not see the Lord, and this could only be St. Mark, of whom Papias in the same context had explicitly stated οὔτε γὰρ ἤκουσε τοῦ κυρίου, οὔτε παρηκολούθησεν αὐτῷ. Therefore we have sufficient evidence to assume that Papias was responsible for the fragmentary remark about St. Mark in the Muratorian Fragment. Whether he was also responsible for that about St. Luke is a moot question. G. Salmon has boldly stated that Papias even based his chronology of Jesus' life upon the Third Gospel,[2] but this is highly improbable in view of its Marcionite contamination. In any case, there is nothing to suggest that the comment on the Third Gospel in the Muratorian Fragment was his. There is, however, sufficient reason to assume that Papias was the source for the remark on the Second Gospel, and it will also appear that one of the comments on the Fourth Gospel in the Fragment is, at least in part, under obligation to him. This does not, of course, constitute an argument in favour of an eastern origin of the Muratorian Fragment, but it raises the question whether there were any special reasons for the Church at Rome to use this source of information. There is no doubt that it was information at first hand. The Roman Church had an easy access to the work of Papias through Irenaeus of Lyons, for the fact that he was acquainted with Papias is beyond question. Not only is it stated by Eusebius[3] that Irenaeus was under obligation to Papias for his theory about the millennium, but Irenaeus even

---

[1] The same source was used by Victorinus of Pöttau, *Commentary in Revelation* 4, ed. W. Haussleiter, 1916, p.50, l.19f. 'Marcus interpres Petri ea quae in munere docebat (scil. Petrus) commemoratus conscripsit, sed non ordine', cf. Harnack, op. cit., p.9.

[2] G. Salmon in Murray, *Dict. of Chr. Biography*, 1912, p.801b.

[3] Euseb., *H.E.*, III.39.13.

quoted Papias by name in his *magnum opus*.[1] This was rather exceptional for Irenaeus who commonly referred to his authorities as 'the Elder' or in the plural 'the Elders', and goes to show that Papias' book was in his hands and he did not just quote from memory.

Irenaeus' influence upon the Muratorian Fragment scarcely extended beyond a commendation of Papias. His own views as to the necessity of a four-Gospel canon,[2] based upon the allegorical interpretation of the four living creatures, Rev. 4:6f., was not taken up in the Muratorian document. However, there seems to be one unmistakable trace of his influence in the paragraph which contains the first justification of the canonization of the Fourth Gospel. I shall analyse this passage in detail later on, and therefore limit my reference here to the words which are needed for my argument: l.9f., 'Quarti Evangeliorum: Johannes ex discipulis . . dixit . . . eadem nocte revelatum Andreae ex Apostolis.' We find here an obvious difference between the description of St. John as 'Johannes ex discipulis' on the one hand, and of St. Andrew as 'ex Apostolis' on the other, and this difference seems to be intentional. St. John is represented as a disciple, but not an Apostle, i.e. one of the Twelve. This ties up with the fact that Irenaeus nowhere calls St. John the Evangelist the son of Zebedee and brother of St. James, but invariably Ἰωάννης ὁ τοῦ κυρίου μαθητής.[3] This, it seems, was an established formula. If it is admitted that it does not prevent the identification of St. John the son of Zebedee and brother of St. James with St. John the Evangelist, it does not demand it either; and it seems likely that Irenaeus would have avoided the ambiguity if his information had allowed him to do so. For we find him hard pressed by his adversaries who claimed that the Fourth Gospel was spurious.[4] If his evidence had permitted him to do so, he could have countered their false assertions

---

[1] Irenaeus, *Adv. Haer.*, V.33.3 (ed. Harvey, vol.2, p.417).

[2] Ibid., III.11.8 (Harvey, vol.2, p.46f.). Victorinus, op. cit. (Haussleiter, p.5of.) has combined Irenaeus' and Papias' theories.

[3] Ibid., II.22.5; III.3.4; III.11.1 and 3 (Harvey, vol.1, p.331; vol.2, pp.13, 40, 43).

[4] Ibid., III.11.9 (Harvey, vol.2, p.51) alii vero ut donum Spiritus frustrentur, quod in novissimis temporibus secundum placitum Patris effusum est in

easily by naming John of Zebedee as the author of the Fourth Gospel. The same reserve is used in the Muratorian Fragment when it excludes St. John the Evangelist from membership in the council of the Twelve. Papias, however, had more elaborate information: He duplicated the figure of St. John. He too referred to 'Johannes discipulus Domini' as his own teacher,[1] but he also mentioned St. John the son of Zebedee as a member of the Twelve,[2] and it appears from a reference in Jerome that he ventured to ascribe the Fourth Gospel and 1.John to the son of Zebedee, a view which was taken up in Egypt—apparently on the authority of Origen—by Dionysius of Alexandria.[3]

It appears that Irenaeus' information came from a gnostic source. He himself quotes Ptolemaeus, the gnostic, the head of the eastern branch of the school of Valentinus, as describing the author of the Fourth Gospel as Ἰωάννης ὁ μαθητὴς τοῦ κυρίου.[4] This was a verbatim quotation, and since Irenaeus himself made use of the same description of St. John the Evangelist only two lines earlier, i.e. with Ptolemaeus' book open on his desk, it is safe to conclude that leading Catholics and heretics in Asia were united in the assumption that the author of the Fourth Gospel had been 'the disciple'—the beloved disciple: the article being used emphatically—but not a member of the Twelve.[5] It must have been a man of exceptional authority who succeeded in imposing this view upon the Church at Rome; but the influence of Irenaeus

---

humanum genus, illam speciem non admittunt quae est secundum Johannis evangelium, in qua Paracletum se missurum Dominus promisit: sed simul et evangelium et propheticum repellunt Spiritum. Infelices vere qui pseudoprophetae quidem esse volunt, prophetiae veri gratiam repellunt ab ecclesia: similia patientes his qui, propter eos qui in hypocrisi veniunt, etiam a fratrum communicatione se abstinent.

[1] In Iren., *Adv. Haer.*, V.33.3f.   [2] In Euseb., III.39.4.

[3] Jerome, *De Vir. Illustr.*, ch.18; Origen, *Comm. Joh.*, I:6 (Migne Gr., vol.14, pp.29–32); Dionys. in Euseb., *H.E.*, VII.25.7. Right to the end of the fourth century this point had to be stressed, cf. Greg. Naz., *Ad Seleucum*, vv.289ff. (Migne Gr., vol.37, p.1536).

[4] Iren., *Adv. Haer.*, I.8.5 (Harvey, vol.1, p.75).

[5] It is perhaps useful to remind readers that the Fourth Gospel, in contrast to the Synoptists, does not limit Jesus' *haburah* at the last Supper to the Twelve, nor does it use 'Apostle' for the disciples.

upon the Roman Church was indeed unparalleled. Thus, in spite of such eastern features, in spite of such sponsors as Papias and Ptolemaeus, the probability that the Muratorian Fragment is Roman remains unshaken, thanks to the mediation of the great bishop of Lyons. In the next section it will appear that there are certain aspects of the Muratorian Fragment which can only be satisfactorily explained by the assumption of a Roman origin.[1]

II

Two arguments are mainly given for the Latin and Roman origin of the Muratorian Fragment, the one that the play on words in l.67, 'fel enim cum melle misceri non congruit', is only possible in Latin, the other that the date in l.75, 'sedente in cathedra urbis Romae . . . Pio episcopo', patently refers to the Roman Church.[1] These reasons are good, but not too good. The first is a Latin proverb which may easily have slipped into a translation,[2] the second may be in favour of a western origin, but Irenaeus, for instance, used this very method of dating Valentinus' stay at Rome, and Eusebius in his Ecclesiastical History copied it from him.[3] Our knowledge of the Roman Church at the end of the second century is almost limited to its Greek speaking and writing members. Of its Latin majority there remains, apart from a few inscriptions and the Octavius by Minucius Felix, which offers no help to us, only the Muratorian Fragment. We are, therefore, fortunate to find a remark pointing to Roman secular life which, in this form, could not have been made anywhere but at Rome. We find this typically Roman remark in the account of the Muratorian Fragment about the Third Gospel:

> 2. Tertio Evangelii librum secundum Lucam.
> 3. Lucas iste medicus post ascensum Christi
> 4. cum eum Paulus quasi ut iuris studiosum

[1] Joh. Leipoldt, *Gesch. d. N. T. Kanons*, 1907, vol.1, p.35n.
[2] Cf. e.g. Plaut., *Cist.*, I.1.71 'amor et melle et felle fecundissimus'; Auson., *Epigr.*, 15 'qui melle carmen atque felle temperans'. On the possible Greek equivalent, cf. Harnack, *Z.N.W.*, 24, 1925, 6f.
[3] Iren., *Adv. Haer.*, III.4.2 (Harvey, vol.2, p.17); Euseb., *H.E.*, IV.11.1-2.

5. secum adsumsisset, nomine suo
6. ex opinione (sc. Pauli) conscripsit.

The author of the Muratorian document was aware of the fact that St. Luke was the 'beloved physician', so it calls for an explanation that St. Paul had taken him 'quasi ut iuris studiosum', as a student of law. One might suggest that St. Paul, the trained Rabbi, took St. Luke, the Hellenist, to be trained in the Jewish Law, the Torah, but I am not aware of any instance where Latin writers described students of the Torah as 'iuris studiosi'. 'Iuris studiosus' is rather a technical expression for a student of Roman law.[1] It would, therefore, be possible to understand the phrase 'cum eum Paulus quasi ut iuris studiosum secum adsumsisset' in the sense that St. Luke was articled to St. Paul. For the 'institutio' of law-students with a famous lawyer at Rome was similar to our articles, which a student of law takes with some solicitor.[2] However, it is not certain whether this 'institutio' was still practised at the end of the second century A.D., and the words 'nomine suo ex opinione conscripsit' demand a different explanation.[3]

The description of 'iuris studiosus' does not only apply to somebody who is being trained in the law, but also to a legal expert who acts on behalf of a Roman official, provincial governor and the like. Most instructive is the following passage:

[*Dig. Just.* 1.22.1] Paul. sing. assess. Omne officium adsessoris, quo iuris studiosi partibus suis funguntur in his fere constat: in cognitionibus, postulationibus, libellis, edictis, decretis, epistulis.

Such an 'adsessor' or 'iuris studiosus' issued an 'edictum, decretum' or 'epistula' either in the name of the Roman official to whom he was attached, or else 'suo nomine ex opinione' of his superior. The appointment of such a member of his staff by a Roman official was technically described as 'in consilium adsumere',[4] and we thus

---

[1] Cf. *Dig. Just.*, 1.22.1; 48.19.9 §4; 50.13.4.

[2] Cf. *Dig. Just.*, 1.2.2 §§43;47, and J. P. Bremer, *Die Rechtslehrer und Rechtsschulen im Röm. Kaiserreich*, 1867, p.7f.

[3] For the following remarks I am under obligation to the advice of my friend, Professor W. Kunkel, Munich.

[4] *Dig. Just.*, 27.1.30 pr. *Papinian V. resp.*

find here a description of St. Luke's ministry in the technical language of Roman Law. It is most unlikely that such a description should have sprung from anywhere but Rome. The paradox that St. Paul should have attached his 'beloved physician' to himself 'quasi ut iuris studiosum' is only made tolerable by the consideration that the author of the Muratorian Fragment intended to explain in this way that the Third Gospel derived its 'Apostolic' authority 'ex opinione' of the Apostle St. Paul; but the way in which he expressed this idea is exclusively Roman.

Thus we may confidently state that the actual compilation of the Muratorian document took place at Rome. This being so, its author was in a position to draw on numerous sources of information. Irenaeus was one of his authorities, and probably directed his attention to Ptolemaeus, the gnostic, with regard to the author of the Fourth Gospel. Papias was the source of information regarding St. Mark and also, as we shall see, of part of that about St. John. Where the information about the Third Gospel came from I cannot say; but if it should be the same as that about the Acts, ll.38–9, 'sed et profectionem Pauli ab urbe ad Spaniam proficiscentis', clearly points to the 'Vercelli Acts', the apocryphal Acts of Peter.[1]

III

There are two remarks about the Fourth Gospel in the Muratorian Fragment, each being longer than that concerning the Third Gospel. The reason for this duplication is commonly and rightly found in the opposition of the so-called *Alogi*, who objected to the Fourth Gospel in no uncertain terms, ascribing it to Cerinthus,[2] one of the earliest leaders of gnosticism and reputed to be a pupil of Simon Magus. A. Harnack[3] has taken exception to this view, and although he did not find many followers,[4] the

[1] Acts of Peter, chapters 1–3, M. R. James, *Apocryphal N. T.*, 1926, p.304f.
[2] Leipoldt, op. cit., vol.1, p.147.
[3] Harnack, *Das N. T. um das Jahr 200*, 1889, p.68n.**
[4] Leipoldt, op. cit, p.152, seems his most noteworthy adherent, although his thesis that the Fragmentist duplicated the justification for sheer joy seems singularly feeble.

reasons for my disagreement with him will be set out in detail later. Here I shall concentrate upon the first justification given in the Muratorian Fragment for the canonization of the Fourth Gospel. It is the legend of the three days' fast, part of which has been touched upon already:

9. Quarti evangeliorum: Johannes ex discipulis
10. cohortantibus condiscipulis et episcopis suis
11. dixit, Conieiunate mihi hodie triduo et quid
12. cuique fuerit revelatum alterutrum
13. nobis enarremus. eadem nocte reve-
14. latum Andreae ex Apostolis ut recognos-
15. centibus cunctis Johannes suo nomine
16. cuncta describeret.

I have already stated that the description of St. John as 'ex discipulis' betrays its origin from Irenaeus and his gnostic adversary Ptolemaeus. However, this does not affect the subject matter of the story. Although the Muratorian Fragment is the only source which records this legend in detail, there are traces which show that it was widely circulated, and which point unmistakably to its origin. Our first task is to show that it was not the author of the Muratorian document who gave the legend its literary form. As to the rise of such a story, we can state that the method of forcing a vision by means of a fast was common enough in those days. We may refer to the Apocalypse of Ezra 1:5, 'then I fasted two times sixty weeks; and then I saw the mysteries of God'.[1] This is a Jewish analogy, and we may gather from one of the Montanist writings of Tertullian[2] that similar analogies existed in the rites of Isis and of the *Magna Mater*. Thus the legend could have arisen anywhere; but in the Muratorian Fragment it is clearly defective and therefore not original. St. John, so we are told, demanded a three days' fast; but the decisive vision was seen by St. Andrew already in the first night, i.e. right at the beginning of the fast. No further vision is recorded, neither are we told

[1] C. Tischendorf, *Apocalypses Apocryphae*, 1866, p.24, cf. P. Rießler, *Altjüd. Schrifttum*, 1928, pp.126,1273, on the Jewish origin of this source.
[2] Tertullian, *De Ieiuniis*, ch.1.

whether St. John and his companions continued their fast or began immediately to compile their analects. Thus it appears that the Muratorian Fragment gives no more than an allusion to an earlier and well-known anecdote.

Similar allusions are found in the East and in the West. From the East comes a remark which Eusebius incorporated in his Ecclesiastical History from the *Hypotyposeis* of Clement of Alexandria:[1]

> St. John wrote as the last, when he saw that the physical things were made known in the Gospels, being urged by the 'Elders' and taken up in the Spirit to God, a spiritual Gospel.

The similarity between this passage and the Muratorian Fragment is to be found in the words 'being urged by the Elders' on the one hand and 'cohortantibus condiscipulis et episcopis suis' on the other. There exists, however, a difference in that Clement maintains that it was St. John who was 'taken up in the Spirit of God', whereas the Muratorian Fragment has it that St. Andrew was granted the vision that all the surviving disciples of the Lord should pool their analects. This difference, however, is perhaps not altogether conclusive because the record in the Muratorian Fragment is defective. Nevertheless, it makes it clear that the two stories are not identical, but two separate branches of an established tradition, of which Clement's is the later.[2] The common source is indicated by Eusebius[3] who calls it παράδοσιν τῶν ἀνέκαθεν πρεσβυτέρων. We are thus once more faced with the 'Elders', that puzzling source from which Irenaeus derived so much of his information.

In the West the same information comes from Victorinus of Pöttau:[4]

> Johannes evangelium postea conscripsit. cum essent Valentinus et

---

[1] Euseb, *H.E.*, VI.14.7.

[2] This fact has been overlooked by G. Salmon, op. cit., p.663a.—Since the mention of St. Andrew contradicts the thesis that St. John wrote as the last survivor of the Twelve, this must be a very early feature.

[3] Euseb., *H.E.*, VI.14.5.

[4] Victorinus, op. cit., 11.1 (Haussleiter 94).

Cerinthus et Ebion et cetera scola Satanae sparsa per orbem, convenerunt ad illum (sc. Johannem) de finitimis civitatibus episcopi et compulerunt eum, ut ipse testimonium conscriberet in Dominum.

A. Harnack[1] has suggested that this report came from Papias, and the following parallel, which comes from Jerome, makes this suggestion very credible.[2]

Johannes apostolus quem Jesus amabat plurimum, filius Zebedaei et frater Jacobi apostoli . . . novissimus omnium scripsit evangelium, rogatus ab Asiae episcopis, adversus Cerinthum aliosque haereticos et maxime tunc Ebionitarum dogma, qui adserunt Christum ante Mariam non fuisse.

Both these passages betray their knowledge of the legend of the three days' fast by the words 'convenerunt ad illum . . . et compulerunt eum' and 'rogatus ab Asiae episcopis' respectively, and evidently come from the same source. However, that cannot have been a copy of Eusebius-Clement, neither has Jerome copied Victorinus. It is also evident that none of them copied the Muratorian Fragment. On the other hand, there is an inter-relation between all these sources, and the two Latin texts even explain by their reference to the polemical purpose against the Ebionites in the Fourth Gospel, what is meant by Clement-Eusebius' obscure reference to τὰ σωματικά. Moreover, Jerome shortly afterwards refers to Papias as his authority on St. John,[3] and the impression that Papias was the source of information in our particular case is strengthened by the fact that he was one of the 'Elders' to whom Clement-Eusebius refer, and confirmed by the XIXth fragment of Papias.[4]

This external evidence agrees with the internal evidence. The two Saints in the legend, St. John and St. Andrew, were Papias' Saints. If St. John might also be called a Roman local Saint because of Tertullian's report that he had been martyred at Rome

[1] Harnack, *Z.N.W.*, 24, 1925, 9.
[2] Hieron., *De Vir. Illustr.*, 9, ed. A. Bernoulli, 1895, p.12f.
[3] Hieron., op. cit., p.13, ll.23–4; ch.18, p.19, ll.14–16.
[4] Gebhardt–Harnack–Zahn, *Patr. Apost. Opera*, 6th ed., 1920, p. 78, 'as the last of them St. John . . . when at that time terrible heresies sprang up, dictated the Gospel to his pupil Papias'.

before being relegated to Patmos,[1] Rome would not have produced St. Andrew as the sponsor of this legendary tradition. At the same time St. Andrew belongs to the Johannine circle in which Papias was specially interested. According to John 1:40 St. Andrew was the first of the Twelve to be called by Jesus;[2] in John 6:1f. he and St. Philip are the two active members of the Twelve at the miraculous feeding; and in John 12:22 the same two Apostles introduce the Greeks to Jesus. St. Andrew and St. Philip thus form a pair in the Johannine circle. Now St. Philip was the local Saint in the district of Hierapolis, Laodicea and Colossae. His grave between his prophetic daughters was kept at Hierapolis, and if modern scholars believe that this information refers to St. Philip the Evangelist, whose prophetic daughters are mentioned in Acts 21:8-9, the Hierapolitan tradition, and even the great bishop Polycrates of Ephesus, regarded him as the Apostle St. Philip, the member of the Twelve.[3]

In Hierapolis St. Andrew was given the first place among the Twelve. In his preface to the 'Sayings of the Lord' Papias stated, 'if, however, someone should refer to the Elders, (he will find that) I have made critical use of the sayings of the Elders: all that Andrew and Peter reported, or Philip or Thomas or James or John or Matthew or any other of the Lord's disciples'.[4] St. Andrew is mentioned here before St. Peter, in accordance with John 1:41-2, but contrary to those Roman claims which were based upon Matt.16:18-19.[5] The second place was not withheld from St. Peter,[6] but it is noteworthy that St. Philip comes third and St.

---

[1] Tertullian, *Praescr. Haer.*, ch.8, §.15; ch.37, §5.

[2] Since early times, cf. John Chrysostom, *Hom.*, 18, ch.3, tom.8, 107c, the attempt was made to identify St. Andrew's companion there with the author of the Fourth Gospel. The Muratorian Fragment may already be a witness for this.

[3] Euseb., *H.E.*, III.31.3; 39.9 (Papias); V.24.2 (Polycrates).

[4] Euseb., *H.E.*, III.39.4, partly translated into Latin in Jerome, op. cit., 18.

[5] A similar polemical purpose may be found in the correspondence between St. James of Jerusalem and St. Peter at the beginning of the Ps. Clementine Homilies.

[6] In the Acts of Philip, ch.32, ed. Bonnet, vol.II, part 2, 1903, p.16, we have only St. John, St. Philip, St. Andrew, St. Thomas and St. Matthew. Why was St. Peter left out? E. Peterson, *Z.N.W.*, 31, 1932, p.97f., has shown that these

Thomas fourth, whilst they only take the fifth and seventh place respectively in the Synoptic lists of the Twelve.[1] The sons of Zebedee rank below them. This seems to indicate that the 'beloved disciple', the author of the Fourth Gospel, was not identified with St. John of Zebedee by Papias, and that the words to this effect in *De Viris Illustribus* 9 are only Jerome's; but the conclusion is not absolutely certain. What is certain is the fact that the Muratorian Fragment, a Roman document, gave prominence to St. Andrew who, in the Hierapolitan group of churches in Asia Minor, was exalted above the 'Roman' Apostle St. Peter.

Another list of the Twelve originating from Asia and showing a preference for the Johannine circle comes from the so-called Epistle of the Apostles, a second-century document which, in the part which interests us, is only preserved in Ethiopic.[2] It runs, 'John, Thomas, Peter, Andrew, James, Philip, Bartholomew, Matthew, Nathanael, Judas Zelotes, Cephas (read: Simon Zelotes)'.[3] Here the equation of the 'beloved disciple' with John of Zebedee is accomplished, and he is consequently given the first place. St. Thomas holds the second, but the Synoptic pairing of St. Philip with St. Bartholomew[4] has been restored. We can thus conclude that this list was not formed under Hierapolitan influence. Its 'Johannine' character is nevertheless established, not only by St. John taking the first place, but also by the appearance of Nathanael, John 1:45f. Yet St. Andrew is reduced to the ranks of the Twelve; and this list, therefore, witnesses to the fact that there were different groups amongst the supporters of the Fourth Gospel in Asia Minor. That means that the Egyptian branch of the tradition of the three days' fast was not identical with either the Hierapolitan or the Roman tradition.

It is with this latter group of traditions which gave prominence

---

Acts were re-written after the council of Gangra, A.D.343, but not that they did not draw upon earlier material.

[1] Matt.10:3f.; Mark 3:18; Luke 6:14; Acts 1:13.

[2] Published by C. Schmidt, *Gespräche Jesu*, *T.U.*, 43, 1919, cf. James, *Apocryphal N.T.*, p.486.

[3] The translator is responsible for the error which gives the epithet of Zelotes to Judas and mistakes Simon Zelotes for Simon Cephas.

[4] Only broken up in Acts 1:13 by St. Thomas who is moved once more.

to St. Andrew that we must deal still further. Perhaps its trace can be followed into the Acts of Andrew (20)[1] where St. Andrew in his vision before his martyrdom sees St. John, not Jesus, in the part of the Saviour;[2] it made its mark also in the Apostolic History of Abdias where, in the tenth book,[3] St. Philip is sent to Scythia which, according to Eusebius,[4] was the domain of St. Andrew, a tradition also belonging to Asia Minor.[5] The fact that the tenth book of Abdias sprang from a tradition closely connected with Papias, is shown by its third chapter, which reports St. Philip's return to Hierapolis where he is subsequently martyred and buried.[6] Although the tomb of St. Philip at Hierapolis was a great memorial for all the churches in Asia Minor, as we know from Eusebius, Papias' record of it is the most likely source for this remark. Finally, there is an almost obliterated clue to the connection between St. Andrew and St. Philip, i.e. Hierapolis, in the Slavonic Acts of Peter and Andrew.[7] There in §16 we have a report about 'a huckster in that town who had been converted by Philip', a wholly unmotivated intrusion in the record of the missionary journey of St. Peter with St. Andrew, which may find its explanation when it is understood as a late reflection of the customary combination of St. Andrew with St. Philip.

Internal evidence, even if it is supported by a number of sources, is of necessity circumstantial, and therefore ambiguous. However, it has appeared that Papias accorded to St. Andrew the first place in the council of the Twelve, something not done elsewhere, not even in the Epistle of the Apostles, although this document too may come from Asia Minor and bears a 'Johannine' character. It has also appeared that in several apocryphal Acts of Apostles the close connection between St. Andrew and St. Philip was main-

---

[1] James, op. cit., p.343f.
[2] This has to be connected with the curious substitution of St. John for Jesus in Origen's exegesis of John 19:26-7, *Comm. Joh.*, book I, ch.6 (M. Gr. vol.14, p.32), repeated by Cyril of Jerusalem, *Catech.*7.9 (M. Gr., vol.33, p.616).
[3] James, op. cit., p.469.
[4] Euseb., *H.E.*, III.3.1.
[5] Ehrhardt, *The Apostolic Succession in the first two centuries of the Church*, 1953, p.68.
[6] For if Acts 21:8 had been consulted, he would have gone to Caesarea.
[7] James, op. cit., p.459.

tained which, although it is stated in the Fourth Gospel, was of a special interest to the district of Hierapolis, as St. Philip was the local Saint there. On the other hand, we find that the majority of the existing fragments of Papias' book[1] bear witness to his special interest in the Fourth Gospel. We also find that the close relation between St. Andrew and St. John found a most unusual expression in the vision seen by St. Andrew in his ancient Acts.[2] Finally, we may state that the West took little interest in the apocryphal Acts of Andrew before the beginning of the fifth century.[3] All this points in the one direction that Papias was the authority for the legend of the three days' fast in the Muratorian Fragment.

IV

The hypothesis that the first justification of the canonization of the Fourth Gospel in the Muratorian Fragment comes from Papias is also supported by the remarks in the next paragraph of the Fragment. This paragraph which contains the justification of the four-Gospel canon is styled after the fashion of a Creed which follows the Roman *regula fidei*, a fact which, however, has not been noted in the recent literature on the development of early Christian Creeds.[4]

16. et ideo licet varia sin-
17. gulis evangeliorum libris principia
18. doceantur, nihil tamen differt creden-
19. tium fidei, cum uno ac principali spiritu de-
20. clarata sint in omnibus omnia: de nativi-
21. tate, de passione, de resurrectione,

[1] Cf. their collection in Gebhardt–Harnack–Zahn, op. cit., p.69f. St. John is mentioned in ten out of nineteen fragments.

[2] I would suggest that these Acts combine otherwise more easily with the Epistle of the Apostles than with the Hierapolitan tradition.

[3] The first western Father who took a genuine interest in the Acts of Andrew was Paulinus of Nola, *Carm.*, 27, l.406f., in which he gave a poetical reflection on the *Passio Sti. Andreae*.

[4] Neither F. J. Badcock, *The History of the Creeds*, 2nd ed., 1938, nor J. N. D. Kelly, *Early Christian Creeds*, 1950, have dealt with the Muratorian Fragment.

22. de conversatione cum discipulis suis,
23. ac de gemino eius adventu,
24. primo in humilitate despectus quod fu-
25. it; secundo potestate regali prae-
26. claro quod futurum est.

The reference to the Creed is explicit: 'nihil tamen differt credentium fidei', 'there is (in the four Gospels) no deviation from the belief of the faithful', can have no other meaning than that the author of the Muratorian Fragment had tested them by the *regula fidei* of his, the Roman Church. The elements of the Roman Creed, even the reference to the earthly ministry of Jesus, which appears in the Apostolic Tradition of Hippolytus,[1] are all present; but the strong emphasis which is laid upon His Second Advent points to influences from Asia Minor. The same emphasis is found in the 'Profession of the Presbyters at Smyrna',[2] but in other Roman sources, like Justin Martyr,[3] we vainly seek for it. It is also well known that, with the exception of the Pastoral Epistles,[4] this element is lacking in credal formulas in the New Testament, or even in the Apostolic Fathers. Thus I venture to suggest that its intrusion here is yet another vestige of the influence of Papias upon the Muratorian Fragment, since we know of the impact of his millennarian theories, mediated in particular by Irenaeus.

V

The passage just quoted was meant as a summary drawn up in justification of the four-Gospel canon. It therefore comes as a surprise that it should be followed by another justification of the canonization of the Fourth Gospel. The position in which

---

[1] In the canon at the consecration of bishops, *Ap. Trad.*, ch.4, §6, ed. G. Dix, 1937, 7.

[2] In Badcock, op. cit., p.35, cf. T. Hahn-Harnack, *Bibliothek d. Symbole*, 3rd ed., 1897, p.5f.

[3] Hahn-Harnack, op. cit., p.4f.

[4] 2.Tim.4:1 seems to contain the Second Advent as an element of a credal formula, but it is less easy to agree with Kelly, op. cit., p.20, that 1.Tim.6:13f. should be in the same case.

this paragraph occurs makes it probable that it came from a different source, and was added for a special purpose. For it is a certain sign that a new source was used when such a general remark, as the one in ll.16–26, is followed by another which resumes the discussion of a subject seemingly closed by this general remark. We are faced with an intrusion into the Muratorian Fragment when reading the following paragraph:

26. Quid ergo
27. mirum, si Johannes tam constanter
28. singula etiam in epistulis suis proferat
29. dicens in semet ipsum, 'Quae vidimus oculis
30. nostris et auribus audivimus et manus
31. nostrae palpaverunt, haec scripsimus vobis'.

fol. 10b.   32. sic enim non solum visorem sed et auditorem
33. sed et scriptorem omnium mirabilium domini per ordi-
34. nem profitetur (sc. se esse).

This passage contains, so it seems, the key to the problem of the Muratorian Fragment. The previous passages have been shown to be either dependent upon Papias, with minor influences from Irenaeus, or of genuinely Roman origin. They have thus borne out Harnack's thesis[1] that the Muratorian Fragment is an official pronouncement of the Catholic Church at Rome.[2] This passage is, on a general showing, unlikely to have come from Papias. Consequently we must enquire into the reasons which may have caused the Roman Church to add it, and into the sources from which it is drawn.

[1] Harnack, *Z.N.W.*, 24, 1925, p.6. H.'s thesis is based especially upon l.66f., 'in catholicam ecclesiam recipi non potest'; l.71f., 'Apocalypses Johannis et Petri tantum recipimus'; 82, 'nihil in totum recipimus'; 84f., 'una cum Basilide Asianum Cataphrygum (eicimus)', which no private person could have written.

[2] Since the days of Pope Cornelius (A.D. 250–3) we know that the official self-description of the Roman Church was just *ecclesia catholica*; cf. Harnack, *Mission u. Ausbreitung*, 4th ed., 1923, p.860 n.2. H. Koch, *Z.N.W.*, 25, 1926, p.154f., rightly assumes that this use is likely to have obtained already when the Muratorian document was written.

Regarding the source, I shall begin with the similarity between ll.29–31 of the Muratorian Fragment and 1.John 1:1. The author of the Muratorian Fragment has consciously referred to 1.John 1:1, in the belief that it was written by the author of the Fourth Gospel. It is, however, noteworthy that the Muratorian Fragment exhibits a text-form which has no support from any reputable New Testament MS. They all read, 'what we have heard, what we have seen with our eyes, what we beheld and our hands have touched'. The differences are considerable. The Muratorian Fragment places the seeing before the hearing, abandoning in the process ὃ ἐθεασάμεθα and adding 'auribus'. In short, it has combined 1.John 1:1 with 1.John 1:3, 'what we have seen and heard'. The result is a much closer parallelism of its constituent parts than is found in 1.John 1:1. There is also the plural 'quae' in the Muratorian Fragment instead of the singular ὃ in 1.John, but this may be due to the Latin, although both *Vetus Latina* and the Vulgate read 'quod'. The next form in the Muratorian Fragment suggests by its highly rhetorical tone that its author did not consult 1.John in the original.

A great classical scholar, E. Schwartz, has seriously doubted whether the beginning of 1.John is not spurious.[1] This radical solution of his *aporia* with regard to the beginning of 1.John finds no support from the Muratorian Fragment; but on the other hand, I find it difficult to share Professor C. H. Dodd's view[2] that 1.John 1:1–2 is no more than the overture to the main theme of the Epistle, which is the reality of Christ's incarnation. Already in its original form 1.John 1:1 had clearly a polemical ring.[3] In this way it was also used by Christians from Asia Minor in the defence of the Fourth Gospel.[4]

[1] E. Schwartz, 'Aporien', *Nachr. Ges. d. Wiss.*, Göttingen, 1907, p.366.
[2] C. H. Dodd, *The Johannine Epistles*, 1946, p. xxx. His is the Catholic interpretation; but in *Acta Joh.*, 93, ed. Bonnet, II.1, 1898, p.196, we find 1.John 1:1 used to prove the docetic doctrine that the body of Jesus was not a natural body.
[3] Ambrose of Milan has shown a fine instinct for this when choosing this text to slay his Arian adversaries, *Explan. in XII Psalm.*, ed. Petschenig, 1919, p.99, interpreting Ps.36:1.
[4] The proof that the Fourth Gospel is later than 1.John is generally found in the fact that the latter has a more primitive, 'futurist' eschatology, cf. e.g. J. N. Sanders, *The Fourth Gospel*, etc., 1943, p.9. This argument may suggest

We have already encountered the list of the Twelve from the Epistle of the Apostles, and have seen that, although it was an Asiatic production, it represented a different 'Johannine' tradition from that of Hierapolis-Laodicea. It is, on the other hand, clearly related to our passage from the Muratorian Fragment:

We John, Thomas, Peter, Andrew, James, Philip, Bartholomew, Matthew, Nathanael, Judas Zelotes and Cephas write unto the churches of the East and the West, the North and the South, declaring unto you that which concerns our Lord Jesus Christ: we do write according as we have seen and heard and touched Him, after that He was risen from the dead.

In this §3 of the Epistle of the Apostles the phrase 'as we have seen and heard and touched Him' follows the sequence of the Muratorian Fragment, and the polemical ring is quite unmistakable. For it is certain that the author of the Epistle of the Apostles, whoever he was, was not an eye-witness to Christ's resurrection but represented a certain well-known Judaizing party within the Church.[1] He claims to speak in the name of those who saw and heard and—St. Thomas—touched the risen Lord. The reference here, as in 1.John 1:1, is to John 20:19-29. This accounts for the positions at the head of the list: St. John, who was supposed to have formulated the claim stated here, leads it; St. Thomas follows because he had the distinction of having touched the risen Christ; St. Peter heads the ranks of the Twelve.

Having established that this attack was started by a Judaizing group, it is easy to find its objective in the Pauline Epistles. The motto of its adversaries was 1.Cor.2:9:

Things which eye saw not and ear heard not
and which entered not into the heart of man,
whatsoever things God prepared for them that love Him.

---

a different authorship, but is historically unavailing: Papias, who held a much cruder eschatology than 1.John, was later than the Fourth Gospel, and the Epistle may in its entirety be based upon it.

[1] We refer to K. Holl, *Gesammelte Schriften*, 1928, vol.2, p.50, who emphasizes that 1.Cor.15:7 marks the last occasion when Jerusalem Apostles were created.

The analogy of this Pauline quotation from an unknown Jewish apocryphal writing[1] explains the change in the sequence—first seeing and then hearing—from 1.John 1:1, which we observe both in the Muratorian Fragment and in the Epistle of the Apostles. It makes it clear that we have here the watchwords of two strictly opposed parties, of which the 'Pauline' party was stronger since it forced its adversaries to adapt their slogan. This adaptation, incidentally, suggests that 1.John 1:1 was aimed at another adversary, and therefore no interpolation.

The fact that 1.Cor.2:9 was first in the field is borne out by its ample attestation. It has a well established place in the Clementine literature;[2] it is found in inter-related pseudo-Petrine sources,[3] in authoritative sources of the churches of Smyrna[4] and Antioch.[5] However, it was only to be expected that gnostic teachers too would make use of 1.Cor.2:9, which suited their purpose so well. It is not only found in the Pistis Sophia,[6] and in the Acts of Thomas 36, but even in a Manichaean fragment from Turfan.[7] It is thus not surprising to see that its adversaries put a fair amount of energy into the fight. We have the witness of Stephan Gobaras, quoted by Photius, that Hegesippus condemned as 'liars against the sacred Scriptures and the Lord' all those who ventured to adduce 1.Cor.2:9 as evidence.[8]

This quotation makes it plain that we are faced with a conflict in which the authority of the 'sacred Scriptures' was at stake.

---

[1] The actual source of the verse is unknown, but the fact that it is quoted in *Asc. Is.*, 11.34, ed. Charles (1900), p.80f., and that Jerome, *Comm. Is.*, 64.4, says that it occurred in the Apocalypse of Elias, although it is not found in the fragment which has come down to us as an appendix of Sophonias, and Justin the Ophite read it in his Book of Baruch, Hippol. *Philos.*, V.24.1; 26.16; 27.1, makes its Jewish origin certain.

[2] 1.Clem.34.8; 2.Clem.11.7; Ps. Clem., *De Virgin.*, I.9.4.

[3] *Apocalypse of Peter in Syriac*, ed. A. Mingana, Woodbrooke Studies (1933), p.110; *Acts of Peter* 20.

[4] *Martyr. Polycarpi*, 2.3.

[5] Theophilus, *Ad Autolyc.*, I.14, ed. J. C. T. Otto, 1861, p.44.

[6] In *Griech. Christl. Schriftst.*, 1905, 13, §114.

[7] F. W. K. Müller, *Anhang z. d. Abhandl. d. Preuß. Akad. d. Wiss.*, 1904, M.789, p.68.

[8] W. Bauer, *Johannes-Evangelium*, 3rd ed., 1933, p.4f., who has collected most of the evidence quoted here.

Moreover, a considerable number of the sources quoted in the preceding paragraph shows a connection with either Rome or Asia Minor or both: 1. Clement is Roman, and pseudo-Clement *De Virginitate* comes from Asia Minor; the Apocalypse of Peter is even treated as canonical in the Muratorian Fragment, although we cannot say whether its Roman form was the same as the Syriac.[1] The Latin Vercelli Acts of Peter, which quote 1.Cor.2:9 in a special form, will be discussed soon: they too are Roman. Above all, Irenaeus, in whose person the Church of the West had its strongest link with the Church at Smyrna, one of the most important churches in Asia Minor, made prominent use of 1.Cor.2:9.[2] Was there really such a great danger for the 'sacred Scriptures' that Rome had to perform such a volte-face? The answer is that at the end of the second century the Fourth Gospel and St. John's Revelation were indeed hotly discussed, and the arguments brought forward by Irenaeus in favour of their canonicity seem to have appeared insufficient in the position in which Rome found itself.

The Roman leaders must have been put under a very heavy pressure to make them abandon such a well established use as that of 1.Cor.2:9. A. Harnack[3] has very justly stressed the exceptional consideration with which they treated the opponents of the Fourth Gospel, the *Alogi*. The names of their leaders are unknown to history, which means that no excommunications took place. This is understandable, for Hegesippus, the exponent of anti-Paulinism, was a dangerous ally. The *Alogi* were probably staunch partisans of St. Paul, and the Roman Church revered in him one of its founders. It would have preferred to follow Irenaeus' lead who, although he resisted the *Alogi*, was imbued with Pauline theology; but apparently the opportunity did not arise. The Church at Smyrna and Papias, who were close allies,[4] were not

---

[1] In the Ethiopic, cf. James, *Apocryphal N.T.*, p.505f., 1.Cor.2:9 is not quoted.

[2] As the conclusion of *Adv. Haer.*, V.36.2 (Harvey, vol.2, p.436). By contrast, 1.John 1:1 is not quoted in *Adv. Haer.*

[3] Harnack, *Das N.T. um das Jahr 200*, p.67f.

[4] One might conceive of a less aggressive way to express the alliance than to say that Irenaeus was 'revelling in the childish fancies of Papias', J. Lawson, *The Biblical Theology of Irenaeus*, 1948, p.287.

the parties addressed in this paragraph of the Muratorian Fragment, however much Papias may have valued 1.John.[1]

Undoubtedly it was the authority of 1.John in the first instance which prompted the Roman Church to go with Hegesippus.[2] Its leaders were faced with the alternative of either accepting the bold statement, 'what we have seen and heard, we write unto you', 1.John 1:3, as true or of treating it as an untruth. Now, since the authenticity of 1.John was not even questioned by the *Alogi*, the Roman Church saw no reason to reject it. Neither did Rome take the way of distinguishing between the author of 1.John and the author of the Fourth Gospel, attempted by those *Alogi* who ascribed the Gospel to Cerinthus. But all this does not explain the adoption of the formula 'what we have seen with our eyes and heard with our ears and our hands have touched'. This formula points to an alliance between churches in Asia Minor other than Smyrna, which are represented by the Epistle of the Apostles, and the Jerusalem Church, as represented by Hegesippus. Such a coalition against Rome is known to have existed on account of the third Easter-conflict so-called. Evidence for its existence may be found in the letters of protest against the excommunication of the churches in Asia Minor sent by the bishops Polycrates of Ephesus[3] and Narcissus of Jerusalem.[4]

Thus we are led to assume that the second justification for the canonization of the Fourth Gospel in the Muratorian Fragment was the olive branch of peace which Rome held out to the churches in Asia at the end of the third Easter-conflict. For it is well known that the Quartadecimans based their conviction that the date of Easter should be 14 Nisan upon the Fourth Gospel, and

[1] Euseb., *H.E.*, III.39.17.

[2] P. Corssen, *Monarchianische Prologe*, T.U., 15.1, 1896, p.50, has held that the *Alogi* did not object to 1.John, because this Epistle had as yet no authority. This view seems to me absurd.

[3] Euseb., *H.E.*, V.24.2f. The fact that Polycrates did not speak for all the bishops in Asia Minor may be deduced from ibid. §8: 'I might have enumerated all the bishops whom you asked me to call together, and whom I have called. But if I had added their names, there would have been [too] many.' Narcissus, however, has mentioned at least three names, among whom the bishop of Caesarea is conspicuous.

[4] Euseb., *H.E.*, V.23.3; 25.

the Roman attitude towards this Gospel was therefore a main subject of discussion between the conflicting parties.[1] Here the Roman Church was quick to seize its opportunity. Since the *Alogi* did not object to the Apostolicity of 1.John, Rome found there a chance of covering the admission of partial defeat which is contained in this paragraph of the Muratorian Fragment. This paragraph shows that Rome had to sacrifice her allies. The *Alogi* were not the only ones who were abandoned, but even Papias' reputation was questioned. The famous remark in Eusebius' *Ecclesiastical History*,[2] σφόδρα γὰρ μικρὸς ἦν τὸν νοῦν, seems to take its origin from these troubles. Papias' reputation was not as bad as that elsewhere. Another school of thought added the following remark to the first mention of his name in the same book:[3] ἀνὴρ τὰ πάντα ὅτι μάλιστα λογιώτατος καὶ τῆς γραφῆς εἰδήμων, and others refer to him as Πάπιας ὁ πάνυ and ὁ πολύς.[4] Therefore, it is perhaps unsafe to put too much stress upon the alleged intellectual shortcomings of a man whom a genius like Irenaeus chose for his guide. In any case, it was certainly not his small-mindedness which caused the Roman Church to add his adversaries' testimony to the reasons in favour of the Fourth Gospel, but the fact that he was not an undoubted authority in the Church in Asia. The Asiatic opposition, however, was not due to the general incredibility of his millennarian theories, but to the fact that they had become the shibboleth of the Cataphrygian heresy, which also derived its Apostolic succession from St. Philip and his prophetic daughters.[5]

Rome had been somewhat uncertain in her attitude towards Montanism, as we learn from Tertullian.[6] The Montanists were at least ambiguous in their attitude towards the Fourth Gospel.[7]

---

[1] Leipoldt, op. cit., 1, p.147, n.3.
[2] Euseb., *H.E.*, III.39.13.
[3] Euseb., *H.E.*, III.36.3.
[4] Papias, frg. 6 and 7, Gebhardt–Harnack–Zahn, op. cit., 6th ed., p.74.
[5] Cf. Ehrhardt, op. cit.
[6] E. Evans, *Tertullian's Treatise against Praxeas*, 1948, p.75f.
[7] The old view of Harvey, *Sti. Irenaei Adversus Haereses*, 1857, 2, p.51, n.2, that the Montanists rejected the Fourth Gospel, has been renewed by Evans, op. cit, p.77, n.1, and deserves a careful examination.

This makes us see the conflict between Rome and the churches in Asia Minor in a new light. It was a confused fight. Rome had been critical of the Fourth Gospel, as much as the *Alogi*, but now Montanism put a new aspect on the case. The bishops in Asia and the Monarchianists at Rome forced Victor I to a decision by which he sacrificed the views of the *Alogi*, although he did not sacrifice their persons, as may be seen in the case of the Roman presbyter Caius.[1] Therefore, since 1.John 1:1 provided an answer to the objections of the *Alogi*, and since it was offered by the Christians in Asia[2] and Jerusalem to Rome as an argument, the Roman authorities used it to support the Apostolicity of the Fourth Gospel against the *Alogi*, even though the Epistles were considered inferior to the Gospels in canonical rank.[3] In other words, in the second justification of the canonization of the Fourth Gospel Rome let down its allies—admittedly, as gently as possible—in no uncertain fashion.

Can anything be said about the Roman Pope who accepted Rome's set-back so plainly? The question is whether it was Victor I himself or his successor Zephyrinus. In favour of Victor two things may be said, first that he excommunicated the Montanists,[4] and secondly that this paragraph could be interpreted as a come-back upon Irenaeus who had strongly advocated peace with the oriental churches,[5] and now found himself a victim of this peace. For his sympathies lay with the supporters of 1.Cor.2:9.

[*Adv. Haer.* v.36.2] In all these things and by them all God the Father is made manifest, who fashioned man and promised the Patriarchs that they would inherit the earth; who accomplished it in the resurrection of the just and fulfils His promise in the kingdom of His Son: afterwards granting that which neither eye has seen nor ear has heard nor man's heart has attained.

In favour of Zephyrinus, on the other hand, speaks the special

---

[1] Cf. W. Bauer, *Rechtgläubigkeit und Ketzerei*, 1934, p.209f.
[2] The same argument is found in a weaker form in *Acts of John*, 88, ed. Bonnet II.1, 1898, p.194.
[3] Harnack, *Das N.T. um das Jahr 200*, p.68n.**, is widely off the mark.
[4] That, to my mind, lies behind Tert. *Adv. Prax.*, 1, 'litteras pacis revocare'.
[5] Euseb., *H.E.*, V.24.12.

esteem in which this rather nondescript Pope was held in the East. There he was even represented as the direct successor of St. Peter as bishop of Rome.[1] Moreover, on a general showing it seems more likely that Victor's successor reversed his predecessor's policy of excommunicating the bishops in Asia Minor than that Victor did it himself. For this paragraph of the Muratorian Fragment marks a defeat for Rome and we know from Hippolytus that Zephyrinus, who sheltered the Monarchianists, was not highly respected at Rome.[2]

There developed a reaction at Rome against the Muratorian document, leaving its mark on the Vercelli Acts of Peter which show a characteristic change from the Greek original:

[*Acta Petri*, 20] . . . This God who is great and small, fair and foul, young and old, seen in time and unto eternity invisible; whom the hand of man has not held, yet is He held by His servants; whom no flesh has seen, yet now seeth; who is the Word proclaimed by the prophets, *not heard of but* now known.

The Latin enlargement upon the Greek has been put in *italics*. The Greek has only 'the Word proclaimed by the prophets now appearing'; the Latin 'the Word proclaimed by the prophets, *not heard of but* now known'. It is clear that this cannot be the original. For the Greek makes sense, whereas the Latin does not. What is meant by 'the Word proclaimed by the prophets not heard of'? If the Word was proclaimed by the prophets, they at least must have heard of Him, even if no one heeded their message. Thus we are led to believe that *inauditum* was an intentional addition. Rome did not abandon the view adopted even by a Pope like Zephyrinus, but would make it innocuous. The Roman addition suggests a compromise, assigning 1.Cor.2:9 to the prophets, i.e. the Old Testament, and 1.John 1:1, 'but now known', to the New Testament. Perhaps this was an echo of the Alexandrian

---

[1] In the two earliest documents of the Church at Edessa, the *Doctrina Addai* and the Martyrdom of Barsamya, it is said that Sarapion of Antioch, who consecrated Palût, the first Catholic bishop of Edessa, had been consecrated in his turn by Zephyrinus, St. Peter's successor at Rome, F. C. Burkitt, *Early Eastern Christianity*, 1904, p.26.

[2] Hippolyt. *Philos.*, IX.11, cf. Harnack, *Mission u. Ausbreitung*, p.117, n.1.

mediation in the Easter-conflict, for we find the same suggestion in Didymus of Alexandria.[1]

This then became the Roman view; but the second justification
of the canonization of the Fourth Gospel was quietly passed over.
In Jerome's *Prologues to the Four Gospels* the first only is repeated in a form which combines the western and eastern
traditions:

> 9 . . . coactus est ab omnibus paene tunc Asia episcopis et multarum
> ecclesiarum legationibus de divinitate Salvatoris altius scribere et ad
> ipsum, ut ita dicam, Dei Verbum non tam audaci quam felici temeritate
> praerumpere, ut ecclesiastica narrat historia . . .

This, as is shown by the open reference to Eusebius' *Ecclesiastical
History*, and a faint echo from Epiphanius,[2] is a slightly elaborated
repetition of the eastern tradition about the conception of the
Fourth Gospel. The following passage then comes very near
Papias' account as preserved in the Muratorian Fragment:

> cum a fratribus cogeretur ut scriberet, ita facturum respondisse, si
> indicto ieiunio in commune Deo deprecarentur; quo expleto revelatione
> saturatus in illud prooemium caelo veniens eructavit: In principio erat
> Verbum etc.

Whether or not Jerome knew the Muratorian document may be
left open; but it is plain that Rome, abandoning St. Andrew's
part, made this its reason for the canonization of the Fourth
Gospel, and thus overcame the set-back which is so clearly marked
in the second justification given for the canonization of the Fourth
Gospel, which it had suffered in the conflict with the churches in
Asia Minor.[3]

---

[1] Didym. Alex., *In Epist. Joh.I* (M.Gr.39, 1776).
[2] Epiphan. *Adv. Haer.*, II.51.11 (M.Gr,41, 909).
[3] Koch, *Zeitschr. f. wiss. Theologie*, vol.55, 1914, p.312, rightly calls it a set-
back, but cf. E. Caspar, *Gesch. d. Papsttums*, vol.1, 1930, p.21, n.1.

3

JESUS CHRIST
AND ALEXANDER THE GREAT

I

PHIL.2:5–11 has been exhaustively dealt with, especially by German scholars,[1] but an interesting parallel in Plutarch seems so far to have escaped attention, although it illustrates the meaning of ἁρπαγμός and helps to throw light on the Pauline passage. Here are the two passages with a translation of the Plutarch.

Phil. 2:5–11. Τοῦτο φρονεῖτε ἐν ὑμῖν ὃ καὶ ἐν Χριστῷ Ἰησοῦ, ὃς ἐν μορφῇ Θεοῦ ὑπάρχων οὐχ ἁρπαγμὸν ἡγήσατο τὸ εἶναι ἴσα Θεῷ, ἀλλὰ ἑαυτὸν ἐκένωσεν μορφὴν δούλου λαβὼν ἐν ὁμοιώματι ἀνθρώπου γενόμενος. καὶ σχήματι εὑρεθεὶς ὡς ἄνθρωπος ἐταπείνωσεν ἑαυτόν, γενόμενος ὑπήκοος μέχρι θανάτου, θανάτου δὲ σταυροῦ. Διὸ καὶ ὁ Θεὸς αὐτὸν ὑπερύψωσεν, καὶ ἐχαρίσατο αὐτῷ τὸ ὄνομα τὸ ὑπὲρ πᾶν ὄνομα, ἵνα ἐν τῷ ὀνόματι Ἰησοῦ πᾶν γόνυ κάμψῃ ἐπουρανίων καὶ ἐπιγείων καὶ καταχθονίων, καὶ πᾶσα γλῶσσα ἐξομολογήσηται ὅτι Κύριος Ἰησοῦς Χριστὸς εἰς δόξαν Θεοῦ Πατρός.

Plut., Alex. Virt. s. Fort., 1:8 fin. Οὐ γὰρ λῃστρικῶς τὴν Ἀσίαν καταδραμών, οὐδὲ ὥσπερ ἄρπαγμα καὶ λάφυρον εὐτυχίας ἀνελπίστου σπαράξαι καὶ ἀνασύρασθαι διανοηθείς, ... ἀλλ' ἑνὸς ὑπήκοα λόγου τὰ ἐπὶ γῆς, καὶ μιᾶς πολιτείας, ἕνα δῆμον ἀνθρώπους ἅπαντας ἀποφῆναι βουλόμενος, οὕτως ἑαυτὸν ἐσχημάτιζεν. Εἰ δὲ μὴ ταχέως ὁ δεῦρο καταπέμψας τὴν Ἀλεξάνδρου ψυχὴν ἀνεκαλέσατο δαίμων, εἷς ἂν νόμος ἅπαντας ἀνθρώπους ἐνέβλεπε, καὶ πρὸς ἐν δίκαιον ὡς πρὸς κοινὸν διῳκοῦντο φῶς. Νῦν δὲ τῆς γῆς ἀνήλιον μέρος ἔμεινεν, ὅσον Ἀλέξανδρον οὐκ εἶδεν.

For he did not overrun Asia on a looting expedition, treating those territories as falling to him by the fortune of war, and so his to seize and hold, to harry and strip bare. But [his task was to spread the gospel of Hellas over the barbarian world and] he sought to show that earthly things are subject to one *logos* and to one city and that all mankind are one people, and so he fashioned himself.

[1] Cf. especially E. Lohmeyer, *Kyrios Jesus*, Sitzungsberichte Heidelberg, 1928, no.4. Of the commentaries consulted Wettstein quotes the first sentence of the Plutarch passage, and Lightfoot, *Philippians*, 6th ed., 111, mentions it in order to illustrate the meaning of ἁρπαγμός.

If therefore the god which sent Alexander's soul to earth had not so soon recalled him, one law would have illumined all men, and they would have managed their affairs with reference to one justice as a common source of light. But, as it was, part of the world which knew not Alexander remained in darkness, cut off from the light of the sun.

The similarity of the two passages, extending as it does to the use of words like ἅρπαγμα and ἁρπαγμός, or ἐσχημάτιζεν and σχήματι εὑρεθείς, seems to justify an inquiry as to their relation to each other. Both deal with a superhuman being who became man and lived on earth in order to benefit humanity, a saviour sent by the Deity and soon recalled by him to a heavenly abode, who fashioned himself to meet the needs of men. But, similar though the two passages are, direct dependence is out of the question. Plutarch, although the younger of the two by about forty years, can hardly be under obligation to St. Paul. That brilliant courtier, philosopher, and priest of the Delphic Apollo would scarcely have borrowed from an obscure writer of an obscure sect, neither, had he done so, is it likely that he would have reduced the Christian song of triumph to an admission of at least partial failure. St. Paul on the other hand freely admits that he became 'to the Greeks a Greek', and it may be assumed that, at least, both writers are drawing on the language of popular philosophy as employed to expound the divinity of Hellenistic monarchs and, later, Roman emperors. A certain Stoic trend in the immediate context of Plutarch, which is in marked contrast with the anti-Stoic tendency of some of his other writings, makes it tempting to go further and look to some Stoic diatribe as a possible model, and even to hazard the name of Posidonius, and the migration of souls, as a possible common source for both passages.

II

In any case it is abundantly clear that Phil.2:5-11 belongs to this range of ideas, and it is instructive to notice the differences. Alexander in his civilizing mission refrained from looting Asia, refusing to exploit his good fortune. Christ, 'being in the form of

God', refused to regard equality with God as a privilege to be exploited, a piece of good fortune to be enjoyed. The common source, or common tradition, probably embraced some idea of divine descent which is contained in St. Paul's ἴσα θεῷ, but deliberately softened and almost eliminated by Plutarch. Perhaps Plutarch was unduly fastidious, for another Platonist, the author of the Pseudo-Platonic *Axiochus* (364A), quite unblushingly informs us that Heracles, son of Zeus, ἴσα θεοῖς ἐτιμήθη. Heracles was the model ruler of Stoic political doctrine, the prototype of Hellenistic rulership, and was also called ἰσόθεος in another work of that school, the *Bibliotheke* of Diodorus, a writer who gives the same title to a variety of demigods and men.[1]

These ἰσόθεοι are not all rulers, but they are all benefactors of humanity, and in this respect all imitators of Heracles, who is the prototype of all those who are 'equal with god'. His labours and his victories and above all his beneficent deliverance of mankind from so many besetting evils earned him the title. To be 'equal with God' is thus the supreme title of the conqueror who is also the universal benefactor, Jesus Christ according to St. Paul, Alexander the Great according to the Stoics. That Alexander was actually worshipped like Heracles appears from Lucian's *Mort. Dial.*, 13.2, where he is greeted as the 'thirteenth god', a title commonly accorded to Heracles.

On the other hand Plutarch, if he hesitated to call Alexander equal to God, did avail himself of another simile, not employed by St. Paul, Helios, the sun of righteousness. If this is part of the original tradition and St. Paul deliberately left it out, the reason might be theological, to stress the supremacy of Christ over the righteous. It is in fact used of the righteous in Matt.13:43, and there is an instructive passage in the Fourth Book of Maccabees,[2]

---

[1] Diodor., ed. L. Dindorf, book I, ch.2 §3. Further instances for ἰσόθεος from the same author are I.20.5 (Osiris); I.97.6 (Daedalus); IV.1.4 (many demigods and heroes); X.9.9 (Pythagoras as the lawgiver at Croton); XXIX.18 (Philopoemen). Another interesting example is Lucian, *Anacharsis* 10, who calls the Olympian victors ἰσόθεοι, probably because of the close connection of the Olympic games with Heracles, their mythical founder.

[2] 4 Macc.17:5. 'Not so majestic stands the moon in heaven among the stars as thou, lighting to godliness these thy seven sons, equal with the stars, dost

where the Maccabean mother and her sons, as the moon and the stars, give a fair analogy to Alexander, the sun of righteousness on earth.

Alexander, like Jesus, stepped down to his subjects by making himself like them. The ἐσχημάτιζεν of Plutarch corresponds to the σχήματι εὑρεθείς of St. Paul. There is an analogy and a difference. Plutarch clearly regarded Alexander's change of dress as a degradation. In the same context he says that the keeper of a bull discards his red dress, and the keeper of an elephant his white one, so as not to irritate the beasts in their charge. In the same way the just king expresses by his dress his respect for his subjects; and the gesture costs him little enough.

In the case of Christ the change of 'fashion' is something more than a disguise, and it is not made without cost. Christ, 'being in the form of His Father', became a subject to His life's end, His death on the cross. The word ὑπήκοος again has its counterpart in the ὑπήκοα of Plutarch.[1] Alexander, though trying to regard his rule as something other than a piece of personal good fortune— ἁρπαγμός is rightly translated by E. Lohmeyer, loc. cit., 20, as 'res rapta' rather than 'res rapienda'—nevertheless only makes by the change of his attire a gracious gesture, as compared with the complete selfgiving of Christ. As Christ's sacrifice is immeasurably greater so is its result immeasurably more important.

Had Alexander lived a little longer, he would, so Plutarch believes, have achieved his object and have united all mankind under the common law, which corresponds with the common *logos*, to which all things on earth are subject. Plutarch, or his source, demands a natural law for human behaviour, analogous to that common natural law, 'the *logos* which governs all things'. A reference to this common *logos*, it should be noted, appears also

---

stand in honour with God, and art established with them in heaven.' It is significant that the term used for 'equal with the stars', ἰσάστερος, is modelled on ἰσόθεος.

[1] It may be either the adjective 'subject' or 'obedient' or the noun 'the subject'. The choice of the noun rather than of the adjective, although the point is of a minor importance, is suggested by the analogy of the Plutarch passage and by the fact that St. Paul does not mention any specific command, given by the Father to his Son, to do this.

in Phil.2:15f., 'ye shine as lights in the world, holding forth the Word of Life'. But Alexander according to the will of the daemon met with failure; Alexander Helios never shone in the West.

To Jesus Christ, according to St. Paul, is granted success far surpassing that denied to Alexander, and in his case his death is itself the reason why the world has come under the one law of Christ by the will of God his Father. The way in which St. Paul gives expression to this conviction again shows the marks of Stoic philosophy, though Plutarch no longer serves as a parallel. For the exegesis of verses 9–11 we may again turn to Diodorus. It is his description of the rise of Zeus to the throne of the world which explains, if not the actual wording, yet the idea underlying these verses.

[Diodor., III.61.6.] Therefore after his departure from among men he was named Zeus because he seemed to be the source of the good life among men; and he was given his place in the *cosmos* by the worship of those who had received benefactions from him, who all gladly acknowledged him god and lord for ever over the whole world.

There is no reason to suppose that St. Paul copied this passage, or even knew it, but he was familiar with the theology behind it, the theology of the divine name, assumed by the divine man at the time of his death, and with the title 'God and Lord for ever'. Instead of the 'whole world' of Diodorus St. Paul says 'in heaven and on earth and under the earth', which means the same but is more explicit. It is God too, not the beneficiaries, who grants to Christ the 'name above all names'. But here too the difference is less than the modern reader might suppose, especially since the common obeisance of all mankind, and all demons, powers, and angels, is particularly mentioned by St. Paul. It seems to me probable that the whole paragraph is dependent on some pre-Roman Hellenistic model from which Plutarch probably deviated farther than did St. Paul.

III

The Roman Emperor was also called ἰσόθεος,[1] and this fact helps to explain why Plutarch says that the West has not benefited

[1] Cf. F. J. Doelger, *Antike und Christentum*, vol.4, 1934, p.128.

from the light of Alexander Helios. If it had, there would have been no need for the Roman Emperor; 'the *nomos* would have been king', as Pindar, with reference to the redemptive work of Heracles, had affirmed it to be. The same reason no doubt enters into Plutarch's avoidance of the word ἰσόθεος. Alexander, however, the son of Zeus Ammon, did undoubtedly afford a model to imperial Rome[1] and official propaganda even went so far as to allow a miraculous conception both to Caesar and Augustus. It may be noted in passing that Jesus Himself was accused by the Jews because He too said that God was His Father, 'making himself equal with God', John 5:18.

'Remota ergo iustitia, quid sunt regna nisi magna latrocinia?' St. Augustine's question (*Civ.*, 4.4) is only the most prominent restatement of the problem which occupied the minds of Plutarch and of St. Paul and of the common source or tradition which underlies both passages. Taking as his starting point the dispute between Alexander and the captured pirate, Augustine gives the necessary background for the theological discussion of Phil.2:5–11 in the light of its suggested origin. Is it enough to be a Macedonian to the Macedonians and a Persian to the Persians? It is not. Plutarch himself admits that Alexander had, at least partly, failed, though behind this admission there is a certain subtle flattery of his imperial master Hadrian, who had visited the whole world and had made his villa near Tivoli a kind of architectural microcosm of his Empire. Is that enough? Is the 'shepherd of the nations' *ipso facto* the divine monarch because he avoids provoking his bulls by a red coat or his elephants by a white one? St. Paul's answer is in the negative: something more is needed. The king must become like his lowest subject, take upon him 'the form of a slave', and die a slave's death. No heathen succeeded in combining the two ideas. Diogenes took the form of a slave, but he was no king; Alexander was king, but he lowered himself only a little, and these two ideal men were opposed to each other with hardly a point of contact. But the kingdom of Christ could be represented

---

[1] This fact is neglected in 'Divus Alexander' by H. Usener, *Kl. Schr.*, vol.4, 1913, p.396f., whose sources are of importance for our argument, although his conclusions are erroneous.

as embracing both these ideals of Hellenistic philosophy, for He
who was in His Father's fashion, like Alexander wearing by right
his father's royal robe, proved that His reign was not a 'magnum
latrocinium', a ἁρπαγμός, by taking upon Him the form of a
slave.

'We have this treasure in earthen vessels', and the preacher must
always to some extent employ the language of his audience. But if
St. Paul speaks in terms of ideas which were commonplace in his
time, the use which he makes of them is not commonplace. He
was writing to Philippi, 'the chief city of that part of Macedonia
and a colony', Acts 16:12, a town where Roman administration
in the name of the 'Imperator Divus' had its headquarters, and no
doubt sometimes exploited its opportunities. So there is special
point in his insistence that equality with God is no prize of fortune
to be exploited; and in this application of the eternal message to
his own day there lies too the fundamental difference between
St. Paul's use of their common source or tradition and that made
by Plutarch: 'be ye also minded even as Christ was'; how could
that have been said of Alexander, whose Persian attire was still a
royal robe? Phil.2:5–11 is not an academic discussion 'On the
Virtue or Fortune' of some great king, nor an attack on a different
philosophical sect, but an attempt to lay the foundations of a new
way of life for every man. Martin Luther in the introductory sentences of his pamphlet *De Libertate Christiana* gives classical expression to the eternal tension which has ever since characterized
Christian living:

Christianus homo omnium dominus est liberrimus, nulli subiectus;
Christianus homo omnium servus est officiosissimus, omnibus sub-
jectus.

4

GREEK PROVERBS IN THE GOSPEL

I

CHRISTIANITY arose in an environment which was, on the one hand, still dependent upon the traditions of the Jewish Church, but, on the other, wide open to Hellenistic civilization. There exists today a strong and in many respects very healthy tendency to test the Gospels for Aramaic origin, the results of which are at the same time stimulating and challenging.[1] However, even if the view that major portions of the four canonical Gospels are translations from the Aramaic be accepted, we are still faced with the question where the ideas behind the words came from. For it is not only risky to assume that the translations themselves were uncritical, quasi-mechanical versions, especially in view of the fact that the contemporary Greek translations of the Old Testament as well as the early translations of the Greek New Testament into other languages show a fair amount of skill;[2] but also the Aramaic original itself may have been influenced by Greek ideas and in this way may have determined the translator's method. The original Aramaic language does not also guarantee the Semitic origin of the thought expressed thereby.

I want to illustrate here the fact that Jewish texts in Aramaic as well as in Greek lent themselves readily to the adaptation of Hellenistic ideas. For this purpose the material has been chosen from the Apocrypha and from the Sayings of Jesus. With the exception of the one Jewish apocryphal text a Semitic original of the texts under discussion is virtually certain. For just as Jesus' disciples

---

[1] Cf. the excellent study by M. Black, *An Aramaic Approach to the Gospels and Acts*, 1946.

[2] Augustine's verdict on the *Vetus Latina*, *Doctr. Christ.*, 2.11 fin., 'ut enim cuique primis fidei temporibus in manus venit codex Graecus et aliquantulum facultatis sibi utriusque linguae habere videbatur, ausus est interpretari', is hardly fair.

discoursed in their native Galilean (Mark 14:70 par.), so did their Master. Therefore, unless the Sayings quoted are spurious, which seems unlikely as they all come from Q,[1] they were originally spoken—and probably even written—in Aramaic. Yet they also show a close relation to current Greek proverbs. This source is now almost silent, because we mainly possess the remnants of the great literature of the time, but in the Hellenistic period it seems to have influenced Greeks and barbarians very strongly.

It must not be argued, therefore, that the comparatively small number of instances given here proves little, for they are chosen from a much larger store of material. In the eighteenth century J. J. Wettstein collected an abundance of Greek and Latin parallels to the New Testament. This collection, it is true, does not satisfy modern theologians, because sometimes the analogies are only superficial and the foundations of the vast edifice are in any case less sure than those of P. Billerbeck's collection of Talmudic parallels. Wettstein is thus more often used as a quarry than as a theological authority. I hope what I say here will contribute in a small way to the foundations of a new Wettstein which, it is hoped, may one day take its place beside Billerbeck. It is for this reason that only proverbial sayings have been chosen. Proverbs are, so to speak, the lowest common denominator of moral philosophy and will allow for a great variety of ethical conclusions to be drawn. It would be fatal to say Christianity is Hellenistic as much as it would be to say that it is Jewish; but it is essential to see that and how, right from the days of Jesus' ministry in Galilee and Jerusalem, Greek modes of thought were not excluded from the preaching of the Gospel.[2]

II

(a) The first Jewish example is taken from the book of Ecclesiasticus 30:20b. The line in question is preserved in Greek, and also

---

[1] M. Dibelius, *From Tradition to Gospel*, 1934, p.233f., assumes that 'the text (of Q) used by Matthew and Luke was in Greek', but even he, reluctantly, allows for the possibility that the earliest collection of Sayings of Jesus was in Aramaic.

[2] It is with a certain concern that we see Greek and Hebrew thought so

in Hebrew in one of the Genizah MSS. (B).[1] There is no doubt that it contains a thought which was current amongst Alexandrian Jews in the third and second centuries B.C. The Greek version is verbally identical with the Hebrew ὥσπερ εὐνοῦχος περιλαμβάνων πάρθενον [καὶ στενάζων], so that there may be doubts as to its priority over against the extant Hebrew.[2] 'As an eunuch embraceth a virgin' is a very telling simile, and it may be asked whether Ben-Sira himself invented it or not. In favour of an Eastern origin may be the fact that eunuchs were more common in the East than in Greece where they had not been known in earlier times. It may also be said that a comparable remark in Juvenal,[3] who says 'cum tener uxorem ducat spado', is no more than a distant parallel; and even in the case of Lucian[4] the parallel may not be wholly conclusive. He says of an uneducated person buying books, 'sooner should a bald man buy a comb, or a blind man a mirror, or a deaf one a flute-player, or an eunuch a young woman' (οὐ μᾶλλον ἢ φαλακρὸς ἄν τις πρίαιτο κτένα ἢ κάτοπτρον ὁ τυφλὸς ἢ ὁ κωφὸς αὐλητὴν ἢ παλλακὴν ὁ εὐνοῦχος), and this agrees with the saying in Ecclus. 30:19f. 'what good doeth the offering to an idol? For neither can it eat nor smell: so is he that is persecuted of the Lord, he seeth with his eyes and groaneth, as an eunuch that embraceth a virgin.' The proof that these sayings have a common source is to be found in the fact that we find in a collection of Greek proverbs,[5] that εὐνοῦχος παλλακήν was a popular

---

diametrically opposed as black and white, as has been done recently, e.g. by J. A. T. Robinson, *In the End God . . .*, 1950, pp.11,49 and passim.

[1] Cf. the text in H. L. Strack, *Die Sprüche Jesus des Sohnes Sirach*, 1903, p.22; N. Peters, *Der jüngst wiederaufgefundene hebräische Text des Buches Ecclesiasticus*, 1902, p.107. R. Smend, *Die Weisheit des Jesus Sirach*, 1906, has been inaccessible to me.

[2] Καὶ στενάζων is spurious, mechanically repeated from verse 20a. In order to claim the priority of the Hebrew over the Greek, it would have to be assumed either that the mistake was already made by Ben-Sira himself whose ms. was translated by his grandson and served as the ultimate source of the Genizah ms. or that the same mistake was committed by a Greek and a Hebrew copyist independently.

[3] Juvenal, 1.22.

[4] Lucian, *Adv. Indoct.*, 19.

[5] Leutsch-Schneidewin, *Paroemiographi Graeci* I, 1839, p.459.

Greek saying. Therefore it is reasonable to assume that Ben-Sira as well as Lucian, and even Juvenal, used this proverb for their various purposes, which in each case was the description of something which, though desirable in itself, was useless to its owner.[1]

In other words, we have here a verse from a Jewish apocryphal writing witnessing to the popularity of a somewhat disreputable Greek proverb. Perhaps there is another verse too (Ecclus. 20:4) which bears witness to the same proverb. How did it happen that such a proverb made its way into the religious literature of the Jews, a place where it is least expected? It is true, of course, that Alexandria, where Ecclesiasticus was written, was more licentious than the Palestinian country and was also the very centre of Hellenism. It would be misleading, however, to claim that Ben-Sira's simile was therefore altogether detached from Jewish thought of the Palestinian type. For Hellenistic influences were very strong in Palestine under the Seleucid reign. The most that can be said is that 'Ben-Sira's general standpoint was Sadducean',[2] i.e. he was inclined to compromise with Hellenism in a way similar to the later party of the Sadducees in Palestine. His general outlook and wide travels in the Hellenistic kingdoms of his day which caused Jesus ben-Sira to open his mind to the influence of Greek civilization, not only in his thought but even in the expression of his thoughts, were the common experience of many Jews of his time who, like him, still preferred to use the language of their forefathers.

(*b*) A similar tendency to use Hellenistic matter still existed in Jewish circles at the time of the early Church; and in the instance I am now going to analyse, the Greek idea which was adopted had more than a flavour of heathendom. It was the outcome of moral convictions which had long been embodied in the religious teaching of Greece. The saying to which I refer is found in the appendix to the Ezra-Apocalypse which is now usually

---

[1] According to V. Ryssel in E. Kautzsch, *Apokryphen und Pseudepigraphen*, 1900, vol.1, p.382f., 'he that is persecuted of the Lord' is a sick person.

[2] W. O. E. Oesterley, *An Introduction to the Books of the Apocrypha*, 1935, p.242.

described as 6.Ezra, i.e. the 15th and 16th chapters of 2.Esdras in the Apocrypha of the Authorized Version. There we read:

[16.49f (Vulg.)] Tanto magis adzelabo eos super peccata sua, dicit Dominus, 50. quomodo zelatur fornicaria mulierem idoneam et bonam valde, 51. sic zelabitur iustitia iniquitatem, cum exornat se, et accusat eam in facie, cum venerit qui defendat exquirentem omne peccatum super terram.

[16.48f (A.V.)] The more will I be angry with them for their sin, saith the Lord, 49. like as a whore envieth a right honest and virtuous woman: 50. so shall righteousness hate iniquity, when she decketh herself, and shall accuse her to her face, when he cometh that shall defend him that diligently searcheth out every sin upon earth.

Regarding the date of the text quoted, it is generally accepted that the two last chapters of 2.Esdras were added to the Ezra-Apocalypse proper (comprising 2.Esdras 3–14) only in the course of the third century A.D. But this view neither determines the time when these chapters were written nor does it say anything about their origin. Even if the Christian origin of 2.Esdras 1–2, another accretion to the Ezra-Apocalypse, should appear probable, chapters 15 and 16 would have to be judged on their own merit.[1] H. Gunkel[2] has correctly stated that Christian origin cannot be claimed for chapters 15 and 16 with any certainty. In fact, there is not a single feature in these two chapters which would appear to be specifically Christian; there are, on the other hand, references to the temple in Jerusalem (15.25), its priests (16.36), and the prohibition to eat sacrificial meat (16.68f). These seem to be sufficient reasons for assuming that 6.Ezra was written by a Jew before A.D. 70.[3] As to its original language, there is hardly a clue.

[1] E. Schürer, *Gesch. d. Jüd. Volkes*, 4th ed., vol.3, 1900, p.316, and G. H. Box, in R. H. Charles, *Apocrypha and Pseudepigrapha*, 1913, vol.2, p.549, should not have combined 5 and 6.Ezra in claiming their Christian origin, neither is the general argument proposed by P. Riessler, *Altjüd. Schrifttum*, op. cit., p. 1285, convincing, who says that they are Jewish, as 'it is impossible that a Christian should have written a book under the name of an O. T. Saint'.

[2] In Kautzsch, op. cit., vol.2, p.332, Gunkel says of 5 and 6.Ezra, 'das erstere Stück ist sicher christlichen Ursprungs, vielleicht auch das zweite'.

[3] Riessler, op. cit., p.1287, who believes that 6.Ezra was written in the late first century B.C., gives an impressive list of contemporary events to which the book refers—if the date is correct.

Although the predominant view is that it was Greek, frequent Semitisms which make themselves still felt in the Latin and the whole character of the work which is fiercely Pharisaic, make it at least possible that it was originally written in Aramaic. In any case it may well serve as an illustration of the Jewish mind at the time of Jesus Christ.

The passage which has been quoted exhibits an ill-adapted illustration comparing the zealous Lord avenging injustice to 'a whore envying a right honest and virtuous woman'. Before an attempt is made to explain this surprising incongruity, which shows a break in the argument caused by the intrusion of an alien element, it is necessary to refer to the Hellenistic parallel which I have in mind. This is to be found in Pausanias' description of the shrine of Kypselos. There, in one of the scenes depicted on the shrine, was found 'a comely woman punishing an ill-favoured one, justice ($\delta i \varkappa \eta$) overpowering unrighteousness ($\dot{\alpha}\delta i \varkappa i\alpha$)'.[1] This was a scene which became popular among the Greeks, as may be seen from Hellenistic vase paintings.[2] It is understandable that similar Persian ideas were easily combined with this Greek conception.[3] The Persian idea, however, contained only one female figure. It was the Druǧ, the power of evil, which attacked the world of the good God:

[Yašt, 19.90] when the creation will grow deathless—the prosperous creation of the Good Spirit—and the Druǧ shall perish though she may rush on every side to kill the holy beings[4] . . .

Thus it appears that the imagery employed is Hellenistic: the

[1] Pausanias, V.18.2.

[2] Cf. the illustration in J. G. Fraser, *Pausanias Descript. of Greece*, 1898, vol.3, p.612, also in A. Baumeister, *Denkmäler*, 1888, vol.2, p.1300 pl.1442. Cf. also Hitzig-Blümner's commentary and my remark, *Harvard Theol. Rev.* 1945, 182, n.16.

[3] P. Böhlig, *Geisteskultur von Tarsos*, 1913, pp.103, 104 n.2, derives the Pauline idea of the struggle between truth ($\dot{\alpha}\lambda\dot{\eta}\theta\varepsilon\iota\alpha$) and injustice ($\dot{\alpha}\delta\iota\varkappa\dot{\iota}\alpha$) from Persian examples, quoting as evidence Bundahish 30.29, 'afterwards Aûharmazd seizes on the evil spirit . . . true speaking on what is evil speaking', trans. E. W. West, *Pahlavi Texts*, vol.1, 1880, p.128. It seems possible that the fact that these are the only abstract ideas matched in the great struggle may be indicative of an influence of Greek philosophical thought upon the Persian text.

[4] J. Darmsteter, *The Zend Avesta*, vol.2, 1883, p.307, cf. Böhlig, op. cit.

honest woman and the harlot fighting are taken from the complex of ideas alluded to in Pausanias' description of the shrine of
Kypselos. The Persian idea comes in, however, insofar as the
initiative is left to the figure representing the power of evil. This
was not changed by the author of 2.Esdras 16:48(49)f., however
much it disturbed his purpose. It may therefore be concluded that
the Persian conception was firmly established in his mind, so that
he appears as an oriental, probably from Palestine, where such
ideas had taken a firm root since the days of the Achaemenids.

Old Testament ideas of justice—and it must be remembered
that the fight between justice and injustice is expressly mentioned
in 16:49(50)—and Christian ideas too, cannot be adduced to
elucidate the allegory. Whether or not 6.Ezra was originally
written in Aramaic, it is certain that it employs a popular Hellenistic idea of a proverbial character, although this idea was by
origin and intention far removed from the doctrinal system of
Judaism. It is true that the concept which the writer employed
is not so much a proverb in the narrower sense as a proverbial
symbol, representing a popular Hellenistic conviction by means
of a picture rather than a phrase; nevertheless it is an instructive
example for the characterization of the Evangelists' minds, who
so often had to put new wine in old bottles.

III

Jesus himself was just as ready as these Jewish authors to adopt
Hellenistic proverbs. Certain Sayings of his are put in such a form
in the Gospels, that they call to mind Greek proverbs preserved in
secular pagan writings. Of these three have been selected to illustrate his use of the material upon which he worked.[1] They are all
well attested, since they are derived from Q, that early collection
of his Sayings[2] which can claim a fair measure of authenticity,

---

[1] Another instance, the parallel between Matt.8:21-2 par., 'let the dead bury
their dead'—also originating from Q—and Eurip. *Alcest.* 894 schol. ed. E.
Schwartz, vol.2, p.304, l.3f., and related texts, demands a more detailed
examination.

[2] Cf. M. Dibelius, *From Tradition to Gospel*, p.244f.

although it shows here and there 'traces of a more advanced development'.[1] The first two are preserved by Matthew and Luke: Matt.11.17 = Luke 7:32, and Matt.24:28 = Luke 17:37; but even the third, which is only found in Luke 16:8b, and which therefore must have passed through Proto-Luke, shows that it ultimately stems from Q.[2]

(a) Matt.11:17 par.

> We have piped unto you and ye have not danced;
> We have mourned unto you and ye have not lamented.

Since J. Wellhausen's[3] time it seems to be agreed that this verse reproduces an Aramaic original because of 'the antithetic parallelism, rhythm and even rhyme which are found in this couplet' [4] whenever it is read in the various Syriac translations. On the other hand, the first line of the couplet has a very close parallel in an old Greek fable—but not the second. Moreover, the parallel is one of concept rather than of actual wording:

> [Herodot., I.141] a flute-player saw the fish in the sea and played his flute believing that they would come to land. Finding, however, that he was mistaken, he took a net and enclosed a great many of the fish and pulled them ashore. Seeing them jump, he said to the fish, 'Stop dancing, for you did not come to dance when I played for you.'

Herodotus tells us this story as the reply of the victorious Cyrus to the Ionian cities, which had applied for treaties after his conquest of the Lydian kingdom. It comes from the great stock of Aesop, and it would be interesting to know whether Herodotus' or Aesop's version was responsible for Jesus' parable. For, if the former should be the case, the parable would form a telling introduction to Jesus' lament over the Galilean cities by which it is followed in Matthew, whereas Luke has separated the two pieces (7:32 and 10:19f.).

---

[1] M. Dibelius, op. cit., p.245.
[2] B. Weiss, *Die Quellen des Lukas-Evangeliums*, 1907, p.249f.
[3] Quoted from E. Klostermann,*Matthaeus*, 2nd ed., 1927, p.101, who does not refer to any specific work of Wellhausen's.
[4] M. Black, *An Aramaic Approach*, p.118f.

The lack of interest in this parallel shown by both classical scholars and theologians is unjustified. For instance How and Wells[1] merely remark in their commentary on Herodotus: 'the fable is part of a collection bearing Aesop's name. For it cf. St. Matt.11:17'; and Th. Zahn[2] says, 'there is nothing to learn from the parallel in Herod., I:141, cf. Aesop *Fab.* 27^b (Halm), except that playing a flute meant an invitation to dance'.

However, at least one further question has to be answered: when and why was the second line added to the couplet? There is no Greek parallel to it and it seems as if the violent forms in which grief was expressed in the East were more restrained in Greece.[3] Moreover, the line is found independently existing in Ecclus.7:34, 'fail not to be with them that weep and mourn with them that mourn'.

There is a very early Christian source indicating that this Saying of Jesus was known in the form in which we have it in the earliest days of the Church, for it seems evident that Rom.12:15, 'rejoice with them that do rejoice and weep with them that weep', echoes Jesus' Saying in Matt.11:17—or rather Luke 7:32—but we cannot draw the conclusion that it was Jesus himself who was the first to pair the two lines of the couplet. This was done even earlier, as appears from a Jewish proverb, quoted by P. Billerbeck amongst his other parallels:[4]

Rab Papa (ob. A.D. 376) has said: This is what is said by the people (i.e. proverbially): 'whether you cry in the presence of someone who

---

[1] W. W. How and J. Wells, *A Commentary on Herodotus*, 2nd ed., 1928, vol.I, p.118.

[2] Th. Zahn, *Evangelium des Matthaeus*, 1903, p.430, n.27.

[3] This may be the reason for the change from ἐκόψασθε in Matth. to ἐκλαύσατε in Luke, stated but not explained by G. B. Kilpatrick, *The Origins of the Gospel according to St.Matthew*, 1946, p.15. For the law of Solon restricting funeral rites, which is repeatedly quoted by later authorities, e.g. Cic., *De Leg.*, II 59, although it did not prohibit the beating of breasts, contained, according to Plut., *Solon*, 21.5, the words ἀμυχὰς κόπτειν, and consequently made the word κόπτειν obnoxious. For as a legal term κόπτειν was used to describe an activity which, on the authority of Solon, came to be regarded as immoral.

[4] P. Billerbeck, *Kommentar z. N.T. aus Talmud und Midrasch*, vol.I, 1922, p.604. A. Schlatter, *Der Evangelist Matthaeus*, 2nd ed., 1933, p.372f., has no convincing analogy to offer.

does not understand or laugh to someone who does not understand, woe to him who does not know how to distinguish between good and evil'.

Granted, this analogy is only late, yet it contains a reference to an earlier proverb which can hardly be derived from Jesus but which said something very much akin to his teaching. It must have sprung directly from Prov.29:9, 'if a wise man contendeth with a foolish, whether he rage or laugh, there is no rest'. We therefore come to the conclusion that a Jewish proverb, derived from Prov. 29:9 but strongly influenced by Aesop's fable, and possibly by Herodotus, was in existence to be used by Jesus. In any case, the foreign origin of Jesus' Saying is still recognizable by the fact that the allegory does not fit well into the context. Thus the result is reached that in Matt.11:17 par. we have a verse, Aramaic in origin, yet at least partly dependent upon thought which had been fashioned into a proverbial saying in Greek surroundings.[1]

(*b*) Matt.24:28 = Luke 17:37, 'wheresoever the carcase is, there the eagles will be gathered together'. Matthew and Luke have the same Greek wording with one exception: Matthew uses πτῶμα for carcase and Luke σῶμα. With regard to meaning this is a distinction without a difference, for σῶμα is often used by the LXX to mean corpse; for our purpose, however, the change in Luke will prove to be significant.

There can be no doubt that this Saying of Jesus has a proverbial character. Old Testament parallels have been adduced by various writers. Of these Hab.1:8, 'they shall fly as the eagle hasteth to eat', which is frequently referred to, lacks all the mention of the carcase and is therefore rather unconvincing. On condition, it is far better to accept Billerbeck's and Bultmann's reference to Job 39:30, 'where the slain are there they (i.e. the young eagles) also

---

[1] R. Bultmann, *Gesch. d. Synopt. Tradition*, 2nd ed., 1931, p.219, n.1, quotes an Arabic proverb as a parallel to Matt.11:17, saying 'when he applauds you acclaim him'. This is but a remote analogy, for this proverb says hardly more than the Latin 'manus manum lavat', and shows nothing of the 'too late', which is so prominent in Aesop and Matthew. The Talmudic parallels to Rom.12:15 in Billerbeck, are also rather late, especially that from *Derek Erez* which Billerbeck puts first, and prove little. It is, however, interesting to notice that b. Ta'an. 11a, says only 'weep with them that weep', like Ecclus.7:34.

are', the condition being that W. B. Stevenson's thesis be accepted
that this semi-verse 'is a superfluous and disconnected part of the
composition', and that 'it may well be an intrusive proverbial
saying or an adaptation of such a saying'.[1] In order to prove this
thesis we have to resort to another verse of Job, in which both the
name of the bird (which is lacking in Job 39:30b) and also the
word πτῶμα appear (for which the Greek of 39:30b has τεθνεῶτες)
and which is of a proverbial character. So far this verse has not
been compared with Matt.24:28 par.[2] The reason for this apparent
indifference is that in the Hebrew Job 15:23, 'he wandereth for
bread saying, where is it? He knoweth that the day of darkness is
ready at his hand', does not resemble Matt.24:28 par. in the least.
In the Greek, however, it reads differently:

> κατατέτακται δὲ εἰς σῖτα γυψίν.
> οἶδεν δὲ ἐν ἑαυτῷ ὅτι μενεῖ εἰς πτῶμα,
> ἡμέρα δὲ αὐτὸν σκοτινὴ στροβήσει.

He is mown down as food for vultures;
and he knows within himself that he will remain a carcase, and the
dark day will terrify him.[3]

Here indeed we have the birds and the carcase not in a description of natural history, as Job 39:30 pretends to be, but with
reference to the fate of the tyrant, a subject rich in proverbial
wisdom.

The difference between the Greek and the Masoretic texts seems

---

[1]Bultmann, op. cit., pp.84, 103, 112, strongly insists upon a Semitic proverb
as the pattern for Jesus' Saying. However, in an aside on p.179, he allows for
the Saying to have been added in Hellenistic surroundings, and it shows good
judgment that Klostermann, *Matthaeus*, p.195, has taken this up and calls
Matt.24:28 'a Greek secular proverb', although he gives no evidence for it,
and we are not convinced that it was secular.—W. B. Stevenson, *Critical Notes
on the Hebrew Text of the Poem of Job*, 1951, p.159.

[2] It has already been mentioned that neither Bultmann nor Billerbeck,
vol.1, p.955, have noted the parallel. It may be added that Schlatter, op. cit.,
p.709, too, gives only a list of passages from Josephus as parallels, which are
chosen so as to illustrate various grammatical points.

[3] I prefer the future μενεῖ because of the corresponding στροβήσει. The
'dark day' contains a reference to Amos 5:18; Zeph.1:15, cf. also the Hebrew
Apocalypse of Elijah 7:5, German translation by Riessler, *Altjüd. Schrifttum*,
p.238, quoting Is.18:6.

due to different vocalization: the Greek translator read *ayyāh* (a large bird of prey, a hawk or vulture) instead of *ayyēh* (where). This, in connection with the subject of the discourse, the fate of the tyrant, seems to have caused the misreading *pīdō* (his carcase) instead of *bᵉyādō* (at his hand).[1] It seems that the Greek, which may go back to a different Hebrew original,[2] owes its origin to the existence of a Greek proverb which contained the words 'vulture' and 'carcase'. The fate of the tyrant, and in particular his miserable death in battle, formed the subject of rhetorical exercises in the boys' schools of the Hellenistic era since the days of Plato, and came to the fore in the translator's mind when meeting with an apparent 'food for vultures' in connection with the mention of the tyrant in Job.

There are numerous allusions to a Hellenistic proverb such as has been presupposed here in Greek and Latin authors. They bear witness to the fact that it contained a reference to the vultures as well as the word πτῶμα, which is rare in Hellenistic Greek.[3] The nearest parallel to Matt.24:28 par. is found in a little textbook on Greek theology ascribed to the Stoic Cornutus and originating from the first century A.D.[4]

---

[1] These two emendations, first suggested in England by G. H. B. Wright, are repeated here on the authority of J. F. Schleusner, *Novus Thesaurus*, 1820–1, s.vv. γύψ and πτῶμα. The first is virtually certain, and the second has at least the value of a brilliant conjecture. On the question whether they should be taken for the Hebrew original, and the Masoretic text for a later misunderstanding, cf. the following note.

[2] Stevenson, op. cit., p.63f., and E. J. Kissane, *The Book of Job*, 1939, pp.87, 91, regard the LXX text as the original. In this case Hellenistic influence would have to be assumed in the composition of the poem itself.

[3] Πτῶμα occurs in the meaning of 'carcase' occasionally in Polybius, Plutarch and Herodian.—How close Greek and Jewish bird-lore could come may be illustrated by the following instance: in 1.Enoch (aeth.) 96:2 we read,
'on the day of sorrow for the sinners your children will be lifted up and will rise like eagles,
and your nest will be higher than that of the vultures'.
This saying is explained by the legend in Antigon. *Mirab.*42 (48), 'some say that no one has ever seen a young male or female vulture. Therefore it was alleged by Herodorus, the father by some woman of Bryson the Sophist, that they belong to another world beyond the clouds. They have their young ones on inaccessible rocks.'

[4] Cornutus, ed. Lang, 1881, p.41.

21. The vulture is said to be Ares' sacred bird because the birds gather together ὅπου ποτ' ἂν πτώματα πολλὰ 'Αρηΐφθορα ᾖ.

The words quoted in Greek have the poetical flavour which often accompanies a proverb. This is especially true of the adjective 'Αρηΐφθορος which moreover seems to be a 'hapax legomenon',[1] and this leads to the assumption that a coined phrase, a proverb, was in the mind of the author. If this proverb was so popular that it even influenced the mind of the Hellenistic Jew who wrote the Greek version of Job, then it is easy to understand how Jesus could expect his audience to appreciate too the use of the proverb.

The number of witnesses to the proverb is indeed considerable, and their critical analysis will suggest that Jesus may have quoted it verbatim. J. J. Wettstein has collected another five instances, three in Latin and two in Greek. Those in Latin are Seneca *Ep.* 95.43, 'voltur est, cadaver expectat';[2] Martial 6.62.4, 'cuius vulturis hoc erit cadaver'; and Lucan 6:550–1

> Et quodcumque iacet nuda tellure cadaver
> Ante feras volucres sedet.[3]

Those in Greek are Lucian *Navig.* 1 θᾶττον τοὺς γύπας ἕωλος νεκρὸς ἐν φανερῷ κείμενος . . . διαλάθοι; and Aelianus *Hist.*

[1] Liddell and Scott give no other reference. This is also the only explicit witness that the vulture was the sacred bird of Ares. Nevertheless, although the vulture was also associated with Pallas, Eurip., *Troad.*534, and with Hercules, Plutarch, *Quaest. Rom.*, 93, cf. Sir d'Arcy W. Thompson, *A Glossary of Greek Birds*, 2nd ed., 1936, p.85, Stoll in Roscher, *Lexikon der Mythologie*, vol.1, 1890, p.487, was right to accept the evidence. For, were not the vultures observed by Romulus and Remus, Livy I.7.1 par., sent by their father Mars-Quirinus? O. Keller in Pauly-Wiss., R. E., vol.7, 1912, p.934, seems to be wrong when saying that the vulture had no connection with religion outside Egypt.

[2] Wettstein's quotation, Ep.46, is incorrect.

[3] To these may be added: Prudentius *Cathemer.*10.41f.

> Quae pigra cadavera pridem
> tumulis putrefacta iacebant,
> volucres rapientur in aures
> animas comitata priores,

a verse voicing pagan sentiments, though written by a Christian poet. Cf. R. Holland, *Arch. Relig. Wiss.*, vol.23, 1925, p.211, on the vulture as a 'soul-bird'.

Anim.2.46. The Latin quotations all contain the word 'cadaver' which, being etymologically derived from 'cadere', is the equivalent of πτῶμα—from πίπτειν. The Greek, however, with the exception of Cornutus and Matthew and Job, say νεκρός. Nevertheless, πτῶμα must be preserved, since the change of expression is the result of that artificial Atticism which made Greek authors observe the rule laid down by Phrynichus[1] that πτῶμα 'corpse' should be used only when it was followed by a genitive of respect.

None of the passages quoted refers to eagles, except Matt. 24:28 par., and we must now ask why this change was introduced. It is at least uncommon for eagles to eat carrion flesh, whereas this is the natural food for vultures. It is therefore widely held that Matt.24:28 par. should read 'vultures'. The simplest explanation for the change would be that 'eagles' was just a mistake on the part of the Evangelist; but in view of the fact that the Greek translators of the Old Testament in most cases changed the vultures contained in the Hebrew text to eagles,[2] this simple explanation seems to be rather improbable. It is more probable that the translators shared the view expressed by Antoninus Liberalis 21, saying that the vulture is 'the most hateful bird to God and man', and therefore disliked the use of the word γύψ. It is thus to be assumed that the Aramaic original spoke of vultures. Whether Wettstein's view should be accepted that the eagle being the symbol of Roman domination even in Jewish apocalyptic writings,[3] the change may betray a political bias on the part of the Evangelist, may perhaps be left open.

Luke's change fron πτῶμα to σῶμα is an interesting translation variant, which has its analogy in the Greek versions of the Old Testament.[4] It is obvious that in this latter case questions of style

---

[1] *Phrynichus*, ed. Lobeck, 1820, p.375, cf. Rutherford, *The New Phrynichus*, 1881, p.472.

[2] O. Keller in Pauly-Wiss., R.E., vol.7, 1912, p.935, who says that this was done in *all* cases where vultures are mentioned in the Hebrew Old Testament.

[3] Cf., e.g., the vision of the eagle in 2.Esdras 11.

[4] In Nu.14:32f., Aquila and Theodotion say πτώματα, whereas Symmachus whose command of Greek was superior to theirs wrote σώματα. For this reference I am obliged to the late Prof. T. W. Manson.—Suidas' remark that πτῶμα was a body without a head hardly deserves any attention.

were responsible for the change, and the same is true also with regard to Luke, whose Greek is better than that of Matthew. Perhaps style was not the only reason which caused Luke to change from Matthew, although πτῶμα was obnoxious from a stylistic point of view. For Atticism reached its peak only in the second century A.D. when Luke's Gospel was already written. There is a possibility that Luke may have been aware of the religious implications contained in the proverb, such as outlined by Cornutus 21, and may have decided to tone them down. In any case, it appears that Matt.24:28, in spite of the change from 'vultures' to 'eagles', is the most reliable tradition for the wording of the Hellenistic proverb, 'where the carcase is, there the vultures will be gathered together', the existence of which can be deduced otherwise only from numerous allusions in Greek and Latin authors.

(c) The third instance of a Hellenistic proverb making its way into the originally Aramaic Sayings of Jesus also comes from Q, although it is not extant in Matthew. B. Weiss[1] has given sufficient reason to show that Luke 16:1–13 is taken from Q. That should hold good even for the semi-verse 8b, 'the children of this world are in their generation wiser than the children of light'. The whole passage, Luke 16:1–13, is shown to be of Semitic origin by its ample attestation by Talmudic parallels.[2] Where, as in the case of v.8b, this Talmudic attestation fails, we find at least linguistic reasons which point the same way. 'The children of this world' and 'the children of light', *beⁿē hā 'olām hazzeh* and *beⁿē 'ōr*, are expressions which are alien to genuine Greek diction. Thus we are faced with a Saying Semitic in style, yet expressing a thought which does not find support from Rabbinic material.[3]

It is understandable that under these circumstances Luke 16:8b

---

[1] B. Weiss, *Die Quellen*, op. cit., p.249f.

[2] Billerbeck, vol.2, p.220f.

[3] It ought to be remembered, however, that the Dead Sea Scrolls in the possession of the Museum for Jewish Antiquities in Jerusalem contain one which describes the struggle between the sons of light and the sons of darkness and in that way provides a certain amount of support to the Aramaic origin of Luke 16:8b.

has been ascribed by Bultmann[1] to the 'sphere of religious syncretism'. However, it is necessary to find some stronger support for this view than Bultmann himself has given it with the help that he has derived from New Testament and Jewish apocryphal analogies. E. Klostermann[2] has drawn attention to the fact that Luke—possibly in an attempt to write in that refined style which was then as always popular amongst the middle classes— has inserted a Greek proverb in Luke 16:3a, 'to beg I am ashamed'. There is, however, a difference between the ideas that the parable itself was couched in such a style, and that the kerygma of the parable was stated by reference to a current popular proverb. The latter is not the necessary consequence of the former, for in the first case it would seem that the Evangelist was entitled in some measure to use his own discretion; in the second, however, a strict adherence to the traditional words of Jesus is demanded in order that the truth of the Divine Word be not impaired. Nevertheless, there is sufficient evidence to show that a Hellenistic proverb may have lain behind the Aramaic Saying which closed the parable of the unjust steward in its earliest form.

The proverb which we have in mind is referred to in one of the letters of Pliny the Younger. In his correspondence, he mentions several times one M. Aquilius Regulus, his political adversary, and a person whom he treats with a real contempt although he belonged to the Roman nobility and was an extremely rich man.[3] Pliny describes him as a typical go-getter and *nouveau riche*, and his antipathy was not even abated when Regulus had lost his only

---

[1] I cannot find any reason for accepting Bultmann's claim, *Gesch. d. Synopt. Trad.*, op. cit., p.190, that Luke 16:8b is secondary: it is the necessary corollary of the fable. I also feel uneasy with regard to his views stated on p.190, n.1. It has to be realised that even the Dead Sea Scrolls do not provide any immediate analogy to the 'children of this world'. Hellenistic analogies derived from Jewish apocalyptic writings on the present and the future Aeon have been collected by H. Sasse in *Theol. Wörterb.*, vol.1, 1933, p.206, l.25f, who, ibid. p.207, l.30f., refers to pagan parallels.—The 'children of light,' on the other hand, are mentioned in the New Testament in 1.Thess.5:5; Eph.5:8; John 12:36, as well as in the Dead Sea Scrolls and in 1.Enoch (aeth.), 108:11.

[2] E. Klostermann, *Lukas*, 2nd ed., 1929, p.216, n.1.

[3] On M. Aquilius Regulus cf. P. v. Rohden in Pauly-Wiss., *R.E.*, vol.2, 1896, p.331.

son. For he even ridiculed the funeral oration which the father, according to custom, had composed for his child: 'credas non de puero scriptum sed a puero' (4.7.7). Nevertheless, on this occasion Pliny felt compelled to admit that Regulus' activities had been conducted with such an energy that they impressed even his adversary, and stated grudgingly,

[ibid. 3] hanc ille vim, seu quo alio nomine vocanda est intentio quidquid velis optinendi, si ad potiora vertisset, quantum boni efficere potuisset. Quamquam minor vis bonis quam malis inest, ac sicut ἀμαθία μὲν θράσος λογισμὸς δὲ ὄκνον φέρει, ita recta ingenia debilitat verecundia, perversa confirmat audacia.[1]

It may be held that this reflection is a common one. If, on the one hand, we are reminded of the fool who rushes in where angels fear to tread, we may also call to mind Hamlet's

> Thus conscience does make cowards of us all,
> And thus the native hue of resolution
> Is sicklied o'er by the pale cast of thought.

All the same, it is important that Pliny did not express the idea only in his own terms, but employed a Greek quotation[2] to which he attached his remarks. That shows that already at his time the experience to which we have referred was expressed in a proverbial saying. It had long been transformed from a shapeless common conviction into a coined phrase. In its original setting this phrase had had nothing to do with a story like that of the unjust steward. That story had its origin in Jewish surroundings, as has been shown by the analogies which Bultmann has collected,[3] but

---

[1] 'If he had used that forcefulness, or by what other name the firm resolve to obtain one's own ends regardlessly is to be called, for worthier objectives, how much good he might have done. Although the good possess less power than the wicked, and just as "lack of learning creates zeal, deliberation laziness", so also are just minds weakened through respect, whereas perverse ones are encouraged by their impudence.'

[2] The quotation goes back ultimately to Pericles' speech on the fallen Athenians, Thuc.II.40.3, but its proverbial character has been recognized long since, cf. A. Otto, *Sprichwörter der Römer*, 1890, p.172.

[3] Bultmann, op. cit., p.216, n.1. Billerbeck, vol.2, p.217f., does not mention these analogies.

it was well attuned to the moral philosophy of the Stoics[1] which was fashionable in the days of Pliny the Younger.

Pliny's own remarks and his quotation afford the means for a comparison between the New Testament point of view and that of its pagan contemporaries. Greek ethics opposed ἀμαθία and its effects to λογισμός, whereas Roman social convention derived similar conclusions from the contrast between 'audacia' and 'vere-cundia'. In other words, the noetic principles which the Greek Sophists and Stoics opposed were replaced by a social code. The Christian Saying, on the other hand, contrasted this αἰών of per-dition with the world of light. Moreover, the two classical sayings both exhibit a spirit of resignation. Pliny is almost complacent about his conclusion that an honest man will not be able to com-pete in energy with a rogue. The Gospel, however, chastises this complacency: 'and the Lord commended the unjust steward' gives Jesus' own conclusion that the children of light should not be less resourceful than the children of this world.

If, therefore, Pliny's quotation serves to underline the fact that the use of foreign material did not prevent Jesus from driving home his own point, it shows, on the other hand, that the tradi-tional uncertainty about the meaning of 'the Lord' is caused by the intrusion of such material. The ambiguity of 'the Lord' in v.8a has no analogy in other parables and clearly marks the suture. All the same, it seems unlikely that Luke 16:8b should be a later addition, for the parable and its kerygma are very closely knit. It seems a reasonably safe conclusion that v.8b was not only extant in Proto-Luke but already in Q.

IV

Is it possible to draw any general conclusions from the limited material which we have discussed? In affirming this we have to remind the reader once more that the instances given are repre-sentative of a much larger material, and that in each case we have

---

[1] The Stoic background of Pliny's saying may be illustrated by a comparison with Chrysippus' definition of ὄκνος as φόβος μελλούσης ἐνεργείας in v. Arnim, *Stoic. Vet. Fragm.*, vol.3, p.98, l.39; p.101, l.30.

even gone beyond the evidence collected by Wettstein.[1] The adoption of Greek proverbs was a fairly wide-spread practice among the Rabbis, and a recent book[2] has drawn just attention to the fact that they were not only quoted in Greek but even translated into Aramaic. The instances discussed, therefore, only illustrate the fact that this wide-spread practice was already popular at the time of Jesus.

This being so, the choice of instances had to proceed with some care. The first example from Ecclesiasticus is meant to show how early this method of adopting Greek proverbs was taken up, and also upon what extraordinary proverbs it might seize. The second example from 6.Ezra not only shows that the practice continued right down to the time of Jesus, it also shows the dilemma between eastern and western influences in which Palestinian Jewry was placed, the world-wide impact of Hellenic-Oriental syncretism. The examples taken from the New Testament show that even in that early collection of Jesus' Sayings which we call Q, Greek influences are clearly discernible, showing the marks of having been re-translated from the Aramaic. Matt.11:17 = Luke 7:32, was taken from a secular surrounding; Matt. 24:28 par. may have a pagan religious background and also shows traces of an intentional alteration—eagles for vultures—which may perhaps have been partly inspired by political considerations; lastly, Luke 16:8b shows how these foreign importations were used to further and not to obscure the Christian kerygma.

All these points may appear obvious, as is also the fact that the

---

[1] An apt illustration of Rom.12:15, discussed before, may be found in Horace, *Epist.*I.18.89: 'oderunt hilarem tristes, tristemque iocosi'. Other striking analogies are frequent: Rom.7:19, 'for the good that I would I do not; but the evil which I would not that I do', responds to Ovid, *Metamorph.*, 7.19:

> . . . . . aliudque cupido
> Mens aliud suadet. Video meliora proboque,
> Deteriora sequor.

Also 1.John 4:18, 'there is no fear in love, but perfect love casteth out fear', has its analogy in Seneca, *Medea*, 416: amor timere neminem verus potest.
All these quotations, which may be easily multiplied, have a proverbial character.
[2] S. Liebermann, *Greek in Jewish Palestine*, 1942, p.144f.

missionary effort of the early Church was directed towards the conversion of Hellenism; however, we are faced today with a growing tendency to ignore them and, opposing Jewish and Greek methods of thought, solemnly to warn us of Greek philosophy as being a hindrance rather than a help to the understanding of the Gospel. Thus it may not be superfluous to point out the signs that not only the Evangelists but even Jesus himself was not opposed to the use of Greek thought. It would not be wise to follow the Jewish Synagogue into the Ghetto, and it is unhistoric to overlook the fact that Christianity owes a considerable debt to religious syncretism. Admittedly, Old Testament parallels to the Gospels are of paramount importance; but when reserve against and perhaps even contempt for the methods of religious history and comparative religion become the fashion of the day, it is necessary to show that neither the tenets of pre-exilic Israel nor the convictions of the Rabbis will altogether account for the riches of the New Testament, and that its exegesis has to take account also of contemporary views and convictions. Those, however, were under the spell of Hellenistic thought, mediating between East and West with a vigour which, alas, it has not altogether preserved.

5

THE CONSTRUCTION AND PURPOSE
OF THE ACTS OF THE APOSTLES

I

I WISH to discuss here[1] three subjects: the literary art of the
historian St. Luke, his technique, and his purpose in the Book of
Acts. I presuppose that the author of Acts is identical with the
author of the Third Gospel and, at the moment, see no reason
why he should not be called St. Luke, but use this name mainly
for convenience sake, and without prejudice. I am not concerned
with textual criticism. The problem of the so-called 'western'
text of Acts, which to my mind is more pronouncedly Judaistic
than the canonical text,[2] will not be touched upon. My aim is to
give a literary appreciation, and for this purpose I take for my
basis the text which has been proposed in the latest Nestle edition.[3]

In the field of the literary criticism of the Book of Acts it seems
almost incomprehensible how lightly theologians have dismissed
the thesis of Eduard Meyer, who maintained that St. Luke figures
as the one great historian who joins the last of the genuinely
Greek historians, Polybius, to the first great Christian historian,
perhaps the greatest of all, Eusebius of Caesarea.[4] The man who
proposed this view was after all the last European scholar who possessed the learning to write an Ancient History of his own. It
seems too easy to dismiss his views with invective about 'His-
torismus' or to say, as M. Dibelius does,[5] that Christianity, despite

[1] Based on a paper read to the Lightfoot Society of the Durham Colleges
on St. Luke's Day, 1957.
[2] Cf. Ehrhardt, *The Apostolic Succession*, 1953, p.28f. The opposite view was
proposed by Lagrange, see the summary given by C. S. C. Williams, *Alterations
of the text of the Synoptic Gospels and Acts*, 1951, p.55f.
[3] *Novum Testamentum Graece*, 22nd ed., 1956.
[4] E. Meyer, *Ursprung und Anfänge*, vol.1, 1924, p.2f.
[5] M. Dibelius, *Studies in the Acts of the Apostles*, 1956, p.2.

St. Luke's assertion to the contrary, Acts 26:26, was a hole-and-corner affair. We may say that now at any rate H. J. Cadbury has made out a very good case that this was not so.[1] Neither is it so utterly convincing as M. Dibelius—and following him numerous other theologians—has held that St. Luke had no intention of writing history, but rather short stories (Novellen).[2] For it is evident to all that the Book of Acts sheds light, if an uncertain one,[3] on the development of Christianity during the roughly thirty years from the crucifixion in A.D. 30[4] to St. Paul's arrival at Rome in A.D. 61-2 in a way unrivalled by any other canonical, apocryphal or Jewish source. Is it not true to say that the story of the raising of Tabitha, Acts 11:36f., let alone that of St. Peter's miraculous release from captivity, Acts 12:1f., which M. Dibelius has quoted in support of his thesis, are in no way out of proportion considering the short space of time encompassed by Acts? They serve to illumine the personality of the Apostle, as do the reports from the small hospital of Lambarene in Central Africa, with their general interest throughout the Oecumene, the inspired personality of Albert Schweitzer; and is it seriously suggested that St. Peter should rank below Albert Schweitzer?

As to the general qualification of St. Luke as an historian, reference is so often made to the Greek historians.[5] This, however, seems to narrow down the points of reference much too far. History, we believe, is neither an invention nor a characteristic of the Greek genius. We cannot help feeling that the author of the two books of Samuel would have stood a fair chance of the title of 'father of history' in preference to Herodotus, had he not met with two misfortunes, the first that his work was not originally written in Greek, and the second that it forms an integral part of

---

[1] H. J. Cadbury, *The Book of Acts in History*, 1955.

[2] M. Dibelius, *Studies*, op. cit., p.4. It is pleasant to record that F. F. Bruce, *The Acts of the Apostles*, 2nd ed., 1952, p.15f., gives St. Luke the rank of a true historian.

[3] It has to be said that in his appreciation of the respective reliability of St. Luke and Josephus, Bruce, op. cit., p.17f., seems to favour St. Luke too much.

[4] Cf. J. Jeremias, *The Eucharistic Words of Jesus*, 1955, p.12.

[5] So not only by E. Meyer, loc. cit., but also by theologians like Bruce, op. cit., p.15f.

Holy Scripture. His biography of king David seems to us a model of historical biography, unsurpassed by either Plutarch or Suetonius or, for that matter, by any other historical biographer who may come to mind, down to Laurence Housman, Lytton Strachey or André Maurois. It is true to say that this art of historical biography survived amongst the Jews down to the Hellenistic period, as may be seen from the work of Jason of Cyrene, excerpts of which have survived in the second book of the Maccabees. It has to be stated, therefore, that St. Luke, whether or not it was his intention to write a historical work, was in this tradition when using the means of historical biography to great advantage, especially in his descriptions of St. Peter and St. Paul.[1]

An appreciation of the biographical art of St. Luke may well start with analysing the part played by St. Peter in the Primitive Church according to the Book of Acts.[2] Here we find St. Luke carrying out that programme which, in the Gospel, Luke 2:52, he had wished to apply to Jesus Himself: 'And Jesus increased in wisdom and stature, and favour with God and men.' St. Luke also succeeded in Acts in developing the figure of St. Peter from the data provided for him by St. Mark and the other sources of his Gospel. There the potentialities in the Apostle's character were

---

[1] E. Meyer, op. cit., vol.1, 1924, p.1, n.1, has rightly referred to 2.Macc. as a literary parallel to Acts, but he is obviously mistaken when he says that that is the only one in the O.T. and Apocrypha. The books of Esther and Judith show the same biographical technique, whether or not they are historical, and Wilamowitz, quoted with disapproval by E. Meyer, op. cit., vol.3, 1923, p.5, n.2, has judged correctly in this respect, however fantastic his conclusions.

[2] It may seem a slight overstatement when the late Dean of Christ Church, Oxford, said, 'the Evangelists, writing for a more important purpose, were not much interested in the biographical details about the persons they mentioned', J. Lowe, *St. Peter*, 1956, p.4, referring to the omission of remarks about St. Peter's youth. What St. Luke wants us to understand is that the 'new life', the real life of St. Peter, began with his confession, 'I am a sinful man', Luke 5:8, and with his vocation by the Lord, ibid.10; and it is significant that the story of the miraculous catch of fish is missing from the other Synoptists. We therefore disagree with Dean Lowe's summary dismissal of the traditional portrait of St. Peter, and claim that it is to a large extent the portrait that St. Luke wanted to draw.—O. Cullmann, *St. Peter, Disciple, Apostle, Martyr*, 1953, p.23f., does not remark either on the fact that Lk.5:1–11 has no parallel in the two other Synoptists.

made clearly visible; and it is evident that a certain lack of balance, an instability which may have been due to immaturity, brought about his denial of Christ.[1] It is therefore, so it seems, of great importance for St. Luke's appreciation of St. Peter that he—and that as the only among the Synoptists—has preserved the saying of Jesus, Luke 22:31, 'Simon, Simon, behold Satan has desired to have you, that he may sift you as wheat; but I have prayed for you that your faith may not fail; and you, when you are converted, strengthen your brethren.' St. Luke thus gives us to understand that the denial was anything but 'a temporary failure',[2] but rather the deep fall from which St. Peter was rescued by Christ. Now in the Book of Acts we see the potentialities of St. Peter's strong and active character being brought to fruition in his work for Christ. His former self-confidence is developed into real courage, and Christ's command, 'when thou art converted[3] strengthen the brethren', is the main theme of his characterization in Acts. In particular, St. Peter has gained in moral courage. For, although it may be said that he acted in the case of the centurion Cornelius at the direct command of the Holy Spirit,[4] yet he possesses the faith to defend the position which he had thus taken in the face of a critical, if not openly hostile, assembly of the Church at Jerusalem,[5] not only once, Acts 11:2f., but twice, Acts 15:7f.

St. Peter, therefore, is shown to grow in the course of the events

---

[1] It seems probable to us that the Synoptists omitted to mention the name of St. Peter as the disciple who drew the sword at the arrest of Jesus for apologetic reasons, whilst John 18:10 mentions it, as an established tradition, E. Klostermann, *Das Markus Evangelium*, 2nd ed., 1926, p.170.—No discussion of St. Peter's denial is to be found either in Lowe's or in Cullmann's books.

[2] So Lowe, op. cit., p.10.

[3] The participle ἐπιστρέψας should rather be translated in the active voice, 'on thy return', so as to avoid the awkward question by whom St. Peter was to be 'converted'. Liddell-Scott, s.v., i.3b, suggest the translation 'when thou hast repented', but that, I feel, sounds rather too psychological.

[4] M. Dibelius, *Studies*, p.111, says, 'obviously the vision is intended to give Peter courage'. I cannot see that this is at all obvious. The reason given is purely objective, Acts 10:15, 'what God hath cleansed, that call not thou common'.

[5] Lowe, op. cit., p.16, speaks of 'the scruples of some at Jerusalem'; Acts 11:2 has οἱ ἐκ τῆς περιτομῆς, not τινές. We differ from Bruce, op. cit., p.229, saying 'it is possible that the expression does not simply mean "Jews" (as in

recorded in the first half of Acts, not only in staying power and self-assurance, but in faith. Not only in front of the Jewish authorities, Acts 4:19f.; 5:29f., but in the Christian Church itself, he proves that, as a Christian, he has to obey God rather than men, Acts 5:29; and whether or not St. John of Zebedee was martyred together with his brother St. James,[1] it is clearly in accordance with St. Luke's conception of the development of St. Peter's character that he has learnt, even before the martyrdom of St. James, to make for himself his most crucial decision. It is not St. Peter's miraculous escape from prison, which according to St. Luke terminates the partnership between St. Peter and St. John, Luke 5:10, neither is it brought to an end by St. Peter's removal from Jerusalem. For on an earlier occasion they had travelled together to Samaria. St. John is rather eliminated by St. Luke because St. Peter has, in a convincing development of his character, gained the confidence to rely upon God alone.[2] It is thus not the least among the various features of St. Luke's art as a historian that, at the council of the Apostles so-called, he gives St. Peter the chance of answering a second time for his baptism of Cornelius, and thus makes him the agent for establishing the alliance between the Church at Jerusalem and the churches of the Gentiles.[3] The scene of Acts 15:6f. is fitly set by St. Luke to make St. Peter act independently, not with a superior institutional authority to that of James,[4] but—if such a comparison be permitted—as a prophet in

---

10:45), but denotes those Jewish Christians who were specially zealous for the law'. In Acts 15:5, to which Bruce refers, we find τινές. Correct de Wette-Overbeck, *Kurze Erklärung der Apostelgeschichte*, 4th ed., 1870, p.168.

[1] I have found it unprofitable to dispose of views of Schwartz in the strong terms used by Bruce, op. cit., p.243, but feel that his case is indeed not proven.

[2] It is of course true that St. John 'is a pure lay figure', Lowe, op. cit., p.15, but that makes it still more important to enquire why he is mentioned at all.

[3] The fact that St. Luke uses here a literary device which 'cannot be understood by Peter's hearers, but can be understood by the readers of the book' is somewhat overstressed by M. Dibelius, *Studies*, p.94f. For the 'old days', Acts 15:7, were not so very old.

[4] Lowe, op. cit., p.18, says 'Peter, probably largely because of absence on missionary work had tended to fade out at Jerusalem and James had in effect taken his place'. That may be true, though doubtful, but it is hazardous to state somewhat later, p. 61, 'the Primitive Church at Jerusalem is built on and around Peter, and he is its leader'.

the presence of the High Priest. His joining together of the two divergent branches of the Christian Church, the Jewish–Christian Church at Jerusalem and the predominantly Gentile churches of St. Barnabas and St. Paul, is therefore the culmination of St. Peter's ministry according to Acts, after which he disappears from the scene.

The existing tension, which is not even fully suppressed in St. Luke's record of the council of the Apostles,[1] and which makes it impossible for him to ascribe to St. Peter the position which by the whole tenor of Acts he ought to have occupied, that of the leader of the universal Church, causes us here to remark upon the suppression by St. Luke of so many facts which our curiosity would wish to know. If it is true—and it is indeed widely true— that drawing is the art of omission, we cannot but describe the first half of the Book of Acts as a supreme drawing. Especially the famous question of how the rulership of the Twelve in the Church at Jerusalem came to an end is nowhere even touched upon by St. Luke. The conflicts and stresses to which this change must have exposed St. Peter are all concentrated in his one and most consequential triumph over his opponents in the case of Cornelius,[2] and his coming to the rescue of St. Barnabas and St. Paul. For this is the part played by him at the council of the Apostles. It has been often and rightly observed that the whole Book of Acts is almost equally divided between a Petrine and a Pauline, I would rather say between a Jerusalem and a Pauline part. The dividing line, however, is uncertain.[3] I would claim that Acts

[1] Acts 15:7, 'and when there had been much discussion', is completed in 15:12, 'then all kept silence'; very similar: Pausan., VII.8.2 (1). This forms of course a stylized frame to St. Peter's speech; but whilst it emphasizes the prophetic character of the intervening speech it shows at the same time the tension existing between 'the Apostles and Elders', 15:6, and St. Peter.— M. Dibelius, *Studies*, p.95, n.6, has overlooked the fact that vv.7a and 12a are the brackets round St. Peter's sermon.

[2] M. Dibelius, *Studies*, p.109f., sees rightly that 'the story of the centurion Cornelius has a special importance in the Acts of the Apostles', but fails to see its true significance, the conversion of—St. Peter. His assertion, however, that St. Peter's vision is invented by St. Luke should at least be fortified by an analysis of St. Paul's conversion and the vision of Ananias, Acts 9:3–16, where a second vision of St. Paul is mentioned in 9:12.

[3] M. Dibelius, *Studies*, pp.175, 193f., expresses the general view that the

13-15 marks the crisis of the whole book, and is to be treated as a separate entity. Its most important part is the fifteenth chapter with the council of the Apostles. Here the development of the Jerusalem Church comes to an end, and that of the Gentile churches becomes the main theme. For it has to be recognized that until that time St. Paul, even on his first missionary journey, is never a free agent. He is always under the guidance of the representative of Jerusalem, St. Barnabas, just as St. Peter in the first chapters is given St. John as his constant companion. It is equally noteworthy that St. Luke, who most carefully refrains from mentioning any conflicts between the Twelve—or St. Peter—and James, and their respective followers, feels no such misgivings in relating at once the quarrel between St. Paul and St. Barnabas, immediately after their common triumph at the council of the Apostles, Acts 15:36f.[1]

If, therefore, we give St. Luke credit for being an accomplished artist in the field of history, it is now the time to ask why, whilst omitting certain facts, he chooses to record certain others. Admittedly, he had to work with the material at hand, and it is possible that, because of the destruction of Jerusalem, in A.D. 70, certain facts were no longer verifiable since all the records of the mother Church were lost.[2] It would be a bold assumption, however, to believe that St. Luke embodied all that he knew about the Church of the Apostles in the Book of Acts. It is admitted that our information now is most scanty,[3] but that did not apply to the

---

command of the risen Lord, Acts 1:8, 'and you shall be my witnesses in Jerusalem, and in all Judaea, and in Samaria, and unto the ends of the world', contains the disposition of Acts. That may be right, but should not compel us to draw a line already at Acts 13. Cf. also P. H. Menoud, *New Testament Studies*, 1954, p.44f.

[1] Bruce, op. cit., p.306, rightly stresses that παροξυσμός, Acts 15:39, is a very strong term; but 'Luke's honesty' seems an insufficient explanation for its choice.

[2] I am in full accord with S. G. F. Brandon, *The Fall of Jerusalem*, 1951, p.101, that St. Luke probably possessed more data about the circumstances surrounding the rise of the Primitive Church than he disclosed, although I differ from him in his reconstruction of these events.

[3] Cf. e.g. the conjectures as to which 'other place' St. Peter went after his escape from prison, Acts 12:17, in Cullmann, op. cit., p.37f. St. Luke seems to have suppressed the information deliberately, and guesses like those of Roman Catholic scholars (Rome) or Brandon, op. cit., p.211f. (Alexandria), are

end of the first century, seeing there exist to this day two reports of Eusebius about the martyrdom of James which, however fanciful they may be, rest on sound historical tradition.[1] If therefore this tradition survived to the end of the third century—and indeed much later—there is every reason to believe that St. Luke made a deliberate selection of the things he wanted to record.[2]

Thus it seems clear that St. Luke deliberately includes the report on the conflict between St. Paul and St. Barnabas, not because he wants to account for St. Barnabas' vanishing from the scene— St. Peter's and St. John's disappearances remain quite unexplained—but in order that the complete and unimpaired Apostolic authority of St. Paul throughout the second half of Acts should be made manifest from the outset. In doing this St. Luke marks the break between the first and the second part of Acts which, incidentally, is underlined by the well-known uncertainty as to the whereabouts of St. Silas—compare Acts 15:33 with 15:40[3] —in the strongest possible way.

This raises the further question of how St. Luke nevertheless succeeds in maintaining the essential unity of his book. We see him on the one hand stress as strongly as he can the shifting of the centre of gravity from the Church of the circumcision to the churches of the Gentiles; but on the other he ties the leader of Gentile Christianity as closely as possible to the Church at Jerusalem.[4] For this purpose he uses three different devices. The first

---

unavailing. St. Luke's whole interest lies in the fact that St. Peter was no longer in charge of the Jerusalem Church. From Gal.2:11 the conclusion might be drawn that St. Peter came to Antioch, where he was a most disturbing element for the course of St. Luke's narrative, cf. below, pp.83,n.4, 94,n.1.

[1] *H.E.*, II.1.5, from Clem. Alex., *Hypotyp* II.23.3f., from Hegesippus, cf. Jos., *Ant*.XX.9.1, quoted by Euseb., II.23.21f.

[2] I differ from Brandon, op. cit., p.109f., with regard to the principle of selection applied by St. Luke: St. Luke was not an apologetic in the way Justin and his companions were.

[3] Cf. M. Dibelius, *Studies*, p.87; C. S. C. Williams, *Alterations in the text*, op. cit., p.61.

[4] W. L. Knox, *St. Paul and the Church of Jerusalem*, 1925, p.94f., has used the data provided in Acts for a biography of St. Paul in the modern style. His results are, I believe, by and large correct, but I feel strongly that St. Luke never dreamt of such a result of his labours. His intention was to describe what God did through St. Paul—*gesta Dei per Paulum*—and not who St. Paul was.

step is that St. Paul, or Saul as he was then called, is brought as near to the martyrdom of St. Stephen as historical truth will permit. He is described as the representative of Jewish enmity against the Messiah and his witnesses.[1] He fully approves of the stoning of St. Stephen.[2] He is 'breathing out threatening and slaughter against the Lord's disciples', Acts 9:1, and that is the description of a man possessed by Satan.[3] Such was the effect of the sermon by which historic Judaism and its earthly Jerusalem temple were condemned by Christ's earliest martyr; and thus St. Paul's career takes its origin from the first execution of a Christian witness. This is followed by St. Philip's mission to Samaria and the baptism of the Ethiopian eunuch, which are framed significantly by the two sayings just quoted. The importance of these events for Saul's career is underlined by the report on St. Paul's stay with St. Philip at Caesarea, cf. Acts 8:40 with 21:8f.; yet at the same time they are closely linked with St. Peter by the Divine intervention preparing the meeting between St. Philip and the eunuch. The parallelism between St. Philip's baptism of the eunuch and St. Peter's baptism of Cornelius is intentional, and must not be overlooked.[4] Neither is there any reason to assume that the visit of St. Paul at St. Philip's house at Caesarea is merely mentioned because of the warnings of the prophet Agabus. Firstly Agabus himself provides a connecting link with the early days of St. Paul at Antioch, Acts 11:28;[5] and secondly it has to be noticed that St. Luke mentions no intercourse between St. Philip and St. Paul dur-

[1] Nothing can be farther from St. Luke's intention than Knox's, *St. Paul*, op. cit., p.98, assertion, 'the death of Stephen and the fortitude of the Christians under persecution (were they so brave? Acts 8.1 says "all were dispersed", i.e. ran away!) had however shaken his belief in the traditional view of religion'.

[2] Acts 8.1, ἦν συνευδοκῶν. Already the A.V., 'was consenting unto his death', has watered this down.

[3] The hapax legomenon ἐμπνέων, Acts 9.1, contains a clear reference to πνεῦμα, and ἀπειλή is used of Satan in Herm., *Mand*. XII.6.1.

[4] This point has been made forcibly and correctly by M. Dibelius, *Studies*, p.121f., but no deductions regarding the plan of Acts have been drawn.

[5] The curious way in which Agabus is introduced in Acts 21:10, as if he were unknown to the reader of Acts, has often been discussed. The claim of Bruce, op. cit., p.388, 'the sudden appearances and disappearances of Agabus are not fiction but fact', should be qualified. They are rather typical for the Jewish idea of 'prophet'.

ing the two years of his captivity under Felix at Caesarea, although the Apostle was given a certain amount of freedom during this time, Acts 24:26. Such meetings between St. Philip and St. Paul—unlike the previous one—would have had no special significance in the course of events which St. Luke wanted to describe. Thus the baptism of the Samaritans and the eunuch paves the way for Saul to take the Gospel to the Gentiles. However, the baptism of the eunuch, although it defied the law of Moses, Deut.23:1, that no eunuch should be a member of the *ecclesia* of Israel,[1] was still inadequate to serve as a starting point for the later missionary activities of the Apostle to the Gentiles. For the eunuch was still a eunuch, circumcised and sterile. It needed for the third step in the preparation of St. Paul's career the miraculous acceptance of the uncircumcised Cornelius *and his whole house*[2] by the Holy Spirit in the presence of St. Peter, to open the road for St. Paul. We do not wish to belabour the similarity between the conversion of St. Paul himself and of Cornelius; but it is significant that in both cases the Divine action precedes the earthly baptism; and the analogy between the Divine commands to Ananias and St. Peter, and the initial refusal of both,[3] is very close. Thus St. Luke makes it evident that the conversion of St. Paul is for the purpose of the conversion of the Gentiles and at the same time links the leading character of the first half of Acts, St. Peter, so closely with the protagonist of the second, St. Paul, that by the prominence given to the Cornelius story the unity of the whole book is secured.

This result of our enquiry into the historical art of St. Luke stresses the fact that the Church at Jerusalem had a firm hold over St. Paul, who indeed owed it his first allegiance in all his travels.[4] The intervention of St. Peter at the council of the Apostles had

---

[1] This fact is often overlooked, e.g. by L. Goppelt, *Christentum und Judentum*, 1954, p.85n., 'nach Lk. geht es anscheinend nur um die Aufhebung des Zeremonialgesetzes für die Heidenchristen,' etc.

[2] It is rarely realized what this phrase, so often used in Acts, meant to St. Luke for the establishment of the true Israel, the Church. Israel after the flesh consisted of 'houses', cf. Luke 2:4, and so does the Church.

[3] The refusal is however a stylistic principle of St. Luke's: Zacharias, Luke 1:18, and the Blessed Virgin, ibid. 34, react similarly.

[4] I concur with the statements of fact about the collection for the poor Saints

brought about the result that the president of the mother Church, that Church which St. Paul had once distressed and almost ruined, formally acknowledged his commission as Apostle to the Gentiles. The significance of this decision lies in the fact that it bridges the gap between the express command of the Lord, 'go not into the way of the Gentiles', Matt.10:5, a command the validity of which St. Paul clearly recognized in his first sermon, Acts 13:46, 'it was necessary that the word of God should first be spoken unto you', and the rather undisciplined missionary activities of Christians abroad, at Antioch, Acts 11:20, at Alexandria where Apollos received his first instruction in Christianity we know not by whom, Acts 18:24,[1] and at Rome where Aquila and Priscilla probably and those Christians who came to St. Paul at Tres Tavernae, Acts 28:15, certainly had been made Christians by unknown missionaries.[2] I shall not here enlarge upon this matter; my chief concern is still with St. Luke's biographical art, and we find there that in all respects, in his description of the growth of St. Peter's personality, as in that of the connection of St. Paul with Jerusalem, there is an intrinsic verity, but there is at the same time a marked consistency of purpose. The 'Prince of the Apostles' aims on the one hand at abiding by the traditions laid down by Jesus Christ in His earthly ministry; but on the other he is ready to follow the Holy Spirit urging him to go beyond these limits drawn by the Master whilst He was yet on earth. On the opposite side we find St. Paul who, although he is prepared to work on equal terms with the Jerusalem emissary, St. Barnabas, as long as the decision about the Gentiles is still in the balance,[3] yet strains

at Jerusalem, by Knox, *St. Paul and Jerusalem*, p.284f.; but I feel that Knox has nowhere faced up to the fact that the Jewish-Christians' antipathy for St. Paul might have evoked reciprocal feelings in the Apostle.

[1] Brandon, op. cit., p.224, has rightly stressed this point.

[2] Whether or not there were already at that time Gentile Christians at Alexandria cannot be stated with certainty; but there were such at Rome.

[3] I identify the proceedings at the council of the Apostles, Acts 15, with the event described by St. Paul, Gal.2:9. It is typical for St. Luke's historical technique that he evolved the description of the Apostles' council from a document in his possession, so rightly M. Dibelius, *Studies*, p.99, but it seems hazardous to build upon this the far-reaching conclusions with regard to St. Luke's theology drawn by Goppelt, op. cit., p.85n.

his lead to the utmost, longing for the conversion of the Gentiles. We grant that even when he works on his own he continues to address the Jews of the dispersion first; but the spirit of his approach is changed. When he says to those at Corinth, 'your blood be upon your head; I am pure, and from now on I shall go to the Gentiles', Acts 18:6, he no longer recognizes any privilege of the Jews, but only the duty of the prophet as outlined in Ez.3:17f., to which verses Acts 18:6 obviously refers. Nevertheless, it is the same Holy Spirit whom both Apostles obey; and in this there lies the peculiar significance of the famous introduction to the Apostles' decree, Acts 15:28, 'it seemed good to the Holy Spirit and to us'. The many who have taken exception to this formula,[1] ignore the fact that this decree countermands Jesus' own personal command, not to go on the way of the Gentiles,[2] and therefore needs a Divine authorization; and it will appear that it has, perhaps, an even greater significance than we have seen so far. For the whole purpose of the Book of Acts, we may say this already now, is no less than to be the Gospel of the Holy Spirit.

II

Having discussed the historical art St. Luke displays in Acts, particularly in characterizing St. Peter and the introduction of St. Paul into the narrative,[3] we now turn to his technique. It has been stated already that this is the technique of historical bio-

---

[1] Cf. e.g. E. Meyer, op. cit., vol.3, 1923, p.185, 'wird mit aller Naivität der aus den Beratungen hervorgegangene Kompromiss . . . als Wille und Offenbarung des in der Gemeinde wirkenden Geistes hingestellt'.

[2] It is possible that St. Luke did not know Matt.10:5, since it is only preserved in the First Gospel; but he certainly knew the story of the Syro-Phoenician woman, Mark 7:27,—and suppressed it. Nevertheless, the whole attitude of the Jerusalem Church towards Cornelius, St. Barnabas and St. Paul would become unintelligible if Jesus had not been understood by them as the Messiah of Israel. A united Church of Jews and Gentiles, let alone the Magna Carta of Gal.3:28, is nowhere to be found in the preaching of Jesus before His resurrection. The collection of texts by Goppelt, op. cit., p.75, n.2, seems to neglect the critical principle laid down in Eph.2:16, 'that He might reconcile both unto God in one body by the Cross'.

[3] Thorough-going research into the linguistic peculiarities of St. Luke has been made by Knox, *The Acts of the Apostles*, 1948, p.3f.

graphy. The end of the nineteenth century has brought to European historians a new technique, and brought to an end an earlier one.[1] The new technique is that of 'social history', to use a short if somewhat vague term. This type of historiography inquires into the environment of the dramatis personae, and attempts to show how much their actions were preconditioned by their background. This, we believe, is a valuable approach to the general understanding of the history of humanity; but at the time of St. Luke it was quite unknown. On the other hand, we are satisfied today with the assumption that spiritual developments follow the principle of causality as observed in the physical processes, whilst ancient historians made at least the attempt of outlining an interaction between the spiritual powers of cosmic importance and the spiritual powers of man.[2] This approach has now been abandoned since the belief in a spiritual world, which is effective in the world of man, if not generally in the world of nature, has been thrown overboard. However, and here I join issue with such a great scholar as M. Dibelius,[3] and with somewhat pedestrian approaches of more recent time,[4] we cannot understand Acts un-

[1] R. L. Milburn, *Early Christian interpretations of History*, 1954, p.1f., in his thoughtful essay on 'the historian's task', seems to have taken no notice of this Copernican turn in historiography.

[2] Cf. E. Meyer's, op. cit., vol.3, p.7, verdict, 'die Darstellung dieser durchweg durch übernatürliche Einwirkung erfolgten Entwickelung gehört daher notwendig zu der Aufgabe, die er (Luke) sich gestellt hat, der auf zuverlässiger Überlieferung beruhenden Erzählung "der unter uns in Erfüllung gegangenen Vorgänge". Eben weil er die Ereignisse von der Geburt des Johannes und Jesus bis zum Ausgang des Paulus in der neronischen Verfolgung unter diesem Gesichtspunkt zu einer Einheit zusammenfasst, ist Lukas der Geschichtschreiber der Urgeschichte des Christentums geworden und sein Werk ein wirkliches Geschichtswerk', etc. This I feel is, for all its theological shortcomings, a more convincing basis for treating Acts as history than those laid by modern writers as Cadbury, op. cit., p.3f., or M. Dibelius, *Studies*, p.102f.

[3] M. Dibelius, op. cit., p.123f., especially 129f.; 133f., makes allowance for Luke wanting his readers 'to understand what all this means, this invasion of the world of Hellenistic culture by the Christian Church', but gives no precise definition of its meaning.

[4] Milburn, op. cit., p.10, thinks that 'the author of Acts eagerly proclaimed that Christianity was, and deserved to be, officially tolerated in the Roman Empire', that he 'set forth an apology for the Christians as law-abiding citizens'. Cf. against this Cadbury, op. cit., p.26, 'here as elsewhere in Luke–Acts the

less we make allowance for this point of view of St. Luke, which is fundamentally different from our approach to history. St. Luke wrote his history of the earliest Church at a time when, as we may gather from the Pauline Epistles and the Synoptic Apocalypse, Christianity was anxiously waiting for the second coming of Jesus Christ. This situation illumines clearly that he intended to show the way in which this belief in the immediately impending parousia was to be overcome theologically by the preaching of the Holy Spirit.[1]

To apply these general considerations more closely to my subject I would state that none of the biographical sketches by St. Luke shows its object as a purely finite being, like the portraits by great painters of the eighteenth or nineteenth century, Sir Joshua Reynolds, or Romney, Gainsborough, Whistler, etc., but as *persona*, an actor on the Divine stage. St. Peter, St. Stephen, St. Philip, St. Paul, St. Barnabas, or James are not so much fascinating characters as characters in the Divine tragedy; and this Divine tragedy is the Gospel of the Spirit of God.[2] This fact can be proved by the similarity of the opening of the first and second books of the work of St. Luke. As in the first book, the Gospel according to Luke, we have in the first chapter a prologue, containing the annunciation and the birth of John the Baptist, and the annunciation of the birth of Christ, which is then built over as it were by the first great scene, the birth of the Saviour of the world, containing the exposition of St. Luke's real subject, the incarnation of the Son of God, we find exactly the same method applied in the Book of Acts.[3] A heavenly and an earthly prologue, the

---

positive flavour of the antique and the supernatural is as conspicuous, as is the absence of the modern rationalism'.

[1] It is with this qualification that I refer to the thesis of A. Harnack, *Die Apostelgeschichte*, 1908, p.4, 'die Kraft des Geistes Jesu in den Aposteln geschichtlich dargestellt — einzig dieses Thema leistete, was hier nötig war'.

[2] I would underline the remark by Knox, *Acts*, op. cit., p.1, 'the risen Lord, exalted to the right hand of God, had received as a reward for His obedience the privilege of sending down to earth the Holy Spirit, Who was to carry forward on earth the work that He had begun; *but the two stages were entirely distinct*'.

[3] With regard to the Gospel the facts have been stated by Bruce, op. cit. p.15. He also seems to have felt the parallelism here stated, ibid., p.30. Cadbury,

Ascension and the constitution of the new Israel by the appointment of St. Matthias, roughly correspond to the two annunciations
and the visitation of Elizabeth by the Blessed Virgin Mary. It has
to be noticed in particular that two Divine promises are made,
as in Luke 1:13–17; 30–33, so in Acts 1:7–8.[1] The conclusion is at
hand that St. Luke saw the time and task of the Apostolic Church
in close proximity to the time and task of John the Baptist.

If the parallel construction of the two beginnings of the two
books is clearly grasped, something else, so it seems, clicks into
place, the mention of the Emperor Augustus in Luke 2:1.[2] It is
true to say that the Book of Acts is meant to describe the trium-
phant progress of the *ecclesia* of the 'King of the Universe',
Acts 10:36, from the promised land to Rome; but the beginning
of the story is not to be found in Acts, but in the imperial census
mentioned in Luke 2:1. The ancient Fathers of the Church were
right in taking, as they did, a most lively interest in the theological
significance of the mention of the census made in connection with
the birth of the Saviour;[3] and modern theologians who neglect
this point may well be off the scent. We feel at any rate that St.
Luke started his work with a clear conception of the whole subject of the heavenly and earthly monarchy, facing each other in
combat for the rulership over mankind. It will be seen how beautifully the balance between the two is poised when it is considered
that, just as the heavenly monarch meets the procurator of the
earthly Emperor, and defeats him by his resurrection, so also His

---

op. cit., p.15, calls the miracle of Pentecost 'a programmatic opening', but does
not refer back to the Gospel.

[1] Goppelt, op. cit., p.75, n.2, takes Acts 1:8; Luke 24:47; Matt.28:19f., as
secondary. That may be so, for they all depend on Mark 13:10, which I take
to be earlier than Matt.8:11 par.—Mark 10:45 par., the 'ransom for many', and
Matt.22:1f., the parable of the marriage feast, are ambiguous, because they refer
to the parousia.

[2] Goppelt, op. cit., p.99, n.1, says, 'Lk. hat das Übergeschichtliche zu sehr
an das Geschichtliche gebunden, aber in Reaktion dagegen darf das letztere
nicht überhaupt eliminiert oder auf das Kreuzesereignis reduziert werden'. I
see no reason for G.'s 'zu sehr'. If it is abandoned a correct appreciation of the
part played by Luke and Acts in the economy of the N.T. may be arrived at.
Of course, already Marcion has shown why they must not be separated from
the other Gospels.

[3] Cf. e.g. Hippolyt., *Comm. Dan.*, IV.9.2; *de Antichr.*, 49.

ambassador, the Apostle St. Paul, is dispatched to meet the Emperor; and it is indeed a subject worthy of our close examination why no personal interview between St. Paul and Nero is recorded in Acts. One of the reasons, we believe, is a technical one. The Acts of pagan martyrs abound, as is well known, with much buffoonery in describing such scenes,[1] and St. Luke, being the artist of omission that he was, certainly felt that such a scene would not further his purpose, and limited the analogy between Christ and His ambassador in the way he did.

In order to deal with St. Luke's technique more fully still we will now treat of two particular questions which are being widely discussed at the moment, that of his sources in general, and that of the speeches in Acts. Regarding the question of the sources a distinction has to be made between the first (Petrine or Jerusalem) half of Acts and the second (Pauline) half. Sources for the first part can be distinguished with some accuracy.[2] I have already mentioned the fact that the obvious contradiction between Acts 15:33 and 40 has to be explained by the assumption that vv.33 and 35 formed the ending of a document, which St. Luke embodied in his book without much alteration;[3] I would also suggest that the report on St. Philip's mission to Samaria, Acts 8:4–13, together with that about the baptism of the eunuch, ibid. 26–40, comes from a written source into which that of the Apostles' journey to Samaria and their confirmation of the Samaritans was inserted for reasons to be discussed later.[4] However, the battle over the sources of Acts is not fought on this ground—we even find that these questions of the first half are on the whole discussed very amicably

[1] Cf. H. A. Musurillo, *The Acts of the Pagan Martyrs*, 1954, p.247f., on the dependence of these acts of martyrs upon the mime.

[2] We may refer here to the thorough examination conducted by Knox, *Acts*, op. cit., p.16f. Although I disagree with his general inclination to regard the sources of Acts 1–15 mainly as oral tradition, his results are on the whole acceptable.

[3] That was stated already by E. Meyer, op. cit., vol.3, p.186, n.1, and since repeated, e.g. by M. Dibelius, *Studies*, op. cit., p.99. However, since Acts 15:30–35 does not belong to the decree proper, we must at least add 15:22,23a to St. Luke's 'document'. Cf. also Knox, *Acts*, p.41f.

[4] This point, which is suggested by linguistic as well as theological reasons, is not made by Knox, *Acts*, 25f.

—but with regard to the second, Pauline part of Acts. There the author frequently reports that which he finds worthy of mention in the first person plural. These reports are the 'we passages' so-called. From a linguistic point of view they are so similar to the surrounding material that it would seem unwise to insist upon their separation, outlined carefully by A. Harnack.[1] It is rather true to say with him that from Acts 15:36 onwards the individual character of the author of Acts becomes apparent, and he writes 'his own untrammelled style'.[2] Two exceptions should be made, however, the one with regard to St. Paul's speech before the Areopagus,[3] the other perhaps with regard to the description of the riot at Ephesus.[4]

We are thus faced with a kind of Hobson's choice. Since the 'we passages' cannot be detached from their context they show that the second half of Acts makes the claim to have been written by an eye-witness to many of the events recorded. In all probability that person is meant to be 'Luke the beloved physician',[5] a follower of St. Paul's, of whom very little is known otherwise. We are thus faced with the alternative of either following Harnack, Meyer and innumerable others in accepting that claim as true, or more critical scholars in declaring, as they do not,[6] the

[1] A. Harnack, *Lukas der Arzt*, 1906, p.20f.; *Apostelgeschichte*, op. cit., p.159f. Methodically it seems contradictory to assert the unity of Acts, and yet to single out the 'we passages' for special inspection, as Harnack did; but his procedure has made such an impression on E. Meyer, op. cit., vol.3, p.19f., that he even concludes that Luke was absent from the events recorded between Acts 16:17 and 20:4. That seems to me an over-interpretation.

[2] Cadbury, op. cit., p.35.

[3] Cadbury, op. cit., p.51f., has justly warned students of Acts that they should not think of the Areopagus hill.

[4] Wellhausen's spirited attack upon the historicity of this report, cf. Harnack, *Apostelgeschichte*, p.179f., deserves to be kept in mind even if it is not to be accepted in toto.

[5] Cadbury, op. cit., p.155f., refers to an ancient Syriac reading of Acts 13:1, 'Lukas of Cyrene' for Lucius of Cyrene. I venture to assume that it was due to a simple misspelling. On the other hand, the Syriac reading of Acts 20:13, 'I, Luke, and those with me' instead of 'we' is not sufficiently well established to serve as more than an early Christian hypothesis of the type proposed here.

[6] Cf. e.g. Cadbury, op. cit., p.3, 'whom from convention if not from conviction we may call Luke', with references. The opposite course is taken by Knox, *Acts*, p.55, who, though identifying the author of Acts with Luke, writes,

second half of Acts as a forgery. If we take the former position we have furthermore to decide whether St. Luke himself put the whole work of the Gospel and Acts together, or whether an editor added the journal of St. Luke to the second book of his work for the sake of completion.

This last suggestion has, I feel, little to commend it. Authors may find it difficult to explain the abrupt ending of Acts;[1] but that is made no easier by assuming such a compilation, and I have already stressed that St. Luke wanted to avoid too close an analogy between Christ and His Apostle, and thus refrained from a description of St. Paul's martyrdom. It may be freely stated that a third book of St. Luke on the lines suggested by W. L. Knox would have prevented this work from becoming Holy Scripture. In addition I would say that an editor, having such a document as the journal of St. Luke before him when compiling his book, might have made the ties between the first and the second half of Acts, however close they may be, a little more pronounced. It has to be stressed that the break between Acts 15:35 and 36 is evident, and St. Luke left it so without much ado.[2] It should not be held that since the days of Jerome Acts 16 has started six verses later, and that for many centuries this fact has troubled neither theologians nor laymen. We have at last become sensitive with regard to such sutures; and that is a good thing in itself and may cause us to consider their significance more accurately. Moreover, the style of the second half of Acts is in accordance with the general intellectual stature of the writer of Acts. In it he writes consistently a well-balanced, somewhat colloquial but educated Greek,[3]

'his theme was the advance of Christianity from Jerusalem to Rome as a result of the work of his hero, Paul, and the form which imposed itself upon him was that of a travel story'. Cf. the scathing criticism by E. Meyer, op. cit., vol.3, p.5f., of Wilamowitz proposing a similar theory.

[1] Knox, *Acts*, p.59, n.5, suggests without support (for Mur.38 cannot be adduced) that Luke intended to write a third book; the 'British Israelites', however, are known to have circulated a forgery—if it can be so called—entitled 'the long lost last chapter of Acts', conducting St. Paul on a tour via Spain and Ludgate Hill, London, to Switzerland.

[2] That is shown by the late interpolation (now generally accepted as such) of Acts 15:34. Bruce's comment on this fact is unsatisfactory, op. cit., p.305.

[3] The careful and considerate analysis of St. Luke's style by Knox, *Acts*, p.5f.,

which has its parallels not only in Hellenistic novels, but also in scientific works like that of the astrologer Vettius Valens, and historians like Appianus and Herodianus.[1] Traces of rhetoric may be found, but his style lacks the embellishments of professional oratory. It is also true to say that in this part of Acts Semitisms are rare; and if we cannot give much for the peculiarly medical analogies, which Harnack has stressed so much,[2] it seems undeniable that the author was an educated man, mastering his Greek better than the other Evangelists and St. Paul, or authors of popular literature, e.g. the Acts of pagan martyrs. If, therefore, we ascribe the 'we passages' to someone other than the final writer of Acts we should be compelled to assume that this hypothetical person inserted no more than the sermon before the Areopagus into the second half of Acts; and to use this one document as the means for separating the sources of the whole Book of Acts, including its first half, is an impossibility, as careful tests have shown.[3]

Thus the question forger or St. Luke remains. In favour of a forgery—no other expression will meet the fact that the author speaks in the first person plural—there are two main arguments. The first and foremost is that the events reported in Acts are difficult to square with the hints to be found in St. Paul's Epistles.[4] This applies in particular to the report on the riot at Ephesus which, for this reason, has often been described as a construction, even as an insertion of foreign material. It is indeed true to say that Acts 19:23f. bears no relation to St. Paul's own account of the same event—if it is the same event[5]—in 1.Cor.15:32. This argu-

---

seems somewhat too disparaging in its final results. The list of comparable literature in Cadbury, op. cit., p.8, is instructive. Cf. also Bruce, op. cit., p.27f.

[1] Cf. the use of λυμαίνειν, Acts 8:3, with Appian, *Mithridatic War*, chapters 53, 54, 60; Herodian.III.6.9.

[2] Harnack's, *Lukas*, op. cit., p.10, n.1, expostulations against Jülicher, *Einleitung*, 5th ed., p.407f., are unavailing. Hobart, *The Medical Language of St. Luke*, 1882, is not a very critical approach, and Harnack's reliance on his results will be shared only by few.

[3] Cf. my analysis of Acts 17:21f.,—below p.225f.

[4] It appears that Cadbury, op. cit., p.123f., is not perhaps sufficiently thorough-going.

[5] Bruce, op. cit., p.363f., cf. p.34, says nothing about this.

ment is of great importance in that it either questions the veracity of St. Luke or the accuracy of St. Paul, and a solution is not easy to find. For both are open to criticism. If St. Paul did indeed fight with wild beasts at Ephesus, as he asserts, it is difficult to understand how he should have escaped alive from this ordeal and, having escaped, how he should have been set free after it.[1] He would not only have lost his Roman citizenship, but his freedom, and it may be assumed, although it cannot be proved with certainty, that as in the case of people condemned to fight as gladiators, the Roman magistrate was to see that he was killed within a year.[2] If St. Paul was a Roman citizen—all the evidence for this comes from Acts—a most elaborate trial would have been necessary, which a provincial governor, even a Roman proconsul, would have been most reluctant to enter upon. On the whole, therefore, it seems easier for us to assume that St. Paul used figurative speech.[3] This result, I would stress, makes it possible that the report in Acts may be correct, but leads to no more certain conclusions. We have to keep this fact in mind when facing up to the many other uncertainties caused by the constant disagreement between the data arising out of the Pauline Epistles and the stories told us about St. Paul in Acts. There are his journeys to Jerusalem; the quarrel with St. Peter in Antioch, Gal.2:11f.;[4] there is also the enumeration of St. Paul's trials in 2.Cor.11:23f., and nothing of it will fit. It is discouraging too that since the days of Sir William Ramsay little progress has been made in elucidating these conflicts of evidence. Therefore, only the assumption that St. Luke immensely simplified the personal history of St. Paul can help us to maintain that the second half of Acts is not an historical novel but real history. In any case, however, we must abandon the idea of a journal of St. Luke being the basis of it. On the other hand, it

---

[1] Aemilius Macer (under Caracalla) in *Dig. Just.*, 48.19.12, states 'quive ad bestias dantur confestim poenae servi fiunt'.

[2] Cf. J. N. Madvig, *Die Verfassung und Verwaltung*, vol.2, 1882, p.286.

[3] So also H. Lietzmann, *An die Korinther*, 3rd ed., 1931, p.83.

[4] I am of the opinion that St. Peter came to Antioch already before the so-called council of the Apostles, but Acts is silent about this, and Knox's *Acts*, op. cit., p.40f., argumentation contains some special pleading, which is rather apt to shake than to strengthen this conviction.

is of course true to say that these conflicts of evidence show that the second half of Acts was penned before the Pauline Epistles had been made generally accessible to the Church.[1]

Having stated this, I may call to my assistance here my observations about the historical art of St. Luke as well as my thesis that the Book of Acts contains the Gospel of the Holy Spirit. If the art of St. Luke was that of outlining the characteristics of the great leaders of the Primitive Church as well as of St. Paul, all the details which did not serve this purpose had to be omitted. In particular those exploits in which one or several members of St. Paul's circle played a major part—like Titus' journey to Corinth, 2.Cor.7:5f. —were radically suppressed, since they might only have served to distort the picture.[2] The companions of St. Paul mentioned in Acts, Silas, Timothy, Epaphroditus, even St. Luke himself, remain on the whole mere lay figures.[3] Priscilla and Aquila are given a standing of their own for reasons which are yet to be discussed. Thus, despite the numerous instances of the use of the first person plural, the entourage of the Apostle has remained almost invisible. This should make it clear that St. Luke's technique included indeed the most radical pruning of the evidence. And secondly, although M. Dibelius is correct in saying that 'Formgeschichte' is not admissible as an approach to the criticism of Acts,[4] it is still true, as we shall soon see, that St. Luke's theme

---

[1] Bruce, op. cit., p.24.—I cannot subscribe to the assertion of Knox, *Acts*, p.28, n.1, 'that Luke knew more of Paul's epistles . . . than is sometimes allowed'. Even the analogy between Acts 26:18 and Col.1:13, to which Knox refers, proves nothing of the kind.—It is however true to say that the writer of 2.Tim. drew upon Acts, Knox, *Acts*, p.41.

[2] The bare number of names mentioned in Acts is very considerable, and since in most cases little or nothing is said about them, their mere mention does not clash with their occurrence in the Paulines to the great satisfaction of Cadbury, op. cit., p.125. However, Titus is not mentioned at all; Aquila and Priscilla go to Rome without St. Luke mentioning their presence there, Rom.16:3; and of Apollos' stay at Ephesus nothing is said in 1.Cor.—The argument of the names has some weight, but also some holes.

[3] Knox, *Acts*, p.59, says, 'it says much for Luke's veracity that he has preserved Silas and Timothy as Paul's companions, although they are mere lay figures'. A poor argument, as it might be out-balanced by the absence of Titus from St. Luke's record.

[4] M. Dibelius, *Studies*, p.4.

is the work of God the Holy Spirit in, with and through the men described in the Book of Acts;[1] and St. Luke was thus compelled to use his discretion as far as the events to be described were concerned. The Book of Acts is a theological, not a factual, history of the events between the Resurrection or Pentecost and St. Paul's arrival at Rome. It does not endeavour to provide us with a chronicle of all that happened in the Church of Christ in those roughly thirty years. Admittedly, even the events recorded by St. Luke had none of them been preached about in the Christian Church, before they were incorporated in Acts. Nevertheless, St. Luke's intention was to report them in such a way as to make them fit subjects for sermons in Church. With this proviso I would say that the first attack upon St. Luke's good faith has been unsuccessful.

The second reason for seeing the author of Acts as a forger comes from a blatant inaccuracy in the first half of Acts. I mean the famous error about the sequence of the rebellions of Theudas and Judas in the speech of Gamaliel, Acts 5:36. It is well known that the revolt of Theudas occurred only ten years after the speech is supposed to have been made, viz. in A.D. 44, whereas Judas the Galilean is said to have started his rebellion at the time of the census, at least as early as A.D. 6–7. This fact is also correctly stated in Acts 5:37, but Gamaliel is made to place Judas' rebellion after that of Theudas. Not only does this prove that Gamaliel could never have made such a speech; but the treatment of the matter by Josephus, *Ant.* xx:5.1, 97 and 102 (Niese), where for good reasons the same sequence is observed, i.e. Theudas is mentioned before Judas, suggests strongly that the author of Gamaliel's speech had this account before him when composing the speech.[2] If he then

---

[1] This has been correctly stated by Bruce, op. cit., p.30, but not elaborated in his comments.

[2] This is not a matter for deciding the respective trustworthiness of Josephus and Luke, as Bruce, op. cit., p.24f., seems to believe. Josephus was undoubtedly both dishonest and slipshod, and should not be compared with Thucydides and Polybius, as Milburn, op. cit., p.9f., does. 'He is the most unreliable and mendacious of writers', says Knox, *Acts*, p.22f. However, what is being claimed is that this mendacious author served as Luke's source.—I am most critical of Goppelt's assertion, op. cit., p.77, n.4, about Gamaliel's speech, 'erdichtet

used Josephus, whose book was first published under Domitian in A.D. 93, he can hardly have written much earlier than A.D. 100, and that would most probably exclude the authorship of a companion of St. Paul's, like Luke the beloved physician.

There are, however, two reasons which may rule out this seemingly convincing argument. The first is that by A.D. 100 the Pauline Epistles were already widely read. They contributed to 'the extraordinary medley of New Testament phrases and heathen religious and astrological language which forms the Greek of Ignatius' of Antioch.[1] At the same time the Antiochene origin of Acts is more than a mere conjecture; and thus its author must have finished his work some time before Ignatius, whose martyrdom took place at the latest in A.D. 117. The second is that the twentieth book of Josephus' Antiquities is a mere compilation. I have proved the alien origin of its tenth chapter,[2] and would subscribe with confidence to the suggestion made that Josephus lifted the fifth chapter from Nicolas of Damascus.[3] This would mean that St. Luke had access to Josephus' source, which was a literary one; and all that remains to be seen is which of the two made a mistake in the use of this source, Josephus or, more probably, St. Luke. In any case it appears that St. Luke cannot be hitched on to Josephus.[4]

This brings me to the last point I want to make about the technique of St. Luke, the one about the speeches in Acts. M. Dibelius, whom I have had occasion to quote several times already, has maintained frequently that if anything the speeches in Acts ought to be regarded as the work of St. Luke.[5] It has also become a common practice to outline in books on the Apostolic age the

---

braucht sie deshalb nicht zu sein'; I also feel that his book, neither here nor anywhere, has faced up to the problem why in Acts the Pharisees are treated with such tenderness, whilst the Synoptists—even Luke—object to them so sharply. The same stricture applies to G. Strecker, *Evang. Theol.*, 1956, p.458f.

[1] Knox, *Acts*, p.1f.

[2] Ehrhardt, *The Apostolic Succession*, 1953, p.50f.

[3] Knox, *Acts*, p.22.

[4] In so far I agree with Bruce, op. cit., p.10f., but with his suggested date, A.D. 62, I cannot agree, neither with his acceptance of Jerome's hypothesis that the place of origin of Acts was Rome.

[5] M. Dibelius, *Studies*, p.3 and especially p.145f.

normal disposition of the speeches in Acts.[1] It is claimed by some that this normal arrangement followed an old-established Jewish model,[2] and this assertion seems on the whole more convincing than the thesis proposed by M. Dibelius that St. Luke adapted for his own purposes the practice of Greek historians who habitually inserted speeches of their own invention in their works.[3] It may be noted in this connection that in Luke 24:27, the Emmaus story, St. Luke himself outlines the programme for the various missionary speeches in Acts. By all these observations we are led dangerously near the conclusion that 'in trying to find the nature of his source for any particular incident, we must rule out the speeches entirely, since they have no real connection with their context'.[4]

I believe this statement is, however, far too sweeping.[5] Admittedly in Gamaliel's speech we have an instance of St. Luke's inventiveness, which may be classed as poor; but on the other hand we have already found that St. Paul's speech before the Areopagus—surprisingly enough, for St. Luke was not present on the occasion—is entirely sui generis. C. H. Dodd[6] may indeed be right when saying that St. Peter's sermons in Acts 'represent not indeed what Peter said on this or that occasion, but the kerygma of the Church at Jerusalem at an early period'. However, they are so similar in construction that I feel that the old theory of Rendell Harris about the use of *testimonia* in the Primitive Church might well be revived.[7] This would apply also to several of St. Paul's missionary sermons, which to the modern reader appear slightly monotonous. The speeches made by St. Paul in his own defence on the other hand are almost identical, and deliberately so,[8] with very little reference to the changed situation. In general my feeling

---

[1] Cf. e.g., G. B. Caird, *The Apostolic Age*, 1955, p.37f.

[2] So Knox, *Acts*, p.17.

[3] M. Dibelius, *Studies*, op. cit., p.138f.

[4] Knox, *Acts*, p.18.

[5] Knox himself, *Acts*, p.24, n.1, does not adhere to it in the case of St. Stephen's sermon.

[6] C. H. Dodd, *The Apostolic Preaching and its Development*, 1936, p.37.

[7] This point has been made by Bruce, op. cit., p.19f.

[8] Knox, *Acts*, p.27.

is that it was an onerous duty for the author of Acts to insert these speeches, which exhibit so little spontaneity. I therefore find it difficult to see in them a voluntary contribution, of the last compiler of Acts,[1] especially when we observe that he missed occasions on which a sermon would be expected. I would mention in particular Acts 5:21 where, despite the command of the Holy Spirit, no sermon is forthcoming; and Acts 28:16 where the natives of Malta 'said that he (St. Paul) was a god'. This is precisely the situation which evoked St. Paul's sermon at Lystra, Acts 14:15f.,[2] whilst on Malta he remains unexpectedly silent. The one great sermon, on the other hand, which really causes things to happen, that of St. Stephen, Acts 7:2f., can be shown to be of an alien origin, not only on stylistic grounds but particularly because it has a theology entirely of its own,[3] at variance as much with the 'Petrine' theology of the first half of Acts as with the 'Pauline' theology of the second. Once it is clearly grasped what is the significance of the great blunder which St. Luke committed when composing the speech of Gamaliel, viz. that he was not at all an expert at this job, for that speech is plainly his own, it becomes incredible that he should have written speeches as different as St. Peter's pentecostal sermon, St. Stephen's sermon, and St. Paul's sermon before the Areopagus, and at the same time have reiterated the story of St. Paul's conversion in form of a speech twice, and that of the baptism of Cornelius once. These repetitions show, however, that St. Luke was inclined to transpose into direct speech material which he possessed in form of historical reports; but that he was loth to invent speeches freely.[4]

[1] It seems unmethodical when E. Hänchen, *Die Apostelgeschichte*, 1956, p.81, accepts M. Dibelius' thesis that all the speeches belong to the last compiler of Acts, yet rejects his view that Acts was written by St. Luke, a view which follows logically from Dibelius' thesis.

[2] The analogy is correctly stated by Cadbury, op. cit., p.25.

[3] This has been well substantiated by Knox, *Acts*, p.24, n.1.

[4] The consequences of this recognition are important both in the historical and in the theological field: (a) It is not so easy to dismiss the testimony of Acts 24:10 for the duration of Felix' procuratorship as Hänchen, op. cit., p.67, n.1, would have us believe; (b) Ph. Vielhauer, *Evang. Theol.*, 1950, p.1f., basing his criticism of the theology of Acts mainly upon the speeches of St. Paul, cannot claim that the divergence between St. Paul and the Apostles—such as

III

I now come to the last and most important matter to be discussed, the purpose of Acts which, as has been said before, is to serve as the Gospel of the Holy Spirit. In this respect I want to make four points, one of which has appeared already in what has been said about St. Luke's technique. It is that the whole doctrine of the Catholic Church concerning the Holy Spirit rests upon the prominent place accorded to His coming on the day of Pentecost, in the second chapter of Acts.[1] I am fully aware of the fact that the sin against the Holy Spirit, which shall not be forgiven, is mentioned in all the three synoptic Gospels; and that St. Paul in particular mentioned Him in all his Epistles, especially in Romans and in the two Epistles to Corinth. We may also refer to John 14-16. However, having said all this, it remains true nevertheless that the term 'the Holy Spirit' has a peculiarly Lukan ring and belongs especially to the Book of Acts. It is equally true that the Holy Spirit appears as the formative principle in the Lukan writings rather than in any other New Testament books.[2] It therefore appears that there is prima facie evidence that in the Book of Acts there is more to the term 'the Holy Spirit' than elsewhere in the New Testament.[3]

---

it is—is a misunderstanding of a later generation, but should accept it as an historic fact.

[1] Cf. E. Lohse, *Evang. Theol.*, 1953., p.422f., especially pp.430f., 434f.

[2] This point has been well made by G. W. Lampe, 'The Holy Spirit in the writings of St. Luke', *Studies in the Gospels*, ed. D. E. Nineham, 1955, p.159f. I differ from him only in that I feel that Luke was aware of the immense change between the action of the Holy Spirit through Jesus Christ and His action through the Apostles. And yet—remarks like Acts 5:12-16 show how closely together Luke could see Jesus and His Apostles.

[3] This may appear as nothing more than a re-statement of the point made fifty years ago by Harnack, *Apostelgeschichte*, op. cit., p.4f., and ably defended by Bruce, op. cit., p.29f., but it is meant to lead further. Yet I feel that they are certainly nearer the truth than Hänchen, *Apostelgeschichte*, op. cit., p.92f. who calls Acts 'eine Erbauungsschrift'. However, Harnack and Bruce have overlooked the fact that 'the Holy Spirit' was a shibboleth of the Church at Jerusalem, which the Church at Alexandria, for instance, ignored, Acts 18:25.

The second point I want to make is that it was the Primitive Church at Jerusalem which found itself, according to Acts, as the trustee of the Holy Spirit. I can only refer to some few instances which will illustrate what I mean by this proposition. The first is that on the day of Pentecost the Holy Spirit was outpoured over the Church at Jerusalem, despite the promise of Jesus, Mark 14:28, 'but after I am risen I will go before you into Galilee'. Whatever the sources, or their lack, for a Galilean primitive Christianity may signify, this breach in our tradition must be reckoned with, for the cheap comfort offered by some that the Holy Spirit in the early Church was outpoured tumultuously, here, there and everywhere,[1] will not stand up to closer inspection.

The second instance is that of St. Stephen, who was 'full of the Holy Spirit', Acts 7:55, when, before his death, he had the vision of the Divine Shekhinah, 'the glory of God, and Jesus standing at the right hand of God', as he had also been all through his ministry. This, as Dr. Barrett has pointed out,[2] is a peculiarly Lukan touch in so far as no other Gospel except the Third mentions humans, apart from Jesus, who were filled with the Holy Spirit. With regard to St. Stephen I would make two more points. The first is that the appointment of the Seven had begun as a matter of expediency. There had been no Divine warrant for this measure: 'And they chose Stephen, a man full of the Holy Ghost', Acts 6:5. This fact had to be stressed because out of this measure of pure expediency there came the break of the Church with the temple at Jerusalem. It was St. Stephen's martyrdom which made the decision to appoint its own ministers in the Church irrevocable.[3]

---

[1] Cf. e.g. Knox, *Acts*, p.21f.

[2] C. K. Barrett, *The Holy Spirit and the Gospel Tradition*, 1947, p.124.

[3] Caird, *Apostolic Age*, op. cit., p.153, has attacked me on the ground that it is not easy 'to see why, if James was the real founder of episcopacy, the first traces of it should appear more than fifty years after his death'. The sources to which he refers are Ignatius' epistles. I would (a) refer him to my paper on 'The beginnings of Mon-Episcopacy', *Church Qu. Rev.*, 1945, p.113f., dealing with Ignatius, and (b) ask whether there is such a welter of evidence from these years as to make valid his verdict, which seems to betray some confessional prejudice. I would also be much beholden to be informed whose theory I have 'revived', as Caird asserts. I am ignorant of predecessors and a little sensitive to an accusation of plagiarism.

Our third instance is that the relation between the Church and the temple at Jerusalem, so keenly exposed by St. Stephen's apology, forms one of the strong undercurrents in St. Luke's work, from the annunciation of the birth of John the Baptist in the temple, and the scenes at the presentation of Jesus, Luke 1:8f; 2:22f., to St. Paul's arrest in the temple, Acts 21:27f. Dr. Barrett is right when stating that the first two scenes 'form an "island" of the Old Testament',[1] but that is not enough. They also signify the first station on the journey from Jerusalem to Rome. The last incident, so it seems, is almost a recapitulation of St. Paul's whole career, meant to remind us how the Holy Spirit has gone out into all the world. Beginning from St. Philip, Acts 21:8, Agabus, ibid. 10, Mnason the Cypriot, ibid. 16, the reception of St. Paul by James, ibid. 18f., cf. Gal.1:19, the sudden disappearance of 'the thousands of Jews which believe', ibid. 20, it brings us to St. Paul's own account of his conversion, 22:1f. He stands alone, like St. Stephen, and this recapitulation leads up to the conclusion that the time of the temple is now past, and that the Holy Spirit has been 'poured out over all flesh', according to the prophecy of Joel, Acts 2:16f. However, until that final apokatastasis we shall find traces of the problem Church and temple throughout St. Luke's work, which will give an insight into his doctrine of the functioning of the Holy Spirit.[2]

Another instance arising out of the trusteeship for the Holy Spirit exercised by the Church at Jerusalem is the control over foreign missions. Here a distinction has to be made between the Jewish Christians on the one hand, and the Gentile churches on the other. For the control was exercised at the outset as a control over the administration of Holy Baptism.[3] This control therefore did not apply in the case of the baptism of a Jew, however notorious he may have been. I have referred previously to the similarity of the two stories of the visions of Saul and Ananias on the

---

[1] Barrett, op. cit., p.122.

[2] The excellent analysis of the action of the Holy Spirit in Acts by Lampe, op. cit., p.192f., has rather neglected this aspect.

[3] W. F. Flemington, *The N.T. doctrine of baptism*, 1948, p.39, has shown that one trend in the approach to baptism in Acts is the distinction between baptism with water and baptism with the Holy Spirit. This fact has to be kept in mind.

one hand, and of Cornelius and St. Peter on the other. However, the similarity between the two events stops here. The baptism of Saul, Acts 9:18,[1] is taken as a matter of course, and never called into question by the Jerusalem Church, for the persecutor of the Church was a Jew; yet the baptism of Cornelius, the benefactor of the Church, is unsympathetically received by the Church at Jerusalem, because he was a Gentile.[2] However, the breach between the Church and the temple, which had begun at St. Stephen's martyrdom, had also opened the first mission abroad, the mission to Samaria. For St. Philip's mission there must be seen as the logical development out of St. Stephen's condemnation of temple worship; and thus, already at the time of Cornelius' baptism, the baptism of non-Jews had become a mass-problem which was not to be judged from the point of view of personal jealousies. The Jerusalem Church acted on that occasion with great alacrity, sending St. Peter and St. John to Samaria in order to confirm St. Philip's baptism which, so we are given to understand, was in its eyes not fully valid. Only the emissaries from Jerusalem were able to endow the Samaritans with the Holy Spirit.[3] The Church at Jerusalem, therefore, up to this point claimed the full control over the admission of converts. Then a miracle happens:

[1] In Acts 22:16 the command to be baptised is expressly given to Saul by the risen Lord, adding 'and wash away thy sins'. Hänchen, op. cit., p.561, refers us to Acts 2:38 and 1.Cor.6:11 as analogies, and does not mention at all that both these verses speak of the receiving of the Holy Spirit in baptism; but it is a problem why St. Paul omits it in his speech. Hypothetically I would say, the breach with the temple now being complete, the unbelieving Jews are no longer addressed on equal terms, as they were by St. Peter, or as Gentile Christians, like the Corinthians.

[2] Nothing of this has been seen by M. Dibelius, *Studies*, p.117f., and yet the similarity of the two visions is meant by St. Luke to draw attention to the dissimilarity of their effects.

[3] Flemington, op. cit., p.41f., compares Acts 8:17 quite correctly with 19:6, pointing to the 'less obvious stress' in 19:6. May we conjecture (a) that the Simonian Gnostics also claimed to impart the Holy Spirit, and that Acts 8:14–21 contains a polemical insertion into Philip's account, and (b) that the re-baptism of the disciples at Ephesus constitutes a problem which is not solved by pointing to the analogy. Had they been baptised into the name of John? and was Apollos re-baptised, Acts 18:26?

For all the efforts made by the Jerusalem Church, the Holy Spirit is God, and He is free. Therefore, at the conversion of Cornelius,[1] He acted even before St. Peter had baptised the centurion and his whole house. The whole emphasis of St. Peter's defence for his action lies on this point: 'What was I that I could withstand God?' Acts. 11:17. This defence was made against an accusation, 'thou wentest in to men uncircumcised, and didst eat with them', ibid., 3. This is the same accusation as that in Gal.2:11, and if the Jerusalem claim in Acts 15:5 goes farther, demanding the circumcision of the Gentiles, yet the Apostles' decree, ibid., 29, lays down food rules once more. Equally the story of the Syro-Phoenician woman, Mark 7:27, which is meant to establish the principle of the relation between Jesus' earthly ministry and the Gentile world,[2] once more speaks of giving the children's food to unclean animals. Therefore, despite the fact that St. Luke already in the Gospel made various efforts to show that Jesus' message of salvation was directed to Gentiles also, we are entitled to claim that these Jerusalem Christians stood by Jesus' command, 'go not in the way of the heathen', denying the Gentiles participation in the eschatological meal of the Church. Against this St. Peter defended himself with his profession of faith in the Holy Spirit: 'Then I remembered the word of the Lord, "John indeed baptised with water, but ye shall be baptised with the Holy Spirit,"' Acts 11:16. These were words of the risen Lord, Acts 1:5, from the prologue of Acts, and they showed the Jerusalem Christians as remaining in the pre-Resurrection period, whereas they also committed the Apostles, witnesses of the Resurrection, and especially St. Peter, to support the Christian mission to the Gentiles.

It is significant, I feel, that as the next step St. Luke stressed the fact that St. Barnabas was the envoy of the Jerusalem Church to Antioch, where by now the mission to the Gentiles had started on a large scale. We know from Gal.2 that St. Peter too came to Antioch on some occasion, together with St. Barnabas, but St.

---

[1] I am critical of the treatment of this passage by M. Dibelius, *Studies*, p.103f., but that does not concern my argument here.

[2] Goppelt, op. cit., p.39, n.1,

Luke does not so much as mention his presence there. This silence constitutes a real puzzle,[1] which I am unable to solve. Was St. Luke anxious that in the eyes of his readers St. Peter might appear prejudiced in favour of the mission to the Gentiles when casting his vote at the council of the Apostles, being already compromised by his baptism of Cornelius? It is also impossible to say with certainty that St. Barnabas, being a Cypriot himself, Acts 4:36, was better qualified to deal with those 'men of Cyprus and Cyrene', Acts 11:20, who had initiated the mission to the Gentiles at Antioch. For St. Luke the essential point of the story was this, that the Jerusalem Church, not necessarily the Apostles, maintained, as the Church of the Holy Spirit, its privilege of control. At the same time he forged the link between Jerusalem and St. Paul by giving prominence to his mentor, St. Barnabas.[2]—Hypothetically it may be suggested that St. Luke's silence about St. Peter may have been caused by internal changes in the mother Church at Jerusalem, which he was unwilling to put on record.

However, and this is my third point, the connection between Jerusalem and St. Paul is of supreme importance for St. Luke. We have been led to believe by St. Paul's frequent complaints about interference from Jerusalem[3] that the mother Church barely tolerated him. We should realise, however, that St. Paul was one of the greatest assets for the Church at Jerusalem. For there were Christian communities which 'had not so much as heard that there was a Holy Spirit', Acts 19:2. Even if these 'disciples' at Ephesus are to be linked up with the Christian community at Alexandria, where Apollos, the 'Jew from Alexandria', too had learned only about 'the baptism of John', Acts 18:24-5, a point which is at least doubtful, we have here the outlines of a conflict between the Jerusalem churches and a non-Jerusalem church abroad.[4] About

---

[1] I agree with M. Dibelius, *Studies*, p.117, that the story of the conversion of Cornelius is meant as an introduction to the mission to the Gentiles at Antioch. It seems all the more puzzling that St. Peter's stay at Antioch is not mentioned by St. Luke, but—Dibelius is as silent about this as St. Luke himself.

[2] It may not be out of place here to state my full agreement with all that Vielhauer, *Evang. Theol.*, 1950, p.11, said about the 'Jerusalem' Christology in St. Paul's speech in Acts 13.

[3] Cf. especially E. Käsemann, *Die Legitimität des Apostels*, Darmstadt, 1956.

[4] This is stated in contrast to E. Schweizer, *Evang. Theol.*, 1955, p.247f., who

these Christians at Alexandria we may have evidence from the famous letter by the Emperor Claudius to the Jews at Alexandria. This point has been made by H. Janne, and although his arguments may not be conclusive, they are at least highly suggestive, and have been treated as such by H. J. Cadbury.[1] It is at any rate evident that St. Luke wants us to know that St. Paul had a ministry also amongst 'disciples'—and that means Christians—who had not even heard that there was a Holy Spirit, i.e. were not aware of the Jerusalem event of Pentecost.[2] It seems clear to me that, whatever the aim of the short passage, Acts 19:1-7, may be,[3] the fact remains that St. Paul at Ephesus joined, according to St. Luke, Christians to the Jerusalem 'Catholic' Church who up to that time had not belonged to it. As regards Apollos the point must be observed that it was not St. Paul himself, but Priscilla and Aquila, who instructed him in the Jerusalem 'Catholic' faith,[4] and thus made him a member of those Christian churches of the dispersion which were in communion with Jerusalem.[5]

---

finds it difficult to believe that there were non-Jerusalem churches abroad. I would rather assume that the Gnostic heresy at Alexandria originated from a rejection of the Jerusalem doctrine of the Holy Spirit. I do not believe that there was a wide-spread mission of followers of John the Baptist, but rather that 'the baptism of John' was a Christian term, describing the heretical baptism in Apostolic times.—However, this is no place to enter into a controversy about Mandaic origins.

[1] Cadbury, op. cit., p.115f.; p.134, n.13.

[2] I am not concerned with exact chronology, but those who wonder how within the seven weeks between Easter and Pentecost the Gospel of Christ could have spread abroad, I would refer to Lohse's *Evang. Theol.*, 1953, p.422f., analysis of the exceedingly vague date 'when the day of Pentecost was fully come', Acts 2:1. It may be observed that it has a similar ring to the date of Elizabeth's giving birth to John the Baptist, Luke 1:57.

[3] I am in agreement with the statement by Schweizer, op. cit., p.249, 'dass die Zeit der Wassertaufe abgelöst ist durch die Zeit der Geisttaufe, die erst der Erhöhte durch die Taufe auf seinen Namen verleiht'.

[4] This seems to dispose of the old and somewhat wild suggestion that St. Luke 'degraded' Apollos, Schweizer, op. cit., p.248.—The word 'Catholic' is suggested by the word ἀκριβέστερον, Acts 18:26.

[5] Schweizer, op. cit., p.249f., quite rightly asks why St. Luke makes so little of the collection for the poor Saints at Jerusalem. The answer is, I feel, that he wants us to see Jerusalem at the giving, not at the receiving, end. Schweizer's own reference to 'Peter's pence' (also a voluntary contribution) makes the

This meeting between Apollos and Priscilla and Aquila deserves closer inspection.[1] When the mob at Thessalonica accused St. Paul and his companions, 'these that have turned the world upside down have come hither also', Acts 17:6, they seem to have referred to the very words of the decree of Claudius by which the 'Jews' were driven out of Rome.[2] By this decree the Jews had been expelled from Rome according to the testimony of Suetonius, because they had been constantly rioting 'impulsore Chresto'.[3] Actually St. Paul and his friends were not Christians from Rome, but he met two of the expellees, Aquila and Priscilla, at Corinth. Whether they were already Christians cannot be said with certainty; but there is a fair probability for it since their conversion and baptism is not reported by St. Luke.[4] The uncertainty—as in the analogous case of Apollos—is probably due to the fact that a complete separation of Christians and Jews had not yet taken place either at Rome or at Alexandria; and there can be no doubt that Aquila and Priscilla are meant by St. Luke to meet Apollos as the representatives of Roman Christianity meeting the Alexandrian Christian—under the sponsorship of St. Paul. This scene ought to stir our historical imagination.[5] Are we here faced with a prophecy of the later Roman-Alexandrian alliance? Should we treat this event as sheer coincidence? Or is it, as we believe, a pointer given us by St. Luke to the reason for St.

---

situation quite clear—or does Rome use this contribution pronouncedly as a testimony for the unity of the Roman Church?

[1] I can only say that Schweizer's, op. cit., p.251, suggestion that Apollos did not come straight from Alexandria, and was a Jew—not a Christian—has not appeared as 'viel näherliegend' to previous interpreters, and is made impossible by the comparative ἀκριβέστερον. He knew something about Jesus Christ already, and St. Luke does not say anywhere that Christianity is only a 'more perfect' understanding of the O.T.

[2] This is suggested by the similarity of the last words in Claudius' letter to Alexandria and those in Acts, cf. Cadbury, op. cit., pp.13, 94, 115f.

[3] Sueton., *Claudius*, ch.25, §4.

[4] Hänchen, op. cit., p.475, n.4.—The analogy between Aquila, 'a Jew born in Pontus', Acts 18:2, and Apollos, 'a Jew born at Alexandria', ibid.24, ought not to have escaped Schweizer, above p.94, n.4.

[5] Hänchen, op. cit., p.492, treats the whole scene as no more than a matter of course, and so—it seems—do all the earlier interpreters, not considering the kind of typological history which St. Luke wants to write.

Paul's ultimate destination? We feel strongly that, just as Jerusalem despatched St. Peter and St. John to Samaria, and St. Barnabas to Antioch, so St. Paul was urged by the Holy Spirit to go up to Jerusalem in order to be sent from Jerusalem, in the same way as the others were sent from there, to Rome.

This is my last point that the Holy Spirit completed the construction of the Catholic Church, originating from Jerusalem, by sending the Apostle to Rome from the birth-place of the Church. This point of view is commended by the fact that it makes sense of the ending of Acts. Rome undoubtedly was a place of special importance: it was the capital of the Empire. But the fact that it was also the residence of the earthly Emperor is hardly mentioned by St. Luke.[1] This fact was quite secondary in his eyes to the need to establish its Christian Church.[2] The pre-Pauline Church at Rome as represented by St. Luke has to be studied carefully in order to assess the implications of the phrase so often used in connection with Acts: From Jerusalem to Rome. We have seen that at the expulsion of the Jews from Rome in 48–9 A.D. Jews and Christians were still so little drawn apart that St. Luke could describe Aquila as 'a Jew'. If the measures taken at that time by the imperial government were at all radical, as Suetonius gives us to understand,[3] the remaining Christians must have been mostly Gentiles. Even if after Nero's accession to the throne many Jews returned, including Aquila and Priscilla,[4] the character of the Christian Church at Rome was probably completely changed, for its separation from the Jewish synagogues had now become

---

[1] It underlies the reply by Festus, Acts 25:13, 'hast thou applied unto Caesar? Unto Caesar thou shalt go'.

[2] I take exception to many of the assertions made by Hänchen, op. cit., pp.659–65. I am particularly doubtful with regard to St. Luke's alleged loyalty to the Roman rule, ibid., p.664f.

[3] The report in Dio Cass.xi.6.6, τούς τε Ἰουδαίους πλεονάσαντας αὖθις, ὥστε χαλεπῶς ἂν ἄνευ ταραχῆς ὑπὸ τοῦ ὄχλου σφῶν τῆς πόλεως εἰρχθῆναι, οὐκ ἐξέλασε μέν, τῷ δὲ δὴ πατρίῳ βίῳ χρωμένους ἐκέλευσε μὴ συναθροίζεσθαι (the Jews who rioted again, so that it was difficult to exclude them from the capital without mob violence, he did not relegate, but ordered them to observe their paternal law, and not to hold meetings), seems to offer a different aspect.

[4] Rom.16:3.

definite. It is thus not altogether surprising that the Jewish Elders at Rome now ignored the Christians; and 'this sect', Acts 28:22, may only signify the Judaeo-Christians. Again St. Luke—for reasons unknown—may have omitted the description of St. Paul's dealings with the existing Christian community at Rome.

It is obvious that a detailed description of St. Paul's leadership in the Church at Rome could not serve as a satisfactory ending to the Book of Acts. It has to be observed, however, that there is an easily recognizable climax in the treatment of the Jews by St. Paul. In Acts 13:41 he quotes the warning of Hab.1:5, which applies only to 'ye among the heathen', the Jews of the dispersion; in Acts 18:6 he refers to Ezekiel, the prophet sent to the captives of Israel; finally, at Rome, in Acts 28:25f., he refers to the total rejection of Israel prophesied by Isaiah 6:9f. This suggests to me that St. Luke felt that St. Paul had of necessity to suffer martyrdom at Rome. In order to clear up this completion of my last point we have to return once more to his career, as described in Acts.

If we want to know why St. Paul's life had to come to an end with his Roman martyrdom we have to begin with the question of why the Holy Spirit sent him into Macedonia, to Europe. For this was the crucial decision which St. Paul had to make, as St. Luke is at pains to point out to his readers, Acts 16:6–10. It would be rash to assume that the Holy Spirit liked the Macedonians better than the people of Asia, Mysia or Bithynia;[1] and if it is true that St. Luke wished to create the impression that St. Paul was the first Christian to set foot on European soil, he himself shows the incorrectness of this assertion soon enough by quoting Claudius' decree, Acts 17:6, and of course by the reception given to St. Paul by the Christians in Italy, Acts 28:14f. There are two answers to our question which, perhaps, are no more than the two sides of one and the same answer. The first is that the subject of the second half of the Book of Acts is plainly the work and the

---

[1] Neither Hänchen, op. cit., 1956, pp.429-36, nor any other commentator of Acts whom I have consulted, seems to have asked the question why the Holy Spirit should have compelled St. Paul to cross into Macedonia. Such are the results of a faulty theology of God the Holy Spirit!

sufferings of St. Paul; the second is that Ps.2, 'why do the heathen so furiously rage together', to which reference is made in St. Paul's very first sermon, Acts 13:33, seems to provide the real master-key to this part of Acts.[1] Now 'the heathen' were at that time the rulers of the world, the Empire of the West, the unnatural Empire of Rome. Europe, in the opinion of Easterners of that time, was not fit to rule the world. The penetration of the Church into Europe was the beginning of the end of that accursed Babylon of the West. It was thus both the preparation of St. Paul for his last and greatest task as well as the resistance of the Gentile world against Christ the King, which demanded that St. Paul should cross into Europe. From that time onwards the Romans, and the heathen in general, begin to play their part in the struggle against the Church. At Philippi, Thessalonica, Corinth, Ephesus, the heathen enmity and the aloofness of the Roman administration come to the fore. The whole pattern of St. Paul's activity appears to have changed.

This change brought about by the conquering Spirit of God in St. Paul's missionary methods can be illustrated in various ways. Elsewhere[2] I have drawn attention to the change in the constitution of the churches of St. Paul. Whilst working together with St. Barnabas he instituted presbyters in imitation of the Jerusalem system; in his later foundations, however, he changed over to bishops. This also goes to show that Jerusalem, through St. Paul, could still control the mission to the world, but could no longer conduct it. The signs of spiritual growth in St. Paul are well worth noticing too. The power of the Holy Spirit, so we are given to understand, was with him. This in itself appears as a miracle, for St. Paul had neither seen the risen Lord ascend into heaven, nor had he sat at table with the Twelve and the Blessed Virgin[3] when the Holy Spirit had descended upon them at

---

[1] I hope to show elsewhere that it is only the Prussian 'throne and altar' theology which is responsible for the widespread error that St. Luke was a Roman loyalist, and the following statements might be taken as a preview of my findings. Ehrhardt, *Politische Metaphysik*, 1959, vol.2., pp.7f., 29f.

[2] Ehrhardt, *The Apostolic Succession*, p.26f.

[3] Lohse, op. cit., 1953, p.423, refers to Acts 1:15 for the explanation of πάντες in 2:1. I would rather refer to 1:14. However that may be, he is quite

Pentecost. His apostleship was confirmed upon him in the course of his ministry; and the close relation between the apostleship and the Holy Spirit appears indeed in the great majority of cases where the word ἀπόστολος is used in Acts. St. Paul's perfection in his apostleship and in the Holy Spirit is revealed to the world on his journey to Rome, and this is the reason, I believe, for the existence of the last two chapters of Acts. They have the purpose to prove that, as St. Peter and St. John were chosen by the Holy Spirit, not only by the men of the Jerusalem Church, to be ambassadors to Samaria, and St. Barnabas to Antioch (although this Church in later time transferred its allegiance to St. Peter), so St. Paul is indeed the ambassador of the Church of the Holy Spirit to Rome, in the power of the same Spirit. The height of his authority is reached when he, in this power, rejects the Jews as the representatives of God at the capital of the world, Acts 28:25-6. This is an eschatological verdict. The Gentile Christians had to carry on from then onwards. 'And Paul dwelt two whole years in his own hired house . . . preaching the kingdom of God', Acts 28:30-1.

IV

One last question remains to be answered: Is this history? Even if we are convinced of St. Luke's historical art and technique, what are we to say of the events which he records? Did they happen or are they fiction of his or somebody else's invention? It is an amazing fact that the historian Eduard Meyer is much more ready to give an answer, if a qualified one, in the affirmative,[1] than many theologians. It is therefore perhaps not unjust to say that their requirements are put too high, they expect a superhuman knowledge of the historian. It is also true to say that at times their

---

right that St. Luke has designed 'einen ganz verschwommenen Rahmen'. But is there any more to be expected where it is described how God the Holy Spirit Himself takes possession of His instruments? St. Luke's artistic principle, why worry about accidentals, seems to me far more effective than all human curiosity.

[1] E. Meyer, op. cit., vol.3, p.14f., cf. ibid., p.9.

judgment is strangely at fault.[1] It may furthermore be argued that they expect—in addition to a kind of omniscience—too big a share of omnipotence of the historian and his hero.[2] My answer to the question has to be carefully balanced. I feel that the attacks upon those who insist that the author of Acts was an eyewitness[3] suffer frequently from an imperfect knowledge of what may be expected from an eyewitness after a lapse of anything up to twenty years.[4] With this proviso my answer is firstly that in the first half of Acts—as in the Third Gospel—St. Luke can be shown to have relied upon a number of written documents. This goes to prove that he was confident that he recorded events which had really happened. It is in particular worth mentioning that the break after Acts 15:35, marked by the clumsy interpolation of 15:34, shows that his record of the proceedings at the council of the Apostles so-called was copied from documentary evidence of some sort. But secondly, St. Luke selected carefully the events to be included in his account of the thirty years of the Primitive Church in strict accordance with his purpose in the Book of Acts.[5] Only if and when that purpose is correctly defined—and I have suggested here how it should be defined—will it be possible to set his report

[1] Hänchen, op. cit., p.63f., for instance, prefers the harmonious chronology of the notorious scoundrel Josephus to the difficult one of Tacitus, who at any rate cannot be proved to be consciously dishonest, because the latter agrees with a chance remark in Acts about the duration of the procuratorship of Felix.

[2] Hänchen, op, cit., p.431, presupposes an 'Itinerar', a travel journal, of St. Paul. I venture to remark (a) that paper was costly, and that St. Paul was very poor, ibid., p.455; (b) that St. Paul had to walk on foot through Asia Minor, was ill on part of the way, not very young, and had suffered physical violence on various occasions. Would he add a heavy journal to his luggage? And (c) no specimen of any such private journal has been found, so far as I know, amongst the welter of papyrological evidence. Was it at all common to keep such a journal? What is the evidence?

[3] So rightly Cadbury, op. cit., p.66, cf. id., *N.T. Studies*, 1957, p.128, on the explanation of the 'we passages' in Acts.

[4] I cannot help sharing the annoyance of E. Meyer, op. cit., p.18, n.1, at the looseness of the critical approach of many theological students of Acts, including Hänchen, op. cit., p.435. It should be realized that St. Luke's readers no less than any other readers understood 'we' as 'we', i.e. a group of people including the writer.

[5] E. Meyer, op. cit., vol.3, p.17.

into right relations with concurrent reports from St. Paul, Eusebius, the Pseudo-Clementines, Philo, Josephus, etc. However, this
caution has to be applied to all histories written by human
historians.

6

THE BIRTH OF THE SYNAGOGUE
AND R. AKIBA

I

IN his exegesis of Cant.8:8, 'we have a little sister, and she has no breasts; what shall we do for our sister in the day when she shall be spoken for?' Origen, the greatest Christian Father of the third century, maintained that the little sister of Shulamite was the Synagogue of the Jews, the little sister of the Church.[1] No words need be lost on the fact that this is just one of the many allegorical interpretations with which his commentaries abound. However, as a view pronounced by such a representative of third-century Christianity his statement deserves to be carefully tested. Was Origen right when he claimed that the Jewish Synagogue was the 'little sister' of the Christian Church? Can it be held that he was even historically right?

Modern scholars both Christian and Jewish seem to take it for granted that the Jewish Synagogue is, of course, earlier than the Church.[2] In the very same way in which modern High Churchmen hardly ever put the question whether the modern, post-Tridentine, Roman Church may be identified with medieval

---

[1] The actual reference is to Aponius, *Comm. Cantic.*, edd. Bottino et Martini, Rome, 1843, p.227f., cf. E. Peterson, *Theol. Traktate*, 1951, p.241. Peterson has however overlooked the fact that Origen, *Homil. Cant.*, vol.2, p.3, *Gr. Chr. Sch.* vol.8, p.45, l.24, described the Synagogue as the sister of the Church. In view of the fact that (a) Aponius was anything but an original thinker, and (b) Jewry at his time was held in deep contempt, it seems obvious that he only repeated views which were made known to him by Rufinus' translation of Origen.

[2] In this way Billerbeck's commentary is being constantly used nowadays, and may also have been conceived. I do not here oppose this use altogether; but I deplore the uncritical way in which historically later testimonies, collected there, are believed to shed light upon the earlier Christian sources, without any attempts being made at stating the reason for so doing.

Catholicism, our modern Judaizers take it for granted that the Judaism of today is by and large the same as it was before the destruction of the temple in A.D. 70. Reasons for this view are rarely given, but if they were asked for, the chief one would most probably be found in the continuance of the Jewish nation or race.[1] For it is indeed true to say that those who gathered in the Synagogue after A.D. 70 and 135, were the offspring of those who had worshipped in earlier times at the temple in Jerusalem. Christian theologians in particular seem satisfied with the statement that the Jews are still the people of the Old Covenant, concluding from this that the Jewish Synagogue must be the elder sister of the Church,[2] providing that they regard the two as sisters.

It appears, however, that theologians should not deal quite as lightly with the question of the seniority of Church and Synagogue. For this question is of crucial importance for Christians, who are taught to regard themselves as 'the Israel of God', Gal.6:16. Are we really entitled to claim that the Church is the true Israel of the Spirit, if we do not even try to establish the historical sequence of Church and Synagogue? Or is it to be assumed that the modern Church has abandoned that claim? Do we treat the phrase 'the Israel of God' as no more than a phrase? If anyone should be tempted to do so, let him beware lest he lose altogether the right of calling himself a Christian. For how can we take the promises of God made to Israel in the Old Testament, and call the Messiah of Israel our Saviour, if we reject our citizenship in the Israel of God?

We are, therefore, dealing with a question of Christian theology when we examine whether it be possible to maintain from a historical point of view that the Synagogue of the Jews is 'the little

---

[1] K. Kohler, *The Origins of the Synagogue and the Church*, 1929, has given evidence for the use of a number of prayers and rites of the Synagogue in pre-Christian time already, among the Chassidim and the Pharisees. His thesis that the Pharisees sprang from the Chassidim, first promoted by E. Meyer, op. cit., vol.2, p.283f., has been strongly opposed by S. Dubnow, *Weltgesch. d. jüd. Volkes*, 1925, vol.2, p.574.

[2] Cf. as an example E. Peterson, 'Die Kirche aus Juden und Heiden', *Theol, Traktate*, 1951, p.241f. From the sources which he, ibid., p.290, n.20, quotes it appears that already Caesarius of Arles (A.D. 502-42) fell into the same error. Cf. on him E. F. Bruck, *Über Röm. Recht*, 1954, p.150f.

sister' of the Church, or whether we will have to be satisfied with
a purely dialectical basis for the Church's claim to be 'the Israel of
God'. I shall endeavour to answer this theological question, and it
is my thesis that the Jewish Synagogue is indeed historically more
recent than the true Israel of Christ's Church. The Jewish Synagogue, I claim, is indeed by age 'the little sister' of the Church.

II

In maintaining that our problem is a theological one I do not
deny, but rather stress, that the method for its solution must be the
historical method. In fact, we have a much better chance today
than ever before to use this method, thanks to the great find of
documents near the Dead Sea, which has kept the minds of people
all over the world in suspense for more than a decade. I need not
here enter upon the importance of this new evidence for Old
Testament criticism, but rather wish to draw attention to those
writings which bear witness to the life of the community of the
'Sons of light' amongst whom the Dead Sea Scrolls were used:
The Battle Scroll, the Manual of Discipline, and the recently published Book of Psalms. For it may be held with reasonable certainty that there are no analogies to them originating from the
Tannaite period of rabbinical literature.

In contrast to this lack of comparable pieces of Jewish literature
of early rabbinical provenance, there are significant parallels to the
Dead Sea Scrolls of the time before the fall of Jerusalem. There is,
on the one hand, the so-called Zadokite document.[1] This was the
manual of discipline of the Covenanters at Damascus, a Jewish
group which, early in the first century B.C., had migrated there
from the South in order to escape persecution. Various scholars are
inclined even now to identify this community with the brotherhood of the Sons of light on the shore of the Dead Sea, because of
the similarities between the Zadokite document and their 'Manual
of Discipline'. However, such an identification seems premature
in view of the distance between the Dead Sea to the South and

---

[1] I have consulted the new edition by C. Rabin, *The Zadokite Document*,
Oxford, 1953.

Damascus to the North of Palestine. For the time being, at any rate, and until new evidence may cause us to take a different view, it seems safer to assume that these are the literary remnants of two different groups.

In support of this view I would also adduce the fact that there is no evidence for the use of a special book of psalms by the Covenanters at Damascus.[1] There are, however, two apocryphal books of psalms in existence, the 'Psalms of Solomon' so-called, and the 'Odes of Solomon'. With regard to the first, their pre-Christian origin, and the fact that they were produced within the Pharisaic community at Jerusalem, are undisputed. However, there is no striking similarity between them and the newly discovered psalms. The 'Odes of Solomon' are, on the other hand, very similar to the new 'Psalms of Thanksgiving'; and thus the tortured question as to their Christian or Jewish provenance, which appeared to have been closed in favour of the former, is open once more. I have never felt very happy with that final verdict and believe now that they—at least in their original form—were also recited by Jewish sectarians.

If we take this view, the material in hand confronts us with no less than four different religious groups within pre-Christian Judaism. We have met the Covenanters of Damascus, the Pharisees at Jerusalem, the Sons of light from the Dead Sea, and in a place unknown those who composed and recited the 'Odes of Solomon'. Neither is that all. We know at least of two or three more groups of Jewish sectarians. There are first the Therapeutae, whom Philo described in his discourse 'On the contemplative life'; and there are secondly the Essenes, about whom both Philo and Josephus give more or less understandable reports. Once more an identification of the Essenes with the Sons of light has been suggested by various scholars, this time also on local grounds—the Essenes, too, are said to have resided in the regions near the Dead Sea[2]—and again we can only return the verdict, not proven.[3] This multi-

---

[1] Quotations from the Psalter of David are found in *Zad.*, 4, 5 and 7.

[2] Plin. mai., *Hist. Nat.*, V.17.

[3] The reasons for this view are to be found in J. Coppens, *Analecta Lovan. Bibl. et Orient.*, ser.2, fasc.44, 1954.

plicity of sects, however, offers a preview on the numerous rifts, not to say the disintegration, of Jewry in the first century B.C., and beyond that illustrates the way in which St. Paul, 1.Cor.11:19, could write coolly about the many groups within the Church at Corinth, 'for there must be also heresies among you', a remark which in later time was even represented as an extra-canonical Saying of Jesus.[1] It seems, therefore, an erroneous assumption that Judaism before the fall of Jerusalem was one solid block.

III

In order to understand the meaning of these sects to their members we must turn to St. Paul. When he was brought before the Sanhedrin at Jerusalem he exclaimed, according to Acts 23:6, 'I am a Pharisee: Of the hope and resurrection of the dead I am called in question.' All the commentators of Acts have jumped to the conclusion that this was a stratagem on the part of the Apostle, designed to set the Pharisees and Sadducees against each other. This, according to St. Luke, was indeed the effect of his outcry. However, before accusing St. Paul of dishonesty, one may just cast a glance at three obvious facts: The first, that he did not benefit by his ruse, but would have been torn to pieces by the enraged mob if the Roman centurion had not intervened; the second, that St. Paul made the same claim again in his defence before Festus and Agrippa, Acts 26:7, and in a qualified form in Phil. 3:9;[2] the third and most important, that St. Paul strove for the salvation of 'all Israel', Rom.11:26, in the form in which he knew it, distressed by heresies, but united by the holy city and its temple. And so did the other Apostles.[3]

[1] Justin, *Dial.*, xxxv, quoted after M. R. James, *The Apocryphal New Testament*, 1926, p.36, agraphon 11.—A separate problem is that of the 'Synagogues' at Jerusalem, Acts 6:9, cf. Bruce, op. cit., p.155f.

[2] E. Lohmeyer, *Der Brief an die Philipper*, 1928, p.130, stresses the point rightly that St. Paul was a most sincere member of 'the order of the Pharisees'.

[3] Here I cannot but join issue with the modern tendency of treating Acts as an unreliable witness, as exemplified in the brilliant book of Brandon, op. cit. I am unable to disregard the researches of Harnack, *Die Apostelgeschichte*, and E. Meyer, op. cit., vol.3, p.3f., as Brandon and his authorities do. Even if it were true 'that the Acts is at least forty years later in production than the

They formed a new group within the Judaism of their time, the Church, but they found it difficult to abandon an earlier attachment, like that of St. Paul to Pharisaism. That we believe to be the case with all the other groups also, the Sadducees, Essenes, Therapeutae, Covenanters of Damascus, Sons of light, and the authors of the 'Odes of Solomon', whom a quick survey of the available sources has brought to light.[1] New groups, however, were forming, especially the Zealots, and dual allegiances made their appearance. All the same, there appears to have been an enormous differentiation between Jews and Jews, and a true Jew like St. Paul could not be satisfied with the mere fact of being of the seed of Abraham. It is true that rabbinical Judaism laid all the stress upon direct descent from Abraham; however, St. John the Baptist, that prototype of Jewish sectarian, could warn the people, Matt.3:9, 'God is able of these stones to raise up children unto Abraham', and already long before him Trito-Isaiah had said, 'doubtless thou art our Father, though Abraham be ignorant of us'.[2] In Jesus' days the strongest personal effort was demanded of those who wished to qualify as true Jews, but at the same time proselytism was encouraged. Men of this persuasion joined in greater or smaller fellowships, made religious vows, as St. Paul had done, and professed their convictions publicly, courting danger. Doubtless, they were only a minority. Even the strongest of all these factions, the Pharisees, constituted only a fraction of the nation; and above all, as Pharisees, Sadducees, Essenes, etc., their members were proud of being Jews.

---

genuine writings of Paul', Brandon, op. cit., p.23, cf. p.208f., there would yet have been witnesses of the events to be consulted by its author. If we discard the witness of Acts altogether, the biased statements of 1.Cor.15:1f.; Gal. 1:19; 2:10f., and Hegesippus, upon whom Brandon relies a good deal, although he is certainly later than Acts, would give no clue to the attitude of the Twelve and of James.

[1] Neither do we assume that this enumeration is at all exhaustive: The probability that the 'Herodians', mentioned in Matt.22:16, were a religious sect has been established by Peterson, *Theol. Traktate*, 1951, p.164, n.15. Also St. John the Baptist's followers may have formed a sect, Acts 18:25; 19:3.

[2] Cf. Billerbeck, vol.1, p.112f. Cf. the valuable remarks by J. Jeremias, *The Eucharistic Words*, 1955, p.148f., on the change of the interpretation of 'the many', Is.53:11f., from pre-rabbinical to rabbinical times.

The great common possession by which Jews of all persuasions were united, was the temple which Herod had rebuilt at Jerusalem. For this temple was not one sanctuary among many others, but—in spite of the existence of a schismatic temple at Leontopolis in Egypt—the unique rallying point for all the Jews, whatever sect or brotherhood they might belong to.[1] In the same way also the Jewish High Priest at Jerusalem was not one amongst many, but was, as Philo once expressed it,[2] in the succession of Adam; and it was his duty and privilege to continue making intercession for all mankind.

From this temple of the Highest God there sprang the two great universal religions, the Church and the Synagogue, which after its destruction had to make all the earth their home. The Church at Jerusalem had found it difficult enough to understand that by the crucifixion and resurrection of the Saviour the temple made with hands had lost its meaning, whilst it was still standing in its full glory. How deeply they mourned its destruction may be learned from the Epistle to the Hebrews, presupposing, as we do, that Overbeck's hypothesis is correct that it was a message of consolation from the Church at Rome to Christians in the Holy Land after the fall of Jerusalem.[3] This is an important illustration of the fact that Jerusalem was no longer 'the Church'. Throughout the first century the rise of the Church is accompanied by contemporary documents, the Paulines, Hebrews, Acts. The rise of the Synagogue, however, is not so documented. It has to be understood from sources which for centuries were handed down by an unchecked 'oral' tradition. Now the difficulty of arriving at con-

[1] Even here a caveat may be necessary. The temple of Onias at Leontopolis is not only dealt with at length by Josephus, but even mentioned in Mishnah, *Menachoth* xiii.10, and as E. Schürer, *Gesch. d. jüd. Volkes*, 3rd ed., 1898, vol.3, p.99, n.6, has pointed out, also in Sib., v.492f. The fact that Philo has ignored the temple of Onias calls for an explanation. The Pharisees, according to the Mishnah, ignored it too.

[2] Philo, *De spec. leg.*, I.57, cf. id. *Vita Mosis*, II.135, and H. Leisegang, *Der Hl. Geist*, 1919, p.20n.

[3] F. Overbeck, *Zur Geschichte des Kanons*, 1880, p.3f. The arguments against this theory up to the year 1930 have been aptly discussed by H. Windisch, *Der Hebräerbrief*, 2nd ed., 1931, p.122f., who himself has rightly concluded from Heb.13:24, that its author lived in Italy.

vincing conclusions with regard to the Church is well known to all biblical scholars; that of using rabbinical sources for explaining the rise of the Synagogue may even seem unsurmountable. For, quite apart from any partisan colouring, the early Rabbis, authors of the Talmud and the extra-Talmudic legends, held views on time and history which are radically different from our Graeco-Christian ideas.[1] Moreover, these sources are in fact very deeply affected by partisan views of that one Jewish fellowship which emerged victoriously from the period of disaster between A.D. 70–135, Pharisaism.

What impression the fall of Jerusalem and the destruction of Jahweh's temple must have made upon contemporary Jewry cannot be gauged even from the report of Josephus. If the history book of his opponent, Justus of Tiberias, were still extant, it would perhaps make it easier for us to understand their feelings. For Justus was not a Pharisee since, according to Pharisaic doctrine, Tiberias was at the time considered as a place of ritual impurity.[2] Josephus, however, had acted as a traitor, and had only one purpose in life left, to make his readers believe as well as himself that, considering everything, all had turned out for the good. Nevertheless, A.D. 70 had seen an almost unparalleled disaster, in so far as the one and only bond which had held all Jews together had been broken; and the contemporaries knew of no other, but believed fervently that the end of the world was approaching.[3] All the various Jewish sects and fellowships were torn apart by the disruption of the bond formed by the Jerusalem temple; and nobody could foretell how they might ever be joined together again.

The most depressing feature in all this was that the Jewish war

---

[1] Cf. Th. Boman, *Das hebräische Denken*, 2nd ed., 1954, p.109f.

[2] So L. Finkelstein, *Akiba*, 1936, p.3, cf. ibid., p.319, n.2. It has to be stressed, however, that the conclusion that Justus was not a Pharisee has not been drawn by so great an expert as E. Schürer, and that it depends entirely upon the one report from the Jerusalem Talmud quoted by Finkelstein. However, this report is bound to go back to a time before the Patriarchate of Tiberias was founded, and therefore possesses a fair amount of historical probability.

[3] This appears quite clearly in the fourth vision of 4.Ezra (9:26f.), as well as in the vision of the waters in Baruch (syr.) 53.

had come over the Jews 'as a thief in the night'. It is true that the Jews had toyed with Messianic expectations for a long time: One day the Son of David would occupy the throne of the Caesars. It is equally true that this hope could only be realized through war with Rome. Nevertheless, there had been no Messianic leader of the Jews in A.D. 66. The war broke out on account of a common brawl between Jews and Gentiles in the streets of Caesarea, at which the Roman governor Florus had acted more foolishly than wickedly; and right down to its last crisis leaders of a considerable minority amongst the Jews, and in particular the Pharisees, Josephus not the least of them, had pursued a course of appease-ment, even when the time for such a policy was long past. The Zealots, the extremists, had forcibly taken the lead. A number of Pharisees, it is true, were to be found among them and, in spite of Philo's contention that the Essenes were pacifists,[1] one of their leaders, John, even seems to have been an Essene.[2] A change from one sect to another seems to have been possible; and in the case of the Zealots, whose ethos was strongly political, even the com-bination of two memberships. The contention of E. Meyer that the Jewish war had not been a religious but a social uprising,[3] is, as I believe, an ill-stated alternative, for these two motives can never be tidily separated, least of all in Jewry. However, the social element stood out in Zealotism and rendered such combina-tions of loyalties possible.

Only when the siege of the temple drew to a close the eschato-logical hopes of contemporary Judaism soared high amongst its defenders, bringing about their terrible internecine strife. At the last, when all hopes that Jahweh would miraculously save His house from defilement by the victorious Romans were dashed, its last defenders abandoned all resistance. Some allowed themselves to be slaughtered by the implacable Roman legionaries; the others

---

[1] Philo, *Quod omnis probus liber*, 12f.

[2] Jos., *Bell*.II.2.4. I can see no reason whatsoever for postulating a second meaning of 'Εσσαῖος ('from Essa', a place-name otherwise unknown) simply on the strength of Philo's assertion, as has been done by O. Holtzmann, *N.T. Zeitgeschichte*, 1895, p.168, and various other historians following him.

[3] E. Meyer, op. cit., vol.3, p.74, n.4, cf. Brandon, op. cit., p.155, n.6, who erroneously has quoted Meyer's first vol.

threw themselves into the flames of the building from which God had turned His face. With this horrible scene of carnage not only Zealotism came to an end, but also Old Testament Judaism. To this day the Arch of Titus at Rome marks this fact for those who behold its stone carvings.

IV

In the winter of A.D. 69–70, when no reasonable people could doubt any longer the ultimate fate of Jerusalem, two groups of such people left the city. The opportunity for so doing arose because Vespasian, the Roman commander in chief, had been proclaimed Augustus by his troops, and had gone to Egypt to raise forces for the fight for Caesar's throne. Nobody could foresee that the battle of Cremona would be won for him by the Pannonian army alone. The fact that there were such groups of reasonable people amongst the Jews has to be stressed. It is perhaps less surprising in the case of the Christians who, according to Eusebius' trustworthy report, went to Pella, north-east of the river Jordan; [1] it is, however, remarkable that a considerable group of Pharisees should have taken the same decision. They left Jerusalem for Lydda and Jamnia, in the plain near the sea, south-west of Jerusalem. We cannot say why these leaders of the Pharisees dissociated themselves from the last fight for the Holy City, and the legend about their departure from Jerusalem shows the same uneasiness. For the alleged smuggling out of Jochanan ben Zakkai and his subsequent meeting with Vespasian (!), at which he obtained the permission for Gamaliel to follow him in order to found the Jewish Synagogue, cannot be accepted, especially if we believe that Simeon, the father of Gamaliel, had fallen in battle against the Romans as one of the leaders of the insurgents, as the legend asserts.[2] This story, we feel, can only be regarded as a plainly

---

[1] Euseb., *H.E.*, III.5.3, says that the Christians left Jerusalem because of an oracle πρὸ τοῦ πολέμου, which I take to mean 'before the siege'. So already Epiphan., *Adv. haer.*XXIX.7; *de mensur.*15. The criticism of Brandon, op. cit., p.169, does not seem sufficient to discredit Eusebius' report.

[2] This romantic tale is not only told by S. Dubnow, op. cit., vol.2, p.476f.,

apologetic version, produced by the Jewish leaders in order to justify the position which Gamaliel ii. had taken at the head of reconstituted Jewry. It obviously comes from a time when the actual events of his and Jochanan's escape had been forgotten.

The truth is that both these men were outstanding leaders of the Pharisaic party, a party whose heart was not in this fateful war. It must always be remembered how much this war was an affair of the Zealots. Even if a Pharisee, like Josephus, had taken up arms at its outbreak, his participation was half-hearted, and in its course he turned traitor. The bond which the temple had formed had been overstrained long since.[1] The High Priest himself too who, during the first stages of the war, had for a time taken command of the Jewish forces, had not distinguished himself in so doing.[2] The gap between the ideal of the Jewish High Priesthood and the facts about it had turned into a chasm which devoured this sacred office.

With the High Priest and his supporters, the Sadducees, discredited, their late opponents, the Pharisees, became the leaders of the Jewish nation, and in particular the group surrounding Jochanan and Gamaliel, whom I have just mentioned. For they founded the so-called Academy of Jamnia. That is all that even the most scholarly history of the Jews will tell us.[3]

---

but even M. Simon, *Verus Israel*, 1948, p.29f., has repeated it, both with some reserve. I prefer the attitude taken by Er. Havet, *Le Christianisme et ses origines*, 1878, vol.3, p.324, 'que les plus considérables entre eux (the Pharisees) se tinrent à l'écart et s'établirent pendant le siège à Jabnë'.

[1] As a symptom of this I may cite the fact that the Essenes did not participate in its animal sacrifices, although they sent presents to the temple, cf. W. Bousset-Gressmann, *Religion d. Judentums*, 3rd ed., 1926, p.431.

[2] It seems probable that Messianic expectations were at the root of this appointment. The Messiah from Aaron does not only occur in the Zadokite document, but also in the Dead Sea Scrolls, *Man. Disc.* 9.10–11, cf. K. G. Kuhn, *N.T. Studies*, 1955, p.168f., and—a fact not generally appreciated—in the theory which found the χριστὸς ἡγούμενος in the succession of the Jewish High Priests, cf. my *Apostolic Succession*, p.56f.

[3] Dubnow, op. cit., vol.3, p.25f. J. Elbogen, *Gesch. d. Juden seit dem Untergang des jüdischen Staates*, 1919, p.6, 'so richtete das Volk sich eine Märchenwelt auf und vergass über dem schönen Traum einer nahen, idealen Zukunft die traurige Gegenwart', rings also more idyllic than true.

We do not know whether there may be a conspiracy of silence or a complete lack of curiosity on the part of the majority of Jewish historians, for it appears that the sources for an elucidation of the stages by which this result was achieved are available, and have been carefully collected, if fancifully used, by a recent Jewish scholar, L. Finkelstein.[1] It is, however, our first duty to put our question correctly: How was it possible that the centre of Judaism was shifted from the Holy City of David to an insignificant little village in Southern Palestine, Jamnia, of which no ancient writer, before Strabo XVI.28, had ever made mention? that the place of the heroic Zealots should be filled by the Pharisaic appeasers, in whose ranks even traitors like Josephus were still tolerated? and that, instead of the daily sacrifices at the temple, an order of Divine Service was accepted throughout Jewry, which seems to have had hardly any basis in the Torah?[2] This last fact is also amply illustrated by those mournful, nostalgic references to the temple Services of old with which rabbinical literature abounds. I feel it is the historian's duty to find answers to these questions by attempting to throw light upon the origins of the Academy at Jamnia.

V

I have discarded as historically untrue the Jewish tradition that Jochanan ben Zakkai received from Titus, the Roman commander, his commission to found the Academy at Jamnia, after he had been removed by stealth from the invested city of Jerusalem. That was, I have held, no more than an officially inspired account, intended to make the break between the Synagogue and the temple appear as insignificant as possible. The truth is that numbers of fugitives from the war were gathered in various places, not only at Jamnia, but also at Lydda and Pekiin.[3] Neither did all the Jewish survivors crowd those southern parts of Palestine; but considerable groups

---

[1] L. Finkelstein, op. cit., passim.

[2] Cf. Chagiga I.8, quoted after Schürer, op. cit., vol.2, p.333, n.7.

[3] There are only comparatively late Talmudic reports which say that Pekiin was situated between Lydda and Jamnia, cf. Schürer, op. cit., vol.2, p.372, n.94. For reasons I shall discuss later, I would prefer to locate it somewhere in Galilee.

of Jews seem to have gathered in Galilee, where Jochanan ben Zakkai is said to have taught for some time, and where Akiba is reported to have acted as the head of a school at Ziphron.[1]

At all these various places something happened, which I myself was able to observe at the internment in 1940. Under conditions of grim asperity, under canvas, with insufficient food, the interned refugees developed at once an active, responsible administration. Men of recognized learning were put in charge, for scholarship was the only distinction which was generally recognized. Prince Frederick of Prussia, despite his family connections with Queen Mary, was found no place in it; neither did great wealth receive any consideration. This administration set itself three tasks, (a) the registration of everybody present, so that not a single case of distress should go unnoticed; (b) the organisation of assistance for the old, the sick and the destitute; and (c) the satisfaction of cultural demands through libraries, schools, lectures, etc. The general improvement of material conditions at the camp lagged a long way behind.

Allowing for some adjustments, this experience may serve as an analogy for the position in which the fugitives of A.D. 70 found themselves. At Jamnia and Lydda they were surrounded by the desert to the South, the Roman army to the East and the North, and the sea to the West. Like ours, their chances of survival seemed remote. If a Roman force passing by had staged a pogrom, nobody would have cared much. Nevertheless, those Jews of old too began to establish a constitution, an administration, and an educational centre. Their head, Jochanan ben Zakkai, was one of the few survivors—allegedly the only one—of the late Jerusalem Sanhedrin, famous as a scribe long before A.D. 70. Although he was already an old man of limited strength, and seems to have died within the first decade of the Academy's existence, his high ranking scholarship gave to it that distinction which was lacking at the other comparable establishments. The Academy at Jamnia could claim an unbroken succession after the Jewish Sanhedrin from the

---

[1] Sources for this in Finkelstein, op. cit., p.329, n.53. Finkelstein's thesis that this was a voluntary exile of Akiba from the Academy at Jamnia is, on his own admission, pure conjecture.

time before the fall of Jerusalem;[1] and through this claim it gained
the attention of the Jews throughout the Roman Empire. Moreover, its first Nasi, Gamaliel ii., added to his own distinguished
record of scholarship his descent from a family of famous scholars,
men who furthermore had maintained good relations with Rome.

The importance of this last circumstance lay in the fact that for
political reasons Rome needed a religious centre for the Jews.[2]
Whether such a centre should be established at Jamnia, Lydda or
somewhere in Galilee was immaterial for Rome; but the future of
the Jewish religion was for her a political problem. In times past
the God of the Jews had been recognized as a God by Rome, and
this decision could not be reversed, for the gods are eternal. Rome
maintained the fiction that she had made Jehovah captive, like
the gods of other subjected nations, whose images had been
brought in triumph to the Roman Capitolium. Since, however,
there was no statue of its God in the Jerusalem temple, as Pompey
had established in 63 B.C., the Roman government collected the
'fiscus Judaicus', the former temple tithe, which rendered Jehovah
a tributary to the victorious Juppiter Capitolinus.[3]

The reason for this taxation was, therefore, not only fiscal and
financial, but still more political and religious. That appears clearly
from the fact that no special purpose is indicated to which this
revenue was devoted. Since, however, it was a capitation tax, it
served well as a deterrent to Jewish proselytizing. In this way it
became the precursor of the legislation which prohibited the circumcision of proselytes, begun by Hadrian and repeated by several
of his successors.[4] These measures taken by the Roman govern-

[1] I show the importance of the Sanhedrin model for the ordination of the
Rabbis, in ch.7 below.

[2] S. Guterman, *Religious toleration and persecution in ancient Rome*, 1951, p.109,
is right when summing up the Roman attitude thus, 'privileges to Jews who
are Roman citizens are given on the basis of their cult. Privileges which are
granted to members of the Jewish nation are given "because they are our
friends and allies".'

[3] Guterman's remarks on the *fiscus Judaicus*, op. cit., p.114f., suffer, like those
of his predecessors, from the fact that the significance of Juppiter Capitolinus
becoming the beneficiary of the tax is overlooked.

[4] The law preserved in Justinian's *Digest* 48.8.11 pr., 'circumcidere Judaeis
filios suos tantum rescripto divi Pii permittitur; in non eiusdem religionis qui

ment aimed at drawing a boundary line between Jews and non-Jews and coincided with similar tendencies amongst the Jews. In Jewry the increasing strictness of the purity laws[1] did not only bring about a similar drawing apart, but broke the earlier enthusiasm for missionary work among the Gentiles.[2] Juvenal and Tacitus—both under Trajan—were the last pagan authors who mentioned the φοβούμενοι, the 'devout persons'.[3]

It is well known that this tendency towards a tidy separation of the Jews from the Gentiles was strongest amongst the Pharisees. They therefore found it easy to meet the Romans on these terms; and the fact that they did so follows from their surprisingly moderate remarks on the 'fiscus Judaicus'.[4] The interest of the Roman Empire demanded on the other hand that, once the distinction between Jews and non-Jews was clearly drawn, Jehovah should be worshipped by His people according to His commands. For although He was a captive God, He was still a God; and the other gods might determine to take His side if His worship was compulsorily abandoned. Under these presuppositions Palestinian Judaism assumed a special importance, since the traditions of Jehovah's worship were kept there.

---

hoc fecerit poena castrantis irrogatur', comes from Modestinus, *Regul.*, VI (third century). This casts some doubt on the report of *Script. Hist. Aug.*, Severus, 17.1, that conversion to Judaism was forbidden by an edict of Septimius Severus. Ibid., Hadrian, 14.2, 'moverunt ea tempestate et Judaei quod vetabantur mutilare genitalia', also demands a critical approach.—The legislation of the Christian Emperors on this matter comes from entirely different considerations.

[1] Cf. Jeremias, *Hat die älteste Christenheit die Kindertaufe geübt*, 1938, p.9f. It has to be admitted, however, that a certain relaxation of the rules regarding ritual purity took place in the course of the second century A.D., in so far as eating with the Gentiles was concerned, cf. Knox, *St. Paul and Jerusalem*, p.154, n.10.

[2] An illustration is the vision of St. Peter, Acts 10, who is represented as having no intention whatsoever of missionarizing the Gentiles. Whether or not the story is historically true, cf. against its historicity de Wette-Overbeck, op. cit., p.150f., for it Bruce, op. cit., p.214, it shows the complete absence of missionary zeal even amongst the Judaeo-Christians at Jerusalem.

[3] Juvenal, *Sat.*, XIV.101f.; Tac., *Hist.*, V.5. B. M. Bamberger, 'Proselytism in the Talmudic period,' quoted from T. W. Manson, *Scott. Journ. Theol.*, 1949/50, p.393, n.2, has been inaccessible to me.

[4] On the *fiscus Judaicus* cf. J. Juster, *Les Juifs dans l'Empire Romain*, 1914, vol.2, p.282f.

VI

In Palestine Gamaliel ii. was the head of the Academy at Jamnia. We have seen that his family had kept close contacts with Rome and the Romans. He himself was no mean scholar, not only in the Jewish sense, for he spoke Greek and Latin and was conversant with contemporary philosophy.[1] The strength of his position was proved by the triumph which he gained over his competitor, the head of the Academy at Lydda, Eliezer ben Hyrkanos. As a centre Lydda was far more important than Jamnia; and there seems no reason to assume that the Jewish Academy there should have been under the control of Jamnia right from its beginning. Eliezer too was fluent in Greek and Latin, so that he might have conducted the necessary negotiations with the Roman authorities. Nevertheless, Gamaliel excommunicated him and held a strong enough position to make his sentence accepted, although the fact that Eliezer's opinions are still recorded in the Mishnah shows that the issue must have been strongly contested.[2]

The conflict between Gamaliel and Eliezer was only one oi many into which Gamaliel was plunged. The fact that it was his first major success follows from geographical data: Lydda and Jamnia were so close to each other that jealousy between the two Academies would of necessity arise. Another conflict, however, concerned Jewry abroad. The head of the Academy at Pekiin was Joshua ben Chananja, who was a noted authority on astronomical

---

[1] W. Bousset-Gressmann, op. cit., p.95, 'in seiner Familie scheint eine gewisse Vorliebe für griechische Weisheit und Sprache sich erhalten zu haben', is a misleading understatement. Bousset's rabbinic authorities have to be judged by the two facts that Aquila's Greek translation of the O.T. was an absolute necessity for the rise of the Synagogue, and that Justin's interlocutor, Trypho, was proud of his converse with Greek philosophers. The rabbinical rule prohibiting the learning of Greek, if it is at all historical, cannot have been pronounced before A.D. 135.

[2] The point at issue between Eliezer and Gamaliel, cf. Finkelstein, *Akiba*, p.122f., is evidently legendary; but the precedent referred to, the excommunication of Akabia ben Mahalalel for not submitting to a decision of the Jerusalem Sanhedrin, shows that Gamaliel's forte lay in his succession after Jochanan ben Zakkai, the last Sanhedrite, Finkelstein, op. cit., p.89f.

matters.[1] Gamaliel is said to have come into conflict with Joshua about matters of the calendar. Since the lunar year was to be observed in the dating of all Jewish feasts, whereas the civil calendar in the Roman Empire followed the solar year, all Jewish feast days had to be fixed anew every year. Before the fall of Jerusalem this had been done by the High Priest. Now Gamaliel claimed this prerogative for himself, and Joshua, who, however great a scholar he may have been according to Jewish standards, was not a man of the world who could have represented Judaism before the Roman authorities, submitted to Gamaliel. The fact that this conflict was later than that between Gamaliel and Eliezer follows from its semi-political character. For some political recognition of Gamaliel's position is to be presumed if this difference between him and Joshua had to be fought out in earnest.[2] Once more the sources, although they seem to have preserved the issue between the two men correctly, have embroidered the humiliation of Joshua with legendary accretions.[3]

In this way Gamaliel obtained the position of Nasi, or universal Patriarch, but at the same time roused the ire of the followers of Joshua[4] who, so it seems, represented the cause of the plebeians against the patrician Partiarch. Joshua had avoided excommunica-

[1] Finkelstein, op. cit., p.77.—It would be of great advantage to know the exact geographical location of Pekiin, cf. above, p.114, n.3. For if it could be claimed that the place of it was in Galilee, which had surrendered to the Romans already in A.D. 67, Joshua's authority in matters of the calendar could be easily explained by the fact that the Jews abroad had had to rely on him, whilst the normal authority, the High Priest of Jerusalem, had been unable to supply them with the dates of the feast days.

[2] On the personality of Joshua cf. Finkelstein, op. cit., p.77. On the political character of the arrangement of the calendar cf. E. Lohse, *Die Ordination im Spätjudentum*, 1951, p.53.

[3] Finkelstein, op. cit., p.118f., gives a picturesque account of these legends. It is regrettable, however, that he should have treated them as historical.

[4] It has to be noticed that a conflict about the calendar between Gamaliel and Akiba who, according to later sources, was ordained by Joshua, cf. Lohse, op. cit., p.35, n.3, has also been recorded in talmudic sources, Finkelstein, op. cit., p.120f.—The strength of the position which Gamaliel gained by the submission of Joshua is illustrated by the report in *Eduyoth*, VII.7, that the decision about a leap-year, taken by the scholars of the Academy at Jamnia in his absence, was made conditional on his approval, Schürer, op. cit., vol.2, p.370, n.79.

tion by his submission to Gamaliel's decree, although his spiritual authority, depending, as it did, entirely upon his succession after Jochanan ben Zakkai, cannot have been beyond question yet.[1] Understandably the necessity of so doing rankled in Joshua's mind, and in that of his friends. Moreover, Gamaliel's power was extremely dangerous for the future of Pharisaic Judaism. Already once, at the time of the Maccabees, a national revival of the Jews had ended with their leaders losing their soul to Hellenistic civilisation. If Joshua, therefore, had lost the first round, he had yet to win the contest.

The man who made the tide turn was Akiba. Who exactly he was, and where he came from, we do not know. The myth that he was originally a shepherd—or a proselyte—is a myth.[2] The name of his chief teacher, Nahum of Gimzô,[3] conveys very little to us; the alleged association with R. Tarphon may be legendary. For if there is any truth in the identification of R. Tarphon with Trypho, the interlocutor of Justin Martyr, he must have been considerably younger than Akiba. Significant, however, is the unanimous report that Akiba was a pupil of Eliezer ben Hyrkanos, and that Joshua ben Chananja ordained him. For both these men we have found in opposition to the Nasi, Gamaliel ii.

The reported gathering of the heads of various Jewish schools at Jamnia illustrates the strength of Gamaliel's position throughout Palestinian Jewry. For in his relations to all of them he is always represented as the Nasi, the head of the Academy at Jamnia, in which these newcomers, together with his disciples, were or were not accorded a seat. He was also at the head of the administration

---

[1] There is a great bulk of Jewish literature on the organization of the Pharisees before the fall of Jerusalem, which is out of all proportion to the sources originating from this period. We can only repeat that according to the standards of historical research it must be treated with utmost reserve. Contemporary sources, the Gospels, Acts, Philo, Josephus, contain no references to the existence of a Pharisaic Nasi, and thus the assumption of Finkelstein, op. cit., p.73, that Gamaliel was marked out for Nasi right from the fall of Jerusalem is an obvious hysteron-proteron.

[2] Cf. P. Bénoit, *Rev. Bibl.*, 1947, p.55, especially on Akiba being a proselyte ibid., n.3.

[3] What little evidence there is about Nahum of Gimzô has been collected by W. Bacher, *Die Agada der Tannaiten*, 2nd ed., 1903, vol.1, p.57f.

of Jewish affairs, and it is probably only a later construction which maintains that Joshua was the Ab bêth-dîn, and that Akiba was assessor at the Jewish High Court. For it was by the efforts of these two men that Gamaliel's position was overthrown.[1] Stated thus baldly the fact smacks of intrigue; and intrigue may well have been their weapon.[2] It has to be emphasised, however, that it was not intrigue for its own sake. The whole future of Judaism was at stake. In order to make this point clear it is sufficient to point to only one effect of Akiba's action: When he began his career the universal languages were Latin, Greek, and Aramaic. One of his achievements was the substitution of Aquila's translation of the Old Testament in the place of the LXX. Biblical Hebrew had ceased to be used in common speech, and was understood only by a small number of scholars. How carefully they treated it may be seen from the surprising similarity between the text of the first of the new Isaiah scrolls and the masoretic Isaiah. No living language would be treated like that. Today, however, Latin, Greek and Aramaic are dead languages which nobody will resurrect; but Hebrew, which was almost dead then, together with Arabic, are the only living branches on the rich tree of Semitic languages. By the comparison with Arabic, Akiba's achievement becomes still more impressive. For Islam spread Arabic with fire and sword over a conquered world; but Hebrew became the language of a nation which had no political power, no Empire, in short nothing except the inestimable treasure of the Old Testament.

VII

L. Finkelstein who, in spite of his overpowering imagination, has collected the sources for Akiba's life in an admirable way,

---

[1] Schürer, op. cit., vol.2, p.370f., has wrongly minimized this event which, however, in the Synagogue was remembered as 'that day' for centuries, cf. Finkelstein, op. cit., p.330, n.63 and 64. Schürer's seems to me an attempt at criticizing the earliest traditions of the Synagogue which is liable to be accused of being arbitrary.

[2] Such a conclusion is suggested in particular by the reported increase in the number of Academicians from thirty-two to seventy-two, Finkelstein, op. cit., p.330, n.67.

emphasizes the fact that Akiba's victory over Gamaliel was due mainly to social reasons.[1] In various respects this is an useful hypothesis. Gamaliel, being a Jewish aristocrat, was on good terms with the Romans, who based their Empire upon aristocratic principles. He was inclined towards Hellenism, and Greek was the language of the higher classes in the East. Only the people of an inferior status, like the fellahs in Egypt, kept their national idiom. It can also be shown that Akiba was under obligation to the very poor for his victory. For Gamaliel was in an almost unassailable position. Only one province was left to Akiba, the administration of welfare to the distressed amongst the Jews abroad.[2]

It seems that Akiba made several journeys throughout all the East of the Empire, Palestine, Syria, probably even Asia Minor, for the purpose of collecting funds and the distribution of comforts amongst the distressed, similar to Gamaliel's famous journey to Rome.[3] His travels seem to have gained for him the moral support necessary to sway the Academy of Jamnia to pass a vote of no confidence in the Patriarch. Once more the reports about the course of the debate are legendary. Only two facts stand out: one that the fall of Gamaliel made an ineradicable impression upon Jewry. The other is that neither Akiba nor Joshua ben Chananja was made Patriarch. That fell to a younger man, more closely connected with Gamaliel, Eleazar ben Azariah.[4] If tradition may be trusted, Gamaliel, at some later date, received back his office, and a directory was formed to which he, Eleazar, Joshua and Akiba belonged.

[1] The whole book is based on the assumption that the cleft between the Shammaite and Hillelite schools was caused by the social contrast between the rich land owners and the poor tenants and artisans. This I find hard to believe. Neither is it beyond doubt that Gamaliel ii., as Finkelstein has set out, op. cit., p.304f., held only Shammaite views and fell because of them, or that Akiba was an out and out Hillelite.

[2] Finkelstein, op. cit., p.331, n.72.

[3] The traditions about this journey should be carefully scrutinized. It seems to have taken place under Domitian, and should be linked up with the evidence of *Acta Alex.* VIII (under Trajan), *Acts of Pagan Martyrs*, ed. H. A. Musurillo, 1954, p.44f.—Akiba's travels are the source of the many moving legends about his wife Rachel.

[4] It is noteworthy that a very critical remark of Eleazar's about Akiba has survived, Bacher, op. cit., vol.I, p.217, n.1, cf. ibid., p.267, n.4.

VIII

It cannot be doubted that from 'that day' on the leader of the Jews, in whatever capacity, was Akiba. Neither is there any reason to assume that the fall of Gamaliel had by any means cleared the field completely. A rabbinical legend may guide us to the first of the outstanding problems.[1] By this legend Akiba is joined to three other great Jewish scholars of his time who have not been mentioned so far, Simeon ben Zoma, Simeon ben Azzai, and Elisha ben Abuyah. The four of them are said to have explored the heights of Jewish mysticism. However, when they had reached the gates of heaven ben Azzai is said to have lost his life, ben Zoma his reason, and Elisha ben Abuyah his faith. Only Akiba was allowed to enter, and to return with the wisdom obtained by the vision of the Divine.

This legend bears witness to the second great struggle of Akiba's, that about the Jewish 'disciplina arcani',[2] the secret doctrine of Jewish mysticism. It has been rightly pointed out by a recent writer that Jewish apocalyptics made a very deep impression on early gnosticism,[3] even Christian gnosticism, and it seems highly probable that Elisha ben Abuyah himself became a Christian. Later Rabbis, for this reason, did not quote him by name, but called him Acher, the other one, because his name had been struck from the book of the living.[4]

It was Akiba who in this struggle vindicated the supremacy of the Halacha, the legal interpretation, over the Haggada, the visionary interpretation of the Old Testament, i.e. the supremacy of Moses over the prophets. Akiba's victory in this contest confirmed the final separation of the Judaeo-Christians from the

---

[1] Bacher, ibid., vol.1, p.408.

[2] Some valuable observations on this are to be found in Jeremias, *The Eucharistic Words*, 1955, p.75f.

[3] G. Quispel, *Gnosis als Weltreligion*, 1951, cf. the article by the same author in *Evang. Theol.*, 1954, p.474f.

[4] Cf. my 'Dike am Tor des Hades', *Studi mem. E. Albertario*, 1950, vol.2, p.565; Billerbeck, vol.4, 2, p.1089f.—On the celestial vision of Elisha ben Abuyah, *Chag. bab.*, 15a, cf. Quispel, *Evang. Theol.*, 1954, p.478.

Synagogue. That appears clearly from the most famous document of Jewish and Christian polemics, Justin's 'Dialogue with Trypho', written no more than twenty years after Akiba's death.[1] There it can be plainly seen, what a reserved attitude was taken by Trypho, the Jewish representative, towards prophecy, and he is supported in this by talmudic evidence.[2] Yet less than sixty years earlier the Jews, and the Pharisees among them, had been the most prolific producers of apocalyptic literature, even after the fall of Jerusalem, as may be seen from the Apocalypses of Baruch and Ezra.[3] It was Akiba's influence, so we deduce from the legend just retailed, which curtailed this development, although it did not altogether close it. The speculations on Metatron in particular continued, and Third Enoch may have been put into literary form not so long after Akiba's death;[4] but otherwise the period of apocalyptic literature was closed by the beginning of the second century A.D.

The strong diversities in the interpretation of the Torah itself, which by Akiba's efforts had become the very centre of Jewish life, were not abolished by him. In this main field of Jewish scholarship the dialectics of two opposites were necessary. However, the cleavage between the Shammaites and the Hillelites, which had continued for more than a century, since the days of Herod the

---

[1] Cf. infra, ch.7, p.132f.—How fluid the boundaries had been between the Judaeo-Christians and other heterodox Jewish sects appears from the fact that it is still impossible to determine the cases in which the talmudic *minim* may or may not mean Judaeo-Christians, cf. Quispel, *Evang. Theol.*, 1954, p.476, whereas the demarcations of the Synagogue are reasonably clear.

[2] On Trypho cf. my *Apostolic Succession*, p.87, n.3. Cf. δωρεὰ πνευματική in Barn.1:2–3, and H. Windisch. *Handb. z. N.T.*, Erg. Bd., 1920, p.303f.—Talmudic evidence may be found in E. Lohse, op. cit., p.53, n.6.

[3] Cf. on Baruch, Kautzsch, *Apokryphen und Pseudepigraphen*, 1900, vol.2, p.407, who puts the date shortly after A.D. 70. On 4.Ezra cf. Gunkel, ibid., p.352, who dates it rightly under Domitian, but is probably mistaken in making it earlier than Baruch. Important, however, are the 'universalistischen Tendenzen' of the book, established by Gunkel, ibid., p.349, which put its author in the vicinity of Philo, cf. above, 109, n.2.

[4] Cf. H. Odeberg, *3.Enoch*, Cambridge, 1928, p.23f. His dating of the work has, however, been challenged by his critics. In particular G. G. Scholem, *Major trends in Jewish Mysticism*, 1955, p.45, believes that it only belongs to the seventh century A.D.

Great, did not survive Akiba. These two schools may well be compared with those of Proculus and Sabinus amongst the contemporary Roman lawyers. Such rivalries cannot be described by a short formula; and they can be ended only by a complete change in the legal system. Such was the case at Rome, when Salvius Julianus, at the command of the Emperor Hadrian, framed the 'edictum perpetuum', and an analogous development took place in the Jewish Synagogue at almost the same time. Akiba's contribution was as important and as conciliatory as that of his Roman counterpart. He, the moderate Hillelite, had still to face two Shammaite antagonists, Josê the Galilean and Ishmael ben Elisha, just as Salvius Julianus was paired with Celsus, the head of the Proculeian school. Legend even records Josê's brilliant victory at their first encounter.[1] Still more important is the figure of Ishmael. However, an agreement was arrived at, and after Akiba's death the partisanship had vanished. The result before us is this, that Akiba created the famous Mishnaic system, whereas the Synagogue canonized Ishmael's principles of interpretation, the thirteen Middoth.[2] Akiba's preponderance, however, follows from the fact that in the vast majority of cases the Halacha has adopted the teachings of Hillel rather than those of Shammai.

IX

I have tried to outline the contest of Akiba at Jamnia, and it now remains for me to assess its lasting results. Here a short formula seems to offer itself. Akiba, so it is often said, created the Mishnah, that work which has determined the system and the method of Jewish interpretation of the Torah ever since.[3] This has

---

[1] Finkelstein, op. cit., p.165f.

[2] Cf. Schürer, op. cit., vol.2, p.375, n.118.

[3] Whether or not Epiphan., *Adv. Haer.*, XXXIII.9, cf. ibid. XV; XLII, may be regarded as a valid testimony for a written redaction of a first draft of the Mishnah by Akiba himself, seems rather doubtful, in spite of Schürer's assertion that this was the case, op. cit., 3rd ed., §3 E, n.24. I would rather assume that one of his disciples put it into writing 'in his name', after A.D. 135, in order to preserve the records of the teaching at the Academy of Jamnia, which had been closed by the disastrous ending of the Bar Kochba war.

also to be accepted as an established historical fact. Akiba was indeed the common ancestor of all the Jewish commentators of the Torah.[1] What remains is the task of the evaluation of his achievement. Should it make him worthy of immortal fame? An analogy from recent time will make my point clear: The lawyer who devised the method of scientific commentaries on the German law codes was a great scholar of the name of Staub, 'dust'; and his tomb bears the inscription, 'Hier liegt Staub, Kommentar überflüssig'. Being of Jewish extraction, Staub's name was officially banned after 1933, and it remains to be seen how much of his well-earned fame may have survived the German disaster, now, only half a century after his death. Is not that rather a warning signal to any who would connect the birth of the Synagogue with this distinction of Akiba?

I feel, therefore, that his real greatness may be insufficiently described if only his authorship of the Mishnah is mentioned. We may come nearer to it by way of the following considerations: The number of great scholars mentioned by name in the rabbinical writings is very considerable;[2] but they go no further back than to the pupils of Hillel and Shammai, men living at the beginning of the Christian era. Even these, Gamaliel i., the teacher of St. Paul, among them, appear in the rabbinical tradition as mere shadows. Moreover, the names of the non-Pharisaic scribes are entirely forgotten.[3] From earlier times there comes, previously to Hillel and Shammai, the succession list in the first chapter of Pirkê Abboth, which seems to have no support from pre-rabbinic sources.[4] Apart from this, the earlier history of the Jews provides

---

[1] Cf. K. Kohler, op. cit., p.136f.

[2] Cf. the list of names given by Schürer, op. cit., vol.1, p.119f.

[3] The conclusion drawn by Schürer, op. cit., vol.2, p.320, on the strength of Mark 2:16; Luke 5.30; Acts 23:9, 'the scribes of the Pharisees', that there must have been scribes of the Sadducees also, seems valid. It is, however, significant that no other evidence of their existence has survived.

[4] Kohler, op. cit., p.109, who maintains that Josê ben Joezer, *Pirkê Abboth*, I.4, should be identified with that Razis, 2.Macc.14.37f., who was forced to commit suicide by the troops of Nicanor, referring to Gen. R. 65. 22, seems unconvincing. It further appears to me that Dom P. Bénoit, *Rev. Bibl.*, 1947, p.61f., has placed far too much confidence upon the high age of the 'talmudic teaching' of the Jews.

us only with the enigmatic title of 'Ezra the scribe', but with no clear analogies to the type of rabbinic scholar from pre-Christian times. It appears that this new type of spiritual leadership of the Jewish nation was established by the Mishnah. It came into being thanks to the authority given to the oral tradition of rabbinical decisions, which had to be learned by heart, even after R. Jehuda the Prince, a century after Akiba, had put them into writing; and this is what we mean by the birth of the Synagogue.[1]

What we have to ask, therefore, is the question in what way the Rabbis are characteristically distinguished from the leaders of any other nation? To answer this question we have to return once more to the historical situation of A.D. 70.

After the fall of Jerusalem three roads were open for the surviving Jews. The first was that of attempting to restore their political existence, as a suzerain state within the Roman Empire. However great their losses in the war with Titus may have been, the spirit of Jewry was still alive, and its hope for the future was not broken. Just because the war had not been planned, but had only broken out by accident; just because important sections of the nation, above all the Pharisees, had stood aside, the day of reckoning for the universal power was yet to come.[2] In the meantime there need not be war. In the days of Trajan, so we hear mainly from rabbinical sources,[3] a real chance for the reconstruction of the temple at Jerusalem may have arisen. This then was the political programme at the foundation of the Patriarchate of Jamnia. Indeed, throughout the existence of the Jewish Patriarchate, the Jewish Patriarchs had to deal with the Roman government on a political basis, whatever definition of the legal position of the Jews within the Roman Empire may have been used by either party.[4]

However, Akiba's triumph over Gamaliel ii. removed these

---

[1] Cf. Bacher, *Die Tradition und die Tradenten*, 1914, which is not accessible to me.

[2] In this respect the contrast between The Apocalypse of Baruch with its burning desire for retribution, and 4.Ezra with its eschatological resignation, is highly instructive.

[3] For evidence cf. Finkelstein, op. cit., p.313f.

[4] Here the researches of S. Guterman, op. cit., p.103f., mark a definite advance over earlier attempts by Mommsen and Juster.

political ambitions to second rank, and thus prevented the political restoration of the Jewish nation from becoming an actual fact. In doing so Akiba also put an end to those dreams which looked for the rise of a political Messiah amongst the Jews. The figure of the Son of David, who would subject the whole earth, receded to that background of Jewish religious ambition from which it would only emerge in times of extreme crisis. The scheming and plotting of the Zealots was over for good.

The second road which seemed open to the Jews led into the mysterious beyond. The forces of Titus had devastated Samaria just as much as Judaea. Nevertheless, from that minute community of the Samaritans there erupted that torrent of mystical gnosticism which flooded the whole Roman Empire. The names of Dositheus, Simon Magus with his Helena, and Menander may be to us hardly more than names; but if we believe their Christian adversaries, especially Justin Martyr, these greatest amongst the Samaritan gnostics did in fact stamp their mind upon centuries of religious thought within the Roman Empire. It may be said that the certain disparagement which these reports have suffered at the hands of scholars will change, once the bearing of the Jewish elements in the newly discovered gnostic documents has been duly appreciated.[1] Ben Zoma, ben Azzai, and Elisha ben Abuyah seem to have taken this road to perdition; but even Akiba did not close it completely. The miraculous deeds of the Rabbis fill the pages of Jewish history, and it is correct to draw a line from Akiba to all the great Jewish visionaries, right down to Spinoza. All the same, the vigour with which he emphasised Judahs debt of loyalty to the Torah saved his people from the way of the Samaritans and the Chaldeans.

For it was Akiba who found a way for his nation which no other nation had taken before, or may take in future, the way of the Law.[2] He made jurisdiction, the legal principle, the life centre

---

[1] It seems to me insufficient when Quispel, *Evang. Theol.*, 1954, p.477, maintains, 'vorläufig ist es wahrscheinlicher, dass Menander eine schon bestehende, jüdische Häresie weiter entwickelt hat', especially when there is no reason to disbelieve the report of Justin, *1.Apol*,26;56, that Menander was the pupil of Simon Magus.

[2] The Greek idea of life according to the Nomos, although it is essentially

of the Jewish nation. The outstanding importance of this fact has been underlined by yet another Jewish legend:[1] When Moses, so this story tells us, went to heaven, he found the Almighty Himself occupied with putting a little crown upon each letter of the Torah. In his astonishment he asked what the reason for this Divine activity might be; and the Almighty is said to have replied that in the future a scholar would arise, Akiba ben Joseph, who would give to each single letter of the Torah its own specific meaning. Moses thereupon desired that he might be shown this man, and having been told to move backward, after he had reached the eighth row he found himself in the midst of Akiba's pupils, listening to the master interpreting the Torah. Seeing him, Moses exclaimed: 'O Almighty, having such a man before Thee, why hast Thou given through me the Torah to Thy people?' The Lord, however, replied, 'Be quiet, for such is my good pleasure.'

X

A second Moses, and greater than he, as predicted in Deut. 18:15,[2] such is the verdict of this talmudic appreciation of Akiba. But a second Moses meant a new foundation of Judaism, for it had been Moses who had first established Israel as a nation. Can this view stand the test of sober historical examination? Synagogues, meeting places, the Jews had known since the beginning of Pharisaism, i.e. since the days of the Maccabees, although we have to guard against too easy an identification of Pharisaism before and after A.D. 70. The mind of the authors of the Psalms of Solomon, for instance, is widely different from that of early rabbinical

---

different, had been appropriated by Philo, cf. e.g. *Vita Mosis*, II.51, and it is useful to compare his ideas about the Torah as the universal Nomos, which strongly influenced later Christian writers, like Origen, with Akiba's contention that the Torah was 'the Law', beside which there could not be any other.

[1] According to Bacher, *Agada*, op. cit., vol.1, p.263f., the author of this legend was Rabh († 235), cf. also Finkelstein, op. cit., p.156f. Bacher, op. cit., p.264, also records a similar legend about Akiba and Adam. Finkelstein, op. cit., p.157, has not understood its symbolism.

[2] This follows from the eighth row to which Moses is removed—after the period of one Aeon, seven 'days', cf. my remark, *Harv. Theol., Rev.* 1945, p.177f.

testimonies. Nevertheless, Pharisaic teaching comparable to that of Akiba was fully established at the time of Jesus; and when Jerusalem had fallen to the Romans, various teachers, as we have seen, possessed considerable authority. This fact enabled them to assume the leadership of the Jewish nation, even if at the war of Bar Kochba other elements came to the fore for the last time.

Nevertheless, the method of rabbinical teaching, if we can assess it correctly, was still in an amorphous state.[1] Gamaliel ii., as we have seen, centralized the administrative system of the Synagogue;[2] but it was the establishment of the Mishnaic principle which caused the specifically Jewish system of education to become the centre of Jewish life. This task, however, was only achieved by Akiba, almost a century after the birth of Jesus Christ and half a century after the foundation of the Church amongst the Gentiles by St. Paul and the other great, early Christian missionaries. From a historical point of view, therefore, the Christian Church is indeed the elder sister of the Jewish Synagogue.

Akiba's great achievement was the reason why Jewish hopes for the coming of the Messiah palled, hopes which had inspired the Zealots of A.D. 70 to that unsurpassed heroism with which they had fought for the temple of Jahweh. Akiba himself, however, fell a victim of the last Messianic war of the Jews, after having recognized Bar Kochba as the Messiah of the Jews. How is this apparent contradiction to be resolved? Only as a hypothesis I would venture to suggest that at the bottom of Akiba's work there lay an overpowering eschatology, the belief that Jahweh would send His Messiah and bring about the end of all things when justice had been restored to Israel. With the strongest belief in the necessity

---

[1] I can do no better than to quote Kohler, op. cit., p.136, 'it was the marvellous decree of Providence that R. Akiba . . . should also have been the foremost master of the Law who, with his great disciples, was to work out the comprehensive plan for the Mishnah with its six sections comprising all the departments of the Law, performing the mighty task which two generations afterwards enabled Judah the Prince . . . to undertake the edition of the complete Mishnaic code'.

[2] Gamaliel introduced, as I believe, rabbinical ordination, cf. ch.7 below.

of his great achievement, I would think, Akiba proclaimed the 'son of a star', Bar Kochba, as the long expected Messiah.[1]

The Christians, and in particular Origen, saw the pitiful, small remnant of Jewry, which had escaped the massacre of the Hadrianic war, and described it as the Church's little sister. That, I believe, is of great theological significance. Not long ago I attempted to show that the Church at that time based the Apostolic succession of her bishops upon the succession of the High Priests of Israel since Aaron, and thus made it her own. In the Creed of Nicea-Chalcedon the Church claims for herself also the prophetic Spirit of ancient Israel. Both these doctrines agree with the rabbinical convictions that in the Synagogue there is neither room for the priesthood nor for prophecy. Of all the inheritance of Israel only one piece has been claimed for the Synagogue, the Law, that Law which, as Christians profess, has found its fulfilment in Jesus Christ, the Saviour. Already St. Paul, Rom.9:31, had foreseen such a development, apparently by his knowledge of Pharisaism. The promise of God, however, is unshakeable; and upon us, the Christians, there is laid the task of considering 'what shall we do for our sister in the day when she shall be spoken for'— by Christ?

---

[1] For this supposition there are several hints in rabbinical theology. It is remarkable, for instance, that later generations of Rabbis found in Akiba's death the fulfilment of Is.53:12, cf. Bacher, *Agada*, op. cit., vol.1, p.269. Another indication is that the Rabbis hold that the ordinand at his ordination receives forgiveness of sins, like the bridegroom at his wedding, Lohse, *Die Ordination*, op. cit., p.55; another that the day of ordination is to God as dear as that on which the Law was given, ibid., p.56.

7

JEWISH AND CHRISTIAN ORDINATION

I

IN discussions about the Apostolic Ministry of the Church the Jewish factor in its development has proved a disturbing element. Therefore, a book dealing with the early rite of rabbinical ordination, published in Germany in 1951,[1] was certain of an interested reception, even though the main facts could be found already in Billerbeck.[2] Dr. Lohse, its author, shows himself well versed in rabbinical literature, and the evidence which he has collected is well nigh complete. Unfortunately, the author's main thesis, although it is by no means new,[3] is apt to provoke serious misgivings. For he claims (p.101) that 'the Christian ordination was modelled on the pattern of that of Jewish scholars, although early Christianity filled it with a new content'. To support his claim the author has given only one important reason, namely that both rites had the imposition of hands as their centre. The other support which the author has tried to build up to strengthen his thesis is, to say the least, feeble. It is therefore necessary to enquire whether the laying-on-of-hands had the same intention in the early Christian ordination rite as in the rabbinical rite. Such identity of intention is, however, not even to be found in all the various cases of laying-on-of-hands in the New Testament, and the same is also true of contemporary Judaism. Philo, for instance, gives an extensive discussion of the laying-on-of-hands upon Ephraim and Manasse,[4] but he never even mentions the s^emikhah,[5] the laying-

---

[1] E. Lohse, *Die Ordination.*

[2] Billerbeck, vol.2, p.647f.

[3] The same view has been propounded already by F. Gavin, *The Jewish Antecedents of the Christian Sacraments*, 1928, p.101.

[4] Philo, *Leg. alleg.*, III.90f., ed. Cohn-Wendland, vol.1, p.133, l.7f.

[5] How S. New in Lake-Cadbury, *The Beginnings of Christianity*, vol.5, 1933, p.137f., has arrived at the form *seminkah*, I do not know.

on-of-hands, in the ordination of Joshua as the successor of Moses,[1]
the famous precedent of rabbinical ordination (Lohse, p.19f.).
No such considerations have, however, entered into Lohse's
book.

Lohse's contention, if it were true, would have grave theological
consequences, for the ministry of the Church cannot easily be
compared with that of the Synagogue. The latter was, by and
large, a legal, not a spiritual, ministry. The rabbis laid no claim to
being priests; they were functionaries. The reason is that there are
no sacraments in the Synagogue. Even circumcision, which every
pater familias may administer to his own children, whilst the rabbi
is granted the authority of administering it to other persons also,
is not a sacramental but a legal act.[2] Neither does Lohse claim
that the idea of the priesthood was the 'new content' with which
early Christianity had filled the earlier rabbinical ordination rite.
In fact no suggestion as to its nature is made, and the choice of the
term 'early Christianity' instead of the early Church seems to
relegate this proposed new content to the realm of religious senti-
ment.[3]

This vagueness with regard to the difference between early
Christian and early rabbinical ordination is matched with a certain
methodological weakness. Lohse decries (p.89) any conclusions
with regard to the ministry of the Church which can be arrived at
only 'if we venture into the unsafe field of hypotheses or draw
conclusions from later usages, which is not permissible'; yet he
has not observed his own rule where rabbinical ordination is
concerned. He admits freely (p.30) that he believes that only
Assumptio Mosis XII.2 can be adduced as direct evidence that the
s^emikhah was administered in pre-Christian times. Thus it seems
hazardous indeed when he (p.30) assumes a connection between

---

[1] Philo, *de Virtut.*, 66f., ed. Cohn-Wendland, vol.5, p.284, l.8f.

[2] Significant for this is the fact that circumcision does not figure even in the
index of J. Elbogen, *Der Jüdische Gottesdienst*, 2nd ed., 1924.

[3] It appears that Lohse himself does not face all the implications of his own
statement (p.98) that the New Testament does not know the idea of the
ministry 'in our sense', for his two authorities, E. Schlink, *Die Theologie der
lutherischen Bekenntnis-Schriften*, 2nd ed., 1946, p.331, and K. H. Rengstorf,
Apostolat und Predigtamt, 1934, p.82, both comment on the Church's ministry.

early rabbinical ordination and the institution of judges by king Jehoshaphat (2.Chron.19:5), even if this report has to be treated as a reflection of post-exilic conditions back into an earlier period. The hypothesis is so very unsafe, since the technical term of *samakh*, to ordain, is not used in 2.Chron.19:5.

II

Lohse's conclusions have to be approached, therefore, with great caution. All the same, his collection of sources provides us with a useful basis from which to start our enquiry, even if it has to be emphasized that the Talmudic material should have been treated throughout with a slightly stricter critical reserve. If anywhere, the two great Jewish wars of A.D. 70 and A.D. 135 had tremendous repercussions upon the organization of Jewry within the Roman Empire, and the ordination of the rabbis belonged chiefly to this field. The organization of the Jews of the dispersion before Titus and Hadrian gave little scope, so far as we know, to the administrative and judicial activities of Jewish scholars; that after Hadrian was wholly dependent upon both. It is difficult to determine how much judicial autonomy was granted to the Jews of the dispersion before A.D. 70. We once hear of the Jewish ethnarch at Alexandria in Josephus,[1] and the papyri have enabled Zucker to draw a picture of Jewish self-government in Egypt;[2] but it is already doubtful how Josephus' reference to Jewish self-government at Sardes[3] is to be understood, and conditions at Rome suggest an organization of the Jews in numerous private communities.[4] Nowhere were the rabbis as such employed in the administration of civil affairs, and it can be safely said that the leaders of Jewish communities at that time were not, as a rule, scholars. At Jerusalem things were different. The Sanhedrin, although it did not consist of scholars, contained at least a fair

---

[1] Strabo in Joseph., *Ant.*, XIV.7.2, §117, cf. J. Juster, op. cit., vol.2, p.111, n.1.

[2] H. Zucker, *Geschichte der Jüdischen Selbstverwaltung in Ägypten*, 1934.

[3] Jos., *Ant.*, XIV.10.17, §235.

[4] Schürer, op. cit., vol.3, p.81f.

number of them, and it was largely in charge of such administrative and judicial authority as was granted by the Romans to Palestinian Jewry before A.D. 70.

After the destruction of the temple, at least part of the same authority was granted by the Roman government to Jewish communities all over the Empire; and, as far as it was known, the Palestinian model was copied by the people of the dispersion. Thus the Jewish scholars, the only surviving group from which members of the Sanhedrin were elected, obtained the leadership in the Synagogue, very largely because of the genius of one man, Akiba, and the school which he founded. This result was not achieved without internecine strife.[1] For this reason it becomes necessary to test carefully the accounts of early ordinations in the Talmud to see whether they have the purpose of safeguarding Akiba's line of succession. For, if such be the case, they may be suspected of introducing the paraphernalia of a later ordination rite into this early period in order to enhance in this way the impeccability of Akiba's succession-line. Conversely, if a Talmudic report differs from the later rite, so well described by Lohse, its historical value will rise accordingly. Thus we would defer drawing conclusions from the report of R.Ba ($\pm$ A.D. 290) about the ordination by R. Jochanan b. Zakkai of two of his pupils, probably before A.D. 70 (Lohse, p.32f.). For even if the fact as such be historically established, the circumstances reported, especially the technical term *s^emikhah*, which is not to be found in the Old Testament, may prove to be a later appreciation of the event. This is, indeed, suggested by the report on that ordination which in order of time follows next, that of R. Eleazar b. Chisma and R. Jochanan b. Nuri at the hands of Akiba's opponent, the Nasi, R. Gamaliel ii. (Lohse, p.33). For there the term *s^emikhah* is missing from the Talmudic report. Instead of *samakh* the verb used is *hoshebh* (καθίσαι in LXX of 1.Kings 2:8; 3.Kings 20:9f.; Ps.112:8) meaning 'cause to be seated'. Purely legendary, on the other hand, appears to be the report that R. Jehuda b. Baba ordained five of his pupils in A.D. 135, in defiance of a Roman decree

---

[1] This has been brought out clearly by Finkelstein, op. cit., p.92f., however much his work may tend to be an eulogy of Akiba.

prohibiting the ordination of rabbis. No such decree is preserved in non-Talmudic sources and, indeed, any such decree would have been impracticable. For there were, on the one hand, vast regions within the Roman Empire unaffected by the war of Bar Kochba, as may be seen from Justin Martyr's *Dialogue*, where the supervision of the Jews by the Romans was not strict enough to prevent the instruction, and probably also a subsequent ordination in Palestine, of Jewish scholars by their master; and, on the other hand, Babylon with its great Jewish colony was under Persian rule and so was unaffected by any Roman decree. The alleged aim of interrupting the rabbinical succession, if it was at all within the compass of Roman policy, could not be achieved in such a clumsy fashion. The tendentiousness of this report, which aimed at the glorification of Akiba's succession, started by the Academy at Jabne (Jamnia) under his leadership, by adding yet another of its masters to its register of martyrs,[1] should not have escaped Lohse.

Under these circumstances we have to form our own verdict on the evidence provided by earlier witnesses to rabbinical ordination, since the later ones, at least in so far as they provide us with data about actual ordinations, have proved to be subject to serious suspicion. Here we first turn to the terms *samakh* and *s⁰mikhah*[2] which, in most of the Talmudic passages quoted by Lohse, are used as technical terms for ordination, the first of them having in the Old Testament—amongst others—the meaning of 'laying-on-of-hands'.[3] This shows, as Lohse (p.45f.) has correctly pointed out, that the centre of the rabbinical ordination rite consisted in the laying-on-of-hands. He also states rightly (p.47f.) how in the course of the fourth century the laying-on-of-hands was more and more dispensed with in the Synagogue, so that the rite was most popular there at the time of the rise of the early Catholic Church. What Lohse does not tell us is the approximate time at which the rite began to be used by the Synagogue. Apparently he assumes

[1] On the intimate relations between Akiba and Jehuda b. Baba cf. Finkelstein, op. cit., p.76.

[2] Cf. J. Newman, *Semikhah*, Manchester, 1950.

[3] *S⁰mikhah* is not to be found in O.T. Hebrew.

that it arose at the same time as rabbinical ordination made its appearance. This view, however, so it appears, is in need of further clarification.

It has been mentioned already that the 'locus classicus' for rabbinical ordination is to be found in Num.27:15f. It may be asked however, whether no other precedent was ever cited. Lohse (p.21f.) has very correctly referred to Num.11:16f., the institution of the seventy elders by Moses, where no laying-on-of-hands is mentioned; but he seems impressed by the unanimous view of Talmudic rabbis that such a mention was only accidentally omitted. I am not so impressed. It may yet be that this precedent is at the root of those traditions which were collected by A. Büchler in his book on the Sanhedrin and the *bêth-dîn*.[1] The significant number seventy in both cases poses a problem which, I feel, can be solved by the identification of the *bêth-dîn* with the Jerusalem Sanhedrin.

However that may be, it is the use of *hoshebh* in the report on the ordination of the two Rabbis Eleazar b. Chisma and Jochanan b. Nuri at the hands of R. Gamaliel ii, which will serve as our 'leading fossil'. For *hoshebh* points to a rival rite to that of laying-on-of-hands, viz. the enthronement of rabbis. With Lohse (p.31f.) we approach with caution the famous controversy of the five pairs of 'Fathers', as to whether *s^emikhah* should be practised or not, as a doubtful testimony for early ordinations. However, the use of *hoshebh* mentioned, would at any rate provide us with a practicable alternative to the *s^emikhah*, the imposition of hands, if it were assumed that the discussion between the 'Fathers', retailed at length in the Mishnah (*Chagh.*, II.2), was concerned with rabbinical ordination. In favour of this assumption is the fact that the significance of the five pairs of 'Fathers' is just this, that they form the model of a rabbinical chain of succession. The Mishnaic report is suspect historically, but I do not feel inclined to dismiss as summarily as Lohse has done the possibility that the discussion

[1] A. Büchler, *Das Synhedrion in Jerusalem*, 1902, where on p.163, even if the note 144 is discarded, remarks are found about an official decision on ordinations, which Lohse, p.36, n.2, though following Billerbeck, vol.2, p.649, may have dismissed too quickly as bearing only on the post-Hadrianic period.

in *Chagh.*, II.2 was concerned with rabbinical ordinations. For his sole reason for so doing is that the tractate of the Mishnah, in which the discussion is preserved, suggests that the discussion was concerned with the laying of hands on the sacrificial victim rather than on an ordinand, and that is no cogent reason. If, and I admit that I am here once more only offering an hypothesis, the discussion in *Chagh.*, II.2 was concerned with rabbinical ordination, it was at any rate not about ordination as such, but on the question of whether or not at such an ordination the rite of laying-on-of-hands should be practised. It would, therefore, serve as proof that at the time of the Mishnah a valid ordination without laying-on-of-hands was still remembered as having existed in the past.

This very fact seems to follow still more clearly from another Mishnaic source concerning rabbinical ordination quoted by Lohse. This source is *Sanh.*, IV.4. By his treatment of this most valuable testimony he (p.30) has shown how wedded he is to the idea that there never was a rabbinical ordination without laying-on-of-hands. For in belittling its value as an early testimony he has inadvertently disrupted the strongest link between rabbinical and early Christian sources dealing with ordination. As a report about the admission to the Jerusalem Sanhedrin the story told us in *Sanh.*, IV.4 contains inconsistencies; but it shows what would be done in an ideal synagogue of the second century in an attempt to imitate this model. It describes how the rabbis were seated in a semi-circle, the secretaries standing on each wing. Facing the rabbis their pupils squatted on the floor, and behind them stood the general public, *qahal*. One of the chairs of the court being vacant, one of the pupils in the front row was elevated to it, whilst his place was filled by his juniors moving up, till the most junior place was taken by a member of the *qahal*.[1] Although the word *s^emikhah* is used for ordination in this context, no laying-on-of-hands is mentioned. Thus it becomes clear how a discussion may have arisen as to whether the new rabbi was to be supported (*samakh*) by the chairman to his new eminence or not.

[1] Cf. Schürer, op. cit., vol.2, p.250, n.36.

The centre of the rite, however, lay in the *hoshebh*, the elevation of the new rabbi to the vacant chair.[1]

The same fact arises out of the reports on the ordination of Joshua by Moses in the Tannaite *midrashim*: In *Sifre* §140 to Num. 27:18 it is said that Moses made Joshua rise and be seated on a chair. The laying-on-of-hands is, of course, not omitted as it occurs in Num.27:18, but the ordination of Joshua to the office of teacher and judge is mainly symbolized by his enthronement. The interesting fact is that the enthronement, which in Num.27:18-19 takes only the second place, is so strongly emphasized in this and other *midrashim* (Lohse, p.26), far more so than the laying-on-of-hands. These observations about the *midrashim* find their support in *Ass. Mos.*, XII.2, where we read: 'Then Moses took him (sc. Joshua) by his hand and lifted him up to the chair before him.' We therefore have here two early versions of the interpretation of the 'locus classicus' for rabbinical ordination. The one from the *midrash* makes little of the laying-on-of-hands, whilst the other, still earlier, from the *Assumptio Mosis*, does not mention any laying-on-of-hands at all, but does indeed illustrate the original meaning of *samakh*, 'to support'. Lohse (p.30) has said that there is a high probability that this report too has to be treated as a witness to early Jewish ordination. We can do more: we can prove that it is such a testimony. As such it appears in the light of Jesus's ironical remark in Matt.23:2 ('the scribes and Pharisees sit in Moses' chair') which, in its turn, in the light of the *midrashim* and *Ass. Mos.* XII.2, is shown to be a reference to contemporary Jewish ordination practice. Indeed, the Christian source, not quoted by Lohse,[2] is needed to drive home his argument that ordination was practised in Jewry at the time of Jesus (p.35, n.2). This rite of enthronement was also continued in certain Judaeo-Christian circles, as may be seen from the pseudo-Clementines, where the chair upon which the new bishop was enthroned was still

[1] The scene described ties up with Büchler's description, op. cit., p.163, of the development of the ordination to the Sanhedrin, according to which at first either the chairman (Nasi) or the court as a whole (*bêth-dîn*) had the right to ordain, whereas eventually they had to combine.

[2] Billerbeck, vol. 1, p.909, has also overlooked the analogy.

described as 'Moses' chair'.[1] Thus my conclusion is that Lohse's picture of Jewish ordination in New Testament times is faulty in so far as he has given no attention to the rite of enthronement which, with the help of a New Testament source, I have been able to show as being of supreme importance in Jewish ordination at the time of Jesus, whereas the laying-on-of-hands, if it was practised at all, was at least kept in the background. The reason for its later rise, I would suggest, was the need for individual ordination in the troubled times from Titus to Hadrian, when the precedent of Num.27:18–19 had to be stressed against that of Num.11:16, which had been favoured by the Sanhedrin with its 71 members.[2]

No part of the ordination, but a consequence of it, is the question of the title with which the newly ordained Jewish scholar was endowed. There can be no question that in Talmudic times it was 'Rabbi' (Lohse, p.36), but in the period before A.D. 70 this title was freely given to non-ordained Jewish scholars—a fact which is borne out by the evidence of the New Testament. Lohse (p.51) has, therefore, suggested that the ordained scholars were called $z^e qenim$, πρεσβύτεροι, a fact which I would be glad to accept unquestioned, if his evidence were stronger. For πρεσβύτερος was the title given to members of the Sanhedrin, and all my research so far has pointed to the fact that the earliest Jewish ordination was bound up with admission to this body. However, Lohse's case is weak. His only support is a reference in the post-Talmudic tractate *Sopherim*, of about A.D. 600 (Lohse, p.51, n.1). There it is said that before A.D. 70, on the Day of Atonement, parents at Jerusalem brought their children to the $z^e qenim$ that they should pray for them and bless them. Lohse has referred to J. Jeremias[3] saying that the description of customs at Jerusalem before A.D. 70 which may be gathered from the tractate *Sopherim*, is, generally speaking, reliable; but he has overlooked two facts. The first is that the treatise does not say that these $z^e qenim$ were ordained scribes; the second is that it does not say that their official description was $z^e qenim$ at Jerusalem in those

[1] Cf. my *Apostolic Succession*, p.73.
[2] Schürer, op. cit., vol. 2, p.240f.
[3] Jeremias, *Jerusalem zur Zeit Jesu*, vol.2b, 1937, p.88f.

days. This is indeed questionable in view of the New Testament evidence where the elders and scribes are mentioned side by side as separate groups in Matt.26:57 and Acts 6:12, which suggests that the elders were not necessarily scribes. For it is clear from both these passages that the scribes are not regarded as subordinated to the elders—as an unordained Jewish scholar would be to his rabbi—but co-ordinated. However, when we turn to Philo we receive an unexpected support for Lohse's thesis from his interpretation of Num.11:16f. There, in the LXX, the seventy elders are called πρεσβύτεροι, which is also by far the most common translation of *z²qenim* in the LXX. Now Philo, in one of the passages quoting Num.11:16f.,[1] viz. *Gigant.* 24, says of the Seventy that they 'truly could not have become πρεσβύτεροι, had they not been given part of his all-wise spirit'. It is true that evidence from Philo is not decisive for conditions at Jerusalem, but it is suggestive. If, therefore, Lohse's and my hypothesis is accepted that Jewish ordination before A.D. 70 conferred the title of *zaqen*, πρεσβύτερος, it would strongly argue in favour of the assumption that Jewish ordination before A.D. 70 was by no means a hole-and-corner affair, to be administered by any rabbi to his disciples at will, but the solemn ritual of admission to one of the seats in the Jerusalem Sanhedrin. As an excursus, I would yet mention that this hypothesis cannot contribute anything to the theory that Christian ordination was the copy of some form of Jewish ordination. For the earliest ordination rite of Christian presbyters, which has come down to us in the *Apostolic Tradition* of Hippolytus of Rome, is plainly a copy of the episcopal consecration rite. We do not know at what time and where ordination of presbyters was first introduced. The bishops consecrated in the pseudo-Clementines are all presbyters of Jerusalem; Irenaeus, before he became the bishop, was a presbyter at Lyons. If any of these were ordained presbyters, their consecration with a renewed

---

[1] Cf. also *De sacrif. Abel.*, 77, ed. Cohn-Wendland, vol.1, p.234, l.2f.; *de Sobr.*, 19, ibid., vol.2, p.219, l.10f., where the Seventy are called the παρέδροι of Moses, a reference to their enthronement, which is not mentioned in Num. 11:16f., but supplemented by Philo, just as the rabbis supplemented Moses' laying hands upon the Seventy; *de Fuga*, 186, ibid., vol.3, p.150, l.19f.

laying-on-of-hands would have been contrary to the Jewish rule that the *s⁼mikhah* must not be repeated; if they were not ordained like the confessors who had been in chains,[1] how did they receive the title of presbyter which, in Jewry, presupposed ordination?

Lohse (p.52), however, believes not only in private ordination before A.D. 70, but also that the title of rabbi was already then becoming the mark of rabbinical ordination. His reason is a curious one. He deduces it from an inscription found on an urn in a tomb on mount Olivet.[2] But how should it follow from this inscription which, on the obverse, reads the name of Theodotion, and on the reverse the title of διδάσκαλος, that 'Rabbi as a title of honour received its special meaning as the address due to an or- dained scholar shortly after the time of Jesus'? Was Theodotion an ordained Jewish scholar? Assuming this to be the case, although I know of no evidence in favour of such an assumption, does Lohse suggest that all other persons buried on mount Olivet, whose tombs do not bear the inscription of διδάσκαλος, were scholars who had failed to obtain ordination? Surely, the only reason given for his statement that very few of the ancient tombs on mount Olivet may be dated after A.D. 70, shows nothing even remotely connected with ordination. We cannot even be sure that Theodotion in his lifetime was called rabbi, for the translation of *rabh* as a noun in the LXX is not διδάσκαλος but ἡγεμών, as in Jer. 45(39): 13.

Apparently as an analogy to ordination, Lohse (p.6of.) has included in his book a short chapter on the very complex question of the *shaliach*; but it may well be asked whether there is any ana- logy between the rabbinical ordination and the sending out of a *shaliach*. For, on the one hand, ordained and unordained persons alike could be so sent out, so that it would be difficult—at least in New Testament times[3]—to draw any analogies between a

---

[1] Hippol., *Ap. Tr.*, X.1, ed. G. Dix, 1937, 19. In spite of the concurrence of Dix and B. S. Easton, *The Apostolic Tradition*, 1934, 39, the Greek χειροτονεῖν makes us wonder whether imposition of hands was at all mentioned, as the Sahidic suggests.

[2] L. Sukenik, *Jüd. Gräber Jerusalems um Christi Geburt*, 1931, p.18.

[3] In the inscription 'quei dicerunt trenus duo apostuli et duo rebbites' (J. B. Frey, *Corp. Inscr. Jüd.*, vol.1, p.438) such an analogy is made; but Schürer,

rabbi and a *shaliach*; on the other hand, the sending out of a *shaliach* could be repeated, whereas Lohse (pp.35,47) more than once rightly stresses the fact that rabbinical ordination could not be repeated. There is no need for me to enter more fully into the *shaliach* controversy of recent years.[1] It has been admirably summed up by T. W. Manson,[2] and there seems to be no real chance of further progress in the matter, unless new sources are opened up.

No analogy whatsoever, so it seems, arises out of the survey of persons who were entitled to administer ordination, and Lohse has, therefore, refrained from summing up his findings in this matter.[3] He has merely repeated the current opinion that in early times each rabbi was entitled to ordain his own pupils, whereas by the end of the second century the Jewish Patriarch (and the Exilarch at Babylon) made attempts to centralize ordination, which by and large were successful.[4] However, we have to enquire more closely into this, since it touches upon the crucial question of the apostolic succession. Here I must state first that the line of rabbinical succession of Akiba was of necessity irregular; so was the Academy at Jamnia (Jabne) itself in the period A.D. 70–135, which experienced such grim events as the excommunication of R. Eliezer b. Hyrkanos and his followers—an action directed against the Nasi Gamaliel ii.[5]—and the subsequent deposition of Gamaliel ii himself.[6] On the other hand, we have to refer to the recognition of the later patriarchs by the Roman government, after A.D. 135,[7] to explain why their attempts to centralize the ordination of rabbis who, after all, were in charge of Jewish civil administration, were successful. For both these facts are important

---

op. cit., vol.3, p.81, saying that the conditions under which Italian Jewry lived did not change from the first to the fifth century, only underlines our lack of sufficient information.

[1] Carried on especially in *Theology*.
[2] T. W. Manson, *The Church's Ministry*, 1948, p.35f.
[3] The sources are easily accessible through Billerbeck, vol.2, p.649f., under 3.
[4] So, e.g. Gavin, op. cit., p.102, n.2.
[5] Finkelstein, *Akiba*, p.122f.
[6] Finkelstein, ibid., p.126.
[7] Juster, *Les Juifs*, vol.1, p.393.

for a critical assessment of the analogy between the rabbinical and Christian ordinations.

Once more the ordination of Eleazar b. Chisma and Jochanan b. Nuri, already mentioned, becomes important, and so does A. Büchler's reference to the ruling that ordinations were to be arranged between the Nasi and the whole *bêth-dîn*, the whole school or academy.[1] For these two rabbis were ordained unknown to the Academy, by the Nasi Gamaliel ii. on a sea-voyage to Rome (Lohse, p.33). We have seen that it is unlikely that this rule was applied to some private school, but we may consider its applicability to the Ab-bêth-dîn, the speaker of the Jerusalem Sanhedrin. For if it was applied to him already, it would throw into relief the irregularity of the ordination of Akiba at the hands of Joshua b. Chananja and the tendentiousness of the report that R. Jochanan b. Zakkai had ordained pupils privately before the destruction of the temple. That would also give us reason to assume that private ordination was, at any rate, not officially recognized before A.D. 70, but was a transient phase in the troubled times between A.D. 70 and 135, and not the true origin of rabbinical ordination.

This conclusion is indeed demanded by the conception of rabbinical succession, of which Lohse has said very little. His reference (p.49) to a register of rabbis kept by the patriarchs should have made it clear how irregular private ordination was. Obviously such a register would not contain the names of rabbis who had been privately ordained by their own masters. Moreover, it is evident from the whole Talmud that no difference of rank was made between those ordained privately and those ordained by the patriarch. This goes to show that private ordination had received its status at a time of crisis, when official ordination was not obtainable, between A.D. 70 and 135, and could be revived under similar circumstances, as in the patriarchate of Jehuda ii.[2] Connected with the succession is the rabbinical tradition; yet here we are on still less safe ground. The Talmud, indeed, indicates if a saying comes from a rabbi or from an unordained scholar; but

[1] Büchler, *Synhedrion*, p.163.
[2] ibid., p. 163.

this is historical evidence only for the period after A.D. 135. As to
the preceding period, Lohse (p.52f.) has referred to the 'disciplina arcani'. This is unconvincing, for the references to Jewish
'disciplina arcani', collected especially by J. Jeremias,[1] provide no
evidence that ordination was at any time a prerequisite for either
giving or receiving instruction on this subject. The tradition of
the rabbis was the *halakha*, to which on the whole only ordained
rabbis were able to contribute. This once more emphasizes that
ordination was meant to continue the Jerusalem Sanhedrin, the
Jewish High Court.

III

If it were true that Jewish ordination at the time of Jesus had
been primarily a private ordination of scribes, it would be well
nigh impossible to assume that His disciples at the constituting
of the Church should have begun with ordaining Christian scribes.
The polemical remarks of their Master against 'the Pharisees and
scribes' were so well remembered that such a contingency just
could not arise. In particular I would ask whether it is credible
that the great 'Woe' against the Pharisees and scribes in Matt.23,
the Gospel which, after all, is closest to Jewish conditions, should
have exerted so little influence; and I would reply unreservedly
in the negative. Lohse, so far from dealing with this question, has
apparently not even seen it. Yet it is in the light of this question
that we must try to explain the identity of the rite of laying-on-
of-hands in the Church and the Synagogue, which in both
these communities was practised in the second century and
later.

We have to go beyond the New Testament material in this
matter, for the analogies claimed to exist between the cases of imposition of hands in the New Testament and in rabbinical ordination are fallacious.[2] No analogy can be established between the
sending out of St. Barnabas and St. Paul and any of the Jewish rites
analysed by Lohse. True, it is reported that 'they', presumably

[1] Jeremias, *Abendmahlsworte*, p.60f.
[2] For this purpose cf. my *Apostolic Succession*.

the other teachers and prophets mentioned in Acts 13:1,[1] 'laid their hands on them' (Acts 13:3) but the Jewish antecedent cannot be the sending out of a *shaliach*, as Lohse (p.71f.) suggests. First of all such an assumption would constitute a contradiction of Gal.1:1, not seen by Lohse, that St. Paul was 'an Apostle, not of men';[2] and secondly, a Jewish missionary was never described as *shaliach*, yet the two apostles were sent out as missionaries. Therefore, even if any analogy could be drawn between the sending out of a *shaliach* and the ordination of a rabbi, which, as we have seen, is not the case, it would not help us to understand Acts 13:1–3. Unfortunately, Lohse's interpretation of the crucial word ἀφορίζειν in Acts 13:2 has overlooked the parallel in Num.8:14, which has led me to a very different explanation of the 'separating' of St. Barnabas and St. Paul.[3]

This is only a preliminary step. For the acid test of the theory that Christian and rabbinical ordination are identical lies in its applicability to Acts 6:6. I, too, believe that the laying-on-of-hands upon St. Stephen and his six companions followed an Old Testament precedent. However, the assertion that the rite copied was the ordination of scribes[4] cannot be commended. We have seen how at the time of Jesus the enthronement was the climax of the Jewish ordination rite, yet Acts 6:2 says that the task of the Seven was to 'serve tables', the very opposite of 'sitting in Moses' chair'.[5] To treat this description of their task as spurious (Lohse, p.78) is unmethodical and unjustified. Admittedly serving tables was a task for which rabbinical ordination was not required, but

---

[1] This is assumed by J. E. Belser, *Die Apostelgeschichte*, 1905, p.163, and would provide us with the three persons required in rabbinical ordinations; but it is uncertain since it was the whole Church at Antioch which 'prayed and fasted'.

[2] Cf. Bruce, *Acts*, p.254.

[3] Cf. my *Apostolic Succession*, p.32.

[4] Bruce, op. cit., p.153f., following but not quoting Billerbeck, vol.2, p.647f., refers in his note on Acts 6:6, to the *s*ᵉ*mikhah* in *Sanh.*, IV.4, but does not state that the rite of laying on of hands was a copy of rabbinical ordination, as does Lohse, op. cit., p.78.

[5] Bruce, op. cit., p.152: 'perhaps τράπεζα is used here in the financial sense', is not supported by Mark 11:15 par., to which Bruce refers, and is impossible: the meaning 'bank' for τράπεζα is well established, but that of administering financial assistance does not occur.

it seems far more probable that the mean task is the historical one, and the exalted task of preaching the Gospel a later embellishment, if such a crude operation were called for in this case.[1] However that may be, if Acts 6:2 is spurious, how are we supposed to believe in the historicity of Acts 6:6? In any case, an author at the end of the first century, the 'Luke' of the canonical Acts, states that the Seven were ordained with laying-on-of-hands to 'serve tables', and this has no analogy in the rabbinical rite. Furthermore, on a mere balance of probability, the change in Codex D which makes the Twelve lay their hands on the Seven, shows that the opinion could be held that the whole Christian community might have done so, which is contrary to the rabbinical precedent. If it is assumed that only the Twelve did it, they did not thereby make the Seven their equals, which would have been the result of a rabbinical ordination. Finally, there were either the Twelve or the people (*qahal*) laying hands on the Seven, but not a group of three, as in rabbinical ordination. Consequently, the Jewish rite applied was not the rabbinical ordination.

Finally, there is the laying-on-of-hands upon Timothy, according to the Pastorals. To regard the Pastorals as genuinely Pauline demands a special courage of conviction. They are of early second-century origin.[2] Even assuming, however, that they should be treated as being Pauline, the analogy between 1.Tim.4:14, the ordination of Timothy by a presbytery, and rabbinical ordination would have to be queried in the same way as that between the ordination of the Seven by the Twelve and rabbinical ordination; that is, if we assume that 1.Tim.4:14 refers to ordination and not to baptism and confirmation, as we do. For was Timothy made a presbyter? and were there three ordainers? Even if it were proved that St. Paul, as it is said in 2.Tim.1:6, alone amongst the presbyters of 1.Tim.4:14, laid hands on Timothy (Lohse, p.82), and thus acted as the Nasi of this presbytery, which is highly

---

[1] The tradition in Asia identified Philip the Evangelist, to whom Lohse refers, with the apostle; is it so certain that the identification with Philip the 'deacon' is preferable?

[2] Cf. Knopf-Lietzmann-Weinel, *Einleitung in das N.T.*, 3rd ed., 1930, p.86, not one of whose reasons has been satisfactorily answered by Lohse.

improbable considering his attitude towards the Jewish traditions, the first question would still remain unanswered. And where is it assumed that this should have happened, and at what time?[1]

However, even if we allow for all these improbabilities, this will not complete the case. For Timothy's ordination took place 'with prophecy', St. Stephen was 'full of grace and power' (Acts 6:8). It was the Holy Spirit who commanded the sending out of St. Barnabas and St. Paul according to Acts 13:2. Lohse (p.53f.) has tried hard to find among the rabbis an equivalent for these actions of the Holy Spirit. The sources, however, which he has quoted from the Talmud are all apologetic. We know, especially from Justin Martyr's *Dialogue with Trypho*, what a powerful weapon the cessation of prophecy in the Synagogue had given to the early Church. The rabbis could only claim that they had something almost as good as the prophetic Spirit of the Church. The words 'with prophecy' in 1 Tim.4:14, written, as we believe, in the early second century, sound the anti-Jewish fanfare so clearly that any alleged rabbinical analogies are blown away.

However, the laying-on-of-hands was taken over by the Church from the Jewish religion;[2] the pseudo-Clementines did appropriate Moses's chair for the enthronement of Christian bishops; and there is an analogy between the Jewish and the Christian πρεσβύτεροι. It is necessary to clear up these coincidences. We are far from any final solution of the problem; but we can contribute to it. First of all, before the destruction of the temple the prophetic Spirit was not lacking among the Jews. It was a deliberate amputation when the Synagogue held that, because of the evilness of the time, God's Shekinah was absenting

---

[1] In *Apostolic Succession*, p.34, I have suggested that the presbytery visualized in 1 Tim.4:14, was that of Derbe, Lystra and Antioch in Pisidia. This would open up the possibility that the rite considered was baptism; but it seems that the intention of the Pastorals was to establish a succession after St. Paul.

[2] The claim of S. New, 'the laying on of hands is not only a well-known Jewish custom, but frequent in all ages and in all countries', in Lake-Cadbury, op. cit., vol.5, p.137, is as true as it is unhelpful. Lohse, p.13f., has collected a fair amount of evidence to show that Gentile sources provide no valid analogies to the Church's ordination rite with its laying-on-of-hands.

itself even from the worthiest members of the Synagogue—men like Hillel, the spiritual ancestor of Akiba—although they were of the quality of the prophets (Lohse, p.53f.). Yet in the Old Testament it had been ordained that Joshua, through Moses' laying hands on him, should partake of the Spirit which was in Moses. This was still being stressed in the *midrashim* when they maintained that at his ordination Joshua's face had shone like the moon, but Moses' face like the sun.[1] Justin, too, took up the imparting of the Spirit to Joshua by Moses, in his *Dialogue*, when discussing the prophetic succession in the Church.[2] This goes to show that in pre-rabbinical times the transference of the Spirit was admitted in Judaism, and was connected with the laying-on-of-hands. The same conclusion is to be drawn from two of the Philonic passages quoting Num.11:16–17, the ordination of the seventy elders by Moses:[3]

(a) It is so also with the spirit of Moses which he implants into the seventy elders, to pass it on to others, and to their own improvement.

The connection with the Talmudic sources about ordination is shown by the fact that in the preceding paragraph Philo mentions the inspiration of Bezalel (Exod.31:2), which plays its part also in the Talmudic discussions on rabbinical ordination (Lohse, p.54).

(b) The seventy elders, unto whom the Divine and prophetic Spirit was distributed.

Although the laying-on-of-hands is mentioned in neither of these two passages and an absolute proof showing that they were relevant to ordination as it was practised at the time of Philo cannot be given, the probability is in favour of both assumptions. There is first of all the use of διενέγκειν, 'to pass on', which suggests a line of succession; and secondly the continuation of the passage (a) suggests the same line of thought:[4] 'thus the Divine Spirit is

---

[1] Billerbeck, vol.2, p.647f.

[2] Justin, *Dial.* 49, cf. my *Apostolic Succession*, p.88.

[3] (a) Philo, *Gigant.*, 24, ed. Cohn-Wendland, vol.2, p.46, l.16f; (b) id. *de Fuga*, 186, ibid., vol.3, p.150, l.20f.

[4] Philo, *Gigant.*, 28, ibid., vol.2, p.47, l.10f. On the idea of the Holy Spirit

able, as we have seen, to dwell in the soul, though not able to continue in it'. Perhaps it is not too fanciful to sense in this remark the turning of the tide, the rising despair of prophecy in Judaism.

Several results arise out of these considerations. The first and best founded is that the development of Jewish ordination confirms our assertion[1] that the Christian description of ministers as presbyters was derived from the title of the members of the Jerusalem Sanhedrin. The second is that in the matter of ordination the Church and the Synagogue appear not in the relation of son and mother, but as half-brothers, like Isaac and Ishmael (Gal.4:22f.) both in their way appropriating the Old Testament example. The third is that it may be wise, especially with regard to the rites of imposition of hands and enthronement of bishops to allow for a period of development extending right down to the middle of the second century. Neither the witness of Acts nor that of the Pastorals will in itself be sufficient to enlighten us on the conditions—or even the existence—of an ordination rite in the Primitive Church. When they are unsupported by other sources[2] their witness is valid only with regard to second-century conditions.

---

in the whole passage—and its pagan antecedents—cf. Knox, *St. Paul and the Church of the Gentiles*, 1939, p.117, n.1; p.133, n.5.

[1] *Apostolic Succession*, p.27.

[2] None of the Apostolic Fathers mentions the laying-on-of-hands. Can that be purely accidental? Ignat., *Philad.*, 10,1; *Smyrn.*, 11,2; *Polyc.*, 7,7, χειϱοτονεῖν θεοπϱεσβεύτην etc., has nothing to do with ordination, but may refer to a practice analogous to the sending of a *shaliach* by the Synagogue. It is, moreover, interesting to note that, according to his *vita* by Gregory Nyssene, Gregory Thaumaturge was consecrated bishop of Neo-Caesarea in his absence by Phaedimus of Amasea, and that Jerome, book XVI *in Is.*48, warns against such ordinations *in absentia*; cf. Bingham, *Antiquities*, bk.4, section 6, ch.8, ed. 1875, p.157f.

8

CHRISTIANITY BEFORE THE APOSTLES' CREED

I

The Meaning of 'Creed,' and the 'Gospels' of St. Paul and his Opponents

N O T so long ago a little treatise on the Apostles' Creed was edited by the late Dom R. H. Connolly, and established as the property of Ambrose of Milan.[1] In this treatise the statement may be found that 'when therefore the holy Apostles all came together they compiled a short formula of the faith so that we might shortly be instructed about the whole course of the faith'.[2] We are not concerned here with the question on what occasion the holy Apostles did come together. Apocryphal traditions know of several such meetings of the Apostles, usually with the Virgin Mary, and it was presumably one of these which was in the mind of the great bishop of Milan.[3] The significant fact is rather that he denied here that Christianity ever went through a pre-credal period. His great authority could not fail to make a lasting impression, especially upon the Western Church. It is evidently on the basis of this his assertion that we find, in the orations of Pseudo-Augustine, a Creed that is divided as follows: 'Peter said: "I believe in God the Father Almighty, maker of heaven and earth." Andrew said: "And in Jesus Christ his only son our Lord." James said: "Who was conceived by the Holy Ghost, born of Mary the virgin." John said: "Suffered under Pontius Pilate, was crucified, dead, and buried." Thomas said: "He descended into

---

[1] 'The Explanatio symboli ad initiandos,' etc., *Texts and Studies*, vol.10, 1952.
[2] *Explan. symb.*, 3, ed. Connolly, p.7.
[3] Cf., e.g., 'Gospel of Bartholomew,' II, James, *The apocryphal N.T.*, p. 170f.; E. Hennecke and W. Schneemelcher, *Neutestamentliche Apokryphen*, vol.1, 3rd. ed., 1959, p.364f.

hell; the third day he rose again from the dead," ' and so on till at last Matthias finishes with the words, 'and the life everlasting. Amen.' [1]

From this conviction that there was never a pre-credal period of Christianity theologians have since then hesitated to depart, either consciously or—more often—unconsciously. The belief that 'the Apostles' Creed' was already the Creed of the Apostles, and in particular of the Twelve, assumed great political importance in the century after Nicea, when the Roman Emperors had made their option in favour of the Catholic Church, and used the 'Creed' of Nicea as the chief instrument for binding the State and the Church together. It is only in these our days that the question is being asked why Ambrose and his contemporaries produced such a legendary foundation for their belief in the true Apostolicity of the Apostles' Creed. The question is really a three-fold one. We have to ask first, how far back can we trace the literary form of Creed, a short formula intended to embody all that is absolutely essential for a Christian to believe in order that he might be saved. Secondly, what authority was attached to these formulas in pre-Nicene time, and in particular were they being used as a touch-stone of orthodoxy, and as a means for the excommunication of unbelievers. Thirdly, whether or not it may be assumed that, even if no particular subscription to any formulated Creed is likely to have been exacted in the Apostolic and sub-Apostolic period there was yet at least a unanimity, a clear agreement, with regard to the content of the Christian Faith amongst those who spread and those who held it. These three may appear as logically separate and independent questions; but historical reality is never logically tidy, and it is therefore necessary to keep them together in mind when we enquire into Christianity before the Apostles' Creed.

The fact that the literary form of Creed can be found before the council of Nicea is, of course, indisputable. We need only to refer to the baptismal Creed of the Church at Caesarea which Eusebius of Caesarea, the Church historian, its conditionally excommunicated bishop, produced at Nicea in proof of his ortho-

[1] Hahn-Harnack, *Bibl. der Symbole*, 3rd. ed., 1897, p.51f.

doxy, and which, after it had been somewhat drastically chopped and changed around, was made to serve as the basis for the construction of the Nicene Creed. This very fact, however, makes us wonder how far spread the use of baptismal Creeds may have been in the Eastern Church of the period. For there was apparently no less suspect formula forthcoming from the bishops assembled in council.[1] This must have been due partly to the fact that they did not all use such a formula at baptism, and partly that they were wary of local jealousies. This second reason seems to point to the fact that whilst the East regarded its faith as 'Apostolic', yet its formulated Creeds were not so described, even though they may have gone back to an early time.[2]

If therefore the view that an authoritative Creed was already proposed by the Apostles seems to be untenable, it might yet be held that the literary form of Creed, a short formula which forcibly brings home some or even all the facts to be believed by a Christian for his soul's health, may be found in the canonical writings of the New Testament. A warning has to be issued, however, against assuming that with the form we also have of necessity the thing itself. This assumption has misled Canon Blair, for instance, to propose some quite unaccceptable views.[3] On the other hand, it is probably true to say that the passages from the New Testament Epistles quoted by the Principal of St. Edmund's Hall, Oxford, show the pattern of credal formulae, and perhaps

[1] Kelly, *Early Christian Creeds*, op. cit., p.217f., has tried to prove that the Creed of Caesarea was not the basis for the Nicene Creed. This theory starts from the assumption that the technique of Creed-making was already at that time fully developed in the Eastern Church, a view which I find hard to accept. It also conflicts with Eusebius' own statement in Opitz, *Urk.*, p.22. These are the reasons why I still hesitate to abandon the earlier view on the origin of the Nicene Creed, as expressed above.

[2] Hahn-Harnack, op. cit., p.127f., have made an effort at re-constituting 'the earliest baptismal Creed of the Oriental Church'. The sources quoted are predominantly Syrian, whilst the presumed formula has also been laced with a few Egyptian additions. Thus this attempt should be treated with considerable reserve. The formula produced seems to exclude Antiochene monarchianism as well as Origenian subordinationism somewhat too definitely, and differs widely from Greek formulae (Creeds?) of the second century, ibid., p.1f. Origen's 'Creed' in *De principiis* is again different as are the formulae from Asia Minor, ibid., p.11f.   [3] H. A. Blair, *A Creed before the Creeds*, 1955.

even that they were intended to be memorized by simple Christians so that they should be able to give an account of their faith.[1] Nevertheless, it would appear somewhat hazardous to describe this material as fragments of 'the earliest Christian catechism', as has been done by certain German scholars following the example of Alfred Seeberg.[2] For it is true to say, on the one hand, that the Gospels themselves, perhaps with the exception of the Third Gospel, were written to be memorized,[3] at least in part, and also to some extent written from memory, and on the other that the capacity for memorizing considerable passages, in prose as well as in verse, has steeply declined in recent times, and the need for producing very short formulae has accordingly increased. To assume, therefore, that it was for catechetical reasons that these credal formulae were produced is at least unnecessary.

Nevertheless it is true to say that these short formulae, and in particular 1.Cor.15:1f., embody a pre-Pauline tradition, probably originating from Jerusalem,[4] which above all dealt with the Passion and Resurrection of the Saviour Jesus Christ, and presumably connected these events with the two great Sacraments of Baptism and Eucharist.[5] What we have to ask, however, is first whether they are fragments of one and the same document, and secondly and above all whether the Primitive Church was

---

[1] Kelly, op. cit., p.17f.

[2] Their views may be found set out in an article by E. Lichtenstein, *Zeitschr. f. Kirchengesch.*, vol.61, 1950, p.1f.—C. H. Dodd in *New Testament Essays*, 1959, p.106f., has given another meaning to the term of 'New Testament catechism', more closely related to historical fact.

[3] The method of teaching amongst the Jews in N.T. times was memorizing, cf. W. Bousset-Gressmann, *Die Religion des Judentums*, 3rd ed., 1926, p.168. The fact that the Gospels were still learnt by heart in the sixth century is shown by two Coptic papyri, nr.51 and 52, in W. Till, 'Die koptischen Bürgschaftsurkunden', *Bull. de la Société d'archéologie copte*, vol.14, 1958, p.198f. Iren., *Adv. Haer.*, III.4.1, cf. *Politische Metaphysik*, vol.2, 1959, p.96, n.1, provides evidence that such was also the case in Gaul in the second century.

[4] H. v. Campenhausen, *Tradition und Leben*, 1960, p.58, n.37, assumes that St. Paul in this passage recorded Galilean visitations. I cannot find his argument conclusive, but I agree with him that in any case St. Paul's information came from Jerusalem.

[5] This follows from παρέλαβον, 1.Cor.11:23.

unanimous in accepting them. To the first question no safe answer can be given. All that can be said is that the existence of more than one collection of such formulae cannot be excluded. For instance, the presumably Roman 'credal formula' used by St. Paul in Rom.1:3f. need not be of Jerusalem origin, whilst the mention of James' visitation by the risen Lord makes such an origin probable for 1.Cor.15:1f. The answer to the second question, however, has to be in the negative. It is evident from 1.Cor.15:1 that the Apostle's technical name for the credal formula subsequently quoted was εὐαγγέλιον. In his Epistle to the Galatians we hear from him that his opponents have brought 'another Gospel', ἕτερον εὐαγγέλιον, which he assures the Galatians is 'not a Gospel'.[1] We thus perceive that there were at least two pre-Pauline traditions about the saving work of Jesus Christ, coming from Jerusalem, both apparently—if our interpretation of εὐαγγέλιον is correct—couched in a credal formula, and mutually irreconcilable. If we then put the date of 1.Corinthians as A.D. 55,[2] and that of the Passion of Jesus Christ as A.D. 33,[3]

[1] Gal.1:6f.—As to the character of the Pauline εὐαγγέλιον we may refer to J. Schniewind, *Euangelion*, vol.2, 1931, p.183, 'im Alten Testament der souveräne Gott, der selbst in die Geschichte hineintritt, und der $m^e ba\acute{s}\acute{s}er$, der ihn verkündigt; im Hellenismus der Gott-Kaiser, der kultisch verehrt wird, und das εὐαγγέλιον,, das ihn proklamiert'. Neither W. Schneemelcher nor his critic, A. D. Nock, *J.T.S.*, 1960, p.64f., have referred to Schniewind's work without which the meaning of εὐαγγέλιον cannot be established satisfactorily. It seems to me that Nock is justified when warning against too much emphasis being put on the 'sacred' character of the word, but that he is mistaken in assuming that εὐαγγέλιον may be just any 'good news'. It follows also from Schniewind that St. Paul's adversaries denied probably the Divinity of Christ, and this links up with the character of the ἕτερον εὐαγγέλιον as outlined by H. J. Schoeps in W. D. Davies & D. Daube, *The Background of the N.T.*, pp.116–18. In his book *Paulus*, 1959, p.73f., Schoeps has omitted the discussion of this aspect of the controversy between St. Paul and the Judaizers.— It may also be permissible to refer to the Pauline use of 'my Gospel', Rom. 2:16, or 'our Gospel', 2.Cor.4:3, especially in connection with ibid., 11:4–5, in order that the Apostle may appear to have given to the term εὐαγγέλιον the meaning of 'the quintessence of his message', and to have presupposed the same meaning for the ἕτερον εὐαγγέλιον of his adversaries.

[2] So Knopf-Lietzmann-Weinel, op. cit., p.78.

[3] This is the traditional assumption which, however, is considered 'highly improbable' by the astronomers quoted by Jeremias, *Eucharistic Words*, p.12, n.3. Jeremias pleads for A.D. 30.

we see clearly that already in the first two decades of the new religion the unanimity about the content of its message to the world was lost, if it had ever existed. The differences even amongst those who professed their allegiance to the Church at Jerusalem were so marked that St. Paul pronounced his anathema over that 'other Gospel'.[1]

As to the authority of his own credal formula, it is clear that St. Paul invoked his Apostleship in its support, as in the Epistle to the Romans,[2] so also when addressing the Galatians,[3] or the Corinthians,[4] and indeed in the addresses of all his Epistles. It seems inviting, therefore, to assume that the supremacy of the Apostle over all the other Christian missionaries was recognized in the Primitive Church, and that St. Paul's adversaries were not in a position to claim a similar distinction.[5] However that may be, and I am inclined to accept this conclusion, it does not say that only an 'Apostolic' Creed should be accepted, any more than that the doctrinal pronouncements of one or all of the Apostles were infallible as such. St. Paul's authority to anathematize the Gospel of his opponents was probably derived from his Apostleship; but what he queried was the authenticity of their message, and this without paying much regard to its origin.[6] They preached that which in its content was not a Gospel, and were condemned for this reason. We can check this statement from what we know of the part played by Epaphras, St. Paul's fellow prisoner, in the conversion of the Colossians. There is no evidence for the frequent assumption that he had been a member of St. Paul's missionary team.[7] Neither is there any evidence

---

[1] Gal.1:8.—Obviously St. Paul thought of the possibility of more than one false Gospel springing up, when he omitted the definite article; but his message would be blunted if it were not stressed that his immediate concern was with his Jerusalem adversaries.

[2] Rom. 11:13.

[3] Gal. 1:17f.

[4] 2.Cor.11:5; 12:11f.

[5] 2.Cor.11:15, cf. Käsemann, op. cit., p.12f.

[6] Cf. the 'certain people who came from James', Gal.2:12, where the word τινές is used in a somewhat derogatory sense.

[7] Cf., e.g., E. Lohmeyer, *Der Brief an die Kolosser*, 1930, p.29, referring to the term σύνδουλος. But this term, which in Pauline literature occurs only in

that St. Paul had ever visited Colossae. Epaphras was not even
an Apostle. Nevertheless, St. Paul exhorted the Colossians to
stand fast in the εὐαγγέλιον which they had heard,[1] obviously
from Epaphras. A stranger to St. Paul, therefore, till they met
in prison,[2] a man who was not an Apostle had brought the right
Gospel, 'the Gospel', to a town presumably never visited by
an Apostle. In whose name? In the Name of Jesus Christ. In
whose authority? Certainly not in the authority of his ministry,
whether Epaphras was a prophet, evangelist, teacher or whatsoever, but in the only sufficient authority, that of the Holy
Spirit.[3]

II

*The Various Forms of the Gospel of Christ in the Later New
Testament Writings*

We have seen so far that in the Apostolic period of the Church
the message of St. Paul, the only Apostle whose writings are beyond doubt products of that period, received formal but no
material support from the authority of his Apostolate. The whole
emphasis of his defence against his opponents is this, that all personal matters are without any significance when the question of
truth or falsehood is concerned. His 'Gospel', i.e. his proclamation of Jesus Christ, God and King,[4] was nowhere specifically
characterized as 'Apostolic'. Neither did he derive it from any
visionary or mystic experience on his part, however much he
may have been granted such experiences, and may have referred
to them in his missionary preaching.[5] This fact arises most clearly

---

Col.1:7; 4:7, in the second instance is used for Tychicus who is described as
διάκονος καὶ σύνδουλος. The addition of πιστὸς διάκονος is explained best
by assuming that only Tychicus had been a member of St. Paul's team.

[1] Col.1:23.
[2] Philem. 23.
[3] Col.1:8.
[4] Cf. my *Politische Metaphysik*, vol.2, 1959, p.26f.
[5] This distinction between the 'the Gospel' and its missionary exegesis has
been neglected in the appreciation of 2.Cor. by Schoeps, *Paulus*, p.73f.

from his Epistle to the Galatians, particularly where he refers to his clash with St. Peter at Antioch,[1] and also from his calming of the Corinthian enthusiasm for the 'super'-Apostles.[2] It was rather—and still is—the message of God to mankind, delivered by Apostles as well as by humbler instruments, in the power of the Holy Spirit. And the number of those other messengers was by no means negligible. If we allow for the historicity of Acts 11:20, we learn that some anonymous Cypriots and Cyrenians took the Gospel to the Gentiles at Antioch.[3] Completely unknown to history are the founders of the Christian Church at Rome, to whom St. Paul's Epistle was sent;[4] and equally unknown are the missionaries from whom Apollos, the Jew of Alexandria,[5] and presumably a considerable number of his compatriots,[6] derived their knowledge of the Christian faith.

This question concerning the missionaries to Alexandria is of special interest for us because we learn from the Acts of the Apostles that 'all the baptism that he (Apollos) knew was that of John'.[7] By this it is clearly shown that Christian teaching at Alexandria was considered by St. Luke as having been defective at the time of Apollos—and perhaps at his own time also. We are therefore entitled to find in the teaching of Apollos yet another Gospel, different from that of St. Paul, and still more

[1] Gal.2:11f.—Without entering upon the controversy whether this clash took place before or after the so-called council of the Apostles, I would like to express my appreciation of the charming little study by Père H. M. Féret, O.P., *Pierre et Paul à Antioch et à Jérusalem*, Paris, 1955. Père Féret pleads for 'l'incident d' Antioch' having taken place before the council, in a way which in any case makes it psychologically understandable without any great violence being applied to the sources. The question why St. Paul did not mention that he convinced Peter and Barnabas—if he and not the council succeeded in doing so—is, however, not clearly answered by Père Féret.

[2] 2.Cor.11:5; 12:11.

[3] Εὐαγγελιζόμενοι τὸν κύριον Ἰησοῦν. Note the verb, which is intentionally chosen.

[4] This Church seems to have had numerous Gentile members, whom Claudius did not expel in A.D. 50 like Aquila and Priscilla.

[5] Acts 18:24.

[6] Cf. Cadbury, op. cit., p.116f.

[7] Acts 18:25, Moffatt.—It is noteworthy that Apollos did not receive rebaptism at the hands of Aquila and Priscilla, but only instruction; but we cannot enter here into this question.

so from that of the emissaries of James of Jerusalem, where the miracle of Pentecost had taken place, and become the constituent event of the Church at Jerusalem. For it appears from the way in which St. Paul apostrophized Apollos, 'I did the planting, Apollos did the watering',[1] that he did not regard the message of Apollos as contrary to 'the Gospel', his own Gospel, however defective it may have been at the meeting of Priscilla and Aquila with Apollos. Nevertheless the fact that it was a different Gospel, and not simply a peculiar personal approach to the Gospel by Apollos, is emphasized by St. Luke when he tells of the 'disciples' whom St. Paul met at Ephesus, and who also had received 'the baptism of John' only.[2] Why these 'disciples', a word which, wherever it stands on its own in the New Testament, clearly denotes Christ's followers, should in this one instance be understood as disciples of St. John the Baptist by the great majority of commentaries on Acts,[3] I have never been able to understand any more than the other, that so many commentators fail to see that the story is obviously told us in order to emphasize how necessary the instruction of Apollos by Priscilla and Aquila had been to arm him fully for his missionary task. For it is for this very reason that St. Luke headed the story of the 'disciples' at Ephesus with the name of Apollos.[4] He quite clearly wants us to realize

---

[1] I.Cor.3:6, Moffatt.

[2] Acts 19:1.

[3] So still, without a word of explanation, Hänchen, op. cit., p.493f. Cf. how J. Thomas, *Le mouvement baptiste*, 1935, p.97f., tries, vainly I think, to separate completely Acts 19:1–13 from its context in order to establish the 'disciples' as members of 'la secte Johannite'. The correct view is not only held by Cadbury, *The Beginnings*, throughout, but also by Bruce, op. cit., p.353.—The incorrect interpretation is, of course, largely responsible for the weight attached to the Mandaic sources in the interpretation of the N.T.; but it would be a vicious circle, if these sources were now invoked to prove the interpretation as correct.

[4] This consideration makes it probable that the disciples were Alexandrians, unless gematrical interpretation of the number twelve is preferred, and they are seen as representatives of Judaeo-Christianity, needing the baptism of the Spirit. Hänchen, loc. cit., has managed to miss all the salient points of the incident, treating it as a mere report of fact, unrelated to anything preceding or following. The connection with Apollos, however, had been stated already by Overbeck in W. L. M. de Wette, *Kurze Erklärung* op. cit., p.302, who did not, however, question the traditional 'disciples of St. John Baptist'.

the fact that Apollos' teaching came from a less reliable source than that of St. Paul.

By thus discussing the Book of Acts we have passed the threshold of that part of canonical literature which was produced after the fall of Jerusalem, and simultaneously the Church at Jerusalem, so often called 'the Mother Church of Jerusalem'. We have to guard against being blinded by that affectionate and even somewhat sentimental title. Already from the Acts of the Apostles one may gather the existence of a certain antagonism to the Church at Jerusalem existing in the circle of St. Philip at Caesarea,[1] despite the fact that it was St. Luke of all the Evangelists who located the Twelve after the Resurrection of the Saviour firmly at Jerusalem.[2] The reports in the other Gospels are quite different. St. Mark records Jesus' saying, 'but after my rising I will precede you to Galilee'.[3] The first Gospel too takes us to Galilee where it locates the appearance of the risen Christ on the Holy Mountain,[4] as predicted by the angel of the Resurrection[5] as well as by the risen Christ.[6] Finally, the Fourth Gospel strikes a somewhat clumsy compromise. It has the Jerusalem appearances in chapter 20, but it has preserved that most precious Galilean document in its last

---

[1] Acts. 21:8f.—On the Caesarean antagonism to Jerusalem cf. Brandon, op. cit., p.178, 'Philip, a distinguished representative of the anti-Judaic movement'. The Jerusalem Church is represented in Acts 21:20 as pro-Judaic.

[2] Another question that has to be asked, but cannot be answered here, is just this: Why did Luke, whose 'sense of detachment with which the destruction of Jerusalem is contemplated' is stressed by Brandon, op. cit., p.206, and by whom 'nothing explicit is said of the fortunes of the Christian community there', ibid., p.107, set such great store by the correct relations between St. Paul and James of Jerusalem, if the conflict at Antioch between St. Paul and St. Barnabas had resulted in a final break with the Church at Jerusalem, as Hänchen, op. cit., p.422f., seems to indicate?

[3] Mark 14:28, Moffat.

[4] Matt. 28:16f.

[5] Matt. 28:7.

[6] Matt. 28:10.—I believe that vv.8–10 are meant to pay respect to the 'Jerusalem Gospel'. There seems to me to be little doubt that the whole last chapter of Matthew has undergone more than one revision before receiving its canonical form, but this cannot be shown here. I feel, however, somewhat hesitant to accept the evidence offered by Kilpatrick, op. cit., p.48f., for his thesis that vv.8–10 were written by the evangelist, since it makes too little of the separate character of v.8.

chapter (21), which evidently clashes with the Jerusalem tradition, and in particular with that form of it which we have in the 'Gospel' of the appearances of the risen Lord, as preserved by St. Paul,[1] and also with St. Luke.[2] This short survey therefore leads to the inevitable conclusion that we have to allow for yet another Gospel, the Galilean Gospel.

Let us take yet another step: The fervent friend of 'the Mother Church at Jerusalem', St. Luke himself, cannot hide the fact that from the very Christians at Jerusalem there issued more than one Gospel. I am not referring to the discrepancy between the two reports on the Ascension, in the Third Gospel and in the Acts of the Apostles, although I find it increasingly difficult to reconcile them to each other the closer I look at them.[3] I am rather referring to the part played by the Seven, commonly called deacons, or at least by the three of them who are more than mere names to us, St. Stephen, St. Philip, and Nicolaus. The fact that St. Stephen's sermon exhibits very singular theological features, which it seems impossible to derive from either the Synoptic or the Johannine tradition of the Gospel, is nowadays generally conceded.[4] Still more disquieting, it seems to me, is the report about the dealings between St. Philip and Simon Magus,[5] who

[1] 1.Cor.15:1f.

[2] Luke 24.—I have repeatedly, cf. *Theol. Zeitschr.*, vol.2, 1946, p.424, n.4; *Politische Metaphysik* vol.2, p.28, n.1, referred to the intentional artificiality of the Emmaus story, Luke 24:13f., which shows a close similarity to the report on the appearance of the deified Romulus, Dion. Hal., II.63.3f., cf. Livy, I.16.5f., and thus to the whole literary genre of self-revelation of deified humans.

[3] Luke 24:50f.; Acts 1:9f.—I subscribe to all that J. G. Davies, *He ascended into Heaven*, 1958, p.41, n.5, has stated with regard to one of the more common attempts at harmonizing the two texts.

[4] Only a scholar as convinced of the Lukan origin of the speeches in Acts as M. Dibelius, *Studies*, p.167f., could neglect the obvious theological and, I think, also linguistic singularity of Acts 7:2-53. The most carefully considered statement of the problem of St. Stephen's sermon I have found in Knox, *Acts*, p.24 n.1. E. Hänchen, op. cit., p.243f., gives an outline of the recent history of the interpretation of the sermon, mainly by German theologians, and on p.247, suggests that Luke adopted a 'neutral' exposition of sacred history, and changed it by interpolations in order to make it suit the occasion. I cannot help finding his approach rather arbitrary. Still more recent is L. W. Barnard, 'S. Stephen and early Alexandrian Christianity', *N.T.S.*, vol.7, 1960, p.31f.

[5] Acts 8:9f.

'after his baptism kept close to Philip, utterly astonished to see the signs and striking miracles which were taking place'.[1]

St. Luke's report about the mission to Samaria makes two things strikingly clear, which are both of great importance for our quest for an Apostolic Creed in the Apostolic period. The first is that St. Philip's baptism did not confer the Holy Spirit upon Simon Magus, or indeed upon any of the Samaritans who were baptized by him.[2] After their baptism they were thus left in the same condition in which Apollos and the 'disciples' at Ephesus found themselves, and which we have characterized as resulting from another Gospel. This impression, I would emphasize, is intentionally created by St. Luke. For the 'confirmation of the Samaritans' by St. Peter and St. John in Acts 8:14f. and the re-baptism of the 'disciples' at Ephesus in Acts 19:1f. form one of the several Peter and Paul analogies in Acts. These analogies belong to the continuous themes of St. Luke's second book, and may be regarded as fountain heads of an incipient doctrine of Apostolicity. The Peter and John episode of the 'confirmation of the Samaritans' is, however, demonstrably an interpolation in the course of the Philip document which underlies Acts 6–8. Where it may come from we do not know; St. Luke does not, I believe, customarily resort to additions of his own to an existing document, if his treatment of Mark in the Third Gospel may be adduced in comparison. It is most likely to be of a Petrine source. It is also reasonably certain that it has not replaced any material belonging to the Philip document. For it seems clear that Acts 8:26, 'but an angel said to Philip,' can easily be joined immediately to Simon Magus' astonishment at the miracles worked by St. Philip.

---

[1] Acts 8:13, Moffatt.

[2] Acts 8:16.—Here the remark 'they had simply been baptised in the name of the Lord Jesus', raises the most difficult question, in whose name the 'disciples' at Ephesus, Acts 19:1f., were re-baptized by St. Paul? Since St. John Baptist did not baptize in his own name—how could he?—the hypothesis that they were his disciples would not help. Εἰς τὸ Ἰωάννου βάπτισμα, Acts 19:3, is, however, a curious formula, coined in analogy to εἰς τὸ ὄνομα Ἰησοῦ, but it belongs to St. Luke, not to the disciples.—I would also like to know whether the eunuch of Queen Candace received the Spirit in his baptism, or whether the Spirit made His presence known only by translating St. Philip to Caesarea, Acts 8:39?

The interpolation of the confirmation episode,[1] however, brings home to us the second fact which needs to be stressed in connection with St. Philip's missionary activity. St. Philip did not convert numerous individual Samaritans but a concrete group, the Simonians, beginning with certain of their members, and eventually winning over even their leader, who is afterwards separated from his group, if we may believe the interpolation. We have thus in Acts 8:12–13 a clear testimony for a corporate reception of a pre-Christian Gnostic sect into the communion of that Gospel,[2] which did not teach the reception of the Holy Spirit in baptism, and which for this reason we have characterized previously as a 'defective' Gospel. Acts 8:9–11 make it perfectly clear that this Samaritan group, which for convenience's sake we have called the Simonians, had already existed before St. Philip came to missionarize the Samaritans, and that they believed in the coming of a Divine revelation through a Divinely inspired human agent. This human agent is eventually cursed by St. Peter[3] not, however, for his false doctrine, but for his 'simony'.[4] And his humble reply leaves open the possibility that after that he was still being regarded by St. Luke as a 'Christian'.[5] This leads us to the question of the existence and extent of Samaritan influences upon Primitive Christianity in general, and upon the Fourth Gospel in

[1] This imposition of hands appears in a rather curious light when it is brought into relation to Clem. Alex., *Excerpta e Theodoto* XXII.5, ed. Casey, p.56, l.245f., διὸ καὶ ἐν τῇ χειροθεσίᾳ λέγουσιν ἐπὶ τέλους· εἰς λύτρωσιν ἀγγελικήν, cf. Heb. 9:12.

[2] This is meant as a reply to R. McL. Wilson, *The Gnostic Problem*, 1958, p.99. —I believe, as indicated in the preceding paragraph, that St. Luke drew on information obtained from St. Philip through a 'Philip document' for his account on the Seven in Acts 6–8.

[3] Acts 8:20f.

[4] Acts 8:18f.

[5] Acts 8:24.—Hänchen, op. cit., p.262, regards this verse as a 'harmless Lukan formulation, underlining the dangerous power of the word of the Apostle', an attempt to escape from the question why no reply is given to the demand 'pray for me'. The question was posed already by Overbeck in de Wette, op. cit., p. 126n. Here indeed lay the burning question of 'second penance', cf. *Heb.* 6:4–6, and it seems at least worth asking whether or not St. Luke was aware of it.—The fact that the Valentinians, at any rate, paid attention to this question may be seen from Clem. Alex., *Excerpta e Theodoto*, LXXXIII, Casey, p.90, l.707.

particular. For it cannot be assumed that the story of Jesus' preaching in Samaria[1] is only to be regarded as some record of an event that occurred during His earthly ministry, any more than that the accusation by the Jews, 'are we not right in saying you are a Samaritan, you are mad',[2] is lacking any general significance. At the same time it is fair to mention that archaeological evidence supports the view that at least St. John the Baptist had preached among the Samaritans.[3] I therefore venture to suggest that the inconclusive ending of the Simon Magus episode receives its light from St. Luke's antipathy for the Samaritans,[4] on the one hand, and from the witness of the Fourth Gospel in favour of them on the other. This tension in the Primitive Church could not be relieved—if relief it is—by excommunication of offenders because these early Christians were still insufficiently aware of the Church as an earthly, human organization, but saw in it 'the communion of Saints'. However, it is perhaps dangerous to enter too deeply into this question before the mutual relations between the Fourth Gospel and the Philip document have been thoroughly examined.

If one of the members of the college of the Seven, St. Philip, admitted a pre-Christian Gnostic sect into the communion of his Gospel, however deficient it may have been, and kept in close contact with its leader,[5] and if in the Johannine literature we may detect an approving echo of this truly momentous decision, we may, I think, find it at least possible that it was indeed another member of this group, Nicolaus, the proselyte from Antioch,[6] who gave the name to those Nicolaitans, whom we find so

[1] John 4:40–2.

[2] John 8:48.

[3] W. F. Albright in Davies & Daube, op. cit., 1956, has shown that Aenon near Salim, John 3:23, is to be found in Samaria.

[4] Only the Third Gospel records the rejection of Jesus by the Samaritan village, Luke 9:52, but cf. also Jesus' command, Matt.10:5, 'do not enter a Samaritan town'.

[5] Acts 8:13.—The suggestion that it was St. Philip, not St. Peter, who 'gains his greatest triumph when his most successful opponent, Simon Magus, tries in vain to purchase from him the secret of his power', E. Hänchen, op. cit. p.265, is a product of uncritical imagination. Acts say nothing of an opposition of Simon against St. Philip. Dr. Hänchen, I feel, has paid too little attention to the argument proposed by R. F. Casey, *Beginnings of Christianity*, vol.5, p.151f.

[6] Acts 6:5.

strongly censured in the letters to Ephesus and Pergamum in the Revelation of St. John.[1] This view was unanimously held by the early Church Fathers from the days of Irenaeus and Clement of Alexandria.[2] Nevertheless, even this external attestation is insufficient to prove this assumption beyond reasonable doubt. For none of the Fathers shows any personal knowledge of the sect, which does not seem to have continued for very long.[3] It can only be held as a possible hypothesis, therefore, that Nicolaus the Deacon was indeed the founder of the sect of the Nicolaitans. As such it has yet the advantage for us that it leads us from the Acts of the Apostles to the Johannine literature. Here we now find the battle joined between that group of Christians amongst whom this literature arose, probably in Asia Minor, and amongst whom it was accepted as authoritative, and their local adversaries.

I would stress the word 'local' adversaries. For in this I find the great difference between the struggle of St. Paul with the followers of James of Jerusalem, on the one hand, and the anti-heretical statements in Revelation and in the two lesser Johannine Epistles on the other. St. Paul did not yet deal with any 'local' opposition. He, as well as his adversaries, was convinced that the task was an oecumenical one; and their conflict was therefore entirely a conflict of ideas. The 'Letters to the Seven Churches', however, have a more limited scope. The whole atmosphere seems to have changed, and the Church to have come down to earth in the true sense of the word, despite or perhaps even because of the strenuous effort made by the Seer to endow

---

[1] Rev. 2:6f.; 14f.

[2] Irenaeus, *Adv. Haer.*, I.26.3; III.10.6. Clem. Alex., *Strom.*, III.4.25, quoted by Euseb., *E.H.*, III.29.

[3] It seems that M. Kiddle, *The Revelation of St. John*, 1952, p.33f., accepts the Patristic evidence too unreservedly, whilst Lohmeyer, *Die Offenbarung des Joh.*, 1926, p.29, rejects it too readily. For there are not many cases of Saints being turned into sinners by the early Fathers, although, of course, the treatment meted out to St. Paul in the Ps. Clementines comes to mind. Cf. also Bo Reicke, *Glaube und Leben der Urgemeinde*, 1957, p.121, n.10. Dr. A. D. Nock has referred me to P. Janzon, *Svensk Exegetisk Arsbok*, vol.21, 1956, p.82f., but I cannot find this publication in Manchester, neither do I read Swedish.—W. Bousset, *Die Offenbarung des Joh.*, 2nd ed., 1906, p.205f., deserves attention because he shows a faint trace linking the Nicolaitans to Samaria.

the Letters with transcendental significance.[1] We see that the Church had progressed considerably towards the realization of its earthly status and task. The Nicolaitans appear in the 'Seven Letters' very much as they were, a local Christian Gnostic group like several others, even if it is true, as is indeed very probable, that they held the same views as that 'Jezebel of a woman' at Thyatira and her followers, who are described as her 'paramours' and her 'children'.[2] Admittedly, their leaders are described as false 'apostles', but that cannot be interpreted as indicating that they claimed to have been eye-witnesses to the risen Lord in Palestine.[3] Most probably this description is no more than a reflection from St. Paul,[4] although it may contain a reference to the special conception of Apostleship which existed in Gnosticism, and will be discussed later.[5] But the question of Apostolicity, in the Catholic sense, had probably not yet arisen among the Christians in Asia Minor, although it may be found clearly expressed in that contemporary Roman document, the First Epistle of Clement.[6]

The reason for assuming this for Asia Minor is that the strict separation of the Nicolaitans for which the Church at Ephesus receives a special commendation: 'You hate the works of the Nicolaitans, and I hate them too',[7] had apparently not yet been

---

[1] Kiddle, op. cit., p.18, has overstated the universal significance of the 'Seven Letters', cf. the more cautious and elaborate analysis by Lohmeyer, op. cit., p.37f. The local character of the 'Seven Letters' is clearly discernible, especially with regard to the martyrs mentioned, cf. Joh. Weiss, *Das Urchristentum*, 1917, p.627.

[2] Rev. 2:20–3.—For the identical character of the groups cf. Bousset, op. cit., p.206, to whose remarks, however, a little caution has to be added. These early Christian Gnostics should not be regarded as self-contained groups like the Irvingites or the Jehovah's witnesses. The boundaries were quite fluid, and the most that can be said of them is that they accepted in their life and doctrine the views of the same teacher, Nicolaus.

[3] Rev. 2:2.—Bousset, op. cit., p.204, rightly identifies the 'false apostles' with the teachers of the Nicolaitans.

[4] 2.Cor.11:13.

[5] Cf. infra, p.177f.

[6] 1.Clem.42:2–3, cf. Tertullian, *De praescr.* 37; Irenaeus, *Adv. Haer.*, III.1.1, and similar texts which R. Knopf, *Handb. z. N.T.*, Erg. Bd., 1920, p.116, has quoted.

[7] Rev. 2:6, Moffatt.

achieved by Pergamum. For of this Church it is plainly stated: 'You likewise have some adherents of the tenets of the Nicolaitans'.[1] It is thus made evident that whatever form the separation from the Nicolaitans may have taken in the Church at Ephesus, it cannot have been anything like a general condemnation of their doctrine, and a general excommunication of its followers. Membership in the earthly Church was not, so it seems, visualized by the letter to Pergamum, but rather the pollution of God's elect, which was the effect of their communion with the Nicolaitans. For it is also the Divine retribution with which 'that Jezebel of a woman' with her lovers and children is threatened, which at Thyatira makes an outward separation appear as clearly insufficient, and even alien to the Seer's real meaning. From all this it follows that neither 'John' nor the Christians in the 'Seven Cities' were fully conscious of the fact that they actually formed a corporation, which would be entitled to lay down—by way of a Creed or of demanding some individual confessions of faith—the conditions under which members would be accepted or rejected. For them the vocation to the faith was still entirely an act of Divine election.[2] Baptism, however we may define it, be it as the spiritual regeneration, rebirth, or as the conferment of the Holy Spirit upon the repentant sinner, was to them in no sense a 'rite

---

[1] Rev. 2:15, Moffatt.—Whether or not a distinction has to be made between the 'works', τὰ ἔργα, of the Nicolaitans in 2:6, and their 'tenets', διδαχή, in 2:15, is at least uncertain. Clem. Alex., *Strom.*, III.4.25, it is true, characterizes them as an antinomian, immoral Gnostic sect, and Bousset, op. cit., p.206, suggests that Clement's quotation, if such it is, παραχρήσασθαι τῇ σαρκὶ δεῖ, may be of Nicolaitan origin. In this case their 'works' would have given more cause for a separation than their mere—modern—doctrine. However, Bousset's theory rests on slender foundations. For at least of Irenaeus', *Adv. Haer.*, I.23, more detailed accusations of promiscuity and eating of sacrificial meat, it is evident that they were derived solely from Rev.2:20; and it seems improbable that Clement should have had knowledge of their foremost doctrine. Consequently the formal 'testing of the spirit', 1.John 4:1f., of the 'false apostles' at Ephesus, suggested by Kiddle, op. cit., p. 22, is also uncertain. For it presupposes that they were expelled for bad doctrine and not, as Rev.2:6 makes clear, for bad manners.

[2] The parable of the wheat and the tares, Matt.13:24f., should be brought to mind, even if it is uncertain whether the author of Revelation knew the First Gospel.

of admission', and very probably did not presuppose any formal declaration of assent or confession of faith. It is at any rate significant that the baptismal command of the risen Lord, βαπτίζοντες-διδάσκοντες, if anything places baptism before—and certainly not after—the instruction in Christianity,[1] and even more so that the baptismal question and answer of St. Philip and the Ethiopian is demonstrably a later interpolation.[2]

However, the recognition that the Christian congregations in each particular town formed a distinct group, a corporation which was in need of some definite ruling about its membership, was in western and southern Asia Minor, as one might say, just round the corner when the Johannine literature came into being in the last two decades of the first century. Quite a few years ago I made an effort to prove that the angels of the Seven Churches were, insofar as their earthly reality is concerned, their local leaders or bishops, and I still believe this to be the case.[3] I do not hold a special brief for the term of bishop in this case, and am prepared to admit that 'pastors' will do equally well, provided that it is granted that there was only one angel or 'pastor' to each of the Seven Churches. On this condition I will even grant that not every bishop is of necessity an angel. In fact, 3.John introduces us to one who was decidedly not an angel, 'Diotrephes, who likes to take the lead among them'.[4] We hear the complaint by 'the presbyter' about him that he did not 'receive' him or his

---

[1] Matt.28:19–20, cf. E. Klostermann, *Das Matthäus-Evangelium*, 2nd ed., 1927, p.232.

[2] Acts 8:37.—It seems significant to me that the earliest witness to the use of this Roman legal rite (*stipulatio*) in Baptism, cf. ch.10, should be Vetus Latina, whereas the earliest Greek MS. exhibiting the verse is only Laudianus (E) of the sixth century.

[3] Cf. *Church Quart. Rev.*, 1944, p.115f.

[4] 3.John 9.—'Ο φιλοπρωτεύων αὐτῶν takes its place in a long series of caustic remarks on the πρωτοκαθεδρία of the bishops, and may have a connection with Matt. 23:6 par. This, however, has not been noted by either Dodd, *Johannine Epistles*, p.161f., or H. Windisch, *Die kathol. Briefe*, 2nd ed., 1930, p.141f. It is mentioned here only in order to show that the situation was a typical one. Otherwise the question of the relations between the Synoptists and the Johannine literature is quite sufficiently obscure, and I would not add to that by claiming any direct or indirect interdependence between the two texts.

messengers, and 'expelled' from the Church those who did 'receive' such messengers.[1]

Moffatt translates 'expel' by 'excommunicate',[2] but this translation seems to be inadequate if any legal denotation is attached to the term, for 'to the just there is no law',[3] and the separation from the 'unjust' was much more a natural, social than a legal process. What actually happened may be more clearly seen when the meaning of 'to receive' is more closely scrutinized.[4] For the Greek word for 'to receive' is used here in two meanings. In v.9 'the presbyter' complains that Diotrephes 'does not receive me', and means by that that Diotrephes rejects his 'message', his doctrine; in v.10, however, he complains that Diotrephes 'does not receive' his messengers, and thus fails to fulfil the generally Christian and particularly episcopal duty of hospitality.[5] It is worth noticing how closely the questions of Christian doctrine and Christian duty—and hospitality could be a very onerous duty[6]—are combined; but it may also be held that it was easier for the local 'bishop' to exclude itinerant heretics, even together with their hosts, from the *ecclesia*, the common meeting and the common meal, than resident ones. It may be true, as I believe it is, that the denial of hospitality should be considered as an early step upon the road to ecclesiastical excommunication, but there were still several further steps to be taken. It is, however, interesting to

[1] 3.John 10.

[2] So also, if only among several other possibilities, Dodd, *Johannine Epistles*, p.162f.

[3] I.Tim.1:9, δικαίῳ νόμος οὐ κεῖται. This conviction was so general among the Greeks under the Romans, cf. *Polit. Metaphysik*, vol.2, p.37f., that we need not enter into the question whether or not Diotrephes could have had any knowledge of the Pastoral Epistles.

[4] The fact that ἐπιδέχεσθαι occurs in the N.T. only in 3.John (and is not even discussed by Grundmann in Kittel, *Wörterb.*, vol.2, p.49f.), does not diminish its importance as a technical term, especially in Jewish circles, cf. the passages from Ecclus. and 1/2.Macc. quoted by Bauer, *Wörterb. z. N.T.*, 4th ed., 1952, p.528. Luke preferred ἀποδέχεσθαι, with the same meaning, probably because it was somewhat more common in Greek circles.

[5] Rom.12:13; Heb.13:2; I.Tim.3:2.

[6] Cf. e.g., how in the *Actus S. Sylvestri* the Saint is the only Christian at Rome who 'receives the Egyptian martyr Timotheus in his house', *Bull. of the John Rylands Lib.*, 1960, p.294.

observe how in this case a measure which the presbyter himself had advocated, recoiled upon him. It had been his advice too: 'If anyone comes to you and does not bring this doctrine, do not admit him into the house,' i.e. refuse him all hospitality;[1] and Diotrephes seems to have followed this advice with regard to the presbyter himself. The two lesser Epistles of John undoubtedly bear witness to much personal bitterness and strife among those early Christians of Asia Minor; but these are inextricably mixed up with the wish that the right doctrine and nothing else should be preached, as may be seen from the words written by the presbyter: 'So when I come, I shall bring up what he is doing, babbling against me with wicked words'.[2] It is evident that this sentence would have been written very differently had there been an authoritative 'Apostles' Creed' to pinpoint Diotrephes' heretical views; but it should not be overlooked that such an authoritative statement of the right Christian doctrine seems to have been sought for by the two contestants.[3]

---

[1] 2.John 10, Moffatt.—The interpretation given presupposes, of course, that the author of 2. and 3.John is one and the same person, a theory which seems threatened by certain inconsistencies in the history of the canonization of the two Epistles. Dodd, *Johannine Epistles*, LXVI, after fully examining these difficulties, nevertheless pronounces in favour of the identity of the author, and I accept his authority.

[2] 3.John 10, Moffatt.

[3] It has been suggested that at any rate excommunication for moral lapses took place in the Primitive Church. In favour of this view three passages might be quoted: Matt. 18:17; Acts 5:1f.; and 1.Cor.5:5. As regards the Matthean passage, I would refer to Billerbeck vol.5.1, p.298, and esp. p.329f., 'nowhere can it be shown that the synagogal banishment served as a means of excluding obstreperous elements from the synagogue, etc.' As regards St. Paul's 'consigning that person to Satan . . . in order that his spirit may be saved', I feel that this is still in line with the synagogal banishment. Billerbeck vol.3, p.358f., omitting 'in order that, etc.' is probably off the right track here. Finally, it is the Divine action by which Ananias and Saphira are punished, not a judicial murder at the hands of St. Peter. It thus appears at least highly doubtful whether the Primitive Church arrogated to itself the right of complete expulsion of a baptized person on moral grounds. This is, however, not the place to align this finding with the 'power of the keys' or with the problem of second penance.

III

Orthodoxy and Heresy in the Early Church

There are, one might say, in the two lesser Johannine Epistles the first beginnings of excommunication for holding false doctrines, which was worked by the refusal of hospitality, and thus too the first signs for a consciousness of the need for an authoritative Creed. However, these were as yet only beginnings and signs, and before a suggestion is made as to how they came to fruition, it seems profitable to cast a glance at the Church abroad in order to find out whether this indefiniteness of the boundaries between orthodoxy and heresy was general among Christians of A.D. 100, or whether it was perhaps only characteristic of that corner in Asia Minor from which the Johannine Epistles seem to have sprung.

For the possibility of making such a survey with comparative ease, and indeed for the first attempt at analyzing Christianity before the Apostles' Creed without any doctrinal or denominational bias, we are indebted to that great New Testament scholar, the late Dr. Walter Bauer, whose *Greek Dictionary of the New Testament* alone will secure for him a place among the greatest. In 1934 he published a comparatively small book on orthodoxy and heresy in earliest Christianity,[1] the result of many years of study. However, those were the days when the small still voice of the self-denying theological scholar could hardly hope to penetrate the groans of suffering and the shouts of triumph in the German Protestant Church, where the battle for the preservation of contemporary Christianity was fought, and at best only partly won. No wonder that Dr. Bauer's book found far too little of the attention which it so richly deserved—and still deserves.

---

[1] Bauer, *Rechtgläubigkeit,* op. cit.—The only detailed appreciation of the book in English which I have found, is that of H. E. W. Turner, *The Pattern of Christian Truth,* 1954, p.37f., which to my great regret does not seem to me to do Bauer's book justice, as in the case of East-Syria, so particularly in the case of Egypt.

Dr. Bauer has started his enquiries very differently from me, by describing early regional Christian Churches which were evidently non-orthodox, i.e. whose tenets did not conform to that rule of faith which is embodied in the Apostles' Creed. It may be held that such a beginning is unmethodical, because it presupposes that somewhere in early Christianity a 'regula fidei' was invented as a touch-stone of orthodoxy, at the very outset of the history of the Church, an assumption which seems to leave out of consideration the question whether or not the problem of heresy was at all visualized in the early days of Christianity.[1] However that may be, it is of the highest importance to face the fact that till the second half of the second century there were within and outside the Roman Empire vast regions containing numerous as well as highly active Christian groups, but completely devoid of any Catholic Christians. As such Dr. Bauer has selected East-Syria and Egypt.[2] To begin with East-Syria, or northern Mesopotamia, I believe that in Britain people of my generation are still fascinated by the scintillating description of the origins of the Church at Edessa and its environs by F. C. Burkitt,[3] and I frankly confess to be still under its spell myself. It therefore comes as a big shock when we see how much fiction that great scholar has interspersed among the facts which he related so beautifully. However, it would not be true to say that obscurity has descended again where once there seemed to be light. For whilst Dr. Bauer has proved that Burkitt's trust in the

[1] Cf. the way in which Bauer, op. cit., p.3f. speaks of 'die Kirchenlehre' as if the earthly existence of the Church had already had a theological significance for the earliest Christians. I suggest that just the opposite is true. If, as the reference in 1.Cor.11:19 seems to indicate, the agraphon 'there will be schisms and heresies', E. Klostermann, *Apocrypha*, III, nr.33, *Kl. Texte* 11, Cambridge 1905, p.8, belongs to the earliest kerygma, it appears that the formation of organized groups was suspect in earliest Christianity, and the true Church was not to be seen in such a light at all. The parallel with Israel, and the nations, cf. E. Peterson, *Frühkirche, Judentum und Gnosis*, 1959, p.51f., which from the time of 1.Clem.30:1, may have provided the pattern of Church organization, originally stressed the exclusive Divine prerogative in the election of the Christians, cf. Gal.4:24–8; 6:16.

[2] Bauer, op. cit., p.6f., 49f.

[3] Burkitt, *Early Eastern Christianity*, 1904, cf. especially pp.10f., on the conversion of king Abgar of Edessa.

early Edessene list of bishops[1] before and even after Palût is completely unfounded, he has not called in question the Christianity
of those regions, but only their Catholicity. Palût, so it appears,
was the first to establish a Catholic community at Edessa, at the
end of the second century, for he seems to have been a contemporary of Clement of Alexandria. It is probable that he came to
Edessa from Antioch; but whether he was sent there after he had
been consecrated bishop of Edessa at Antioch seems highly
questionable.[2] When he arrived there, however, he found himself confronted throughout the whole of East-Syria with a strong
and virile Christian movement perhaps rather than Church,
amongst whose Fathers were Marcion, Bardesanes,[3] and I would
add Tatian, who may even have still been alive at the time; and of
which only fifty years later Mani, the founder of Manichaeism,
was the genuine product. Dr. Bauer believes that Marcion had
been the founder of East-Syrian Christianity;[4] but this view may
be open to doubt. For whilst his influence upon the life and belief of these Christians was apparently very great, his *Euangelion*
and his *Apostolos* vanished before the immense popularity of
Tatian's *Diatessaron*, and I know of no evidence showing that
Tatian's Encratites were in reality Marcionites.[5] The fact is, I
believe, that after Marcion he became the most influential teacher
amongst the Christians in East-Syria. It cannot be assumed, however, that these Christians still continued without any outward
organization. It appears that they formed an organized Church, at
the latest by the beginning of the third century, which excluded
non-Marcionite 'heretics'. Amongst these heretics the Catholics

---

[1] Burkitt, op. cit., p.25f.

[2] Bauer, op. cit., p.25f.

[3] So Bauer, p.29f.

[4] Bauer, *Rechtgläubigkeit*, op. cit., p.26f.

[5] It appears from the earliest use of ἐγκρατής in a disparaging sense by Iren.,
Adv. Haer., I.28, cf. Clem. Alex., *Paed.*, II.2. etc.; Hippol. *Ref.*, VIII.20, that no
clearly defined group of heretics was visualized by it; and Irenaeus, for instance,
comprises under it the followers of Satornil and Marcion indiscriminately. It is
quite uncertain whether any store may be set by Jerome's assertion, *De vir. ill.*,
XXIX, 'Tatianus . . . novam condidit haeresin quae Encratitarum dicitur'. I
feel sure that this has been formulated upon lines of thought which only arose
from experiences of the post-Constantinian period.

were prominent, and were dubbed 'Palûtians'.[1] In A.D. 200, therefore, the position in East-Syria was to some extent inversely analogous to that in the more westerly parts of the Roman Empire. There was an organized 'Marcionite' Christian Church, opposed by an 'heretical', much smaller group of Catholics, described by that Church as 'Palûtians'. The development of the doctrine and the life of the Church had therefore progressed in East-Syria in a similar manner to that in the West, and far beyond what we have found in the Johannine congregations of Asia Minor in A.D. 100. The only marked difference is that we do not hear of any Marcionite 'regula fidei'.

With regard to Egypt, it is true to say that Dr. Bauer has made one of the most signal discoveries in early Church History. It is a case of Goethe's famous distich:

> What is the most difficult? What you believe to be easiest:
> To behold with your eyes what lies in front of your eyes.

For Dr. Bauer has met the ever-repeated complaints about the scarcity of sources bearing on the history of early Egyptian Christianity[2] with the wholly convincing claim that early Egyptian Christianity was Gnostic Christianity, for which there is an abundance of sources; whereas Catholic Christianity was only a late arrival upon Egyptian soil.[3] This theory, which I accept to the full, may help to clarify even what has been said previously about Apollos, the Jew from Alexandria.[4] For with the support of Dr. Bauer we may here add to what has been said before about his

---

[1] Bauer, *Rechtgläubigkeit*, p.26.—The acerbity of the conflict is reflected in Adamantius, *Dial.*, I.8, where the Marcionite says: 'I am called Christian, and if you (the Catholic) call me a Marcionite, then I will call you a Socratian.' The name and person of Palût seem to have been omitted on purpose by the Catholic author of the Dialogue.

[2] Cf., in place of many, the complaint by E. R. Hardy, *Christian Egypt*, 1952, p.11, 'the obscurity that surrounds its (the Church of Alexandria's) early days, ends with the episcopate of Demetrius (190–233)'. On the artificiality of the Alexandrian succession-list cf., however, E. Caspar, *Die älteste römische Bischofsliste*, p.153f. I feel sure that even the accession-date of Demetrius is suspect.

[3] Bauer, *Rechtgläubigkeit*, p.49f.

[4] Cf. also my remarks about the rejection of the Jerusalem doctrine of the Holy Spirit by Alexandrian Christianity, see above, pp. 89,n3; 94,n4.

'different' Gospel a reference to the Alexandrian 'Gospel according to the Hebrews',[1] and also to its correlative, the 'Gospel according to the Egyptians';[2] and, without having any means of answering the question, we may wonder whether these two Gospels obtained in Egypt some sort of quasi-canonical authority, similar to that of the Diatessaron in East-Syria, and perhaps earlier than the Four-Gospel canon among the Catholics.

In other respects, however, this Egyptian Christianity bore quite a different aspect from that which we have encountered in East-Syria. For whilst in East-Syria, in the course of the second century, an organized Church was formed, largely founded upon the basis of Marcionite doctrines, Egyptian Gnosticism never achieved that goal. It is, I believe, fanciful to talk about Gnostic 'sects' in Egypt in the second century.[3] The careful distinctions,

---

[1] Bauer, *Rechtgläubigkeit*, p.55f.—It may be stated that the 'Gospel according to the Hebrews' exhibited a very individual doctrine of the Holy Spirit, cf. Hennecke-Schneemelcher, op. cit., vol. 1, p.108, nr.3, cf. the parallel in *Epist. Apost.*, 14, ed. Duensing, ibid., p.133, where Christ Himself is the angel of the annunciation and enters Mary's womb. P. Vielhauer, who in this edition is responsible for collecting and arranging the fragments of the three Judaeo-Christian Gospels, has also rightly stated, p.104, 'the fact that the Easter stories in the "Gospel according to the Hebrews" differ widely from the canonical reports, is clear'; but has not there referred to the analogy between its frg.7, op. cit., p.108, and 1.Cor.15:7. It may be asked, therefore, whether this parallel to the report of the appearance of the risen Lord before James, and the tremendous respect for James in the 'Gospel according to Thomas' log. 12, which obviously derives from it, do not point to an earlier date than that suggested by Vielhauer, p. 107, the first half of the second century.

[2] Bauer, op. cit., p.54f.—Schneemelcher in Hennecke-Schneemelcher, op. cit., p. 109, dashes our hopes that the find of Nag'Hammadi may help on our knowledge of this Gospel beyond that which Bauer, loc. cit., has stated.

[3] Cf. the use of *ecclesia* in the Gnostic 'Sophia of Jesus Christ,' ed. Walter C. Till, *Die gnostischen Schriften*, etc., *T.U.*, 60, 1955, p.260f., which is similar to that made in the excommunication rite of the third century 'Pistis Sophia', 105, ed. C. Schmidt, 2nd ed. by W. Till, 1954, p.173f. This in its turn finds a parallel in *Epist. Apost.*, 48, Hennecke-Schneemelcher, p.154, and may not depend immediately upon Matt. 18:15–17, but upon the 'Gospel according to the Hebrews,' which was either a corruption or an imitation of the canonical First Gospel.—I hear now that Professor Morton Smith of Columbia University, New York, has discovered a letter by Clement of Alexandria quoting from a non-canonical version of the Gospel according to Mark. Markan quotations are on the whole rare in Egyptian Christian literature; but I do not feel that

which may be found in the anti-heretical writers, from Irenaeus to Epiphanius, between the Valentinians—who admittedly formed a sect in the West—the Ophites, the Carpocratians, etc. make curious reading when they are compared with the attitude taken by the Catholics on the spot in Egypt. Even if we omit the 'Epistle of the Apostles', the orthodoxy of which seems to me just as doubtful as its place of origin,[1] our main witnesses are Clement of Alexandria and Origen. Of these two we find Clement making a collection of excerpts from Theodotus, probably a pupil of Valentinus, which he was going to use for the continuation of his 'Stromateis',[2] the work which he produced in defence of the Catholic doctrine. The method employed by him in using such material may be studied in his earlier literary productions.[3] The preservation of this raw material is of course due to the fact that the persecution by Septimius Severus in A.D. 202 prevented him from finishing his work.[4] In a very similar way Origen too chose

---

such a find, and still less the use of the Fourth Gospel in Egypt, cf. Turner, op. cit., p.53f., will constitute an argument either for or against the assumption that the separation of the Catholics from the Gnostics in Egypt had taken place in Alexandria at any time before the episcopate of Demetrius. There can be no doubt at any rate that the succession line of Alexandrian bishops from St. Mark down to Demetrius is altogether fictitious.

[1] G. Bardy, whom James, op. cit., p.485, has quoted without comment, has questioned the orthodoxy of the *Epist. Apost.*, which C. Schmidt, *Gespräche Jesu*, op. cit., had maintained. It is supported by the attack upon Simon Magus and Cerinthus, *Epist. Apost.*, 1f., who may be regarded as the representatives of Gnosticism in general, since they are allegedly the only Gnostic contemporaries of the Apostles, and also by the numbering of Gnosis among the five foolish virgins, *Epist. Apost.*, 42 fin. It is, on the other hand, seriously put into question because of the analogies with the 'Gospel according to the Hebrews' which are to be found in the *Epist. Apost.*, 48. These analogies also point to an Egyptian origin of the *Epist. Apost.*

[2] Cf. R. P. Casey, 'The excerpta ex Theodoto', *Studies and Documents*, I, 1934, p.4, n.1.

[3] A selection from Clement's more extensive quotations may be found in W. Völker, *Quellen zur Gesch. d. Gnosis*, 1932, cf. also Th. Hopfner, *Fontes hist. rel. Aegypt.*, 1922–5, p.365f.

[4] This view would be untenable if A. Ehrhard, *Die Kirche der Märtyrer*, 1932, p.49, were right in maintaining that this persecution was solely directed against Christian catechumens. This assertion, however, falls with the recognition that the addition to the report of Septimius Severus' prohibition of conversion to Judaism, *Hist. Aug.*, Severus XXVIII.1, 'idem et de Christianis', is no more

the commentary by the Gnostic Heracleon, also a member of the Valentinian school, for the basis of his own commentary on the Fourth Gospel.[1] Once the meaning of these and other related observations[2] is clearly grasped, it will be understood that in the second century in Egypt Gnosticism and Christianity were largely exchangeable terms, and that in any case Egyptian Christianity was Gnostic Christianity. Men like Basilides and his son Isidorus, Valentinus, Carpocrates and Epiphanes, and all the others should be seen as the teachers of Christianity in Egypt, and as 'heresiarchs' only in the sense that they were school-heads who, like so many other famous theologians, sometimes joined forces, and at other times engaged in furious conflict.[3] There are signs that in its beginning even the famous Catholic 'Catechetical School' held no stricter views about its competitors.[4] Clement also stated dolefully that these Gnostics had been great teachers, who had, however, come to grief because of their excessive pride.

It appears from this as well as generally that these Gnostic leaders claimed a 'prophetic' ministry in the early Christian sense, in constant touch with the Logos, and that it was for this reason that they used for their works the literary forms of 'inspired'

---

than a shameless interpolation. The reasons for this verdict are (a) the inanity of the addition: Christianity was prohibited altogether, what purpose could be served by adding a special prohibition of joining it? Papinianus, Severus' minister of Justice, was anything but such a fool. (b) The form 'idem et de' is common for so-called 'glosses' in Roman legal sources.

[1] Cf. the fragments of Heracleon collected by Völker, op. cit., pp.63–86.

[2] Amongst these I count the fact that the *Epist. Apost.*, although it has at the beginning, in para. 3, an evident credal formula, uses the agraphon, 'there will be schisms and heresies' in para.29, Hennecke-Schneemelcher, vol.1, p.142, just in the sense in which I have interpreted it above, p. 172, n.1.

[3] I consider as clearly attacking what is to be read in Apocr. Joh. 68, 13f., ed. W. Till, p.177, 'but I said: "Christ, those who have not recognised the All, what are their souls or where will they go?"' the saying in the Gospel of Thomas, log.67, 'Jesus says: Whoever knows the All but fails to know himself lacks everything.'

[4] Cf. how Euseb., *E.H.*, VI.2.13f., tries to explain the fact that Origen, apparently without hesitation, accepted after the persecution of A.D. 202 the patronage of the 'renowned Alexandrian heresiarch' Paul and his patroness, cf. Bauer, *Rechtgläubigkeit*, p.62f. For the assurance that Origen never consented to pray with Paul, is obviously an attempt of the pious Eusebius to make the bitter truth a little more palatable to his contemporaries.

writings, Gospel, Prophecy, and Revelation.[1] For they believed
that 'Gnosis' was no mere human achievement, but the result of a
kind of a mystical union with the eternal Logos. This accounts for
the large number of such books which have been discovered in
the Gnostic Library of Chenoboscion or Nag'Hammadi.[2] It has
to be said, however, that they are different in kind from our
canonical Gospels, and probably also from the two Gospels
according to the Hebrews and the Egyptians.[3] One feature in
particular is common to all the Egyptian Gnostic writings of
which I know, Pistis Sophia, Book of Jeû, Gospel of Mary,
Apocryphon of John, Sophia of Jesus Christ, Gospel of Truth,
and Gospel of Thomas, and I confidently predict that it will also
appear in all the unpublished Gospels from Nag'Hammadi. It is
that they are all post-Resurrection Gospels, Sayings of the risen
Lord, the Logos purged of His earthly flesh. Here, I believe, lay
the dividing line between Gnosticism and Catholicism in Egypt,
and this incidentally is the representative significance of that great
little book *On the Incarnation of the Logos* ascribed to Athanasius.
The Egyptian Gnostic concentration on the risen Logos, on the
other hand, made a separate theology of the Holy Spirit appear to
be rather superfluous, and this may already form the background
of that enigmatic saying of the twelve 'disciples' at Ephesus, 'we
never heard the Holy Spirit existed',[4] whom we have tried to

[1] Schneemelcher in Hennecke-Schneemelcher, op. cit., p.32, calls this a
'loaned authority'. Whilst fully agreeing with his distinction between an earlier
and a later type of apocryphal Gospel, I consider this an unfortunate term, cf.,
e.g., Valentinus (?), *Gospel of Truth*, ed. K. Grobel, 1960, p.198, 'Having been
in the place of rest', for the authorization claimed by these Gnostics.

[2] Ch. Puech in Hennecke-Schneemelcher, op. cit., p.158f., enumerates more
than thirty of such 'Gnostic Gospels and related documents', the largest part of
which is contained in the codices of Nag'Hammadi.—One wonders about the
relation between this library and the monastery of Pachomius at Chenoboscion,
near whose site the find was made, cf. Ch. Puech in F. L. Cross, *The Jung Codex*,
1955, p.13.

[3] The 'Gospel according to the Hebrews' may have been a mixture of the two
types: Frg.1–2, 7, are of the narrative type of the canonical Gospels, frg.3–5 of
the Gnostic sayings type. Similarly the *Epist. Apost.* exhibits in 4–12 the pre-
Resurrection narrative type, and after that (13–51) the post-Resurrection sayings type.

[4] Acts 19:2, Moffatt.—Foakes-Jackson, *The Acts of the Apostles*, 1931, p.176,

place in the nearest neighbourhood of Apollos, the Jew of Alexandria. The miracle of Pentecost seems to have exerted little influence over Egyptian Gnosticism.[1]

After the analyses of East-Syrian and Egyptian Christianity, Dr. Bauer proceeds to examine West-Syria in the light of the Epistles of Ignatius of Antioch, Smyrna and its districts judged by the evidence about Polycarp, Macedonia, and Crete.[2] Of these only the part about Ignatius is of importance for us since Ignatius is known for the Creed which is contained in his Epistles. However, it seems to me that in the case of West-Syria Dr. Bauer's approach is somewhat lacking in punch, especially since he has completely neglected the evidence of the Didache. This is an unfortunate omission, for as B. H. Streeter has shown,[3] the constitutive force

---

very pertinently asks, 'whether the doctrine of the Spirit and Baptism here implied is that of St. Paul'? But he seems not to have found sufficient confirmatory evidence for this in the Pauline letters. I should say that St. Luke wanted it to appear as the unanimous doctrine of the Twelve and St. Paul, but not of the Churches founded independently, e.g., at Samaria.

[1] It seems to me no longer possible to adduce Clem. Alex., *Excerpta e Theodoto* 24, ed. Casey, p.58, l.269, in favour of the opposite view, since we have learned from Apocr. Joh., 47, 1f., ed. W. Till, *T.U.*, 60, 1955, p.135, that the Valentinians had their own theory of the 'outpouring of the Spirit', which is quite different from that in Acts 2:1f. But even the 'Catholics' in Egypt showed great reserve towards Pentecost. It is perhaps not altogether surprising to see the *Epist. Apost.*, which is of doubtful Catholicity, quoting the promise of the Holy Spirit, as in Acts 1:8, in its para.30, Hennecke-Schneemelcher, op. cit., vol.1, p.143f., yet never referring to Pentecost; but this fact assumes a special significance when we see from Stählin's Index that Clement of Alexandria never quoted Acts 2:1f. either.—Reference may also be made to the question of the Arian daemon in an enlargement of the *Historia Lausiaca* (not to be found in Dom C. Butler's edition, quoted here after E. Preuschen, *Palladius und Rufinus*, 1897, p.118, l.9f.) in the Life of Evagrius: 'He said, "concerning the Holy Spirit and the Body of Christ, is this truly of Christ, or truly of Mary?" And the Abbot Evagrius replied, "The Holy Spirit is neither begotten nor created. For everything created occupies a limited space, etc.",' cf. also Clem. Alex., *Excerpta e Theodoto* 60.1, ed. Casey, p.78, l.556f.—Equally puzzling is the fact that the epiclesis in the liturgy of Serapion calls for the descent of the Logos upon the elements, cf. Clem. Alex., op. cit. 13.1-3, p.50, l.153f. A special enquiry into the development of the doctrine of the Holy Spirit in Alexandrian theology would, I believe, pay a rich dividend.

[2] W. Bauer, *Rechtgläubigkeit*, pp.65-80.

[3] B. H. Streeter, *The Primitive Church*, 1929, p.144f. Dr. Bauer does not seem to have referred to Streeter's book at all.

exercised by the Didache within the Churches of West-Syria was very considerable indeed. The fact that Ignatius in his Epistles struggles against docetic Gnosticism[1] is, of course, well-known, and it may be permissible to draw the conclusion from this that he had a similar conflict in hand in his Church at Antioch.[2] However, the evidence for a strong Gnostic movement in Antioch at the time of Ignatius is hardly overwhelming. The only notable name is Menander, the pupil of Simon Magus, who by his time was probably dead.[3] Above all, there are two good reasons which should prevent us from accepting Dr. Bauer's claim that on the evidence of the Ignatian Epistles it can be made probable that Christianity at Antioch was predominantly or even to a large extent Gnostic. The first is that Ignatius can hardly be called a representative witness for that Church from which the Pseudo-Clementine literature as well as the VII and VIII books of the 'Apostolic Constitutions' with their strong admixture of Jewish liturgical elements took their origin, unless his praise of St. Paul,[4] and his protests against Judaeo-Christian practices,[5] were sheer hypocrisy. The second reason is that the objectives for which Ignatius fought were not purges and excommunications—these are nowhere even mentioned in his Epistles—but rather the reclaiming of the various Christian cliques for the common 'parish' Service which the bishop conducted. A definite separation of a group of Christians (αἵρεσις = sect) is only mentioned for Tralles,[6] and its members appear as irretrievably lost; but in all other cases Ignatius advocated a policy of reconciliation,[7] which

---

[1] A useful example of the docetic protest against the Catholics may be found in Acts of John 100 fin., ed. M. Bonnet, reprinted 1959, p.201,l.10f.

[2] Bauer, *Rechtgläubigkeit*, p.69, says, 'Ignatius had come to know, loathe, and fear "the mad dogs", "the beasts in human form", as he calls them, in his home town.' This does not follow from Ign., *Eph.*, 7.1 and *Smyrn.* 4.1, the texts to which Bauer refers.

[3] Bauer, *Rechtgläubigkeit*, p.70, refers also to Satornil and Cerdo as 'Syrians', but that probably meant East-Syrians; and the story of Epiphanius that Basilides had imported the Gnosticism, which he had learned from Menander at Antioch, to Alexandria, *Haer.* XXIII.1, will not bear critical inspection.

[4] Ign., *Eph.* 12:2.   [5] Ign., *Magn.* 8; *Philad.* 6f.

[6] Ign., *Trall.* 6.

[7] Cf., e.g., Ign., *Eph.* 2:3.

aimed at the maintenance of a common worship by and for all local Christians. These two facts once stated make clear in their turn the significance which is to be ascribed to Ignatius' Creed in our investigation. Firstly, if Ignatius is not representative for the Church at Antioch, his Creed cannot have had much local importance, and perhaps it was not even known there at all.[1] Secondly, although Ignatius' credal declarations have a polemical purpose against the Docetics, they are apparently not used for excommunication. Still less can I find in them any reference to the instruction to be given to catechumens. What is to be found in them is the closest connection between Ignatius' declarations of his faith and his eagerly expected martyrdom.[2] Ignatius' Creed then is the Creed of the martyr—perhaps, the martyrs. It is, therefore, still *Euangelion*, as in Apostolic time, the proclamation of the present Lord, 'who suffered under Pontius Pilate', and is present in His martyr.[3]

The other provinces of the Roman Empire whose Christianity is examined by Dr. Bauer, seem to yield much less fruit for our enquiry. The same applies also to his challenging if not wholly convincing scrutiny of 'Asia Minor before Ignatius of Antioch'.[4]

[1] The two credal formulae from the third century Didascalia, Const. Apost. VI.11 & 14, quoted after Hahn-Harnack, *Bibl. d. Symbole*, op. cit., p.13f., which are of Antiochene origin, and were valid for centuries in the Church there, exhibit no similarity at all with Ignatius' Creed. F. J. Badcock, *The History of the Creeds*, 2nd ed., 1938, p.47, offers a reconstruction of the Antiochene baptismal Creed which, I think, is highly misleading. Of Badcock's sources, to be found in Hahn-Harnack, op. cit., mostly at p.141f., only the Didascalia is pre-Nicene, and of its characteristic additions as ἕνα μόνον θεὸν τῶν ὄντων δημιουργόν, ἑνὸς Παρακλήτου and omissions, as the virgin birth and Pontius Pilate (both prominent in Ignatius) no mention is made by Badcock, not even in a footnote.

[2] If, of course, this part is arbitrarily omitted from the quotations of Ign., *Trall*.9; *Smyrn*.1:1-2, as in Kelly *Early Christian Creeds*, op. cit., p.68f., the understanding of one of the important factors in the formation of the Creeds is lost, and the significance of occasional triadic formulations as in Ign., *Magn.* 13:1, is highly over-emphasized.

[3] It is significant that Pontius Pilate is mentioned in both the elaborate credal formulae by Ignatius, probably in imitation of 1.Tim.6:13.

[4] Bauer, *Rechtgläubigkeit*, pp.81-98.—I am doubtful with regard to the Asiatic origin of several of Bauer's sources, especially of Jude—and 2.Peter—of which the earliest witnesses, according to Windisch, *Die Kathol. Briefe*, p.38, are from the West, Canon Muratori and Tertullian, and from Alexandria. The

This chapter, however, puts the question what became of Christianity in Asia Minor in the later years of the second century, a question which, unfortunately, Dr. Bauer has not tackled in its entirety. It is, however, in two respects of importance for our enquiry. The Montanist crisis in particular reveals, on the one hand, the unifying effect of the establishment of a resident ministry, the beginnings of which appeared—in a somewhat unfavourable light—in 3.John, and the consolidation of which was the main purpose of Ignatius; on the other hand, the Montanist crisis shows, perhaps, the unsettling effects of the conversion of national religious groups, like the Phrygians, of which, although in a much smaller frame, we have had an example in the conversion of the Samaritans together with their religious leader, Simon Magus. However, by thus concentrating upon the Montanist crisis, we do not intend to belittle the range of Gnosticism in Asia Minor, of which some words will have to be said first.[1] The main similarity and difference between the Asiatic and the Egyptian Gnosticism may be characterized by its chief literary productions. Both these groups felt themselves in an immediate contact with the risen Logos; but whilst this feeling led to the production of Gnostic Gospels in Egypt, it made Asia Minor the home of Gnostic Acts of the various Apostles. Of these Acts a selection was made before the end of the second century in the so-called corpus of Leucius, which seems to have had as wide a circulation in Catholic[2] as in Gnostic circles. Only since the time when the Manichees, the genuine upshot of East-Syrian Gnosticism, made

---

Asiatic origin of the Pastoral Epistles is not altogether beyond doubt either. Since Ignatius and Tatian, cf. M. Dibelius, *Die Pastoralbriefe*, 2nd ed., 1931, p.6, used them, they may well have their origin in Syria. If, on the other hand, 1.Peter were not of Roman origin, as is now widely assumed, cf., e.g., Cullmann, *Peter, Disciple*, p.82f., but written in the South of Asia Minor, the famous problem of the omission of this region in the address of this Epistle, of which Bauer, op. cit., p.82f., makes so much, would find a natural solution.

[1] R. McL. Wilson, op. cit., p.97f., has treated the Asiatic Gnosticism in its entirety as 'earlier Gnosticism', and ibid., p.116f., the 'later Gnosticism' as almost exclusively Egyptian. The regional difference between the two schools is overlooked. But the regional differences between 'Gnostics' were, I believe, at least as marked as the regional differences among the Catholics.

[2] Cf. the proof offered for this in my *Apostolic Succession*, p.68f.

the Leucian corpus into their canonical 'Book of Acts' was a fair amount of reserve towards them created in the circle of Catholic theologians. We find, for example, a cover of Catholic varnish spread over the ancient Gnostic daub of the Acts of John in their fourth century Latin version.[1] At the time of their origin, however, we find a kind of Catholic and Gnostic co-operation in the production of the constituents of the Leucian corpus. For while the Acts of Thomas quite unashamedly exhibits its Gnostic origin, and those of John and Andrew, and probably of Peter also, if less pronouncedly, seem to come from similar sources, we find Tertullian accusing a Catholic presbyter of being the author of the 'Acts of Paul'.[2] Admittedly, this may not mean much more than that the book was officially rejected by the Montanist leaders in Asia Minor; but it enhances the recognition of the fluidity of the boundaries between Catholicism and Gnosticism amongst the Christians in Asia Minor. Dr. Bauer too in his chapter on Asia Minor starts his argument from the regional divisions of Asia Minor, which he then attempts to equate with doctrinal divisions. Whilst reserving our judgment as far as Asiatic Gnosticism is concerned, I would state that this method is of great importance in the analysis of the fundamental crisis which was experienced by Asiatic Christianity at the rise of Montanism.

Montanism, it has to be remembered, started as a regional movement. Its earliest name, I believe, was 'the heresy according to the Phrygians', the 'Cataphrygian' heresy. This name, so it has been held by W. Schepelern,[3] a Danish scholar, whose study

---

[1] Cf. James, op. cit., p.228.

[2] James, op. cit., p.270.—The reprint of R. Lipsius-M. Bonnet, *Acta Apostolorum Apocrypha*, 1959, however welcome, must not blind us to the fact that a new edition, at least of the Acts of Paul, incorporating in particular all the new papyrological evidence, is an absolute necessity, Cf. also Peterson, *Frühkirche*, p.189f.

[3] W. Schepelern, *Der Montanismus und die phrygischen Kulte*, 1929, cf. K. Aland, *Z. N. W.* 46, 1955, p.109f., whose scepticism with regard to the connections between Montanism and the Phrygian cults established by Schepelern seems to me to be too radical. It is, on the other hand, useful to be reminded of the fact that millenarianism is an Asiatic doctrine, ibid., p.113f.—An evident parallel between the Attis mythos in Pausanias, VII.17.10–12 and in Arnobius, V.5–7 may be found in H. Hepding, *Attis, RVV*.1, 1903, p.37f.

seems to have found less attention than it deserves,[1] tells a tale:
The districts of Phrygia and Cappadocia, where the new movement started, undoubtedly held many Christian congregations,
but they were far less hellenized than, in particular, the two 'senatorial' provinces of Asia and Bithynia.[2] Although it seems true
to say that Dr. Bauer has greatly exaggerated the relative failure
of Polycarp's attempts at expanding the influence of his Church
at Smyrna upon the other Christian communities of Asia
Minor (and incidentally has shown no reason why Smyrnaean
Christianity only should have been Catholic, when it is true
to say that local jealousies played an enormous part in all
secular, political affairs in Asia Minor), he was nevertheless quite
right in drawing his readers' attention to the struggles of Polycarp.[3] For it seems indeed most improbable that Smyrna of all
places should have exercised a spiritual control over the central districts of Asia Minor. It will be found, however, that
Melito of Sardes was striving for the (re-?) establishment of
such an influence on the part of his Church upon Phrygian
Christianity.

These cities in the province of Asia were, of course, centres
of Hellenistic civilization; but Phrygia was not deeply hellenized.
Underneath this thin veneer there continued a savage and ecstatic
religiosity, which nevertheless proved strangely attractive to the
more civilized inhabitants of the West.[4] From amongst the
adherents of these cults Montanus, who seems to have been a

---

[1] I notice with regret that J. Lebreton in Lebreton-Zeiller, *De la fin du 2e
siècle à la paix constantinienne*, 1946, p.35, has nowhere even quoted it.

[2] On the reason for this cf. my article 'Imperium und Humanitas' in *Studium
generale*, 1961, p.646f.

[3] Bauer, *Rechtgläubigkeit*, p.73f., has given a colourful description of Polycarp's various difficulties. This now led him to a conflict with Harnack about
Polycarp's controversy with Marcion. In this conflict honours are about even,
both parties holding too extreme views. Bauer has shown no evidence that
Marcionitism, as distinct from a somewhat vague Gnosticism which was quite
ready to reject at least one of its fathers, Cerinthus, was wide-spread in second-
century Asia Minor. Harnack has failed to show that this relative insignificance
of Marcionitism in the regions west of the River Halys, was to any great extent
due to Polycarp's efforts.

[4] Cf. Schepelern, op. cit., p.79f., especially on the 'prophetic' character of
the Phrygian religion.

pagan priest (of Cybele?),[1] was converted to Christianity together with his two prophetesses, Priscilla and Maximilla. This, I would suggest, points to a group conversion under religious leaders in a way comparable to the conversion of the Samaritans under Simon Magus, and with a similar effect upon 'organized Christianity'. This happened at a time not so very far removed from that earlier time when the district surrounding Sardes and stretching as far as Pergamum in the North-West, and Laodicea in the South-East, had been at least partly ministered to by an ambulant ministry, similar in kind to the wandering 'prophets' of the Didache,[2] as has been deduced from 2 and 3.John.[3] It is evident, therefore, that the trouble into which these Phrygian ecstatics and their 'prophets' were running, and which was partly caused by national religious tradition, was akin to that between 'the presbyter' and Diotrephes some fifty years earlier. However, the established local ministry was by this time much stronger than at the turn of the first century, largely because of the efforts of Polycarp and his contemporaries, and Montanism thus appears to us as a reactionary, not a progressive, movement.

Regarding the Catholic defence against the Montanist movement, Dr. Bauer voices his disgust at the two or three samples of it which Eusebius has preserved for posterity in his *Ecclesiastical History*,[4] and in this we cannot but join him wholeheartedly. The use of calumny and special pleading as well as the apparent lack of all pity, let alone any kind of fellow-feeling, for the numerous

---

[1] The sources for Montanus' pagan priesthood are an express statement to the effect in Didym., *De trin.* III, 41, cf. N. Bonwetsch, *Texte z. Gesch. d. Montanismus*, 1914, p.23, and his description as 'abscissum et semivirum Montanum' in Jerome, *Epist. ad Marcellum*, XLI.4, ed. J. Labourt vol.2, 1951, p.89. The antischismatic fervour of the Church Fathers did not cool down in the course of the fourth century, and we have to use our discretion with regard to their assertions. It seems, however, unmethodical to reject their statements without giving the reasons for so doing, as in K. Müller-v. Campenhausen, *Kirchengesch.* vol.1, 3rd ed., 1938f., p.172, n.2.

[2] Did. 11:1f.

[3] Dodd, *Johannine Epistles*, LXVIII, stresses the fact that 2. & 3.John 'were written in the same province of Asia, and very likely addressed to the same churches' as Revelation. Cf. also my reference to the—anti-Montanist—list of succession of Christian prophets in Asia Minor, *Apostolic Succession*, p.69.

[4] Bauer, *Rechtgläubigkeit*, pp.136–49, discussing Euseb., *E.H.*, V.16–18.

Montanist martyrs is simply appalling, and it is difficult to find any argument in favour of such polemics, even if the Montanists themselves, as Dr. Bauer surmises,[1] attacked the Catholics in a similar manner. It is, however, questionable whether this type of polemics arose already before the Church at large had withdrawn from the communion with the Montanists. For it appears that both the anti-Montanist Anonymus and Apollonius, the two witnesses of Eusebius, belong to a later period.[2] Consequently the doctrinal conflict seems to have lost its interest for the somewhat barren and primitive minds of these two writers who now saw no other task left open to them than that of discrediting their adversaries. However, a doctrinal conflict undoubtedly had existed, and it seems to have been conducted in a much more objective way by both Melito of Sardes and Apollinaris of Hierapolis.[3] It may have been no more than a regrettable accident that Eusebius found in Pamphilus' library no other anti-Montanist writings than the two low specimens which he has quoted. We learn from him, however, that the applicability of Revelation to the 'new prophecy' formed one of the issues which had been hotly discussed;[4] and it is interesting—if somewhat puzzling—to notice how the anti-Montanist Roman presbyter Caius[5] summed up the anti-Montanist polemics of his Asiatic allies, the Alogi, by ascribing the canonical book of Revelation to that Gnostic archheretic Cerinthus.[6] There is, therefore, at least some possibility that the Montanists had made good their claim that their 'new prophecy' was of the same kind as that of John the Divine.

Two conclusions are at hand from these our considerations

---

[1] Bauer, op. cit., p.148.

[2] Bauer, op. cit., p.136, gives the last decade of the second century as the date of both writings.

[3] Melito seems to have written three tracts dealing with Montanism, the titles of which have been preserved by Euseb., *E.H.*, IV.26.2, 'On conduct of life and prophecy', 'On the Church', and 'On prophecy', and it is remarkable that Tertullian is represented as 'praising his elegant rhetoric' by Jerome, *De vir. ill.*,24. On Apollinaris cf. Euseb., *E.H.*, V.19.1f.,

[4] Euseb., *E.H.*, V.18.14.

[5] Euseb., *E.H.*, II.25.6.

[6] For a complete collection of relevant sources cf. Leipoldt, op. cit., pp. 43-7.

about the development of Christianity in Asia Minor during the Montanist crisis. The first is that in addition to the 'Apostolic' ministry, which in the synods about Montanism and in the polemical literature against it played a significant part on the Catholic side in the contest, it was the closing of the 'Apostolic' canon of sacred books, which prevented the 'new prophecy' of the 'Cataphrygians' from making its mark in the Catholic Church. The second is that even in the doctrinal conflict about the Holy Spirit and the Church no recourse to any 'Apostolic' credal formula was made. It appears in fact that the boundaries between Catholicism and Gnosticism at any rate were too fluid in Asia Minor during the second century to warrant any attempt at the conception of such a formula. For only in this way can it be understood that the allegation of Cerinthus' authorship of Revelation could be credibly made by Caius, a member of the Roman clergy enjoying great authority far beyond his own Church, without his being deposed or excommunicated for making it.

IV

The Formation of the Creed and the Church of Rome

If our analysis is correct it shows that the two great crises of Christianity in the second century, the Gnostic crisis and the Montanist crisis, were different in kind from all the later heresies which beset the Church in the Roman Empire in the subsequent centuries of its existence. They were not caused by misapprehension of any specific doctrines, but rather by the two dangers which of necessity accompany the Church on its way through human history. The one, represented by Gnosticism in all its various forms, is the danger of a mystic rationalism or rationalistic mysticism, which concentrates its efforts upon the fact that the Saviour, the Son of God, is the Logos, the highest ideal of reason. The other, which is all the more dangerous because its necessity for the Christian life is more easily recognized than the pernicious effects of its abuse, came to the surface most clearly in the terrifying eruption of Montanism. This is the danger of sentimental enthusiasm or enthusiastic sentimentality, which took its origin from the recognition that He who calls men into communion with God, is the Holy Spirit, the Spirit of Love which is the very essence of God, the Spirit of that God who is Love. Over against these two, Catholicism, the form of Christianity which we have chosen for our starting point, insisted very markedly upon the fact that it is the Church of the Father, the God of Law and peace, who is not a God of disorder, but of peace.[1] It has to be stressed, however, that excessive legalism may lead into heresy—of a Judaeo-Christian type—just as easily as the over-emphasis laid on reason and the Logos in Gnosticism, or on enthusiasm and the Spirit in Montanism, had done.

It is thus clearly not enough that our considerations have shown us that Gnosticism, Montanism, and Catholicism are the three sources of the trinitarian Creed which, existing as they did from Apostolic time—even if the crisis of the 'Cataphrygian' prophecy did not come to a head till a hundred years later—gave rise to the various attempts made during the first hundred years of Christianity to create such a formula summarizing the convictions contained in the 'fides quae creditur'. No more has it been sufficient simply to point out that group conversions, as of the Samaritans in Gnosticism, which was its cause as Catholic theologians from the days of Justin Martyr down have always maintained,[2] so of the Phrygians in Montanism, were responsible for the catastrophic over-emphasis which ensued in both cases. We feel that due attention should also be given to the claim of Dr. Bauer that it was the particular Roman character of Western Catholicism which crushed these two movements, and perilously over-weighed the requirements of Law and organization in the resulting Catholic Church. His theory is that it was the imperialistic character of the Church at Rome and its power politics, which by establishing its rigid organization, based upon an early conceived and formulated 'rule of faith', throughout the Christian congregations of the East made Catholicism victorious even

[1] 1.Cor.14:33, cf. Hermas, *Mand.* 1.1.
[2] Cf. Wilson, op. cit., p.99.—As to the exact type of Simon's 'Gnosticism', cf. the quotation from L. Cerfaux, ibid., p.109, n.5.

in those regions where primarily another Gospel and a freer organization of the faithful had been the rule.[1] It should be seen in particular, so Dr. Bauer claims, that the part played by men like Ignatius, Polycarp, and Dionysius of Corinth in establishing 'organized Christianity' in their respective spheres of influence in the course of the second century would be inexplicable, and their lasting renown in the Catholic Church impossible, if they had not acted as the confidants of that ambitious Church at Rome.

In stating at once that this conclusion of Dr. Bauer's seems to be very far from the truth I have to apologize for the fact that within my limits of space only the most cursory enquiry into the early history of the Church at Rome can be given. I feel, however, that the chief reason for Dr. Bauer's failure to grasp what is really behind the evolution of 'organized Christianity' is that he has nowhere given an account of the character and the organization of the Church at Rome in the second century, as has been done for the end of that century by G. La Piana.[2] La Piana's article has in fact invalidated such earlier research into second-century Roman Christianity as has in one way or another influenced the judgment on Roman Church policy by numerous Church-Historians.[3] One illustration only may be given in order to show the comprehensiveness of the Church at Rome in the second century, that of Valentinus' stay at Rome.[4] For about twenty years this head of one of the most influential Gnostic schools had his habitat at Rome and was to all intents and purposes a member of the

---

[1] Bauer, *Rechtgläubigkeit*, p.99f.

[2] G. La Piana, *Harv. Theol. Rev.*, 1925, p.276f.

[3] I do not refer to such productions of an excited imagination as G. Edmundson, *The Church in Rome in the First Century*, 1913, or H. D. M. Spence-Jones, *The Early Christians in Rome*, 1910, although traces of their influence may be found, e.g., in R. Smith Wilson, *Marcion*, 1933, p.19f.; but rather to an attitude which is expressed even in such a meritorious treatise as H. E. Symonds, *The Church Universal and the See of Rome*, 1939, p.51f., or in that great book by Caspar, *Gesch. d. Papsttums*, vol. 1, p.2f., both of which, like Bauer, treat 1.Clement as the representative document of early Roman Church policy, although it seems that for almost a century it found no successor, and an equivalent perhaps only in the correspondence between the two Dionysii of Rome and Alexandria in the second half of the third century.

[4] Cf. Grobel, *Gospel of Truth*, op. cit., p.12f.

Catholic Church there. He was even, so Tertullian asserts,[1] seriously considered as a candidate for the Roman see; and Tertullian's concurrent statement that he was 'once or twice' ('semel et iterum') ejected from that Church does not seem to me to carry much weight.[2] The common Christian within the Roman Christian community may have felt much uneasiness about what was going on in the various Christian schools there, for he seems to have voiced it in the *Shepherd* by Hermas.[3] The situation showed, on the other hand, much similarity to that of the Gnostic teachers in the Churches in Asia Minor, who were attacked by Ignatius at a slightly earlier date.[4] The school-heads there and at Rome were, however, not ejected, but rather the opposite. They aspired to the first ranks in the general congregation, if they demeaned themselves to attend it, and Hermas had angrily to admit that they obtained them. All this appears to me as a fitting background to Valentinus' teaching and candidature at Rome, which are roughly contemporary to the later parts of the *Shepherd*; but it casts a shadow of doubt upon the homogeneity of the Church at Rome in the middle of the second century, at least in matters of doctrine.

Returning to Dr. Bauer, his first and indeed very weighty argument in favour of his thesis is the theological character of that

---

[1] Tertullian, *De praescr.* 30.

[2] Tertullian, op. cit.; Grobel, loc. cit., tries to make sense of the remark, which in the first instance refers to Marcion whose banishment from the Roman Church is, of course, an established fact, cf. E. C. Blackman, *Marcion and his Influence*, 1948, p.1f., but was caused by his resignation, if we may trust Epiphan., *Adv. Haer.*, XLII.2. In the case of Valentinus Tertullian may have done no more than to venture a conclusion by analogy.

[3] Hermas, *Mand.* 11.—M. Dibelius, *Handb. z. N.T., Erg. Bd.*, 1923, p.538, assumes that προφητεύειν in *Mand.* 11:12 has the meaning of 'predict the future'. This I find hard to believe not only because of the analogy of Did.11.12, but particularly because of the widespread conviction among the ancients that it was immoral to teach for money. Did.13:1, quoted by M. Dibelius, op. cit., p.539, seems to me to deal with a very different situation, and to have no bearing upon our case.

[4] Ign., *Eph.* 8:1; *Smyrn.* 4:1, may indeed refer to migrating 'prophets' as R. Knopf, *Handb. z. N.T., Erg. Bd.*, 1920, p.206, assumes, but the Judaeo-Christian teachers who are mentioned in Ign., *Philad.* 6:1, were evidently resident ones.

earliest document of the sub-Apostolic Church at Rome, the First Epistle of Clement so-called. It cannot be doubted that this epistle made a profound impression upon two Eastern Churches, the Church at Corinth, which was the recipient, and the Church at Antioch, where it engendered the Pseudo-Clementine literature, if somewhat belatedly, only in the second half of the second century.[1] A resounding blow for Roman supremacy was thus struck, and Dr. Bauer claims that this was also the purpose of the epistle. He argues as follows: The immediate cause for writing the epistle was a clearly defined, and perhaps not even particularly important conflict in the Church at Corinth. However, the epistle hardly deals with this at all, but consists of a long-drawn-out doctrinal exposition, scarcely connected with the real issue. This, Dr. Bauer says, shows that Rome already at that juncture claimed the doctrinal supremacy even over Churches of Apostolic foundation.

I have heard this argument before,[2] and have been amazed both at its inconclusiveness and its persuasiveness. For it could be argued at least as well that not the doctrinal exposition, which nowhere claims to be authoritative, but a definite interference in its disciplinary affairs would show that the Church at Corinth was subject to Roman supremacy. Yet the infinite tact and caution shown when dealing with the matter in hand proves that Rome claimed no such authority.[3] This interpretation finds support from the fact that Ignatius, almost at the same time, sent out a whole bundle of hortatory letters, indiscriminately to Churches of Apostolic and later foundation, dealing with Church organization,

[1] Even in the course of the third century an uncertainty about the authority of Clement of Rome seems still to have existed in the East-Syrian Church: The *Doctrina Addai* maintains that Palût was consecrated first bishop of Edessa at the hands of Serapion of Antioch, who in turn had received consecration from Zephyrinus of Rome, 'whom Simon Cephas . . . had selected as his successor', Bauer, *Rechtgläubigkeit*, p.22. This description seems to me to clash somehow with that of 'Clement, the disciple of Simon Cephas' in the East-Syrian Acts of Clement ed. A. Mingana, 'Some early Judaeo-Christian Documents', *The Bull. of the John Rylands Library*, 4, 1917, p.10.

[2] Cf., e.g., the quotation from A. Loisy in S. Herbert Scott, *The Eastern Church and the Papacy*, 1928, p.16f., who adopts it.

[3] A very cautious assessment of the authority of the Church at Rome according to 1.Clem., to which on the whole I would subscribe, may be found in W.K. Lowther Clarke, *The First Epistle of Clement*, 1937, p.18f.

discipline and doctrine. Neither is there any evidence that it was the authority of the martyr which he used to justify this practice, although he was conscious of it, and it certainly had an effect upon the recipients. The same appears to me to be the case with regard to the first paragraph of 1 Clement, which by implication aspires to the same authority.[1] The analogy between 1 Clement and Ignatius can also be shown from the effect of the example which they set. For just as Dionysius of Corinth valued 1 Clement,[2] so was Polycarp of Smyrna under the spell of Ignatius and his epistles, and both these bishops were prompted by their respective authorities to embark upon a correspondence offering spiritual guidance to other Churches. I believe, therefore, that 1 Clement has to be seen not in isolation, but against the background of all the other early Christian epistles, even including the 'Letters to the Seven Churches' from Revelation, the Epistle to the Hebrews, and St. Paul's Epistle to the Romans. It will then become clear that the step taken by the Church at Rome was less extraordinary than it appears to be. It will also be realized that the one uncommon feature of 1 Clement (which it shares with the Epistle to the Hebrews), a feature which at the same time is very Roman, its anonymity by which the name of the author was suppressed in favour of the name of the Church at Rome, has so far hardly found sufficient attention, because his name was preserved by reliable secondary tradition.—But even if 1 Clement is treated in isolation it will not bear out Dr. Bauer's thesis of Roman intolerance in cases of doctrinal divergencies. For the epistle rejects expressly the excommunication by the refusal of hospitality, as we have found it in 2. and 3.John. It says of the leaders of the 'young men' at Corinth, who had apparently started the trouble in the Church: 'If anyone will do so,' i.e. go into voluntary exile, 'he will obtain great glory in Christ, and all the world will receive him.'[3] Whether or not Harnack and

---

[1] 1.Clem.1:1, 'owing to the sudden and repeated misfortunes which have befallen us, brethren, we are somewhat late, we think, in concerning ourselves with the matters disputed among you. . . .'

[2] Cf. Euseb., *E.H.*, IV.29.11.

[3] 1.Clem.54:3, cf. my *Politische Metaphysik*, vol.2, p.56, n.5.—'To receive' is

Lietzmann were right in maintaining that no doctrinal issue was involved in the Corinthian conflict[1]—and I frankly confess that I am very doubtful about this—the Church at Rome offered the leaders of the rebellion Christian hospitality throughout the oecumene. By whatever authority this offer may have been made, it certainly does not look like drawing rigid boundaries between Catholics and schismatics or heretics.

Dr. Bauer tries to reinforce his argument by reference to the famous excommunication of all the Churches in Asia Minor by Pope Victor I in the so-called third Easter conflict.[2] It appears, I venture to say, to be somewhat unmethodical to connect this event with the sending of the First Epistle of Clement to the Church at Corinth, which had taken place almost a century earlier. For personalities and conditions had substantially changed in the course of these one hundred or slightly less years. Especially in Asia Minor the Montanist crisis had brought about a considerable consolidation of 'organized Christianity' which, according to the whole tenor of Eusebius' *Ecclesiastical History*, regarded itself as the Catholic Church in Asia Minor, and was so regarded by its sister Churches. Rome, on the other hand, had established her supremacy in the Latin-speaking West, as Irenaeus and Tertullian testify, probably by means of its creation of 'Vetus Latina', the earliest Latin translation of the Bible including the New Testament.[3] In the beginnings of the Montanist struggle, and throughout

here expressed by the simplex δέχεσθαι, cf. above, p.169, n.4. It is nevertheless certain that the canonical duty of hospitality is referred to here as in 3.John 10.

[1] Harnack, *Einführung in die alte Kirchengesch.*, 1929, p.92; H. Lietzmann, *Gesch. d. alten Kirche*, vol.1, 1932, p.201, both quoted with approval by Bauer, *Rechtgläubigkeit*, 100, who, however, continues, 'das "Amt" war in Gefahr und Rom stellt sich schützend davor'. To liberal Lutheranism, of course, the ministry appears as *adiaphoron*, and not as a doctrinal issue. But was that really the attitude of the early Church?

[2] Bauer, *Rechtgläubigkeit*, p. 101f., cf. S. L. Greenslade, *Schism in the early Church*, 1953, p.99f.

[3] It is salutary for those stressing too much the importance of the liturgy for the development of the Church to consider the fact that the Roman liturgy was, at least in parts, celebrated in Greek till the middle of the fourth century, cf. Th. Klauser, *Miscellanea Mercati*, I, 1946, p.467f., quoted from Chr. Mohrmann, *Études sur le Latin des Chrétiens*, I, 1958, p.54, n.7, whilst the Latin Bible had been in existence for almost 200 years. For it follows from this that the Roman

most of its duration,[1] the Western Church had wavered in its attitude towards the 'new prophecy'; it is even possible that the martyrs at Lyons had actually favoured it.[2] Rome finally came to the conclusion that she must sever her relations with the Montanists not, as we hear from Tertullian, by the free and unbiased decision of Pope Victor I, but moved by the influence of the confessor Praxeas, who himself was an Easterner, and not a resident member of the Roman Church.[3] It also appears probable that it was Praxeas, and not Pope Victor himself, who established the doctrinal basis for this decision with an undeniable admixture of monarchianism. The Roman Pope, it seems, was at this time rather reluctant to formulate any doctrine unless he was compelled to do so.[4]

Having broken off Rome's relations with the Montanists, and in doing so reversed his earlier decision,[5] Pope Victor, so we may

---

Church neither feared nor suffered any harm from this practice for maintaining her primacy over the West; but translations of the Bible into the vernacular, Gallic or Berber, tongues would have been dangerous, and were never encouraged.—The Latin version, including the O.T., had existed at Rome since the second half of the second century, as Mohrmann, op. cit., p.109f., has shown. Whether or not there had been an independent Latin version of the Bible originating from Africa, I am not certain, but the results of G. Bardy, *La question des langues dans l'église ancienne*, I, 1948, p.58f., should not be treated as final.

[1] It appears from Tertullian, *Adv. Prax*, I, that Pope Eleutherus had actually taken a stand against Montanism, cf. Evans, *Tertullian's treatise*, op. cit., p.76, but that his successor, Victor I, was almost prevailed upon to reverse this policy. The interpretation of the veiled allusion in Tertullian's words, 'et praecessorum eius auctoritates defendendo', cf. Evans, op. cit., p.185, is still a very thorny task.

[2] Euseb., *E.H.* V.3, was evidently reluctant to give a verbatim quotation from the martyrs' letter although, no doubt, it was extant in Pamphilus' library. This observation supports the view of Evans, op. cit., p.76, n.1. which has been adopted here.

[3] Evans, op. cit., p.10. His suggestion, somewhat hesitantly made, that Praxeas 'is a nick-name designed to cover some well-known person, possibly Calixtus, who afterwards became Pope', seems unacceptable if we believe Tertullian that Praxeas came from the East.

[4] The appreciation of Zephyrinus' attitude in the monarchian controversy between Hippolytus and Callistus by Dom G. Dix, *The Treatise on the Apostolic Tradition*, 1937, XXIII f., is meant to be, and to my mind is, representative for the general attitude to doctrine taken by the Popes of this time.

[5] G. Krüger, *Handb. d. Kirchengesch.* vol.1, 2nd ed., 1923, p.84, n.1, says that it

reasonably assume, expected a certain amount of gratitude and good will on the part of the Catholics in Asia Minor when he now turned to that urgent problem of the Church at Rome, the Easter date.[1] It is, however, equally reasonable to assume that the Churches in Asia Minor had not forgotten Rome's vacillations during their recent predicament, and therefore remembered all the more vividly how Polycarp of Smyrna in A.D. 154, perhaps forty years earlier, had celebrated the (Easter?) Mass at Rome on their Easter date, the fourteenth of Nisan, at the express invitation of the then Pope Anicetus.[2] On the other hand, it is yet one more reasonable assumption that Pope Victor had not forgotten that he had almost excommunicated the now recalcitrant Asiatics, and thrown in his lot with the Montanists, not so long ago. It may even be that the doctrinal differences about Praxeas' monarchian heresy contributed to sharpen his resentment at not having done so.[3] These personal points have to be taken into consideration when it is claimed that it was nonetheless the general character of the Roman Church which showed itself in the third Easter conflict.

Dr. Bauer has made this claim, and in order to elucidate and support it has referred to the Roman doctrine of the Apostolic succession of the Roman bishops after St. Peter and St. Paul.[4] It is, of course, quite impossible once more to take up the problem of the Apostolic succession, and all that can be done here is to give an analysis of the influence this doctrine had upon the conflict between Pope Victor I of Rome and the Catholic Churches

---

is 'probable' that Victor excommunicated the Montanists. Surely, scepticism is not criticism.

[1] Cf. G. La Piana, *Harv. Theol. Rev.*, 1925, p.276f.; Greenslade, *Schism*, op. cit., 99f.

[2] Irenaeus in Euseb., *E.H.* V.24.16.—I disagree with the discussion of this incident by earlier historians of the Church, still to be found in Greenslade, op. cit., p.99, because I do not believe that the feast of Easter was at that time annually kept at Rome.

[3] If K. Holl, *Ges. Aufsätze*, vol.2, 1928, p.194, should be right, which I doubt, even the earliest British Church would have embraced already at this time the Quartadeciman cause, and thus have asserted its independence from the Church at Rome.

[4] Bauer, *Rechtgläubigkeit*, p.115f.

of Asia Minor. In this respect two things have to be distinguished. The first is the justifiable pride of the Church at Rome at being the guardian of the 'trophies' of the martyrdom of the two chief Apostles, St. Peter and St. Paul, and in this sense a Church of Apostolic foundation. It is evident from a letter written by Poly-crates of Ephesus that Pope Victor in his epistle to the Asian Churches concerning the Easter date had made use of this argu-ment with great vigour, in preference to the second that he him-self was the successor of these great Apostles.[1] The effect of Victor's plea proved, however, to be negligible, for the bishop of Ephesus coolly replied that Asia Minor was at least as great a repository of Apostolic remains as Rome, and then proceeded to enumerate them. What was the reason that Pope Victor refrained from basing his authority upon the unbroken list of succession of Roman bishops? There can be no doubt that such a list, beginning with St. Peter and St. Paul, was in his day officially circulated by the Church at Rome. The testimony of Irenaeus makes this quite clear.[2] Why then, we ask again, did Victor hesitate to support the Italian decision about the right date of Easter by this means? The answer seems to be that the observation of the feast of Easter had begun in the Church at Rome only within living memory, prob-ably as late as A.D. 170, whereas in the Churches of Asia Minor it did go right back to Apostolic times.[3] The Apostolic succession at Rome was thus unsupported by a concurrent tradition, and conse-quently not sufficiently authoritative. Another Church, however, Jerusalem, was less squeamish: Although it is evident that its custom to celebrate Easter on a Sunday, as in Rome, was contrary to the earlier, sub-Apostolic usage there, and had only arisen in its gentile-Christian Church when after A.D. 135 no circumcized person was allowed to visit Jerusalem more than once a year, bishop Narcissus of Jerusalem together with the other Palestinian bishops claimed the authority of their Apostolic tradition and suc-

---

[1] Euseb., *E.H.*, V.22.2f.—It appears from my analysis of Polycrates' letter, *Apostolic Succession*, op. cit., p.66f., that Polycrates, and presumably the entire Catholic Church in Asia Minor, had as yet at best only a somewhat hazy con-ception of the doctrine of the Apostolic succession of bishops.

[2] Irenaeus, *Adv. Haer.*, III.3.2, cf. my *Apostolic Succession*, 38f.

[3] Cf. Müller-v. Campenhausen, *Kirchengesch.*, vol.1, p.226f.

cession for it.[1] This makes us hesitate to admit that the basing of his decision upon his 'Apostolic' authority showed Victor's typically Roman attitude. I would rather suggest that Victor had seriously misjudged the situation. Himself an African, coming from a province which traditionally recognized the Roman primacy,[2] he naturally expected that the Eastern Churches would do the same, and was most painfully disappointed.[3] Victor thus had committed a major diplomatic blunder, even though the Quartadeciman practice in Asia Minor was subsequently abandoned, and this was long remembered. Sixty years later clear vestiges of resentment against Roman presumptuousness may still be found in the letter by Firmilian of Caesarea in Cappadocia to Cyprian when Pope Stephen of Rome once more tried 'to cut off whole Churches of God'.[4]

From what we have seen so far it follows that the influence of the Church at Rome, such as it was,[5] did not aim at a doctrinal unification, although the successful elimination of Montanism, and before that of Marcion and his followers, must not be overlooked.[6] Thus it seems doubtful from the start that this Church

---

[1] The facts have been carefully assembled and discussed by K. Holl, *Gesammelte Aufsätze*, vol. 2, 1928, p.215f.

[2] Tertullian, *De praescr.* 36, cf. Cyprian, *De unitate* 4; *Epist.* LIX.5, and B. J. Kidd, *The Roman Primacy*, 1936, p.29, n.1.

[3] I would suggest that the attitude of Irenaeus, himself an Asiatic, who by this time had made public his recognition of the Roman primacy, *Adv. Haer.*, III.3.1, but nevertheless now 'fittingly exhorted him not to cut off whole Churches of God . . . and he wrote to many other bishops on the same subject', Euseb., *E.H.*, V.24.11f., cf. Symonds, op. cit., p.54f., was probably the cause for the petering out of the conflict. A similar view is held by Krüger, op. cit., p.89, n.3, who even assumes that by Irenaeus' intervention 'peace was restored', a fact which is not recorded by Eusebius, our only source.

[4] Cyprian, *Epist.* LXXXV.

[5] The strongest signs of the Roman influence upon the Church universal are not to be found in the actions of the Roman Popes, nor in Rome's literary production, although not only the Pseudo-Clementines, but also the numerous writings ascribed to Justin Martyr in the East witness to its considerable influence upon Christian thought there, but its great attractiveness for so many prominent Christians, orthodox as well as heterodox: Marcion, Valentinus, Hegesippus, Justin, Polycarp, Tatian, and many more came on a visit or for a more prolonged stay.

[6] As far as I can see, Bauer, *Rechtgläubigkeit*, has omitted to deal with Justin,

should have been responsible for the spreading of the Apostles' Creed, and Dr. Bauer has understandably refrained from enquiring into the propagation of the Roman 'regula fidei'. This is nevertheless to be regretted, even if it is true to say that the conclusions drawn by F. Kattenbusch from his considerable collections of material,[1] which some fifty years ago were widely accepted by Church historians, have now been discarded in so far as they refer to the Roman origin of the Apostles' Creed.[2] There is no more time here to enter into this question. Let it be sufficient to state that by and large we accept the verdict by the Principal of St. Edmund's Hall, Oxford, 'in itself the theory of the sudden codification of the Church's belief, even in so go-ahead a community as that of Rome, shortly after A.D. 100 is improbable.'[3]

A short summary may, perhaps, be welcome to show what has been attempted in this chapter: It appears as a miracle that, in contrast, for example, to Buddhism in East Asia, where right from the beginning numerous doctrinal and regional groups were formed whose tenets and traditions bear hardly any resemblance to each other, Christianity in all its denominations has maintained its spiritual unity. The danger here was no less than in Buddhism, for right from its earliest days there existed numerous traditions about Jesus Christ, and several attempts to concentrate the essentials of the new faith in a short formula did not meet with unanimous approval. Group conversions and personal jealousies in their turn threatened Christian unity, and the mysticism of the Gnosis as well as the asceticism of the Cataphrygians, these inevitable companions of all new religious movements, showed an extraordinarily strong disruptive force. The unity of Christianity was not preserved by outward means. Pre-baptismal instruction

---

1.*Apol.*, 26; 58, and the curious refund of Marcion's donation by the Church at Rome, Tertullian, *De praescr.*30, cf. J. Stevenson, *A new Eusebius*, 1957, p.98f.

[1] F. Kattenbusch, *Das apostolische Symbol*, 1894–1900.

[2] Badcock, op. cit., p.1f.

[3] Kelly, op. cit., p.63.—It may, however, be remarked first, that the idea of the Apostolicity of the *regula fidei* was probably evolved in the Roman Church; and secondly that Hermas, *Mand.* I.1, shows a remarkable similarity with the first article of the Apostles' Creed, both, of course, dependent upon the First Commandment.

was, of course, given from an early time onward, and credal formulae were evolved for the purpose, as a 'disciplina arcani'; but it was only after some considerable time that they found a somewhat uncertain place in the baptismal liturgy. For Baptism was not originally considered as an admission rite, a 'rite of initiation', demanding the conscious assent of the candidate, but rather as the free gift of regeneration in the Holy Spirit, made to the neophyte by the heavenly Father. The Latin Church made the closest approach to the doctrine of contractual assent in Baptism,[1] and it is to the eternal glory of Pope Stephen of Rome that he resisted this tendency, and recognized heretical baptism. This reveals that the Creed even at that late date was not considered as a constituent part of Baptism, since the heretics would not have used it, but only as declaratory, and almost accidental. Whence then came its authority? In answer to this question it should be considered that there is no evidence for it to have been used as a touch-stone of orthodoxy anywhere before the end of the second century, but that in the terrible days of persecution the martyrs —and indeed the whole Church—needed a short formula of their faith; and the Holy Spirit taught them what to say, as Jesus Himself had promised.[2]

[1] Cf. chapter 10 below.
[2] Luke 12:12.

9

CREATIO EX NIHILO

I

GOD created this world out of nothing. This statement which, as a rule, theologians will pass as a genuine interpretation of Gen.1:1, 'in the beginning God created the heaven and the earth', deserves a critical inspection. In this essay the attempt will be made, to show that these two statements, so far from being identical, are largely contradictory, and that the first involves us in consequences which Christian theology has to qualify and often to avoid altogether. The stubbornness with which biblical, and in particular Old Testament, tradition preserved the formula that God 'created the heaven and the earth, the sea and all that in them is',[1] will appear to exhibit a healthy and, indeed, a very necessary reserve towards the more scientific language which asserts that God created the world out of nothing.

It is commonly known that the ancient Hebrew language had no word which might serve as an adequate equivalent for the modern term of 'universe', and it has been said by critics that this was due to a certain lack of philosophical insight. However that may be, it is highly significant that a religious literature of the high standard of the Old Testament never felt the need for describing the entirety of God's creation by one single term. For thereby it is shown that the idea of 'all things' or of the universe is a product of philosophical considerations which are not common to all mankind.

Indeed, the popular idea of a universe comprising 'all things visible and invisible' will not stand close examination. It starts from the assumption that 'all things' may be subjected to one ordering principle which, in the case of the modern popular idea

[1] Exod.20:11, cf. Nehem. 9:6; Ps.146:6; Jonah 1:9; Acts 4:24; 14:15; Rev. 10:6; 14:7.

of the universe, is that of number. Once the fact has been clearly grasped, it becomes very questionable whether numbers can in all cases be applied as an ordering principle. For even if we neglect the moral and spiritual side of God's creation, the thoughts and desires, the impressions and sentiments, the 'thrones or dominions or principalities' (Col.1:16), it is still true that there are physical phenomena like rays or waves or energies, to which the principle of number, if at all, can be applied only in a special way, very different from that which is used for the measuring of quantities. There are also indeterminate quantities and, in short, the whole principle breaks down when confronted with the complexity of those phenomena which are open to human observation. Consequently, the words 'all' or 'universe', when used for the totality of God's creation, should be regarded as a convenient but at the same time wholly inadequate expression, if they are meant in the sense of the whole number of things created by God. The accusation of a philosophical deficiency on the part of Hebrew religious thought may, therefore, recoil upon those who regard the formulation of this idea of one universe as an accomplishment of human progress.

Furthermore, the accusation is, perhaps, even incorrect in some way. For at least in one instance, under the influence of Greek thought, a biblical writer has used the term *'olam* for a description of the 'universe'. If such was the case, he came very close to a certain mode of thought which was found among the early Teutons, if we may trust the results of modern etymology. For our English word 'world' is a compound of two elements, 'wer-alde', the first meaning 'man'—akin to the Latin 'vir'—and the second 'age', etymologically the same as 'old'. The world, therefore, was to the ancient Teutons the 'age of man', the time for man, the stage set for human history. In this conception it was not the principle of number, but that of history or—to use a less common but perhaps more adequate term—of dispensation, which was used as a common denominator of all things created. The world as such, the objectively existing system of things created, was neglected in favour of a world for man, a world which was the field of human activity, the world as man's task. In short, the mathematical approach was replaced by the moral approach.

It is evident that in the conception of the universe as the world the time factor plays the decisive part, and in particular one of its aspects, the present. Neither the origin nor the final destiny of the universe are taken into consideration. Nor has the attempt been made to combine all the items which may possibly exist, but have not yet been discovered, under the supreme principle, which is man as he exists here and now. If we criticize the popular idea of 'all things' or universe because of the actual inadequacy of the principle of number, but may yet hold that a more complicated mathematical process might be evolved which unites all things created under one common mathematical principle, we can definitely state that the idea of the world defeats its own object. For, as the moral decision is taken here and now, the stage for human activities is constantly changing. Just now we have passed from a pre-atomic age into an atomic age, and thus the world has a radically different aspect from what it was twenty years ago. The same is true about the geographical discoveries of old and will be true with regard to the expected inter-planetary discoveries of the future. The world in this sense will not be the same in the future as it has been in the past. This consideration is essential even now in the field of history, essential in particular when examples of the past are discussed as models for any future moral conduct. The idea of 'the world' as used by the historians is totally different from the scientific aspect of the universe: inferior with regard to its range, yet superior insofar as it attempts to include man himself and in particular the moral side of his being which, as we have seen, is excluded from the scientific conception of the universe.

With the incessant change which is characteristic for this moral, historical aspect of the world, there is, however, one constant factor, we might even say a mathematical factor: that of time. In the two cases in which the Old Testament literature attempted to state an idea which would embrace the entirety of all things created, under one single heading, it appears from the two terms used that this common denominator of time was in the mind of the writers. For the expressions used for this purpose, *cheled* and *'olam*, both

denoted the eternity of time—not just the time of man, the 'world'
—but probably all the ages since the day when 'in the beginning'
God created the heaven and the earth. Both these Hebrew words
are used, once each, in this way in the Old Testament, and Hellenistic influence is certain. The English versions using 'world'
frequently in the Old Testament are misleading, insofar as the
Hebrew has a more limited expression, earth, countries, etc. As a
matter of fact the case for *cheled* need not trouble us very much
either:

Ps.49:1 hear this all ye people, give ear all the inhabitants of *the world*.

For the LXX translated this term as 'oecumene,' as if it had been
Hebrew *tebel*, and *cheled* has not been used to mean 'world' again,
but only to mean 'life'. *'Olam*, on the other hand, assumed the
meaning of world in Rabbinic Judaism, and it is the use of this
term in Eccl. 3:11, which we have to consider now:

He has made everything beautiful in His time; also He has set the
world in their heart; so that no man can find out His work that God
maketh from the beginning to the end.

It is significant that the Greek confirmed the use of *'olam* as 'world'
in Eccl.3:11, by translating it by 'aeon', as follows:

He has also made the universe beautiful in His good time, and He has
given the aeon in their heart,
so that man should not find out
the work, that God has made from the beginning to the end.

'The world' in this context (aeon) is this world of perdition, the
phantom world of temporality. Aeon, the god of eternity, the
universal godhead of Alexandria,[1] is used as the travesty of the true
God, the creator of heaven and earth, with a palpable reference to
the Greek theory of micro- and macrocosm. For it was the Greeks
who believed that in the heart of the just man the true likeness
of the Divine world was engraved;[2] the author of Ecclesiastes,

[1] Cf. O. Weinreich, *Arch. Relig. Wiss.*, 19, 1919, p.189; E. Norden, *Die Geburt des Kindes*, 1924, p.24f.
[2] Cf. my 'Vir bonus quadrato lapidi comparatur', *Harv. Theol. Rev.*, 38, 1945, p.177f.

however, regarded it as the image of 'this aeon' only, which prevented man from perceiving the reality of God's creation. Obviously, the idea of the universe was consciously repudiated by him; but, insofar as he considered it, he saw it from the point of view of time. This was the view of the universe commonly taken in the Near East at the time when Ecclesiastes and the LXX were written.

This idea of the universe as a system 'in time' has to be understood as a deliberate if unsuccessful attempt at combining the universe of science and the world of history. However, an investigation into the objective existence of time will show that this idea of aeon does not work, although it has been held by many that time is entirely man-made, a standard for human thought only, and that therefore the conception of the universe as a system 'in time' is philosophically possible. Such views, so it seems, were held by the people who are criticized in Eccl.3:11. However, the purely subjective view of time is incorrect. For time must always have one fixed point to which it refers. It must be B.C. or A.D. Abstract time is nonsense. Time is, therefore, at least in one instant immanent in the world. For this reason it cannot serve as the principle of the world. Accordingly, if we endeavour to find a common denominator for the world, time being inadmissible, space, because of its close proximity to time, has to be rejected on analogous grounds. This has been recognized by modern physics which limits its arguments to a finite, if expanding, universe as the field in which human observations are valid. This view does not deny the existence of something created beyond those limits, but it questions the intelligible character of all the statements concerning it.[1]

II

A more promising attempt at combining the two conceptions of 'world' in a moral, historical sense and 'universe' in a scientific

[1] In a way this is a return to the idea of a multitude of universes, so prominently displayed by Lucretius, even if Prof. Einstein, *Antike und Abendland*, 2, 1946, p.198, rightly denies any immediate connection.

sense was made in Greek philosophy. For, although the word 'aeon' was a Greek word, the Greek approach to the idea of the universe was a different one. If the people of the Near East tried to derive the ordering principle from the idea of time, and thus came to the conclusion that the universe had a beginning (and possibly an ending) in time, or else that it would repeat itself periodically in exactly the same way from conflagration to conflagration, as the Stoics believed, or from conflagration to flood and flood to conflagration, as Plato (*Tim.*, 22B) had taught, apparently under the influence of oriental beliefs, the genuine Greek view maintained the eternity of the world. This means that the classical philosophy of Greece claimed that the cosmos as such was everlasting, although traces of other doctrines, assuming the creation of the world, and probably its annihilation in the future, have been discovered in early Greek theology. Under the classical Greek aspect time ceased to be of paramount significance for the conception of the universe. It had its importance for the arrangement of human history, but it was unsuited for an ordering principle of the universe as such. For the Greek claim was that the natural phenomena and the processes of nature should be fundamentally unchangeable, however manifold they were; and it was this conviction which formed the basis for the construction of the Greek idea of cosmos. In adopting this idea, and in rejecting that of the aeon, the Greeks seem to have made a conscious choice. For the convictions upon which the worship of the god Aeon of Alexandria rested were of long standing in the Near East and certainly not unknown to the classical philosophers of Greece.[1] The decision in favour of cosmos was ascribed by later generations to the great genius who is hidden behind the name of Pythagoras. If that should be true, his theory must have met with an immediate and general success. For according to the evidence of our sources, the earliest philosophers who used cosmos in the sense of universe did not belong to the Pythagorean school. They were

---

[1] Cf. R. Reitzenstein, *Hellenist. Myster. Relig.*, 3rd ed., 1927, p.180; E. Peterson, *Heis Theos*, 1926, p.296f; W. Bousset-Gressmann, *Relig. d. Judent.*, 3rd ed., 1926, p.243f.—A Jewish tribute to *Aeon* may be found in *Orac. Sib.*, 3, l.785f., cf. W. Weber, *Der Prophet und sein Gott*, 1925, p.59.

Anaximenes of Lampsacus, Heraclitus of Ephesus and the Sicilian Empedocles.[1]

The term *cosmos* was political. Its use arose together with the rise of the Greek city state. Homer had used it only in the sense of good order and ornament; but in the course of Greek history it came to denote the political constitution, especially in the early oligarchies. Therefore, when the term was chosen to mean the universe, it pointed to the analogy between the civil law and the universal law. This analogy is particularly impressive, when it is applied to the city on the one hand and the starry sky on the other; and it is indeed true that the earliest use of cosmos in the sense of universe, and perhaps even the Pythagorean use,[2] referred exclusively to the sky and the stars. This usage also continued until much later times, witness for instance the LXX, where in Deut.4:19 'all the host of heaven' was translated as πάντα τὸν κόσμον τοῦ οὐρανοῦ. The ordering principle of the universe was therefore, according to the view taken by classical Greek philosophy, the beauty of a good and firmly established order, which was manifest in the unchanging courses of the stars in the sky, and upon earth in the stability of the city state. In due course the permanent changes from summer to winter, day to night and birth to death were added to that number of unchangeable laws of nature upon which the idea of the cosmos was founded. The continuity of all these changes and movements suggested to the Greek mind the existence of a supreme power which controlled the constant regularity of all natural processes. Consequently it was assumed that the constitution of the universal city was monarchical and Zeus, the father of gods and men, emerged as the universal king. However, the monotheistic theory was never proved conclusively, and soon critical voices arose.

The trend of this criticism will be more easily understood when 'mundus', the Latin term for world, is compared with the Greek

---

[1] The tradition that Pythagoras was the first to give to 'cosmos' the denotation of universe is found e.g. in Ps. Plutarch, *Placit. Philos.*, 2.1 (Areios Didymos). Anaximenes, frg.2, Diels-Kranz, *Fragm. d. Vor-Sokr.*, 5th ed., vol.1, p.95, l.18. Heraclitus frg.30 ib., vol.1, p.124, l.11. Empedocles, frg.134, ibid., vol.1, p.366, l.4.

[2] Cf. Diels-Kranz, op. cit., vol.1, p.225, l.13f. from Diog. Laert., VIII, 48.

'cosmos.' It has been frequently and justly assumed that the Latin word was no more than a translation of the Greek term.[1] There are two meanings of 'mundus' which support this theory: as an adjective it meant 'clean' and 'neat' and had the connotation of adorned or decorated. As a noun 'mundus' originally meant heaven or sky. There was, however, another meaning of 'mundus,' that of a sacrificial pit, which was dug in the ground to receive the blood of the victims.[2] The word, therefore, had a certain connotation of magic related, so it seems, to the Roman conception of 'pax deorum'. For the Romans were inclined to regard their worship not so much as a routine fulfilment of natural obligations than as a constant revindication of the covenant between Rome and her deities. It was a precaution by which the gods were constantly placated, in order that the mutual relations between them and the state should not be disturbed: the use of 'mundus' for the universe, therefore, called into question the very assumption upon which the idea of cosmos was built, the intelligible, recognizable regularity of the processes constituting it. The idea of laws of nature was removed and replaced by that of a pact, a contract with powers whose final intentions were inaccessible to human recognition. The joy and confidence felt by the Greeks when observing the cosmos of nature was replaced by fear and trembling.

It is evident, that the Greek conception of the cosmos is superior to the other conceptions of the universe described, in that it sets up an idea as the common denominator of the universe which is purely spiritual, the idea of law and order. This idea appeared to be capable of embracing both the realms of nature and morals. Nevertheless, it could be attacked from the point of view of truth.

---

[1] W. Kroll, *Festschr. f. Kretschmar*, 1926, p.125, objecting to this thesis has defeated rather than strengthened his own case by his proof that the earliest meaning of *mundus* was 'the sky'.

[2] On *mundus* denoting the sacrificial pit in the Roman *comitium*, cf. Varro in Macrob. *Sat.*, 1.16, discussed by L. Deubner, *Hermes*, 68, 1933, p.53f. F. Cumont, *Lux Perpetua*, 1949, p.59f., says, 'selon toute probabilité cette fosse était formée d'un puits vertical aboutissant à un caveau cintré comme la calotte du ciel; de là le nom de *mundus* qui lui était donné'. This is a very tempting hypothesis, only—the stone-slab covering the *mundus* had the shape of a square.

For, assuming that those dark, demoniacal, magic powers which were taken into consideration in the Roman conception of 'mundus' had indeed a part to play in nature, the universe was neither orderly nor beautiful. This fact was realised by Hellenistic theologians and philosophers when they contrasted the cosmos of the supra-lunar spheres, those beyond the moon, with the blind rule of 'Tyche', Fortune, which was exercised in the sub-lunar sphere and upon earth. Hellenistic astrologers went even further, pointing to the irregular position in the sky of the constellation of Hydra,[1] which could not be fitted into the circle of the zodiac. This objection was, however, treated with a neglect which it did not deserve, because it was raised by a school which failed to gain an unquestioned authority. Significant was also the state of panic which was created in Rome in the years of the great revolution before the pacification of the world by Augustus, because of the subversion of the earthly counterpart of the cosmos, the state; for it largely arose on metaphysical grounds.[2]

However, the argument derived from the insecurity of man in the sub-lunar sphere was too weak in itself to disprove the existence of the cosmos. It was much rather the means of putting the idea of the cosmos in a new and interesting light. For the evidence provided by the changeless movements of the celestial bodies argued too strongly in favour of the existence of an universal order, a supreme natural law. It was, therefore, alleged, that the supra-lunar spheres represented to human eyes the order of the heavens, the kingdom of the supreme monarch, Zeus, the ruler of the gods. His rule was the nomos by which they were kept in perfect subjection, yet without losing their personalities, but rather by joining in the chorus of the spheres with its unending praise, that perfect cosmos of a most beautiful order. The sub-lunar sphere, however, was far removed from this ideal of a perfect order. The earth was handed over to 'the little god of the world'

---

[1] F. Boll, *Aus der Apokalypse*, 1914, p.101f., derived from this astrological protest far-reaching consequences for the interpretation of Rev.12.

[2] Weber, op. cit., p.42f., has given a vivid picture of this state of affairs at the time of Cicero, mistakenly assuming, however, that the classical Greek approach was the 'natural' approach (J. J. Rousseau).

(Goethe), to man, and to his special kind of liberty, the liberty of chance. The perfect order of the supra-lunar spheres, expressed by the indicative statement 'it is', which is characteristic for all the laws of nature, had its counterpart in the imperfect order of the moral and civil laws with their imperative demand 'it ought to be'. Indeed, the natural laws were not in abeyance in the sub-lunar sphere: birth and death, day and night, summer and winter, witnessed to their effectiveness; but within this frame-work of natural laws man was given the freedom of chance just mentioned which was characteristically his. It enabled him to choose between right and wrong. This alternative too, so most of the philosophers believed, had its basis in nature. The moral law was inborn in man, and the king was charged with enforcing it, insofar as man refused to observe it. Insofar the king appeared as the representative of the universal monarch:

> Iuppiter omnipotens *regum* rerumque deumque
> progenitor genetrixque deum, deus unus et idem,

the king of the gods was called by the Roman republican poet Valerius Soranus.[1]

The assumption of a moral law in-born in man led logically to the demand that it should be realized in life. The sub-lunar sphere was to be transformed by human efforts into a replica of the supra-lunar cosmos. The liberty of chance, 'eleutheria', which allowed man to go wherever he desired,[2] had to be used according to the moral law, which was part of the natural law, the law of the gods with their monarchical constitution. It was for this reason that the ancient nations bowed to the kings and their images. The Hellenistic theologians stated it quite plainly that 'the king is the last of the gods and the first of men', the connecting link between the supra-lunar cosmos and the sub-lunar 'chaos',[3] and that he was of

---

[1] Augustine, *Civ. Dei*, 7.9, cf. Weber, op. cit., p.42, n.1, who is certainly mistaken when he regards these verses as something exceptional.

[2] The etymological connection between *eleutheria* and *eleusomai* seems to be very close.

[3] The quotation from the Hermetic *Core Cosmou*, ed. W. Scott, vol.1, p.475. must not be altered—with Scott—for it has numerous parallels, cf. e.g. W. Gundel, *Abh. Munich phil. hist.*, 1933, pp.41; 75, n.4. They all resort in the last instance from Aristotle, *Pol.* I.13.13, 1284a, 'like a god among men is the king'.

the kindred of Zeus. The willingness of the masses in the Hellenistic kingdoms to acclaim the king not only as the 'Euergetes,' the benefactor, but also as the 'Epiphanes', the present god, and as the 'Soter', the saviour, will not be properly appreciated, unless its cosmological background is fully understood. It was not rank flattery, but religion, the result of strong sentiments based upon a genuine and, in its way, competent theological and philosophical attempt at understanding the universe as a political system with a monarchical constitution. For this very reason, the Jews, even in such a late composition as 4.Macc.4:15, took the strongest exception to Antiochus Epiphanes among all the Hellenistic kings— Antiochus the present god.

III

The really effective criticism of the idea of a cosmos had to start by calling into doubt the assumption of its infinity. The theory that the universe had had its origin 'in the beginning' was traced back by Aristotle and subsequent generations to no less a poet than Hesiod, the father of Greek theology.[1] There is no doubt that it was at least co-equal with the school of Elea, that philosophical school which first discussed the theory of recognition. For this school showed itself anxious to prove that 'nothing arises out of nothing' and therefore must have had opponents who asserted that the universe had arisen out of nothing. The Eleatic theory was brought to a head by Parmenides. In order to prove his case, he had to draw the conclusion that the apparent world with its constant change of rise and decay was a delusion of the senses, and that a true eternity belonged only to the world of the spirit. Therefore, if all observation of nature was a delusion of sensual apperception, the argument derived from the observation of the cosmos of the stars became inadmissible, and thus the whole idea of the cosmos fell to the ground. Parmenides in particular, when warning men not to concern themselves with the μὴ ὄν, nothing,

---

[1] J. Bernays, *Abh. Berlin*, 1882, p.14. R. Bultmann's assertion, *Das Urchristentum*, 1949, p. 13, that the conception of 'creatio ex nihilo' was unthinkable for the Greeks, is erroneous.

aimed at the natural philosophers with their theories based upon the observation of the phenomena of the apparent world. Just because he opposed the idea that the real universe could have a beginning, he found himself compelled to denounce the apparent world which exhibits innumerable beginnings as nothing.

The Eleatic thesis that nothing arises out of nothing was widely accepted by Greek philosophers—surprisingly enough—in many cases without a discussion of the conclusions drawn by Parmenides. Thus we learn from Diogenes Laertius 9:44, that Democritus had stated as an axiom of his philosophy that nothing arises out of nothing, but in spite of his general scepticism there is no evidence of a discussion of Parmenides' views in the fragments of the work of Democritus which have survived.[1] It seems that no thought was given to the important question, whether or not the first and second 'nothing' in this very ambiguous statement did indeed mean the same thing and, if so, what its exact meaning was. At the time of Aristotle 'nothing arises out of nothing' had become a stereotyped formula, and was incorporated in the philosophy of Epicurus, like so many other leaves taken by him out of the book of Democritus. However, it was not yet destined to rest there. That may be seen from the way in which Lucretius, 1.150, quoted his master's doctrine: 'nullam rem e nilo gigni divinitus unquam.' H. J. Munro in his famous commentary has treated this as a truism; it is, however, evident from Lucretius' own addition of 'divinitus' that the matter was at his time hotly discussed between the faithful and the atheists.[2]

As a matter of fact, the discussion about the origin of the universe had never been quiet in Greek philosophical circles. J. Bernays has rightly deduced this fact from two passages, the one in

---

[1] General scepticism, cf. frg.6, Diels-Kranz, op. cit., v.2, p.138, l.26f., 'man must know by this standard, how far from the truth he is', frg.9, ibid., p.139, l.16f., 'and we do not perceive anything essentially certain, but only changeable impressions, according to the constitution of the body and the onslaught and resistance of the atoms'. A general reference to the Eleatic philosophy may be found in frg.10, ibid., p.139, l.20f.

[2] Epicurus' own statement, Diog. Laert., 10.38, Lucretius, H. A. J. Munro, *T. Lucretii Cari De R. N.*, 3rd ed., 1873, p.342. Bernays, op. cit., p.13, has drawn attention to the significance of the *divinitus* in Lucr., I.150.

Aristotle, the other in Pseudo-Aristotle, both however belonging to the pre-Christian era. It may, perhaps, be held that their Peripatetic provenance is of some significance, as indeed no other Greek philosopher stated the case for and against the eternity of the cosmos more clearly than did Aristotle. However, it will be seen that other philosophical schools, in the time before Christ as well as later on, had their own particular contribution to make. The two passages of Bernays are:

[Aristotle, *De Coelo*, 3.1, 298b] [1] For there are some who say that there are no uncreated things but that they all have a beginning, and that of the things created some are permanent and others will perish again.

[Ps. Aristot., *De X.Z.G.*, 1, p.975a, 8f.] [2] That things which are non-existent come into being, and that many things have come into being out of non-existence, has been said not just by some nobodies, but by men who have a reputation of being wise. Already Hesiod holds that 'the Chaos was made first and after that the wide earth (Gaia), the everlasting, safe foundation of the universe, and after that Eros who stands out amongst all the immortals,' and they say everything arose out of that triad, and that out of nothing.

To these we may add,

[Plut., *De Anim. Procr.*, 5, p.1014B] for the creation did not take place out of the non-existent, but out of that which was not beautiful and insufficient.

Having quoted these texts, so to speak the impressions left in the ground by a body of opinion that has vanished long ago, it is necessary to state exactly what their implications may be. Aristotle's report that his opponents taught that 'no things' existed which had not previously been created leaves open the possibility of an existence of primeval matter, of which they might have been created; even Pseudo-Aristotle's thesis that Hesiod's triad of Chaos, Gaia and Eros arose out of nothing seems to come only as an afterthought, and leaves some doubt as to whether 'the men

---

[1] Quoted by Bernays, op. cit., p.14, n.2. C. Prantl assumes for some good reason, *Aristoteles Werke*, vol.2, 1857, p.321, n.3, that Aristotle referred mainly to Orphic speculations.

[2] Translated from Bernays, op. cit., p.145, n.3.

who had the reputation of being wise' really denied the existence of any primeval matter. Only Plutarch is perfectly precise on this point. Now these three testimonies are of different ages. Aristotle is the oldest, Plutarch the most recent. We are therefore entitled to assume that in the centuries after Aristotle the pagan doctrine of 'creatio ex nihilo' gained some considerable ground. This impression is reinforced by the perusal of the creation myths found in the various magical and mystery texts which also show the reason why the more serious thinkers of the period would not have anything to do with the theory.

It is probable that there were oriental influences at work in this development; but it is, on the other hand, certain that the main progress had been made before Aristotle and can be explained sufficiently with the help of those Greek sources which are at our disposal, so that any oriental influences that may be established had only the importance of stimulants. It is, furthermore, possible to determine the starting point of the doctrine. For early Greek philosophy was concerned with the definition of the μὴ ὄν, and right from the beginning connected with it a certain definite meaning. For, although the term was destined to serve for a limitation of natural science, it did not so much convey the idea of something vacant, something which was just not there, but of untruth, something which had no right to be there. It was in this sense that Parmenides[1] had held that 'there are two causes and two elements, warmth and cold, so to speak fire and earth'. Of these two he had put 'on the side of existence the warmth but the other on the side of the non-existent'.[2] In connection with the turning of this largely physical contrast into a moral contrast, we even hear of the name of a philosopher who maintained the creation of the world 'ex nihilo,' Xeniades of Corinth, one of the adversaries of Democritus:

[Sext. Emp., *Adv. Math.*, 7.53] Xeniades of Corinth, who is also mentioned by Democritus, holds that everything is false and that every imagination and opinion is lying, and that all that exists arises out of

[1] According to Aristotle, *Metaph.*, 5, 986b, 27f.
[2] Cf. again Aristotle, *Metaph*, 1.3,318b, 6.

the non-existent, and that all that perishes goes down into the non-existent.[1]

It is impossible here to enter into the whole doctrine of the μὴ ὄν.[2] It may suffice to mention that it was the positivism of the Sophists which rather shelved than solved the problem and transferred it to the field of metaphysics. This was achieved by the famous statement of Protagoras, saying:

[Sext. Emp., *Adv. Math.*, 7.60] the standard for all things is man, stating of the existing ones that they exist, and of the non-existent that they do not exist.[3]

In the same vein was the famous proof of Gorgias that neither existence nor non-existence had any real being.[4] It was on account of such criticisms that the problem of the μὴ ὄν was removed from the field of natural philosophy. The power which restored it to that pseudo-science which lay at the bottom of later—Hellenistic —philosophy probably came from abroad; whether or not the abstract idea of matter was of Greek origin is perhaps immaterial, but the oriental idea that matter was evil entered into a close union with the Greek idea that the μὴ ὄν was an untruth. This fact is illustrated especially by the close resemblance between the view attributed to Xeniades of Corinth and the famous speech of the Maccabean mother in 2. Macc.7:28, to which we now shall turn.

IV

2.Macc.7:28 takes its stand not so much on the side of popular religion which demanded that the liberty of the creative spirit of the deity should not be limited by the pre-existence of that matter upon which it would have to work, but in support of the Eleatic point of view. The Maccabean mother protested against the pre-

---

[1] Diels-Kranz, op. cit., vol.2, p.271, l.16f., c.f. Sext. Emp., *Pyrrhon. Hyp.*, 2.18.

[2] O. Gilbert, *Religionsphilosophie*, 1911, p.181f., maintains that the particular kind of μὴ ὄν which Parmenides considered, was matter. L. Troje has recently contributed an essay on 'disordered motion' as the Platonic—and Manichean— conception of matter, *Museum Helveticum*, vol.5, 1948, p.96f.

[3] Diels-Kranz, op. cit., vol.2, p.263, p.3f.

[4] Sext. Emp., *Adv. Math.*, 7.66f.

sumptuousness of the 'present god' Antiochus Epiphanes, i.e.
against the political conclusions drawn from the Greek theory of
the cosmos. This is what she had to say to her youngest son:

> I beseech thee, my son, look upon the heaven and the earth and all
> that is therein, and consider that God made them of things that were
> not; and so was mankind made likewise: fear not this tormentor, but,
> being worthy of thy brethren, take thy death.

In other words, it was the lack of reality of this **cosmos** which was
adduced as an encouragement to martyrdom. For through martyrdom, the Maccabean mother continued, she would be enabled
to 'receive thee again in mercy and with thy brethren'.

Surprisingly enough J. Bernays himself, as well as the scholars
who followed him, have failed to remark upon the significance of
the context in which this earliest and probably unique statement in
pre-Christian biblical literature concerning the 'creatio ex nihilo'
is found. It should be realised, however, that it was drawn most
carefully and had a pungent flavour. The first point to mark is that
in the general exhortation of her other sons, 2.Macc.7:23, the
Maccabean mother could speak of God as 'the creator of the
cosmos', but in countering the 'Epiphanes' she was made to use
the age-old formula 'the heaven and the earth and all that therein
is'. With other words, the exhortation of the Maccabean mother
to her youngest son shows a recalling to the paternal religion
which avoided the idea of cosmos. The expression 'creator of the
cosmos' is a most exceptional one in biblical literature. The second
point is the description of the king, the 'Epiphanes', as δήμιος.
Of course, this word meant the hangman, and it was quite an
apt description of the part played by king Antiochus IV, but it
also underlined the claim that he was just one among 'the kindred
of men'.[1] For the etymological connection with 'demos', a term
which carried some connotation of contempt, would not be over-
heard. In short, we are faced with a Jewish adaptation of philosophical polemics of a non-Jewish origin.

This polemical character is also found in the next two passages

---

[1] The A. V. which has been quoted above weakens the argument by simply
saying 'mankind'.

which will be jointly discussed, the first from the book of Jubilees
12:4, and the other from Heb.11:3. For it is only by their joint
discussion that the meaning of both these texts can be fully appreciated:

[Jub.12:4] The worship of the God of heaven who makes the rain
and the dew to fall upon the earth, and makes everything upon earth,
and has made everything by his Word, and from whose face everything takes its origin . . .

[Heb.11:3] Through faith we understand that the worlds are
framed by God, so that things which are seen were not made of things
which do appear.

The first passage deals with the worship of idols, and contrasts
them as man-made to the Divine creation of the worlds by the
Word of God, as in John 1:3. It is, however, evident that in
Jub.12:4 nothing is said regarding the origin of the matter out of
which they were created, so R. Bultmann's assertion that this is a
case exhibiting a doctrine of 'creatio ex nihilo'[1] is erroneous. The
Logos may have worked with or without primeval matter. For
instance, it is true to say that the creative activity of the Logos
according to the Hermetic religion was directed upon primeval
matter, whereas Philo used expressions which pointed the opposite way:[2]

For God called the non-existent into being, order out of disorder,
quality out of unqualified matter, similarities out of dissimilarity etc.
To introduce the non-existent into existence . . .

The author of Hebrews too enlarged upon his pre-Christian,
Jewish model, whether it was the passage from the book of
Jubilees quoted or—more probably—a more recent Jewish writing[3] which in its turn may have depended upon Jub.12:4. For it
should be realised how keenly these Hellenistic Jews were interested in this theory.

[1] *Das Urchristentum*, 1949, p.13.

[2] On the creative activity of the Hermetic Logos, cf. R. Reitzenstein,
Poimandres, 1904, p.36f. The following quotations from Philo are *Spec. Leg.*,
IV.187; *Opif. Mundi*, 31.

[3] The book of Jubilees was written either at the beginning or shortly before
the beginning of the Maccabean period, cf. Bousset-Gressmann, op. cit., p.13f.

Heb.11:3 states therefore, either 'that things which are seen were not made of things which do appear', as the Authorized Version has it or, as modern scholars prefer, 'that the things which are seen were made of that which does not appear'. The difference is not very important, although the latter version would affirm that which is only hinted at in the former negative translation.[1] On the whole, it is likely that the Authorized Version is nearer to the intention of the author of Hebrews than the modern view, because the author, having no wish to express his opinion on a question of natural philosophy, wanted to make a statement similar to St. Paul's:

[Rom.1:20] For the invisible things of Him from the beginning of the world are clearly seen, being understood by the things that are made, even His eternal power and Godhead.

This parallel makes it clear that the author of Hebrews, although he was obviously conversant with the Jewish form of the theory of the 'creatio ex nihilo', had it in his mind that 'by faith' we should understand the 'invisible things' of God from His visible works. It is, on the other hand, certain that he drew more closely to the Jewish formulation, because he addressed a church which had to endure persecution,[2] and the comfort given in Heb.11:3 was, therefore, closely related to that which the Maccabean mother gave to her youngest son in 2.Macc.7:28.

In none of these cases, however, is there an unambiguous statement of an absolute creation out of nothing. Even when the words used are seemingly quite definite, as in 2.Macc.7:28, or in the two quotations from Philo, there is always a Divine reality behind the apparent world, 'the invisible things of Him' as St. Paul has called it in Rom.1:20, and this too had a tradition in the philosophy of Hellenistic Judaism. There is the reference to God's mercy (ἔλεος, Heb. *rechem*), where the Maccabean mother would find her martyred son again; there is also in Philo's *De Opificio Mundi*, 16, and passim, a fairly elaborate exposition maintaining that the apparent world had been created according to an invisible cosmos

---

[1] Cf. e.g. the commentary of Windisch, *Der Hebräer-Brief*, 2nd ed., 1931, p.99f.   [2] Windisch, op. cit., p.98f.

of celestial originals, closely related to the Platonic world of ideas. On the whole, it seems quite in vain to expect any consistency on the part of Philo with regard to the creation of the cosmos. Drummond seems to have assumed that Philo's general approach was in favour of a 'creatio ex nihilo'. E. Bréhier, on the other hand, has shown strong reasons why it should be assumed that Philo inclined towards a theory of primeval matter, wherever he chose to state his views on the matter more extensively. Still more impressive is the proof of R. Reitzenstein, how strongly Philo was influenced by current pagan creation myths.[1] It is probably fair to say that Philo submitted to the combined strength of the Platonic and Stoic arguments of his teachers in the philosophical school at Alexandria—if somewhat unwillingly.

Nevertheless, this capitulation of Philo before the overpowering might of the arguments of Hellenistic philosophers did not mean that the theory of 'creatio ex nihilo' was altogether defeated amongst the Jews. Not only did the Armenian translator of Philo, *De Deo*, 6, represent matter as created by God,[2] not only did Rabbinic Jewry strongly support the doctrine, but we find in Justin's Dialogue with Trypho, 5, an interesting testimony for the popularity of the doctrine among the Jews. Justin, who otherwise was somewhat uncertain about it,[3] had in his Dialogue the aim of inviting the Jews to join the Christian Church. For this reason he started by recording his own conversion. The arguments which he put in the mouth of the venerable old man who converted him were calculated in such a way that they should be acceptable to his Jewish interlocutors. Thus the subject of the world's creation was discussed, as follows:

'And do you say that the world is uncreated?'

[1] Drummond, *Philo Judaeus on the Jewish Alexandrian Philosophy*, 1888, v.1, p.304, quoted here from E. Bréhier, *Les Idées Philosophiques et Religieuses de Philon*, 1925, p.81, n.4, cf. p.78f. Reitzenstein, *Poimandres*, pp.39–41, comparing Plut., *De Iside* 53f. with Philo, *De Ebrietate* 30, ed. Wendland p.176, l.3f.

[2] Bréhier, op. cit., p.81, n.2.

[3] F. Loofs, *Dogmengeschichte*, 4th ed., 1906, p.119, n.4, derives from Justin, 1. *Apol.*67.8, that Justin taught an absolute creation; but I have arrived at the opposite conclusion. Here is the text: 'on Sunday we all gather together in one place, because it is the first day in which God changed darkness and matter making the *cosmos*'.

'Some say so, but I do not agree.'

'You are right. For what reason (logos) is there to be found in a body so hard and refractory, being a compound and changing, perishing and rising again every day, that it should not be thought of as having arisen at some beginning?'

It is true, as Otto in his edition has pointed out,[1] that this argument was soaked in Platonic philosophy. Nevertheless, it is stated once more that the cosmos had been created 'in the beginning'; and it is evident from a collection of contemporary sources,[2] the number of which could probably be increased, that the early Fathers of the Church were convinced followers of this theory.

Some of them have indeed expressly stated the creation of matter as an article of faith, as in the following passages:

[Hermas, *Mand.*, I.1.1] First of all you have to believe that there is one God who has founded and organised the universe and has brought the universe out of the non-existent into existence.

[Theophil., *Ad Autolyc.*, II.4] What a small thing, if God had created the cosmos out of existing matter. For even a human craftsman, if he may take his material from somewhere, can make of it what he wants. But the power of God shows itself in this that He creates out of the non-existent whatsoever He wants, just as also the giving of souls and of movement belongs to no one else but God alone. For man may well fashion an image, but reason (logos) and breath and senses he cannot give to the work of his hands. Beyond this, however, God has the property that He may create reasonable, breathing beings, capable of sensual apprehension. As God is now in all those things mightier than man, He can also create out of the non-existent that which exists in quantity and quality, as it is His will.

These passages only draw the logical conclusion from the Jewish polemics against that ideology upon which the Hellenistic states with their ruler cults were based. A theory of the Logos lay behind

---

[1] Justin, *Opera*, 2nd ed., 1848, v.1, p.23, n.3, referring to Plato, *Tim.*, 28B. It has not, however, seemed expedient to enter more fully into this question.

[2] Apart from the texts which will be quoted in the next paragraph I have noted Theophil, *Ad Autol.*, II.10, ed. Otto, vol.1, p.78f.; Iren., *Adv. Haer.* (Harvey), I.15.1; II.10.2; IV.34.2.

these polemics in Jewish[1] as well as in Christian circles, which probably accounted for the noticeable development away from the original concrete situation of martyrdom in which the theory of a 'creatio ex nihilo' had made its first appearance in Jewish literature. Still, even Hermas and Theophilus made their statements in the defence of the Christian faith against its persecutors. However, there was a tendency towards the statement of an abstract truth,[2] which brought the Christian doctrine into close proximity with those views of ancient Greek philosophers who had denied the eternity of the cosmos. For of the two new elements in the Jewish and Christian doctrines of 'creatio ex nihilo,' the protest against the political conclusions drawn from the idea of the cosmos and the teaching of the creative activity of the Logos, only the second was strictly preserved. There is yet a riddle to be solved, viz. why the Apostles' Creed, already in its earliest forms, although it described God the Father as the 'maker of heaven and earth', did not embrace the idea of 'creatio ex nihilo.' Was there a line to the evil 'Demiourgos' of Marcion and other Gnostics, which had to be avoided? Hermas and Theophilus sound sufficiently orthodox; but did they, perhaps, venture too far?

The answer to this question is not to be found in any of those sources which have been examined here, but it may be possible to arrive at some probable solution by an examination of the idea of nothingness. It has to be realized that the idea of nothingness is indeed derived from that of negation, that is, it is man who states that something is absent when it was expected to be present. In case that the place where the absent was expected to be present has not been taken by something else, man will be in a position to state that there is 'nothing', that the place is indeed vacant. In this respect Protagoras was right when he held that 'man is the

---

[1] Thus we find in *Apocal. Baruch* (syr.), 48.8, 'thou callest into life by thy Word that which is not'.

[2] Hermas, *Mand.*, I.I.I, has been regarded as an early Creed by Bousset, *Kyrios Christos*, 4th ed., 1935, p.291, n.4, but cf. M. Dibelius, *Handb. z. N. T.*, *Erg. Bd.*, 1923, p.497f. who connects it, more convincingly, with early Jewish precedents. *Universorum conditor* is, however, found as part of an early Creed in Justin, 1.*Apol.*, 61, and in Tertullian, Badcock, op. cit., pp.11,19.

standard of all things, stating of the existent that they exist, and of the non-existent that they do not exist'. In accepting this statement of Protagoras, however, the true problem of nothingness has not yet been touched. For this problem is that of the limits of the universe. In order to illustrate the problem, reference may be made to the similar one of two parallel straight rails of a railway line, which seem to get closer and closer in the distance. If this apparent process is followed up to its logical conclusion, the two rails will finally join into one, if only we have sufficiently keen eyes to follow them and then, continuing as one, form an angle to their previous course (which is impossible) or they will cross and then open out again (which is no less impossible).

It is, of course, true that they never meet, and the whole problem is imaginary. It remains, however, to be seen whether the same is true with regard to the problem of absolute nothingness which provides us with an equally puzzling alternative. Aristotle[1] has neatly circumscribed the alternative which offers itself here with the following words: 'the one side maintains that the existing things arise out of nothing; the others, in order to escape from this conclusion, state that all things combine into one whole'.[2] With other words, the ideas of nothingness and of the universe are mutually exclusive. The idea of the universe demands that it should embrace all things, and thus be limitless; whereas the idea of nothingness, insofar as it has any meaning at all, demands that all things, i.e. the universe, should be opposed to it, and consequently be limited. Therefore, if the theory is proposed that the universe is created out of nothing, we are faced with a logical impossibility; whereas, if it is assumed that each one individual thing takes its origin out of nothing, and returns again into nothing without a connection with any other thing, the absolute 'nothing' may be held responsible for a relative appearance of any one thing. In view of the fact that the three conceptions of 'universe', 'world'

---

[1] *Metaph.* X, 1075b., 14f.

[2] This may contain a reference to Xenophanes, cf. Sext. Emp., *Pyrrhon. Hyp.*, I. 225, ἐδογμάτιζε δὲ ὁ Ξενόφανης παρὰ τὰς τῶν ἄλλων ἀνθρώπων προλήψεις ἓν εἶναι τὸ πᾶν, καὶ τὸν θεὸν συμφυῆ τοῖς πᾶσιν, εἶναι δὲ σφαιροειδῆ καὶ ἀπαθῆ καὶ ἀμετάβλητον καὶ λογικόν.

and 'cosmos', each in its way, have proved to be highly question-able, we are driven dangerously near the conclusion drawn by the Maccabean mother, 2.Macc.7:28, that this world is only sham.

However, Aristotle's alternative omits every reference to a creative deity. Where it is assumed that God's creation took place out of nothing, whatever this 'nothing' may be, it would be pri-meval, a competitor with the godhead; in short we are faced with some sort of dualism. In particular, if the Christian position is taken, as we find it described by Christ Himself, Matt.19:17, 'there is none good but one, that is God', then this nothing could not be regarded as good. Yet it cannot be regarded as neutral either; at any rate not as neutral in the sense in which natural science regards its objects as neutral. For there cannot be any room for the application of the principles of natural science before the creation of 'nature'. It therefore remains to be seen whether 'nothing' may be regarded as neutral—neither good nor evil—in a moral sense. This solution seems to recommend itself on account of the fact that nothingness is incapable of having any quality and therefore should hold a neutral position between the contrast-ing qualities of good and evil.

In dealing with this question we have to avoid the logical diffi-culty that in proving that there is 'nothing' which might be neutral in the struggle between good and evil we allow absolute nothingness to be neutral. It is, therefore, necessary to turn to an analogous case, and such an analogous case did indeed occupy the minds of Christians in the Middle Ages, of Dante, Wolfram von Eschenbach and especially of popular theologians: the case of the neutral angels.[1] Legend had it that, at the fall of Lucifer, one-third of the heavenly host followed the rebellious prince of darkness, one-third obeyed the Divine command and the remaining part

[1] I am under obligation to the late Prof. Friedrich Ranke, Basel, for the fol-lowing references: Dante, *Div. Comm.*, I.3.34f.; Wolfram, *Parzival*, 454, 21f.; 471, 15f.; Legend of St. Brandon; Jans Jansen Enikel, *Weltchronik* (A.D. 1280); *Zimmerische Chronik* (16.century), as mentioning these neutral angels. Another reference may be found in J. and W. Grimm, *Irische Elfen-Märchen*, 1826, XIII. It seems probable that the legend may have originated from some Celtic source,

stayed neutral. The minds of laymen rather than of the theologians were troubled with the question regarding the fate of these neutral angels. The answers given, although they varied in degree, were unanimous in one point, that even such a neutrality was an offence in the eyes of God. Therefore nothingness, just because it is incapable of quality, is in a very subtle way evil. Consequently, although we have no proof to offer that this happened intentionally, and even less that the legend of the neutral angels was already known at such an early time, it is at least clear that the words of the Apostles' Creed, 'maker of heaven and earth', barred that way to Gnostic dualism, which Herm., *Mand*.I.I.I. might have opened up, just as effectively as they excluded the faulty ideas of 'universe', 'world' or 'cosmos'.

V

The previous section has made it clear that the earliest Christian Creed had a good reason for preserving the age-old Hebrew term of 'heaven and earth'. It is now the time to examine whether or not in doing so the Apostles' Creed stepped back behind a line which had already been crossed by early Judaism and by the New Testament writers. It has been seen in the course of our argument that at least Heb.11:3 had a somewhat ambiguous wording, which made it possible to understand this verse in favour of a 'creatio ex nihilo'. It has also been seen that even 2.Macc.7:28 may have overstepped its mark in this direction, although, by using the words 'heaven and earth' instead of cosmos, it showed itself conscious of the danger. It is, however, fair to say that those are the exceptions to the rule. In the biblical Apocrypha the reference to the cosmos in this sense is, nevertheless, made sometimes. It can be stated, however, that cosmos in this context did not always have its full philosophical significance.

Thus we find in the Wisdom of Solomon 7:17, 'He has given me certain knowledge of the things that are, namely to know the construction of the cosmos', and in 9:9, 'and wisdom was with Thee: which knows Thy works and was present when Thou madest the cosmos'. The Valentinian Gnosis understood these

words as meaning that a personified Sophia or Achamoth penetrated into the presence of the Almighty to watch Him at His
work, but Christian belief has always shrunk from this conclusion.[1] A last—and decisive—gesture of Christian orthodoxy was
that St. Jerome in both these cases decided to translate cosmos by
'orbis terrarum'. This made it evident that the Catholic Church
regarded the use of cosmos in these texts as a mere figure of
speech. However, in these two verses as well as in Wisdom 11:17
(18) 'for the almighty hand that made the cosmos of matter
without form', the danger line was definitely touched and Greek
influence was clearly discernible. But it may be seen from ibid.,
10:1, 'she preserved the first formed father of the *cosmos*', namely
man, that St. Jerome had some support for his limitation of the
meaning of cosmos in the book of Wisdom, unless, that is, 10:1
referred to the myth of the original man, that centre-piece of
Gnostic anthropology. It is therefore permissible to classify even
the author of the Wisdom of Solomon as at least an uncertain
witness for the Divine creation of one cosmos, even if 11:17 (18)
shows a close affinity to Greek philosophical thought.

In the other canonical Apocrypha of the Old Testament no
similar references to the creation of the cosmos are to be found, and
the same applies to the canonical Gospels. Although St. John's
Gospel uses the word cosmos in many instances and with various
meanings, the creation of the world is referred to only in John
17:24, 'Thou lovedst me before the foundation of the cosmos.'
This term 'before the foundation of the cosmos' is also found in
the Synoptic Gospels, for instance in Matt. 25:34 and Luke 11:50.
It was no more than a reference popular at the time, to Ps.78:2,
enlarged by the addition of the word cosmos.[2] If the intrinsic

---

[1] On the part played by Sophia in the Valentinian Gnosis cf. G. Quispel,
Theol. Zeitschr., 5, 1949, p.433f. On the character of the Hellenistic influence
upon the Wisdom of Solomon, cf. the very balanced analysis by I. Heinemann, ibid., 4, 1948, p.241f.

[2] Ps.78:2 reads ἀπὸ καταβολῆς, Matt.13:35; 25:34; Luke 11:50; Heb.9:26;
Rev.13:8; 17:8 read ἀπὸ καταβολῆς κόσμου. On the other hand John 17:24;
Eph.1:4; 1.Pet.1:20 read πρὸ καταβολῆς κόσμου and Rom.1:20 ἀπὸ κτίσεως
κόσμου. Similar is the quotation in Matt.24:21 from Joel 2:2 (LXX), ἀπ'
ἀρχῆς κόσμου.

value of all these sayings is rightly assessed as a mere figure of speech, the impression will disappear that the New Testament writers possessed an elaborate and well established doctrine of the creation of the cosmos. In fact, there are only two passages which deal ex professo with the creation, John 1:3f., a passage which has been referred to previously,[1] and St. Paul's sermon on the Areopagus.

In order to understand St. Paul's point of view, it is necessary to have first of all an outline of the whole of his sermon. For, whoever may have been its author, the little piece Acts 17:22–31 forms one self-contained whole, which agrees with the rhetorical principles of the time. It appears clearly, when St. Luke's report is critically analysed, that it is an outline of a speech actually made rather than an invented address:

I. v. 22–23	Introduction; the unknown God.
IIa. v. 24a.	He is the God who made 'the cosmos and all things therein', the 'Lord of heaven and earth'.
IIb. v. 24b–25	He is independent of the works of men.
IIIa. v. 26	For He has made the lives of all mankind.
IIIb. v. 27	For 'they should seek the Lord'.
IIIc. v. 28	'For we are also His offspring.'
IV. v. 29–30	'Therefore repent'.
V. v. 31	For through the resurrection of Christ God's judgment has come upon mankind.

By this analysis it is shown, first of all, that the reference to the resurrection of Christ is the necessary, logical completion of the sermon on the Areopagus, and not a pious Christian addition to an already existing pagan scheme of a missionary sermon. Such a view has been put forward by E. Norden,[2] but it has in reality nothing more to commend it than the unquestionable existence of allusions to and quotations from Greek philosophical writings. The most famous of these quotations, that from Aratus, *Phaen.*, 5, would be ill placed if the concluding verses 29–31 were missing, however weighty the authority of that poet philosopher may have been.

[1] See above, p.216.
[2] Norden, *Agnostos Theos*, 1913.

The result of our analysis, by which it is shown that the sermon on the Areopagus was a Christian production—either St. Luke's or St. Paul's—makes it necessary to examine its allusions to pagan tenets in order to find out how far the Christian author was committed to any Greek cosmogony. The excuse that we are only faced with a Christian adaptation of pagan material is inadmissible. Under this responsibility towards both sides, it is the most necessary part of our research to fix the point where Christian and pagan doctrines were forced to disagree. It was the very point where the philosophers refused to follow St. Paul's argument any further, the resurrection of Jesus Christ. For, as Christ was risen in His earthly body, St. Paul was not only prevented from accepting the statement of the Maccabean mother, 2.Macc. 7:28, 'so was mankind made likewise', viz. out of nothing, but this world was by the resurrection of Christ accorded a reality which Greek philosophy in general was not prepared to grant it.[1] Thus the old contrast between those who taught the 'creatio ex nihilo' and those who denied it was put on a new level and actually resolved.

Consequently St. Paul's failure at Athens was not due to any philosophical incompetence either on his part or on the part of the author of Acts 17:22f. His address was rather a deliberate challenge of a widely accepted pantheistic theory derived, so it seems, from Orphic sources by the masters of Greek philosophy. The Orphic poem which lay behind it was already referred to in Plato's *Laws* and preserved at some length in Pseudo-Aristotle's treatise *De Mundo*:[2]

---

[1] Norden, op. cit., 6f. has almost the same analysis of the speech, which has been given here, and compares it with *Poim.*, 1.27; *Od. Sol.*, 33; *Kerygma Petri*, p.13f. and the sermon of Barnabas from the Ps. Clementine *Homilies*, p.15, l.10f. (Lagarde), but he fails to perceive the significance of the mention of the resurrection in Acts 17:31. He also errs in that he does not see that the rhetorical pattern is a common one.

[2] Plato, *Legg.*, IV, 715E; *De Mundo*, 7, p.401a, ed. Lorimer-König, 1935, p.99f. cf. O. Kern, *Orphic. Fragm.*, 1922, nr.21, p.91. The last two verses are an obvious addition, based upon the Stoic theory of periodical conflagrations of the universe. How the poem grew and changed in the course of time, may be seen from Porphyry in Kern nr.168, p.201f., who gave the official version of his time, omitting the two lines of Ps. Aristotle.

Zeus is the first; Zeus with flashing lightnings is the last.
Zeus is the head, Zeus the middle, out of Zeus the universe is fashioned.
Zeus is the foundation of the earth and of the starry sky.
Zeus is male, the immortal Zeus was made woman.
Zeus is the breath of the universe, Zeus the force of the
indefatigable flame.
Zeus is the root of the sea, Zeus the Sun and the Moon.
Zeus is king, Zeus with flashing lightnings is the leader of all.
[For hiding all things, he has brought them again
into the joyful light from his sacred heart, achieving the enormous.]

Out of this pantheistic approach many theories could be evolved, and it proved especially fruitful in Neo-Platonic theology. However, at the time of St. Paul it proved to be the most valuable support for the political cosmology. The verses of Valerius Soranus quoted above show a genuine kinship with this Orphic poem:

> Iuppiter omnipotens regum rerumque deumque
> progenitor genetrixque deum, deus unus et idem.

These lines could not have been invented by a Roman poet—Rome had no kings—they must have had an Hellenistic ancestry. They were, however, popular enough, being characteristic for that theory of royal prerogative based upon cosmological considerations, which has been discussed before. Horace[1] echoed them in his famous lines:

> Caelo tonantem credidimus Iovem
> Regnare: praesens divus habebitur
> Augustus . . .,

where the 'praesens divus' is neither more nor less than the ancient Hellenistic 'Epiphanes'.

The stage was therefore set for a repetition of the Maccabean protests; but the Christian author was prevented from using the arguments of the Maccabean mother. He, therefore, first stressed the things which the Christians had in common with the philosophers. Consequently allusions to the Old Testament had to be

---

[1] Horace, *Carm.*, III.5.109.

slight; those to Greek philosophy on the other hand were conspicuous. An outstanding example for this is v. 24a, 'God that
made the cosmos and all things therein': how strikingly similar
this is to 'out of Zeus the universe is fashioned'. Yet St. Paul added
the 'Lord of heaven and earth', apparently as a safeguard, although
it corresponded once more to 'Zeus is the foundation of the earth
and the starry sky'.[1] If, therefore, this verse marks the closest
approach to the pagan doctrine of cosmogony, the quotation from
Aratus in v. 28, 'for we are also his offspring', shows a definite
protest against the idea of the 'Divine right of kings'. God is not
only 'regum rerumque deumque progenitor', but 'we are also His
offspring'. Once more the view held in 2.Macc.7:28 is reversed:
'He has made of one blood all the nations of men' is very close to
'so was mankind made likewise', but St Paul did not continue in
Acts 17:26, that they were made out of nothing, but went rather
the opposite way, 'for in Him we live and move and have our
being' v. 28.

Once more we are face to face with Greek philosophical
thought. Porphyry's version of the Orphic poem quoted above,
contains the famous line 10,

> for all this is lying in the great body of Zeus.

Again this line is only chosen as representative for a whole trend
of thought in Greek philosophy. It is also evident that it was
familiar to St. Paul. For Norden[2] has proved that the genuinely
Pauline formula, Rom.11:36, 'for of Him and through Him
and in Him are all things', which is akin to St. Paul's reported
remark in Acts 17:28, has any amount of contemporary philosophical support. It is, so it seems, a thought which St. Paul loved to
express, as in Romans so also in 1.Cor.8:6; Col.1:16f.; Eph.4:6.
Not only Acts 17:28, 'for in Him we live and move and have our

---

[1] How close the relation was felt to be, may be seen from Lactant., *Epit.*, 3,
Kern, op. cit., nr.88, p.160, saying, 'Ovidius principalem deum dicit qui caelum
solemque cum ceteris astris, qui terram qui maria condiderit', a formula
accepted by Lactantius as being virtually Christian.

[2] Norden, op. cit., p.240f., refers mainly to Marc. Aurel. 4.23; Plut., *Platon.
Quaest.*, 2.2, p.1001C and Manil., V.915, 'in eo sunt omnia et in omnibus ipse
est solus'.

being', but Heb.2:10, 'Him for whom are all things and by whom are all things', shows the deep impression which this repetition of the formula made upon the other members of his circle. They copied willingly the saying of their master, but the adoption of this formula did not mean their adoption of the Stoic conception underlying it, any more than it did with St. Paul himself.

However, the difference may appear to be only slight: It lies mainly in the word 'we', although this word is not to be found in Rom.11:36 and Heb.2:10. Nevertheless, it is of great significance that there is no pagan parallel for this emphasis laid upon the personal side of the formula. Moreover, it is a fact that its origin from the ancient doctrine of the unity of the universe, first proclaimed by Xenophanes, made it impossible for ancient philosophers to draw any such conclusion. However, if the author of the sermon on the Areopagus intended to continue not only with his reference to Aratus, *Phaen.*5, 'for we are also his offspring', but also with his reference to Christ's resurrection, he had to change the emphasis, because the resurrection of Christ concerned in the first line the redemption of mankind. He thus paid attention to the peculiar position of sinful man within the entirety of God's creation, altogether neglected by the Greeks. It is instructive to see how his statement answers the resignation of 2.Macc.7:36, 'for our brethren who now have suffered a short pain, are dead under God's covenant of everlasting life'. This is answered in Acts 17:31, which holds that God 'has given assurance to all men, in that He has raised Him from the dead'. In this way the argument of the sermon on the Areopagus actually leads up to the great dialogue between Jesus and Martha in the story of the raising of Lazarus:

[John 11:24] Martha saith to Him: 'I know that he shall rise again in the resurrection at the last day.'
[25] Jesus said unto her: 'I am the resurrection and the life'.

VI

It is essential that the theological research on the creation of the world should lead straight to the resurrection of Christ. For

without the incarnation the Aristotelean alternative—that either
this world must be one, ἓν καὶ πᾶν, as the Orphics said, and consequently the world itself, the cosmos, identical with the supreme
deity, because there would be no room left for it beyond the infinite universe, or else that the apparent phenomena of nature
would have to take their origin out of that nothingness which is
untruth—would be unavoidable. There would be on the fringe of
his latter theory a possibility for that pious hope of a 'true' world
in the 'mercy of God' far distant, to which the Maccabean mother
referred, a belief in such divine reality as Parmenides had described
and an enthusiastic desire for it as is found in pagan as well as in
Gnostic mysteries. All this is superseded by the incarnation of the
Word of God, who by his resurrection has taken up His earthly
body—the vestiges of the created world—into the reality of the
Godhead. 'All things were made by Him and without Him was
not anything made that was made', John 1:3;[1] this sentence, so far
from being in opposition to the first article of the Nicene Creed,
describing the Father as the Maker of heaven and earth and of all
things visible and invisible, interprets this article. For it turns the
idea of a creation which was accomplished once and for all 'in the
beginning' into that which to the human mind appears as a continuous process: 'behold I make all things new', Rev.21:5.

The importance of Christ's resurrection for the doctrine of the
creation lies in the fact that He rose in His earthly body and, at the
ascension, took His risen body into the presence of the Divine
Majesty. This signifies the reality of His body, and incidentally of
all those who are members of His body. It is, therefore, not just
symbolic language but a statement of fact when, in one of our
most popular hymns, it is said of the Church 'she is His new creation'. This, however, applies to humanity only, not to nature. Of
the various meanings of words expressing the entirety of God's
creation, the resurrection of Christ gives validity first of all to that
of 'world', the stage set for man's activity, the world as the age of

---

[1] John 1:10, has been omitted here, because many believe that in this verse
cosmos meant only the world of man, cf. e.g. K. Meyer, *Prolog des Johannes*,
1902, p.46; R. Bultmann, *Johannes Ev.*, 1937/41, p.33. Different, Bauer,
Johannes Ev., 3rd ed., 1933, p.19f.

man. It is indeed true that, from the point of view of a continuing, perpetual Divine creation, the present moment, each present moment, is hallowed and made real to be used to the full by man as the inheritor of the Divine promises. This, we take it, is the principal meaning behind the Johannine terms of 'Saviour of the cosmos' and 'Light of the cosmos'.[1] On the other hand, it is evident that, in so far as this cosmos is not hallowed by the incarnate Word, is not organized as members of His body, there is indeed no other interrelation between the individuals comprised under this term, and the numerous cases in which cosmos is used in a derogatory sense in St. John's Gospel[2] all witness to its origin out of that nothingness which is untruth. In other words Aristotle's alternative appears in the light of Christ's resurrection as the 'judgment of this cosmos', John 12:31, whose master is described in John 8:44 as 'a liar and the father of it'.

This conception of the universe as the world of man is indeed very pronounced in the New Testament. It may therefore be asked whether the stress laid upon the human aspect did not prevent Christianity from having a correct approach to nature. Is it not true that, by stressing the human point of view, the Church was brought very near that dangerous thesis of Protagoras that 'man is the standard of all things', even though we claim that He who is the standard is the God-man. There can be no doubt that Church history supports the criticism inherent in this question, not only by the recording of those staggering mistakes made in condemning men like Galileo for their great discoveries, but still more by that perpetual tendency of the Fathers of the Church of suspecting the powers of nature of being evil because they are 'neutral', if not in a moral yet at least in a scientific sense. The most serious mistake in this respect was made by the Church at the fourth Lateran Council of 1215 when the caution of the earlier Creeds was abandoned in favour of making the 'creatio ex nihilo' an article of the Christian faith.[3]

[1] John 3.16f.; 4:42; 6:33, 51; 12:46f.; 1.John 4:9, 14.
[2] Cf. the references given in Cremer-Kögel, *Bibl. Theol. Wörterbuch*, 11th ed., 1923, p.622 under d).
[3] Mansi, *Conc.*, vol.22, 982.

In order to disentangle Christian doctrine from this maze, it has to be remembered that the personal note in those various sayings related to Rom.11:36, although it is very important, nevertheless is not exclusive. Rom.11:36 itself lacks it and proves that St. Paul saw beyond the 'world of man' even if, according to Acts 17:28, he had no reason to say so in his sermon on the Areopagus. The question, therefore, which has to be asked, is this, what did the New Testament writers wish to express by adopting the Stoic formula 'of Him and through Him and to Him are all things'? The answer has to be found in Christian eschatology,[1] for beyond the world of man there are 'the new heaven and the new earth where justice dwelleth', 2.Pet.3:13. It is essential to see St. Paul's quotation from the Stoics in this special light, for only thus does it become quite clear that man is part of God's creation and not just banished from some 'spiritual' place, to live in the 'material' universe as an exile and to be recalled through the ivory gate of death to his original home. 2.Pet.3:13 took up the Greek idea of the cosmos: the new heaven and the new earth were qualified in such a way as to re-establish the idea of a universe representing the Divine law of righteousness. It is essential to notice the differences between 2.Pet.3:13 and Is.65:17; 66:22, on the one hand, where the new heaven and the new earth are promised but no reference to their 'justice' is made, and Slavonic Enoch 65:8 on the other, which promises 'the new aeon of the just'. For in 2.Pet.3:13 'dikaiosyne' is represented as a quality of the whole creation of God, not only of the redeemed race of man. This was an idea characteristic for and of long standing amongst the Greeks. It may not be sufficient as an interpretation when Karl Barth comments upon Rom.11:36,[2] 'how could St. Paul close this chapter more significantly than by stating plainly, menacingly and in a hope provoking fashion that which was known already to those outside', but it is an important point. The ambiguous conception of the cosmos with its Divine law has, so Barth argues

---

[1] Lietzmann, *Römer*, 4th ed., 1933, p.107, rightly stresses 'the formula which appears to be quite common-place, receives its special meaning from its connection with verse 32, i.e. in view of the redemption of the *cosmos*'.

[2] K. Barth, *Römerbrief*, 5th ed., 1926, p.409.

rightly, received its Divine sanction through Christ's resurrection.

In this respect it is essential to notice that 2.Pet.3:13 has the present tense: 'wherein dwelleth righteousness'. The change from the future tense, 'the heavens shall pass away', etc., in verses 10f. to this one and only present in v.13 is highly significant, warning us not to regard this new heaven and new earth as some future event, in the same way as also the Revelation of St. John insists upon the eschaton being present already. In other words, Christ's resurrection is effective not only in the redemption of mankind, but in the true and perpetual creation of the world. The new heaven and the new earth are just as much a Divine reality as the new Jerusalem and the new and redeemed nature of man. One thing only remains open to conjecture, whether human science is able to express the truth about the redeemed universe. The question to which we are thus led is whether scientific truth can be related to Him who has said 'I am the way and the truth and the life'. To this there are two main answers: first, that the truth about God's creation must have life spelt over it and not death, for He is 'the God of the living and not of the dead'. Unless we learn to understand and to use God's creation as living and life-giving, we shall still remain in the thrall of 'the last enemy which is death'. Secondly, 'we walk by faith, not by sight'; therefore, the axioms upon which natural science is built must not contradict God's infinity. That means to say that space and time must be related to the basic facts of Christ's incarnation and resurrection. If this demand is neglected, science will do no more than add to the many deceptions of 'this aeon'.

10

CHRISTIAN BAPTISM AND ROMAN LAW

I

SOME fifty years ago W. E. Ball maintained, in a book entitled *St. Paul and the Roman Law*, that the assent to the Christian Creed given by the catechumens in baptism was fashioned after the manner of a Roman 'stipulatio'.[1] Although the book itself hardly deserves any attention, this idea is worthy of closer testing. For the rite of solemn interrogation by the priest and response by the candidate as practised in the baptismal liturgy of the Church of England is indeed reminiscent of Roman verbal contracts. It therefore seems a promising enquiry to establish the time and reason for its introduction. In both respects W. E. Ball has made no progress, but after making his claim and giving a superficial account of the Roman 'stipulatio', he proceeded to another subject. However, if such an analogy could be proved, it might throw light upon the way in which the term 'sacramentum', 'military oath', came to be used for the description of the Christian initiation rite as well as for those other rites which accompany the Christian 'via vitae'.

It must be said at once that it was not St. Paul who introduced the Roman 'stipulatio' into the Christian baptismal rite.[2] The earliest allusion to a rite of question and answer may perhaps be found in 1.Pet.3.21, ὃ καὶ ὑμᾶς ἀντίτυπον νῦν σώζει βάπτισμα, οὐ σαρκὸς ἀπόθεσις ῥύπου ἀλλὰ συνειδήσεως ἀγαθῆς ἐπερώτημα εἰς θεόν, δι' ἀναστάσεως Ἰησοῦ Χριστοῦ κτλ., 'the interrogation of a good conscience toward God through the resurrection of Jesus Christ' (Revised Version). The word ἐπερώτημα is the technical term for

---

[1] W. E. Ball, *St. Paul and the Roman Law*, 1901, p.38f.
[2] It has been suggested that 1.Tim.5.8, τὴν πίστιν ἤρνηται, refers to a question-answer rite. The suggestion is extremely weak and the verse non-Pauline.

the 'stipulatio' in the eastern provinces of the Roman Empire.[1]
The formula ἐπερωτηθεὶς ὡμολόγησα was customarily added to contracts on papyrus. Here the word described the creditor, not the
debtor. Thus the verse sees the catechumen as receiving in baptism
the Divine promise, not as making any baptismal vow as in the
later rite.[2] The making of a formal confession of faith in reply to
the interrogation by a Christian minister has come into the New
Testament only in the interpolated verse, Acts 8:37, 'and Philip
said, If thou believest with all thy heart, thou mayest. And he
answered and said, I believe that Jesus Christ is the Son of God'.[3]
The story of the baptism of the Ethiopian eunuch by Philip was
apparently enriched by the addition of v.37,[4] because it lacked
an explicit confession of faith on the part of the eunuch.[5] The
question-answer form was chosen, because it was the customary
rite in the interpolator's Church,[6] i.e. accidentally. Acts 8:37,
therefore, provides us with a *terminus a quo* for the rise of the
question-answer confession of faith in Christian baptism. We can
state for certain that it was not practised in Antioch or Asia Minor,
where St. Luke's book was probably composed,[7] at the time when

[1] So much is admitted even by Windisch, op. cit., p.73, who by misjudging
the juridical problem, rejects the solution suggested here.

[2] Greeven's interpretation of 1.Pet.3.21, *Theol. Wörterbuch z. N.T.*, v.2, 1935,
p.686, is superficial. He ignores the question in what way ('through the resurrection of Jesus Christ') the ἐπερώτημα of (or for) a good conscience is addressed.
Dean Selwyn, *The First Epistle of St. Peter*, 1947, p.205f., has seen that a legal
analogy is used, whereas Flemington, *N.T. Doctrine*, op. cit., 1948, p.99, n.3,
has ignored it, and thus failed to offer a solution. The whole passage is treated
by Reicke, *The Disobedient Spirits and Holy Baptism*, 1946, p.182f., who has seen
the legal connotation but interpreted it incorrectly.

[3] The fact that a Creed was said in baptism already in very early times is
admitted by Kelly, op. cit., p.30f., but if E. Lichtenstein, *Z.K.G.*, 1950, p.45f.,
is right, the earliest Christian Creed, 1.Cor.15:3, was not a baptismal Creed.

[4] The MS. evidence makes the interpolation certain. Only codex E, the
Laudianus of the sixth century, a 'western' type, together with some few
minuscules, and a Syriac version of the seventh century have it. *Vetus Latina*
probably had it, but in the Vulgate it is a later addition. Among the Fathers,
Irenaeus is its strongest support.

[5] Cf. Foakes-Jackson, *Acts of the Apostles*, p.76.

[6] There is little information forthcoming as to the use of the question-
answer rite in the ante-Nicene Church. It was not very widespread. Cf. Kelly,
op. cit., p.38f.

[7] Antioch was the origin, according to Knopf-Lietzmann-Weinel, op. cit.,

it was written, some time during the second half of the first century. This result is important since it makes it unlikely that this form of confession of faith came from Jewish sources.[1] The introduction of Jewish rites into the baptismal liturgy of the Church, though by no means impossible, is very much less likely to have happened in the second century than in the first, owing to the continued hostility of the Jews, so much so that we need not pursue it any further in this connection.

The *terminus a quo* for the introduction of the question-answer form of the Creed, insofar as the manuscript evidence for Acts 8:37 is concerned, lies no further back than the sixth century. However, Irenaeus witnesses to the verse being known already at the end of the second century, and even that seems to be later than the actual introduction of the rite. For already Justin Martyr made reference to a formal baptismal vow.[2] In this he seems to have been preceded by gnostic sects,[3] but it cannot be stated with certainty in either case that the question-answer rite was used. In the case of Justin Martyr it may be alleged that a certain probability exists in favour of his presupposing such a rite, since Rome seems to have been the Church where this rite was first introduced. Justin, as we know, was the representative Roman theologian in the middle of the second century.

The Roman origin of the rite follows from the use which Irenaeus made of the story of the baptism of the eunuch. In his *magnum opus*, *Adversus Haereses*, he referred to the incident twice,[4] but only in the earlier of the two passages did he mention

---

p.134, whereas Harnack, *Lukas der Arzt*, p.117, has suggested Asia Minor or Achaia.

[1] On the other hand, it seems probable that the learning of the Creed by heart and its recital by catechumens, which was widely practised, was of Jewish origin, cf. Flemington, op. cit., p.7f.

[2] 1.*Apol*.61, 2 καὶ βιοῦν οὕτως ὑπισχνοῦνται,, a remark turning upside down the parallel to 1.Pet.3:21 in Polycarp, *Phil*.5:2, καθὼς ὑπίσχετο ἡμῖν ἐγεῖραι ἡμᾶς ἐκ νεκρῶν.

[3] Windisch, *Taufe und Sünde*, 1908, p.378, has rightly referred to the vow made by the Elkesaïtes at their second baptism, according to Hippol., *Philos*., IX.13f.

[4] Iren., *Adv. Haer*., III.12.8 (H.2,62), and IV.40 (H.2,231).

Acts 8:37. Moreover, his wording shows a curious restraint with regard to the question-answer rite: ὁ εὐνοῦχος πεισθεὶς καὶ παραυτίκα ἀξιῶν βαπτισθῆναι ἔλεγε· Πιστεύω τὸν υἱὸν τοῦ θεοῦ εἶναι Ἰησοῦν Χριστόν. It thus appears that Irenaeus omitted Philip's question and preserved no more than the eunuch's Creed. That means that in Smyrna—and probably in Antioch too—in the middle of the second century the Creed was recited by candidates for baptism. Nevertheless, the question-answer rite was practised where Acts 8:37 originated, for the manuscript evidence does not permit us to assume that verse 37b, the part quoted by Irenaeus, ever existed separately. The probability that Irenaeus drew on Roman traditions follows from the similarity of his remark to the words preceding our previous quotation from Justin Martyr, 1.*Apol*.61.2[a], ὅσοι ἂν πεισθῶσι καὶ πιστεύωσιν ἀληθῆ ταῦτα τὰ ὑφ' ἡμῶν διδασκόμενα καὶ λεγόμενα εἶναι κτλ. 'Πεισθείς' and 'πεισθῶσι' in connection with baptism point to a common source. On general grounds, too, it seems credible that Irenaeus at Lyons used the Roman text of Acts; but that as a pupil of Polycarp, he felt like his master—and 1.Pet.3:21—that God's promise should be stressed rather than man's vows.

If Rome was the place where the interpolation of Acts 8:37 was effected, it is also the place of origin of the earliest Creeds conceived in the form of question and answer, added to a similarly made renunciation of the devil.[1] The earliest document containing the baptismal Creed in form of question and answer, if genuine, takes us back to A.D. 220 and comes from Rome.[2] It is, of course, hard to prove that this rite was not at the same time practised elsewhere, and it will appear that it had certainly, at an early date, spread to Africa. However, oriental synods laid it down that the Creed should be learned by heart in the twenty days before baptism, and that it should be recited on Maundy Thursday

---

[1] Both of these have probably sprung from the exorcism which was practised in baptism since the earliest times, cf. W. Heitmüller, *Im Namen Jesu*, 1903, p.384f.

[2] The sources for this form of interrogatory Creeds in Hahn-Harnack, op. cit., p.34f., are all of Roman origin. Add Hippol., *Apost. Trad.*, 21.12–18, ed. G. Dix, 1937, p.36f., and note the oriental variants 21.11 ab, ibid., p.35f.

by all the catechumens then assembled in Church.[1] This, incidentally, was the only day of the year on which the Creed was publicly recited in the eastern Church. Since recital rather than question and answer was the practice in the Jewish baptisms, we may assume that the recital of the Creed was the earlier rite. That being the case, Irenaeus quoted verbatim only Acts 8:37b, for Philip's question was without special significance for him; but the eunuch's confession of faith was essential. In other words, Irenaeus persisted in the earlier oriental baptismal rite.

This rite was also practised in the West. We find it mentioned in Gaul at the council of Agde,[2] and in Spain, where it was expressly laid down at the second council of Braccara.[3] In Italy and Africa, however, the interrogation of the catechumens seems to have been practised. The view that Ambrose of Milan should have referred to a recital of the Creed[4] can easily be proved wrong from his other sayings; but even if he had the Creed recited in his baptismal liturgy, he certainly had the question-answer rite practised at the renunciation of the devil and the world. Moreover, he gave a clearly legal description to his catechumens of the effect which their renunciation of Satan and their confession of faith in Jesus Christ made in the course of the baptismal liturgy was to have upon those who took this step:[5]

respondisti, Abrenuntio. Memor esto sermonis tui et numquam tibi excidat series cautionis tuae.—Ubi promiseris considera vel quibus

---

[1] Cf. *Conc. Laodic.*, can.46 ὅτι δεῖ τοὺς φωτιζομένους τὴν πίστιν ἐκμανθάνειν καὶ τῇ πέμπτῃ τῆς ἑβδομάδος ἀπαγγέλλειν τῷ ἐπισκόπῳ ἢ τοῖς πρεσβυτέροις.

[2] *Conc. Agathen.* (A.D. 506) can.9.

[3] 2.*Conc. Bracc.* (A.D. 563), can.1, 'ante viginti dies baptismi catechumeni symbolum quod est, Credo in Deum Patrem omnipotentem, specialiter doceantur'.

[4] This view was tentatively proposed by Bingham, *Antiquities*, op. cit., 10.2.10, edit. London, 1875, p.437b, n.48. To this store-house of learning I am indebted for several references to little known sources. However, Ambros., *de Sacram.*, 2.7 (M.L., 16, 448) and Bingham's references to (Ambros.) *de Init.*, 2, 'ingressus es regenerationis sacrarium, repete quid interrogatus sis, recognosce quid responderis'; Ambrosiaster, *Comm.* 1 *Tim*, 6.12, 'cuius confessio inter ipsa rudimenta fidei teste interrogante et respondente monumentis ecclesiasticis continentur', prove my case.

[5] Ambrose, *de Sacram.*, 1.2, cf. Bingham, op. cit., 9.7.6, ibid., 518a.

promiseris: Levitam vidisti, sed minister est Christi. Vidisti illum ad altare ministrare: ergo chirographum tuum tenetur non in terra sed in coelo.

Two legal analogies have been used in this context, 'series cautionis tuae' and 'chirographum'. 'Series cautionis tuae excidat' means 'the content of thy promise may become void'. 'Cautio' in the language of the late Roman law was almost synonymous with 'a written acknowledgment of a debt',[1] and was commonly used by Ambrose in this meaning.[2] What kind of a written acknowledgment he had in mind appears from the second term he used, 'chirographum', 'note of hand'.[3] Such documents were at that time invariably concluded by a clausula referring to an accompanying 'stipulatio': on Egyptian papyri the formula ἐπερωτηθεὶς ὡμολόγησα. In Italy, too, this concluding formula had gained popularity since the second century A.D., as may be seen from the well-known 'donatio' of Flavius Artemidorus,[4] an inscription on stone headed 'chirographum' and concluded as follows:

se hac re dari, fieri praestarique stipulatus est M. Herennius Agricola spopondit Titus Flavius Artemidorus.

The original document was written in A.D. 176; and by the beginning of the third century the addition of such a 'stipulatio' to any 'chirographum' of whatever purpose had become universal.[5] It is, therefore, certain that by using the words 'cautio' and 'chirographum' Ambrose referred to the formal contract of Roman civil law as an analogy to the baptismal vows. People at his time were still aware that the 'stipulatio' was a verbal contract. In this

---

[1] Cf. Heumann-Seckel, *Handlexikon d. römischen Rechts*, 9th ed., 1914, p.61, s.v. *cautio* 2.

[2] B. Brissonius, *De Verborum Significatione*, ed. J. G. Heineccius, 1743, p.173a, s.v. *cautio* 2.

[3] Theologians should be warned not to compare Col.2:14. The legal differences between the χειρόγραφον of the early Empire and of post-Constantinian Italy are very considerable. Cf. H. Steinacker, *Die antiken Grundlagen der frühmittelalterlichen Privaturkunde*, 1927, p.29f.

[4] Cf. C. G. Bruns-O. Gradenwitz, *Fontes Iuris Romani*, 7th ed., 1909, v.1, p.335.

[5] L. Mitteis, *Reichsrecht und Volksrecht*, 1891, p.485f.

sense Ambrose himself said:[1] 'tenetur vox tua non in tumulo mortuorum sed in libro credentium'. 'Vox tua' obviously refers to the verbal contract.

Ambrose's views, however, do not seem to have had a very long tradition. They may have arisen in a somewhat earlier time, since the 'stipulatio' in the late fourth century had become a written clause added to all sorts of legal documents, and the ancient solemnity of the verbal contract had very largely passed out of legal practice. 'Cautio' and 'chirographum' may have been his modernization of an earlier scheme.[2] If so, Ambrose's testimony may witness to the fact that the baptismal interrogations and responses were traditionally regarded in Italy in the light of the ancient Roman verbal contract, concluded between the bishop as God's representative, and the catechumen. Nevertheless the analogy of the civil contract, the 'stipulatio', is no more than an episode. The ancient name for the baptismal vow, 'sacramentum', leads us to another and more stringent analogy, the military oath. In order to prove this we have to turn to Africa, for at Rome, as we shall see, the understanding of 'sacramentum' was in the third century[3] very largely influenced by its eastern counterpart

---

[1] *De Init.*, 2.—C. P. Caspari, *Ungedruckte . . . Quellen zur Geschichte des Taufsymbols*, v.2, 1869, p.50f., has unearthed another instruction of catechumens containing an interesting legal description of the XII Apostles as a co-operative society in creating the Creed: 'symbolum Graece dicitur, Latine autem collatio: et maxime symbolam negotiatores dicere consuerunt, quando conferunt pecuniam suam et quasi ex singulorum collatione in unum constipata integra et inviolabilis conservatur, ut nemo fraudem collationi facere conetur, nemo negotiationi: denique inter ipsos negotiatores ista est consuetudo, ut, si quis fraudem fecerit quasi fraudulentus reiciatur.' This interesting treatise has now been re-published by Dom R. Connolly, *The explanatio symboli ad initiandos*, 1952, and proved to be a genuine work of Ambrose.

[2] Cf. the entirely different use which Tertullian made of the term 'chirographum' when he said, *Pudic.*, 19, 'nam et solvit, liberans hominem per lavacrum, donato chirographo mortis'.

[3] According to H. v. Soden, *Z.N.W.*, 12, 1911, p.201f., μυστήριον in Justin Martyr had no connection with Christian baptism, but either meant the mystery of Christ's passion, death and resurrection, or 'religion'—especially pagan religion—in general. In Irenaeus, cf. ibid., p.204f., and Hippolytus, ibid., p.205, n.1, the word was used to describe gnostic liturgies in a slightly derogatory way.

μυστήριον: the initiation rite of the adherents of the mystery religions.[1]

The use of a question-answer rite in the African Church can be proved for the time of Cyprian. For this Father refers to it as an old-established custom in one of his letters:[2]

sed et ipsa interrogatio quae fit in baptismo testis est veritatis. Nam cum dicimus, Credis in vitam aeternam et remissionem peccatorum per sanctam ecclesiam? etc.

This evidence should go a long way to prove that the same rite was already practised at the time of Tertullian, even though his own words may sound ambiguous:[3]

cum aquam ingressi Christianam fidem in legis suae verba profitemur renuntiasse nos diabolo et pompae et angelis eius ore nostro contestamur.

If, therefore, Tertullian knew the solemn question-answer rite, it is surprising that he, the keen lawyer, nowhere used the Roman 'stipulatio' as an analogy for the baptismal vows, especially since he inclined to the doctrine that remission of sins was obtained by the good works of the catechumen.[4] For, although his chief analogy to the baptismal vows was the military oath, the 'sacramentum' of the Roman legionary, he was quite capable of introducing other parallels, as for instance that of 'Dei census', the enrolment in the citizen list of God's city.[5] It will appear, however, that the analogies of 'stipulatio' and 'sacramentum' were mutually exclusive.

[1] Cf. the use of μυστήριον in Clem. Alex., *Protr.*, 12.120.1.
[2] *Ep.*70.2.
[3] *De Spect.*, 4, cf. *Corona*, 3 'aquam inituri ibidem, sed et aliquanto prius in ecclesia sub antistitis manu contestamur nos renuntiare diabolo et angelis eius. Dehinc ter mergitamur amplius aliquid respondentes quam Dominus in evangelio determinavit'. 'Contestari' is ambiguous, but 'respondentes' points to the question-answer rite. The intentional vagueness is due to the 'regula fidei' being part of the 'disciplina arcani'.
[4] Loofs, op. cit., p.165, referring to Tert., de Paenit., 6.
[5] Tert., de Bapt., 17.

II

The oath of allegiance which the Roman legionary had to swear was called 'sacramentum'. It expressed his personal allegiance to the Emperor since the days of Augustus.[1] We know little about the ceremony performed, no doubt, when he first joined the ranks; for in the Empire the rite was repeated at least twice annually, on the day of the Emperor's accession and at the New Year, and the oath was sworn on these days not only by soldiers, magistrates and other officials, but also by the Roman citizens and subjects abroad.[2] Th. Mommsen was inclined to believe that a certain amount of compulsion was exercised by the Roman authorities to insure the regular repetition of these oaths, and in an extremity that may have been the case.[3] However, under normal circumstances the solemnity of the occasion was sufficient to guarantee the attendance of a large crowd and to make compulsion unnecessary. Neither the available number of officers who were entitled to demand the 'sacramentum' nor the existing census-lists were at all adequate to the task of exacting the oath from everybody. The Emperor Decius, it is true, tried to use this rite in his persecution of the Church, but the Christian historians have rightly regarded his action as an innovation, and the documents attesting the swearing of the oath on this occasion make it clear that universal compulsion was not the normal procedure.[4] Not only was the administrative problem insuperable—we know that thousands of African Christians under Decius successfully evaded the census—but also the value of such a compulsory oath would have been insignificant in comparison to the effort needed.

[1] Th. Mommsen, *Röm. Staatsrecht*, vol.2, 3rd ed., 1887, p.792f.

[2] Ibid., p.793, n.2.

[3] The two instances quoted, ibid., p.793, n.4, do not seem to bear out Mommsen's case.

[4] A. v. Domaszewski, *Die Religion d. röm. Heeres*, 1895, p.8, says that the essential symbols in the presence of which the Roman soldiers swore their oaths were the field-signs, and that it was only by accident that these surrounded the Emperor's bust, Tac., *Hist.*, I.55. This I find hard to believe: the statue of the Emperor seems rather to have taken the place of the republican general who received the *sacramentum* in person.

Even in the army the days of swearing were feast-days, and the repetition of the 'sacramentum' was part of their solemnities.[1]

We know now that Augustus not only slightly re-fashioned the terms of the military oath, as Mommsen believed,[2] but also established a military calendar for the use of all the forces. Yet it appears that Mommsen was right in assuming that the tenor of the oath and the ritual of swearing it was not greatly interfered with by Augustus. It is, therefore, as he has pointed out, permissible to refer in so far to republican antecedents. Copious collections of the formulae used were made by B. Brissonius,[3] and on these both J. Marquardt[4] and J. N. Madvig[5] have drawn for their descriptions of the procedure at the taking of the soldiers' 'sacramentum'. The best information comes from M. Verrius Flaccus, the tutor of the princes of the Julian house at the time of Augustus, who died as an old man under Tiberius.[6] In an excerpt of his work in Festus[7] we read, 'praeiurationes facere dicuntur qui ante alios conceptis verbis iurant; post quos in eadem verba iurantes tantummodo dicunt: idem in me'. From this we learn that the representative from each garrison spoke the 'verba concepta' of the oath, whilst the execration formula by which every oath was confirmed was adopted by each soldier severally with the words 'idem in me'. Only in exceptional cases do we hear that each soldier individually was asked to repeat the whole oath.[8] For the binding part was the clause condemning to eternal punishment all persons whatsoever who would break the oath. This, by the way, explains Ambrose's somewhat obscure remark,[9] 'tenetur vox tua

[1] Cf. Nock, *Harvard Theol. Rev.*, 1952, p.187f.—A similar annual oath was provided for the religious community of the Dead Sea, cf. V and VI of the 'Manual of Discipline', H. Wildberger, *Evangel. Theologie*, 1953, p.31f.

[2] Op. cit., 2, p.792, n.5, referring to Cassius Dio, LVII.3.2, τοὺς μὲν γὰρ ἐν τῇ Ἰταλίᾳ ὄντας τοῖς ὅρκοις τοῖς ὑπὸ τοῦ Αὐγούστου καταδειχθεῖσι προκατέλαβεν. This remark has assumed a new significance in the light of the newly discovered military calendar from Dura-Europos.

[3] Brissonius-Conradi-Bach, *De Formulis*, 1755, p.319.

[4] J. Marquardt, etc., *Röm. Staatsverwaltung*, 2nd ed., 1884, vol.2, p.385, n.4.

[5] Madvig, op. cit., vol.2, p.479.

[6] Sueton, *Gramm.*, 17.

[7] Festus in Bruns-Gradenwitz, op. cit., vol.2, p.26.

[8] Cf. Marquardt, op. cit., vol.2, p.385, n.3, referring to Tac., *Hist.*, IV.31.

[9] (Ambros.), *de Init.*, 2.

non in tumulo mortuorum sed in libro credentium': not the infernal deities will record the Christian baptismal vow, but the angels in heaven who keep the book of life (Rev.20:12).

The significant term for the legal understanding of 'sacramentum' used by Verrius is 'concepta verba', for this is a technical expression of Roman law. Just like 'sacramentum' itself, 'concepta verba' was a term used in Roman civil procedure; and there is now no doubt that the parties in a law-suit at Rome agreed before the 'praetor' by way of a formal contract to the 'formula conceptis verbis' which outlined the subject of their difference.[1] Such a contract, too, formed the basis of the 'legis actio sacramento' as much as that of the later form of procedure 'conceptis verbis'. It is thus evident that the 'sacramentum' of the Roman legionaries was closely connected with ideas related to the category of legal contract. Moreover, confirmation of contracts by oath was by no means an uncommon occurrence in Roman law, and we learn from Isidore of Seville that, right down to the bas-Empire, such contracts were considered to be a form of 'sponsio', the last survival of the verbal 'stipulatio'. He says,[2] 'sacramentum est pignus sponsionis; vocatum autem sacramentum quia violare quod quisque promittit perfidia est'. This remark, which is preceded by a quotation from Pauli *Sententiae*, 5.7.1, shows—if no more[3]—that definitions of 'sponsio' as a sacred rite, like that of Festus,[4] 'ex Graeco dictum ait, quod ii σπονδάς interpositis rebus divinis faciant', were never forgotten at Rome. This should be combined with the same author's definition of 'sacramentum':[5] 'sacramento dicitur quod [iure iurandi sacratio]ne interposita actum [est; unde sacramen]to dicitur interrogare quia [ius iurandum interponitur]'. These two texts show how the 'sponsio' could be, and often was, corro-

---

[1] L. Wenger, *Institutionen des röm. Zivilprozesses*, 1925, p.16.

[2] Isidor., *Origin.*, V.24.31.

[3] H. A. A. Danz, *Der sakrale Schutz*, 1857, p.107f., has added 'sacramentum' after 'firmum' in the line preceding our quotation. As there is no MS. evidence to support this addition, I prefer to neglect this precarious ally.

[4] Bruns-Gradenwitz, op. cit., vol.2, p.40.

[5] Ibid. p.33f. The completion of the lacunae marked can be taken as virtually certain.

borated by an oath, for the words 'sacramento interrogari' clearly refer to the scheme of the Roman verbal contract.

The Greeks and Romans generally regarded an oath as a contract between man and the deity,[1] and the texts quoted will help us to understand how the 'sacramentum' of the Roman soldiers, when viewed from a legal point of view, was quite naturally seen in the light of a verbal contract. The swearing of the oath was only one half of the contract, which consisted of the 'sacramento rogare', an expression especially beloved by Julius Caesar, on the part of the Roman commander, or Emperor, and the 'sacramento dicere' on the part of the soldiers.[2] An almost literal statement of this fact may be found in Livy's description of the arrival of the younger Scipio in the camp of the army besieging Numantia:[3] 'citati milites nominatim apud tribunos militum in verba Scipionis iurarunt'. This means that the soldiers by their oath undertook to serve and obey the general according to his terms, his 'verba concepta'. This oath, therefore, instituted a strong personal link between the Roman general and his soldiers as long as he was in command. Whenever a change of commander took place, this relation was re-constituted by a new—and possibly different— oath. Various formulae of Roman military oaths, largely preserved by Greek historians,[4] are not stereotyped; they can only serve to indicate the type of obligation undertaken by the Roman legionaries when they swore their oath of allegiance.[5] The value of the formula preserved by Gellius[6] consists in the fact that being conceived in the second person singular, as a question addressed

---

[1] The fact that in classical times every oath was seen as a contract has been proved by R. Hirzel, *Der Eid*, 1902, p.65f.

[2] The distinction between the two terms has been neatly set out, by Marquardt, op. cit., vol.2, p.385, n.5, but neither he nor Madvig, op. cit., p.479, who has added further material, has drawn the obvious conclusion from it, that the Roman military oath was a formal verbal contract 'iuris publici.'

[3] Livy, XXVIII.29.12.

[4] The formula preserved in Polyb., VI.21.2, ἦ μὴ πειθαρχήσειν καὶ ποιήσειν τὸ προστατόμενον ὑπὸ τῶν ἀρχόντων, has been treated with too much respect even by Marquardt, op. cit., vol.2, p.384, n.10.

[5] Brissonius, *De Formulis*, p.320, although he overstressed the formula in Gellius, *N.A.*, XVI.4.2, made this quite clear by the numerous instances given.

[6] Gellius, *N.A.*, XVI.4.2, from L. Cincius, *de Re Militari* (first century B.C.).

to the soldier who was about to swear the oath, it proves the 'sacramentum' to be a verbal contract of the 'ius publicum'. In one respect this contract differed from the 'stipulatio' of the 'ius civile', and to this Tertullian, the trained lawyer, has drawn attention,[1] the 'sacramentum', being a contract of the 'ius publicum', could be received by a representative of the Roman commander, usually a 'tribunus militum', a staff officer, whereas the civil contract demanded that the parties must meet in person.[2]

III

Two facts have arisen out of our considerations, the first that where the Christian baptismal vows were taken by way of question and answer, they could be likened, and by Ambrose were likened, to the 'stipulatio', the verbal contract of the civil law. The analogy was not drawn, however, by Tertullian, although he was a trained lawyer.[3] The second fact which we can state is that the 'sacramentum' of the Roman legionary was a verbal contract of the 'ius publicum', similar to the 'stipulatio' in that it employed the simple ritual of question and answer. This was the analogy which was repeatedly stressed by Tertullian. In other words, Tertullian rejected the legal analogy to the baptismal vows offered by the Roman 'ius civile' and insisted upon another derived from the Roman 'ius publicum'. It remains to be seen what his reasons were for doing so, and whether his reasons were universally adopted. It may be that his views were purely traditional, in which case, owing to the state of our sources, we would be unable to determine their origin. On the other hand, it may be that Tertullian, although he adopted an earlier view, gave it the mark of his personality. In this case the content and fate of his views are of great importance.

---

[1] Tert., *Bapt.*, 11.

[2] This distinction should throw light on the origin of the Roman 'procuratores', and especially on Cic., *pro Caec.*, 57, cf. Mitteis, *Röm. Privatrecht*, 1908, p.234, n.102.

[3] I can find only one remote allusion, *De Fuga*, 12, 'apud inferos remancipatio nostra est et stipulatio in coelis', cf. A. Beck, *Röm. Recht bei Tertullian u. Cyprian*, 1931, p.94, n.2, and p.106.

The fact that 'sacramentum' in the sense of 'vow' or 'oath' was used in the Latin Church long before Tertullian, seems to follow from the famous report of Pliny the Younger about the Christians in Bithynia, and is admitted by Tertullian himself. This is what Pliny wrote to the Emperor Trajan:[1]

seque sacramento non in scelus aliquod obstringere, sed ne furta, ne latrocinia, ne adulteria committerent, ne fidem fallerent, ne depositum adpellati abnegarent.

No doubt that 'sacramentum' here has the meaning of 'oath',[2] and if Pliny himself was responsible for the surprising choice of the word, there can be no doubt either that Tertullian approved of this choice as being substantially correct, and thus made it clear that he used 'sacramentum' as a traditional term. He said that Pliny[3]

nihil aliud de sacramentis comperisse quam coetus antelucanos ad canendum Christo ut deo et ad confoederandam disciplinam, homicidium, adulterium, fraudem, perfidiam et cetera scelera prohibentes.

At the same time we see that the meaning of 'sacramentum' in this sentence is slightly changed. The vow of abstaining from immoral and criminal practices is still prominent in it, but added to this there appears the hymn-singing as part of the 'sacramenta', something which Pliny had treated separately. This, therefore, is an accretion to the meaning of 'sacramentum' which had enriched it in the time between Pliny and Tertullian. The latter, we believe, strove to restore the meaning of 'oath', and for this purpose stressed the analogy of the military oath.

A. Harnack has by a number of quotations illustrated the fact that Tertullian stressed the analogy between the baptismal vows of the Christians and the 'sacramentum' of the Roman soldiers.[4]

[1] Pliny, *Ep.* 10.96.
[2] The suggestion made in Hastings, *Dictionary of Religion and Ethics*, s.v. *sacramentum* (western) that Pliny may have misunderstood his witnesses is unconvincing; the remarks passed, ibid., on the *legis actio sacramento* are unfounded and incorrect.
[3] Tert., *Apol.*, 2.
[4] Harnack, *Militia Christi*, 1905, p.33.

Before entering upon these passages we must for a moment consider the ethos which lay behind Tertullian's analogy. Wherever an organization which is not recognized by law rejects the analogies offered by civil law and selects those offered by constitutional law, when it shuns the form of private association and models itself upon the army, it is a revolutionary organization. This attitude is clearly discernible in Tertullian. Thus, when he says, *Ad Mart.*, 2, 'vocati sumus ad militiam dei vivi iam tunc cum in sacramenti verba respondimus', we must not only take notice of 'respondimus', which reminds us that the 'sacramentum' was a verbal contract of public law, but also remember that it was the 'sacramentum' which distinguished the 'miles' from the 'latro', and honourable captivity from shameful prison.[1] *Praescr.*, 20,'quae iura non alia ratio regit quam eiusdem sacramenti una traditio', does not only stress the legal character of the 'sacramentum', but much more that the Christian order of life was that of the military camp.[2] *Corona*, 11, 'credimus humanum sacramentum divino, superduci licere et in alium dominum respondere post Christum?' and *De Idol.* 19, 'non convenit sacramento divino et humano, signo Christi et signo diaboli, castris lucis et castris tenebrarum; non potest una duabus deberi deo et Caesari', not only deserve our attention because of the obvious legal allusions in 'respondere' and 'deberi', but because they plainly state the conflict, claiming exclusiveness for the Christian 'sacramentum' and resolutely placing the Emperor and his 'sacramentum humanum'[3] side by side with the powers of darkness. Such views were not encountered among the Christians of Bithynia by Pliny, and they combine ill with the ideas of 'mysterium', hymn-singing, etc. They may be regarded as Tertullian's, and the question arises how strong were they?

It is clear that Tertullian had to take his stand against a deep-rooted tradition. A. Harnack[4] has rightly stated that in addition to

[1] Marquardt, op. cit., vol.2, p.387, n.2.

[2] Similar, *Scorp.*, 4, 'huic sacramento militans ab hostibus provocor; . . . quis hunc militi suo exitum voluit nisi qui tali eum sacramento consignavit?'

[3] This was an obvious 'crimen laesae maiestatis' under Commodus, E. Beurlier, *Le Culte Imperial*, 1891, p.38f., but would just pass in the more sober times of Septimius Severus.

[4] Harnack, op. cit., p.33.

'military oath' 'sacramentum' in Tertullian had a variety of meanings which may be combined under the heading of 'a sign mys-
teriously representing a sacred matter and forming part of it'. In
other words, it was the translation of the Greek μυστήριον. This
is in no way surprising. What is surprising is that E. de Backer[1]
has found that in every four out of seven cases where Tertullian
uses 'sacramentum' it has the clear denotation of 'oath'. It can also
be held that in most of the other cases at least a connotation of
'baptismal vow', either in its liturgical sense or in its material
sense, can be discovered in Tertullian's use of 'sacramentum'. That
may be illustrated by one particular instance. The passage I have
chosen is one recently discussed by that outstanding authority on
Tertullian, Canon E. Evans. He has suggested[2] that *Adv. Prax.*, 2,
'et nihilominus custodiatur οἰκονομίας sacramentum quae unita-
tem in trinitatem disponit', should be translated as follows: 'While
none the less is guarded the mystery of that economy which dis-
poses the unity into trinity'. I venture to suggest that the translation should read, 'the confession of faith in that economy, etc.'.[3]
The difference is not without significance, for although Tertullian
knew that 'sacramentum' could serve as a translation of Greek
μυστήριον,[4] he himself, like other Africans,[5] used the Latin trans-
literation 'mysterium' and seems to have insisted that Christianity
must not be confounded with the pagan mysteries.[6] Tertullian,
therefore, attempted as far as possible to maintain that use of

[1] J. de Ghellinck, E. de Backer, et. al., *Sacramentum*, 1924, p.143f.

[2] E. Evans, *Tertullian's Treatise against Praxeas*, 1947, p.132.

[3] Evans, op. cit., p.45, adding 'though it remains a mystery' has, I believe,
imparted to Tertullian something of his own thought, for I feel that Tertullian
showed little inclination towards 'credo quia absurdum' or the 'mysterium
tremendum'.

[4] Tert., *Adv. Marcion.*, V.18, a *Vetus Latina* version of Eph.5:32.

[5] E.g. *De Rebapt.*, 3.

[6] Tert., *Praescr.*, 40, 'a diabolo, cuius sunt pares intervertendi veritatem, qui
ipsas quoque res sacramentorum divinorum idolorum mysteriis aemulatur,
tingit et ipse quosdam etc.' This attitude towards the word μυστήριον is
identical with that of Justin Martyr and Irenaeus. On the other hand, Tert.,
Adv. Marcion., I.13 'aridae et ardentis naturae sacramenta leones Mithrae philo-
sophantur', may suggest the existence of Mithraic 'sacramenta', and there is one
occasional remark, Tert., *Ad Nat.*, I.7, 'nihil enim unquam retro de Christianis
mysteriis audierant', referring to Christian mysteries.

'sacramentum' which showed the connection of the word with the idea of 'militia Christi', so highly favoured by the Roman centurion's son, and the legal conception of a new covenant between Christ and His soldier, so dear to the lawyer. Very few cases in which 'sacramentum' occurs in his writings show no trace of either of these ideas.[1] I therefore conclude that, once the idea of baptismal vow is fully understood in all its implications, comprising in the baptismal liturgy all the Sacraments in which priestly ministrations are demanded, as penance, immersion, unction, laying on of hands, and the Eucharist, and on the material side both the Christian faith (the Creed) and the 'via vitae' (the Ten Commandments and the renunciation of the devil), no etymological speculations will be needed to explain the use of 'sacramentum' by Tertullian.

Rome, too, had in the second century shown a healthy distrust of the term μυστήριον. However, in the third century, if we may trust Novatian and his compatriot, the author of Ps. Cyprian, *Adv. Judaeos*, the Roman Church took a different line. From the collections of J. de Ghellinck and his collaborators it appears[2] that among the meanings of 'sacramentum' which were prominent in Africa two are not to be found in the writings of third-century Roman theologians. The one is the meaning of 'military oath', the other that of 'Holy Sacrament'. It is the former, of course, which concerns us here. It has to be said that in this instance Novatian deliberately differed from his master Tertullian, whom he followed in most other respects.[3] The reason for this difference cannot be found in any change in the attitude of the Church in Africa. There, the analogy of the baptismal vows and the military oath was still a commonplace: Cyprian as well as his adversary,

[1] Tertullian occasionally spoke of Jewish 'sacramenta', e.g. *Apol.*, 17; but Evans, op. cit., p.331, has brilliantly illumined the situation by his note on *Adv. Prax.*, 31, 'novare sacramentum—make a new covenant', a 'novatio' of the 'sacramentum', contract of public law, and pagan rites are described pointedly, *Ad Nat.*, I.16, as 'vestra non sacramenta'. Neither *Corona*, 15, nor *Exhort. Cast.*, 13, should be adduced as proof that he did not mean what he said.

[2] de Ghellinck, op. cit., p.218.

[3] This verdict of Jerome, *De Viris Illustr.*, 70, has been tested and found substantially correct by Evans, op. cit., p.25f.

the author of *De Rebaptismate*,[1] accepted it, and it found a fervent advocate in Arnobius.[2] At Rome, however, the meaning of μυστήριον, that term which had been unpopular with both Irenaeus and Hippolytus, had gained the field.

IV

The change at Rome may indicate a lessening in the Christian resistance to the state. A similar one in Africa can mean nothing else. Lactantius in his earlier period, when he wrote his *Divinae Institutiones*,[3] made frequent use of the term 'sacramentum' in the sense of 'oath of allegiance'. However, he seems to have become far more cautious in the use of the word after he had left Africa. In his Epitome of the *Institutiones* at any rate he has used a considerable number of circumscriptions for 'sacramentum', which clearly avoid this particular meaning.[4] I suspect that one of the reasons for this reserve towards the use of 'sacramentum', on the part of that African Father to whom Constantine entrusted the education of his son Crispus, is to be found in the revolutionary taint which Tertullian had given it. At the time of the Donatist revolt this revolutionary flavour was bound to come out in various ways, and a loyal Catholic African Christian would find sufficient reason to avoid such an ambiguous expression.

Moreover, the time was approaching when the analogy with the military oath was to become strained and to lose much of its reality. When the Empire turned Christian the military oath had to be changed. How this came about, and at what time, is uncertain. We may assume that Constantine himself, who still not only allowed his soldiers to acclaim him 'dii te nobis servent', but even

---

[1] de Ghellinck, op. cit., p.218.

[2] Cf. e.g. Arnob., *Ad Nat.*, II.5, 'quod ab dominis se servi cruciatibus adfici quibus statuerint malunt, solvi coniuges matrimoniis, exheredari a parentibus liberi, quam fidem rumpere Christianam et salutaris militiae sacramenta deponere'.

[3] Cf. e.g. Lactant., *Div. Inst.*, I.1, 'nobis autem qui sacramentum verae religionis accepimus, cum sit veritas revelata divinitus, cum doctorem sapientiae ducemque virtutis Deum sequamur, universos sine ullo discrimine vel sexus vel aetatis ad caeleste pabulum convocamus'.

[4] de Ghellinck, op. cit., p.241f.

allowed this acclamation to be put on the statute-book,[1] permitted neutral[2] or alternative[3] formularies to be used by Christian and pagan soldiers. However, we know from Vegetius[4] that at the end of the fourth century the military oath was sworn after the enrolment of a soldier in the following terms:

per Deum et Christum et Spiritum Sanctum, et per maiestatem imperatoris . . . omnia se facturos quae praeceperit imperator; numquam deserturos militiam nec mortem recusaturos pro Romana re publica.

This oath, for which we can quote the support of a papyrus of the fifth century, insofar as the trinitarian formula is concerned, though it is otherwise a civilian oath sworn in A.D. 438, under the reign of Theodosius II and Valentinianus III,[5] was still called 'sacramentum'. However, its character had changed. The ancient system of Hellenistic despotism, which had made the king the guarantor rather than a party to the oath, so ably described by Seidl,[6] once more won the day. Thus the basis of an argument with the Emperor about the compelling force of the baptismal vows had shifted.

The argument itself, however, arose with an unparalleled asperity when Constantius II embraced Arianism and persecuted the Catholics. We are fortunate in possessing a reference to the baptismal confession of faith in the pamphlet addressed to Constantius II by Hilary of Poitiers:[7]

[1] *Cod. Theod.*, VII.20.2 (A.D. 320). Justinian, *Cod. Just.*, XII.46.1, piously and discreetly changed this to 'Deus te nobis servet', thus underlining for us the pagan character of the, original.

[2] Such are the oaths on Egyptian papyri of the fourth century, which contain no invocation of the deity whatsoever, but only the mention of the monarch, cf. E. Seidl, *Der Eid im röm.-ägypt. Provinzialrecht*, 1933, vol.2, p.8f.

[3] We know from Tert., *Corona*, 15, that the followers of Mithras were not punished by their military commanders for refusing to wear garlands at the military ceremonies.

[4] Vegetius, *Epitoma Rei Mil.*, 2.5.

[5] *Stud. Pal.*, vol.20, nr.122, Πατέρα, Υἱόν, Ἅγιον Πνεῦμα καὶ τὴν εὐσέβειαν καὶ νίκην τῶν δεσπότων ἡμῶν Θεοδοσίου καὶ Οὐαλεντινιανοῦ τῶν αἰωνίων Αὐγουστῶν, cf. E. Seidl, op. cit., vol.2, p.8, n.7.

[6] Seidl, *Der Eid im Ptolemäischen Recht*, 1929, p.13f., and ibid, pp.23, 31.

[7] Hilar. Pictav., *Ad Const. Aug.*, 2.4 (M.L.10, 565f.).

Recognosce fidem quam olim, optime ac religiosissime imperator ab episcopis optas audire et non audis. Dum enim a quibus ea requiritur, sua scribunt et non quae Dei sunt praedicant, orbem aeternum erroris et redeuntis in se semper certaminis circumtulerunt. Oportuerat enim humanae infirmitatis modestia omne cognitionis divinae sacramentum illis tantum conscientiae suae finibus contineri quibus credidit, neque post confessam et iuratam in baptismo fidem in nomine Patris et Filii et Spiritus Sancti quidquam aliud vel ambigere vel innovitare.[1]

There is much in this accusation which was intentionally left ambiguous. 'Sacramentum' is separated from 'fidem confessam et iuratam', so that it suggests the meaning of 'mystery' rather than that of 'military oath'. Nevertheless, the oath is there: the confession of faith which man may neither change nor break, the competition between God and Caesar. There could be no choice, said Hilary:[2]

et quia in regenerationis nostrae nativitate in haec sacramenta iuramus, renuntiantes diabolo, saeculo, peccatis, cum interrogantibus respondemus, retinendam usque in finem confessionis huius fidem statuit.

Here we even find the military expression 'in haec sacramenta iuramus', which we know from Vegetius. Only—the analogy with the military oath was nowhere expressly drawn. Even at the time of victory, when Ambrose quite openly quoted Tertullian,[3] the analogy of the 'militia Christi' was not very strongly stressed.[4]

[1] Learn the faith, o you best and most religious Emperor, which you desire all along to hear from the bishops, but never hear. For some, when they are asked for it, write their own ideas and fail to profess what is of God: they have carried around that eternal cosmos of error and eternally repeated conflict. Yet it behoved human infirmity in modesty to let the whole mystery of our knowledge of the Divine be contained within those limits of our insight, in which it believes, and not after having confessed by oath in baptism the faith in the name of the Father and the Son and the Holy Spirit, to hanker after something new and different.

[2] Hilar. Pictav., *In Ps.*14.14 (M.L.9, 306).

[3] Ambros. *Comm. Luc.* 9.36 (M.L.15, 1894) 'et bene prius quae Caesaris sunt Caesari reddenda decernit; neque enim potest esse quis Domini nisi prius renuntiaverit mundo. Sed omnes renuntiamus verbis, sed non omnes renuntiamus affectu; nam cum sacramenta suscipimus, renuntiamus', cf. Tert. *De Idol.*, 19, 'non potest una duobus deberi, Deo et Caesari'.

[4] Hilar. Pictav., *Ad Const.*, 10, cf. E. M. Pickman, *The Mind of Latin Christen-*

The struggle for the orthodox faith was not a revolutionary one, and accordingly the analogy of the civil contract was preferred. This is what Hilary said:[1]

venturi enim ad baptismum prius confitentur credere se in Dei Filio et in passione et resurrectione eius; et huius professionis sacramento fides redditur. Atque ut hanc verborum sponsionem quaedam rerum ipsarum veritas sequatur etc.;

his contemporary Zeno of Verona[2] instructed his catechumens in a similar way: 'ligaturis adstringitur cum, renuntians saeculo sponsione facta, spiritaliter sacris interrogationibus obligatur'. The context in both cases leaves us in no doubt that these were descriptions of the effect of the baptismal vows. Finally, the Ambrosiaster twice[3] refers to the 'verba solemnia' used in baptism, a current formula for the description of the question-answer rite at the 'stipulatio'.[4]

This then was the ground upon which the analogy was drawn between the baptismal vows and the 'stipulatio', which we have found in Ambrose. The Arian conflict, as we have seen, was for the Catholics not a revolutionary one, but they resorted to an appeal made 'de imperatore male informato ad imperatorem melius informandum'. For behind the Arians there threatened, throughout the fourth century, the forces of pagan reaction, especially in the city of Rome. The leaders of the Catholics were not inclined to conjure up this enemy once more. However it cannot be denied that revolutionary sentiments came to the fore, not so much with Hilary but particularly among the younger generation who had experienced only the later phases of the struggle,

---

dom, 1935, vol.I, p.22 n. 132, was not even afraid to compare Constantius II. with Judas, and *contra Arian.*, 4, cf. Pickman, op. cit., vol.I, p.17, has given a most moving comparison of the Church under pagan with that under Arian persecution; nevertheless, he has very little to say about 'militia Christi'.

[1] Hilar. Pictav., *Comm. Matth.*, 15.8 (M.L.9, 1006), cf. ibid., *In Ps.*, 118.14 (M.L.9, 652) 'se spondens Christo'.

[2] Zeno Veron., *Tract.* II.27.3 (M.L.11, 470). Cf. on the time of this Father, Palanque-Bardy-Labriolle, *De la Paix Constantinienne . . .* , 1947, p.227f.

[3] Ambrosiaster, *Com. 1.Cor.*, 1:17; 3:6 (M.L.17, 198; 209).

[4] Cf. e.g. Pauli, *Sent.* V.7.1.

such as Jerome (born c. A.D. 340) and Rufinus (born A.D. 345). These men returned to the meaning of 'military oath' for 'sacramentum', the timid Jerome with a tremendous verve when he wrote,[1] 'recordare tirocinii tui diem quo, Christo in baptismate consepultus, in sacramenti verba iurasti'. The whole context breathes a military spirit, but it referred not to the general Christian duties but to the special vocation of hermit. Not so Rufinus,[2] who resolutely took his analogy from the civil wars:

denique et in bellis civilibus hoc observari ferunt, quoniam et armorum habitus par et sonus vocis idem et mos unus est atque eadem instituta bellandi, ne qua doli subreptio fiat, symbola discreta unusquisque dux suis militibus tradit

and he found followers in this.[3] Nevertheless it has to be realized that Rufinus changed the simile: it was no longer the military oath which was compared with the baptismal vows, but the watch-word of an army engaged in civil war which was compared with the Apostles' Creed, a general appeal rather than an individual one. Times had changed and the true 'milites Christi' were now only those who lived a monastic life.[4] To those Ambrose could still address the old challenge which, at the time of Tertullian, had been meant for all Christians,[5] 'quando enim sine militiae sacramento miles in tentorio, bellator in proelio?' As to Christian laymen, common opinion in the West was unanimous to see their baptismal vows only in the light of a civil contract, if no longer as a 'stipulatio' yet still as a 'pactum'.[6]

---

[1] Jerome., *Ad Heliodor.*, *Epist.*14.2 (M.L.22, 548).

[2] Rufin., *In Symb. Apost.*2 (M.L.21, 338).

[3] E.g. Maxim. Taurin., *Hom. de Trad. Symb.*, quoted after Caspari, op. cit., vol.2, p.89, 'quod beati Apostoli, ut ego reor, exemplum sequentes ecclesiae Dei, quam adversum militiam diabolici furoris armabant, mysterium symboli tradiderunt' etc.

[4] K. Holl, *Gesammelte Aufsätze*, 1928, vol.3, p.193, n.1.

[5] Ambrose, *De Virgin.* III.4.20, C.P. Caspari, op. cit., vol.2, p.90, n.62.

[6] Cf. the sources in Caspari, *Alte und Neue Quellen*, 1879, p.294, n.28.

HOLY SACRAMENT AND SUFFERING

I

THE laborious work of textual criticism has been going on for over a century. A new knowledge of New Testament language and grammar has been established which surpasses by far all that was known or believed in at the beginning of the last century, but the theological gain which has accrued from this work has been scanty, although the work was in the main carried on by theologians. Apart from a general uneasiness about the reliability of the New Testament records of the life of Jesus and the conditions in the Church of the Apostles, there are few results of textual criticism which come to one's mind when the question is asked what effect the concentrated energy of so many great Christian scholars has had on the teaching of the Church. When we consider in particular how far the teaching of St. Paul has become clearer by the establishment of a text so infinitely superior to the *textus receptus* as are the modern Souter or Nestle texts, we have to confess that no one has really concerned himself with this question. The work of bringing the results of textual criticism to bear upon the doctrinal teaching of the Church has yet to be done, for otherwise the Church's doctrine will be discredited. I shall try to make here a contribution to this doctrinal re-valuation of a text which has suffered a change at the hands of the textual critics.

The passage which merits such a re-interpretation is 1.Cor.11:29 where a change in the text has been brought about by the careful and not in the least revolutionary critical methods applied by Westcott and Hort. Here the *textus receptus* reads:

He who eateth and drinketh unworthily, eateth and drinketh damnation (or: judgment) to himself not discerning the Lord's body.

We all know the tremendous edifice about fasting communion,

soul-searching, etc., which has been erected upon the words 'un-worthily' and 'the Lord's', yet since Westcott and Hort it is the unanimous verdict of textual critics of the New Testament that these words were not to be found in the original of 1 Corinthians, and this has been borne out of late by the Chester-Beatty papyrus which, like all other reliable witnesses, does not contain the words ἀναξίως and τοῦ κυρίου. Even the modern Roman Catholic editions of the Greek New Testament relegate these words ac-cordingly to the footnotes. It is the Latin and Syriac traditions which support *indigne*, and the Syriac, but only part of the Latin, manuscripts have also *Domini*, a tradition of such little credit that Wordsworth and White have even removed the word *Domini* from their edition of the Vulgate.

Westcott's and Hort's contemporaries, in order to safeguard the traditional interpretation of v. 29, have offered the following translation in the Revised Version:

> For he that eateth and drinketh, eateth and drinketh judgment unto himself, if he does not discern the body.

The translators have thus accepted the alternative offered in the margin of the Authorised Version, 'judgment', instead of 'dam-nation', but even so it remains to be seen whether they have achieved their objective. For it is obvious that the two additions 'unworthily' and 'the Lord's' are explanatory additions made to clear up an uncertainty, and that it is therefore the duty of the interpreter to find out—and if necessary to refute—the other pos-sible interpretation, and not simply to resign himself to Robertson-Plummer's conclusion that 'the exact meaning of v. 29 is uncer-tain'. Their three tentative explanations all presuppose the exis-tence of 'unworthily' and 'the Lord's' in the text. In so doing they reject J. Moffatt's translation, 'he who eats and drinks without a proper sense of the Body, eats and drinks to his own condemna-tion'; but Moffatt's interpretation of the passage is just as tradi-tional as theirs. A. Schlatter, the German theologian, states em-phatically, 'it cannot be Paul's view that whosoever eats and drinks brings judgment upon himself', but since that is the clear meaning of the Greek, I am amazed that he gives no reason whatsoever to support his view. The question whether τὸ σῶμα really means the Lord's body has not been asked at all, although the later addition of τοῦ κυρίου may well lead to the opposite conclusion. Thus it seems true to say that the analysis of 1.Cor.11:29 may yet lead to fresh results and that earlier attempts do not compel us to join unreservedly the chorus of voices claiming that the Apostle was lacking in lucidity and had to be rescued by later generations with the simple expedient of adding three more words. We suggest as a tentative translation of the Apostle's words:

Whosoever eats and drinks, eats and drinks condemnation unto himself, not separating his own person (or: body).

II

My first task is, of course, to justify this translation and to point out where and why earlier translators have gone wrong. The next step will be to examine the results of the earlier exegetes in order to show that they justify making a new start. After that I shall offer reasons to support as well as to correct the Church's doctrine of the Eucharist in the light of the alteration of 1. Cor.11:29.

We begin with the word κρίμα which the Revised Version translates as 'judgment' and of which Robertson–Plummer say, 'it is a neutral word, court or judgment, not condemnation, still less damnation'. The three great dictionaries of the New Testament by Cremer-Koegel, W. Bauer and G. Kittel do not bear out this assertion, which has been the only support for those who feel anxious lest condemnation might be the inevitable result of receiving Communion. It may be defended on the ground that the Vulgate says *iudicium*, but Jerome's inserting *indigne* made it clear in what sense he wanted this ambiguous word to be understood. It is indefensible when modern commentators, like Lietzmann, adduce Jerome as an authority but at the same time omit *indigne*. Particular attention must be drawn to the fact that κρίμα in v. 29 is not isolated, but that there is a surfeit of words derived from the Greek stem κριν- in vv. 27–34. No translator will be able to imitate this, but it is his duty to use the same translation when a word occurs twice in such a paragraph, as κρίμα, in vv. 29 and 34 and διακρίνειν in vv. 29 and 31, and to take notice of the fact that St. Paul by his choice of words shows that his subject is judgment and condemnation in relation to the Eucharist. This fact was stressed already by Tertullian but seems to be imperfectly understood by Lietzmann who describes the repetition of διακρίνειν in vv. 29 and 31 as being in the nature of a pun. Regarding the meaning of διακρίνειν, we find that it means either to judge or to discriminate, and that there is no evidence supporting Lietzmann's thesis that it was ever used as a synonym for δοκιμάζειν (v. 28). 'To judge' seems to make no sense in the context of either v. 29 or 31. Rom.8:33 expressly forbids that men should 'judge' the body of Christ, and to 'judge' the elements, taking 'body' in that very rare and specialised meaning, is hardly feasible and not borne out by the Vulgate translation *diiudicans*. Next comes the translation of σῶμα. It means of course the body, and in v. 27 it has the connotation of the bread which is the body of Christ. But this is a very rare meaning, and why it should be the meaning of σῶμα in v. 29, is not evident. I suggest that it means body = person or 'self', which gives the version 'discerning one-self' (for 'not judging one-self' would take us too close to δοκιμάζειν in v. 28 and would presuppose the 'unworthily', two things which we must avoid). Consequently I prefer—for the time being only as an hypothesis— the translation 'to discriminate' or 'to discern', all the more so as this meaning is borne out by the use of διακρίνειν in 1.Cor.4:7. In this way we have dealt with the most disputed words in v. 29, κρίμα, διακρίνειν, and σῶμα, and have come to the conclusion that the translation proposed is possible.

As regards the interpretation of the context, current opinion makes it extremely difficult to connect v. 29 either with the preceding or with the subsequent verses. The connection backward proposed by current opinion makes v. 29 appear as a mere repetition of v. 27a, from which it is somewhat awkwardly separated by v. 28. Μὴ διακρίνων τὸ σῶμα appears in that light as a special case of unworthy reception of the Sacrament, complementary to the general use of ἀναξίως in v. 27a. But we learn from v. 28 that the

unworthiness contemplated in v. 27a is the neglect of a due preparation for the receiving of the blessed Sacrament. In v. 29,
however, the very act of receiving Holy Communion is envisaged and there is no more time left for preparation. At the
reception itself, so the commentators say, the communicant must
be aware that he receives a special food, otherwise he will 'eat and
drink judgment unto himself'. Such is the unanimous verdict of
Lietzmann, Schlatter, Rengstorf, and all the others. They take for
granted that σῶμα in v. 29 has the same meaning as in the Words
of Institution, although this use is not found elsewhere in the New
Testament, and none of them attempts to justify this view. In
other words, the intention of the interpolator has been imple-
mented by subsequent generations of theologians until it has become sacrilege to doubt the authenticity of his additions. All the
same it can be proved that he was wrong. The same Lietzmann
who in his commentary on Corinthians says 'discriminate, means
to discriminate from profane food', has shown in his *Messe und
Herrenmahl* (p. 228), that the Corinthian church celebrated the
Agape and the Eucharist together, and even states this view
in an earlier passage of his commentary. That means that no discrimination of sacred and profane food was contemplated by the
Corinthians, and it would be a subtle psychologist indeed who
attempted to judge whether or not a mental discrimination of
this kind took place in the minds of newly converted communicants. 'Fasting and bodily preparation' may be, as Luther said,
'a fine outward discipline', although St. Paul prescribes in
1.Cor.11:21, 34, that Christians should not be hungry when
taking the sacred meal, but 'the consciousness of the difference'
as demanded by most of the commentators is to my mind sheer
hypocrisy.

Still more difficult is the link with the verses following v. 29.
In v. 27 it is said that an unworthy communicant will be 'guilty of
the body and blood of the Lord', i.e. he will be treated 'as a
heathen man and a publican', Matt.18:17. That has a genuine
ring: such a man will not be tolerated in the Church of Christ. In
v. 29, however, it is said that 'he eateth and drinketh judgment
unto himself' which, according to v. 30, means that he will fall ill

and die. A. Schweitzer in his *Mysticism of Paul the Apostle*[1] says, 'therefore the Lord by the cases of sickness and death is bringing home to them that a dying which will lose them the glory of the Messianic kingdom may be their fate if they do not use the "Lord's Meal" as an opportunity for strengthening their union with Christ'. In other words, A. Schweitzer holds that St. Paul's mysticism enabled the Apostle to meet Christian mourners at Corinth with an impish 'told you so': if your dead had not taken the Eucharist unworthily, they would still be alive. At the same time the blessed Sacrament appears as a means of dangerous magic which creates physical discomfort to the unbeliever. Does any modern commentator believe that? I hope not; but why then do they burden St. Paul with such heathenish superstition? Still more objectionable is the current interpretation of v. 31f. which altogether eliminates v. 29. The fact that St. Paul made his choice of words to assure us that v. 31f. depends upon v. 29 and not upon v. 28, in that he repeated διακρίνειν in v. 31 and κρίμα in v. 34, but did not use δοκιμάζειν again after v. 28, is completely overlooked. Insofar as German commentators are concerned, that may be because they like to forget how dangerously near their exegesis leads to demanding a fasting communion. Therefore they substitute their demand for self-examination. But this cannot be done. The interpolator clearly held the view that the Corinthians would not have died if they had adhered to the rule of fasting communion, and the same is the logical outcome of Lietzmann's exegesis, if only he did not wear his confessional blinkers. The less thorough commentators repeat the demand for self-examination without reference to either v. 28 or 29, but with complete self-assurance. Human self-examination, so we are told, will save Christian communicants from the Divine judgment: if only we had done God's work in ourselves, we would be safe from sickness and untimely death. Worse still: God's judgment upon the poor Corinthians is only a chastisement, as St. Paul himself has said, but his commentators are of sterner stuff. J. Moffatt, for instance, says: 'they are not yet condemned, but it may well come to that', and A. Schweitzer and A. Schlatter energetically underline this warning

[1] A. Schweitzer, *Mysticism of Paul the Apostle*, 1930, p.283.

which they believe to be an interpretation of v. 32b, 'that they may not be condemned with the world'. For they assume that this semi-verse is the logical outcome of v. 27b, 'guilty of the body and blood of the Lord'. At this instance the interpretation tends to be not only negligent but un-Christian. Human self-examination, so it is held, saves man from eternal punishment. Such indeed was the moral approach of Lucian of Samosata, the Cynic, in his 'Charon', but we should not expect such a view of St. Paul. The true self-examination of a Christian is that described in 1.John 3:20: 'if our own heart condemn us, God is greater than our heart and knoweth all things'. And the true doctrine of the Divine judgment is to be derived from John 3:18, 'he that believeth in Him is not judged; he that believeth not has been judged already', and although both these passages are Johannine, they are also truly Pauline in spirit.

III

To explain the difference between my own interpretation of 1.Cor.11 and that which is now generally accepted, it seems best to begin with four negative statements. I claim (1) that v. 29 is not a repetition of v. 27; (2) that it does not demand that the communicant should distinguish between the body of the Lord and something else; (3) that the verse does not promise that a sincere communicant will be safe from illness and a premature death; (4) that it does not hold out any hope that a Christian by earnest self-examination may avoid the Divine judgment any more than that he may avoid the condemnation of the world. These four statements are meant to give a clear outline of the views held by my opponents.

The interpretation here offered seeks to cover the whole passage 1.Cor.11:17–34, which is clearly divided into four parts: vv. 18–22, which describe the occasion for St. Paul's diatribe, the improprieties committed by the Corinthians at the celebration of the Agape and the Eucharist combined; vv. 23–5, which recite the Words of Institution, so to speak the rule laid down by Jesus Christ for the proper use of the Eucharist; vv. 26–32, which explain how this rule is to be applied in dealing with the matter in hand; and vv. 33-4, in which regulations for the transition period are given. In other words, the passage 1.Cor.11:18-34 exhibits features of a mature and carefully used legal technique. Such was the way in which Church administration, following the example of the Roman administration, began to act already at the time of St. Paul, and so it has continued to this day, despite the sneering of visionaries. Of the four parts, the first and third are complementary in that they oppose the present abuses to the correct usage to be followed in the future. However, this parallelism has not misled the Apostle into the use of an analogous structure for the two parts, for the dialectics of disorder differ from those of peace (1.Cor.14:33), and this differentiation delights the mind of a reader with legal training. For, whilst the first paragraph contains no more than allusions which are now hard to understand, the third shows a perfectly lucid disposition: v. 26 gives the aim and definition of Holy Communion, vv. 27-8 treat of the preparation for making one's communion, v. 29 is concerned with the act of Holy Communion itself, and vv. 30-2 deal with the effects of receiving or neglecting Holy Communion.

Having thus explained the structure of the passage 1.Cor.11:18-34, I shall now explain its meaning and logical progress in a succinct commentary. In v. 18 St. Paul begins with the divergences which, as he has heard, had made themselves felt in the Church Services at Corinth. He says that he has given some credence to these reports, as such divergences of opinion are a necessary test of the sincerity of true Christians, v. 19. However, although they are necessary, they are at the same time to be deplored when they show their effects in the worship of the Church: 'the Lord's meal' must not be celebrated like that, 'this is not to eat the Lord's Supper'. It seems as if the οὐκ ἔστιν has a connotation that the offerings contributed were insufficient to satisfy the hunger of all who came to the Service, for everyone rushed to the table and began to eat, apparently even before Grace had been said. Moreover, as there was no proper arrangement for the distribution of the food provided, some over-ate and others remained hungry. This was because the people who were better off made no proper provision to assist their poorer fellow-Christians privately, but left everything to the common meals. Thus they too dishonoured the Divine Services (τὰς ἐκκλησίας τοῦ θεοῦ), and put the poor to shame who could not control their appetites at these meetings, vv. 20–22a. The rich were thus as much to blame as the poor, v. 22b.

The situation thus described resembles that which obtained at Jerusalem before the ordination of the Seven, Acts 6; but St. Paul's remedy was different. He advised an increase in private charity: 'have you not houses to eat and drink in?' This advice may be understood as suggesting the split-up of the one general Divine Service in the Church at Corinth into house churches, similar to the Roman title-churches, or—more probably—the severing of the Agape from the Eucharist, or at least the first beginnings of this process which led to the celebration of the Agape in private houses as we find it in the Didascalia. Christian life was developing beyond the conditions obtaining in the Primitive Church at Jerusalem. The public feeding of the poor was seen to be discreditable: 'and put them to shame who have not', v. 22. The desire for a liturgical form for the common meal was felt. Therefore, St. Paul introduced the last meal of Jesus as the liturgical pattern of the Eucharist; and he made it clear that it was a ceremonial meal by contrasting the ἴδιον δεῖπνον in v. 21 with the κυριακὸν δεῖπνον in v. 20, for these two terms are meant to illustrate the difference between the private and the solemn royal meal. G. Kittel and A. Schweitzer may be correct that v. 23a, 'for I received from the Lord that which I also delivered unto you', is a rabbinical formula, but we should beware of building a huge superstructure upon this observation. For the gentile Christians who formed the majority in the Church at Corinth would not have discovered the origin of the formula. What is really significant is the fact that this was the most solemn introduction which was at the disposal of St. Paul. The Lord, κύριος, i.e. the absolute ruler in His majesty (even W. Bousset,[1] has said rather too little than too much about this) had acted thus and had ordained the repetition of the rite. Τοῦτο ποιεῖτε has a cultic

---

[1] *Kyrios*, 3rd. ed., 1934, p.104f.

meaning, 'celebrate this', as appears from the parallels quoted by Lietzmann.[1]

Thus we are led to the interpretation of the paragraph which forms our main subject. St. Paul began it in v. 26 with a definition: The Sacrament of the altar is the proclamation of the death of Christ in the consumption of bread and wine, to be continued 'till He comes'. In other words, in the Eucharist the Lord is present as the innocently condemned and executed Lamb of God. This concept links up with v. 27, for the proclamation of the death of Christ is at the same time the judgment pronounced over this world. That is the reason for the use of the legal term ἔνοχος, 'guilty' or 'liable for'. The verse reminds us of the fact that Judas Iscariot was also present at the Last Supper. This verse also contains a much more severe threat of punishment than current opinion will admit. 'Guilty', ἔνοχος, of the body and blood of the Lord is the direct opposite of Heb.3:14, μέτοχοι γὰρ γεγόναμεν τοῦ Χριστοῦ, 'for we are become partakers of Christ'; ibid., 2:14, τὰ παιδία κεκοινώνηκεν αἵματος καὶ σαρκός, 'the children are sharers in flesh and blood'. That is the alternative for the Christians, which will come to pass—notice the future ἔσται—in the reception of the blessed Sacrament and at the last judgment. There is no real distinction between the two, for the reception of the Sacrament is the judgment, the realisation of the judgment over this world which took place in Christ's passion, John 12:31. Neither does it clash with the character of the Sacrament as a 'means of grace', for there can be no grace without judgment and condemnation.

This is what the communicant has to face and to 'prove himself' by accepting it, v. 28. The word δοκιμαζέτω, 'let him prove himself', refers to the δόκιμοι, 'they which are approved', in v. 19. They are the 'approved' Christians and the word contains much more than mere self-examination. For when it is used of God, as in the LXX Ps. 80, cf. Jer.11:20; 17:10, it means 'to test', and the same is true of 1.Cor.3:13, where it is used for the fire of judgment; and even this does not encompass its full meaning. That is shown by a comparison with 2.Cor.13:5, where it is used in

---

[1] *Korinther*, 3rd ed., 1933, p.58.

conjunction with πειράζειν, 'to test'. There, as well as in 1.Cor. 11:28, it means to make it evident that we are not ἀδόκιμοι, 'try your own selves whether you are in the faith'. Thus the word means both self-examination and approval by God and, although it is not certain that formal confession of sins and absolution were prerequisites for Holy Communion in the Pauline Church at Corinth, the word δοκιμάζειν neatly corresponds to the part which the two play in the liturgy of the Eucharist. Consulting Clement of Alexandria (*Strom*, I.5f.) helps us to realise that v. 28 demands a 'Christian life in the communion of faith', and that individual self-examination will be insufficient as well as misleading. God's approval is necessary and those who have received it may eat of the bread and drink of the cup.

This concludes the preparation, and the communicants now go up to receive the Sacrament, eating and drinking 'judgment' or even 'condemnation' to themselves. For just as Jesus Christ in His passion has condemned the world, so also has this world condemned Him. This condemnation of Jesus Christ by this world is the condemnation from which the faithful and approved Christian does not 'discriminate' himself, v. 29. A Christian who has received the approval of His Lord and Saviour takes upon himself the proclamation of the death of Jesus on the cross and embodies it in his life. In this respect his 'unworthiness' plays no part; on the contrary, it may be held that such a Christian is deemed worthy to participate in the sufferings of the Lord. This is indeed a sort of 'mysticism', as A. Schweitzer understands the word, but it is the mysticism of human suffering representing to us the suffering of Christ. The correctness of this interpretation depends largely upon the meaning of the word διακρίνειν, and this I shall now establish in detail.

The first step is to exclude the possibility that the word deals with a duty on the part of the communicant. For this purpose it is sufficient to state that wherever the New Testament uses διακρίνειν in a positive way, the word has a derogatory flavour. Apart from the cases where the word is no more than a synonym of κρίνειν it nowhere occurs in the New Testament as denoting a Christian duty. Moreover, it is evident that ἑαυτοὺς διεκρίνομεν in v. 31 refers back to μὴ διακρίνων τὸ σῶμα in v. 29. Yet v. 31 emphasizes the duty of not διακρίνειν and thus distinguishes the διακρίνειν from the δοκιμάζειν in v. 28, a fact which will become more explicit when we discuss v. 31, but in support of which we may say already that the New Testament use of διακρίνειν nowhere encourages its equation with δοκιμάζειν. Positively we would point out that the Sacrament has the aim of strengthening our communion with Jesus Christ, as A. Schweitzer has rightly stated, and it is therefore the duty of a Christian not to make any discrimination. To discriminate is, on the other hand, the meaning of διακρίνειν in 1.Cor.4:7, which supports our choice of this meaning in 11:29. For, since the idea of Holy Communion demands this translation and another passage in the same Epistle provides us with it, we are entitled to treat it as correct. If that be so, the next question is why St. Paul should have used τὸ σῶμα to mean 'himself', especially since ἑαυτούς, the normal term, occurs in v. 31. Two facts should be stated first, (*a*) that σῶμα has the meaning of the flesh of Jesus in the Words of Institution, but nowhere else in the New Testament. Thus it cannot mean His flesh here unless τοῦ κυρίου be added, and (*b*) that the specifically Pauline meaning of τὸ σῶμα, 'the Church', has no immediate bearing upon v. 29. That being so, we find that Christ's earthly body was the object of the world's condemnation. It was the man Jesus of Nazareth who died on the cross, His body endured the aches and pains which torture and death cause to human beings, and thus the communicant is expected to 'take up his cross'. The physical suffering of Jesus is proclaimed in the suffering and death of the faithful communicant.

This fact is carefully explained in v. 30. A. Schweitzer has correctly held that the human suffering contemplated here is the symbol of something else; but not, as he contends, of that perdition which threatens the faithless, but of the redemptive suffering of the Saviour. This idea is found in several passages of St. Paul's epistles, especially when he says of himself, 'now I rejoice in my sufferings for your sake and fill up on my part that which is lacking of the afflictions of Christ in my flesh for His body's sake, which is the Church', Col.1:24, or when he explains the meaning of Holy Baptism, Rom. 6:3, 'or are you ignorant that all we who are baptised into Christ Jesus were baptised into His death?' Here lies the true kerygma of St. Paul's doctrine of Holy Communion. The sufferings of the faithful have a meaning: they proclaim the death of the Lord till He comes. This exegesis does away with the view which assumes that St. Paul in v. 30 used, so to speak, invectives against those Corinthian Christians who now 'sleep'. The opposite is true: v. 30 is a word of comfort to those 'among you who are weak and sickly' as well as to the bereaved. At the same time it is a warning to all generations of Christians that the Sacrament is not a panacea for physical diseases. Neither is it permissible to conclude that a strong and healthy person has made his communion worthily, or that the sick and suffering are unworthy communicants. Any priest of the Church will know that—and St. Paul should not have known it? The idea that God is glorified through suffering can be illustrated especially from 1.Cor. and in particular from the passage which is so important for the exegesis of 1.Cor.11:29f. because of its use of διακρίνειν, 1.Cor.4:7–13. There we read in v. 9, 'for I think, God has set forth us, the Apostles, last of all, as men doomed to death; for we are made a spectacle unto the world, and to angels and men'. We ask, what kind of a spectacle? The answer is, a Passion play—ὡς ἐπιθανατίους —until He comes, proclaiming the suffering and death of the Lord Jesus. Thus St. Paul connects the sufferings of the Christians with the suffering of Christ; yet he does not forget what their reason is. Suffering and death are the consequences of sin. The condemnation, κρίμα, which Christians take upon themselves in Holy Communion is not undeserved; but in this connection St. Paul inserts in v. 30 the doctrine of atonement as explained in 2.Cor.5:21, 'Him who knew no sin He made to be sin on our behalf; that we might become the righteousness of God.' Thus the communion between Christ and His Christians is made perfect in that Jesus Christ bears our transgressions, and that we Christians are made by Him 'God's fellow workers', 1.Cor.3:9, 'and fellow workers unto the kingdom', Col. 4:11.

Thus the distinction between Christians and non-Christians lies only in this that the Christians may have to suffer more. The dangers of persecution, the dangers of the mission-field, the dangers of working among the sick and suffering multiply the sufferings of the Christians. Under these conditions it is understandable that the Corinthians should ask what advantage there would be in partaking of this Holy Communion, if it was a communion of suffering together with Christ; and this question is taken up and answered by St. Paul in v. 31. Indeed, so he says, if we discriminate ourselves, this judgment will not come upon us. If we desert Christ the world will no longer persecute us, all the roads of selfishness will be open unto us, and if we fall ill and die, that illness and death will have nothing to do with the condemnation of Christ by this world. This verse may remind the reader of Ps. 73:3f.:

> for I was envious at the arrogant
> when I saw the prosperity of the wicked.
> for there are no bands in their death,
> but their strength is firm, etc.

However, St. Paul continues his argument with a thought which once more elucidates the meaning of Christian suffering: 'but when we are judged we are chastened of the Lord', v. 32a. We notice first that the ὑπὸ τοῦ κυρίου is put in a place where it refers to both κρινόμενοι, 'when we are judged', and to παιδευόμεθα, 'we are chastened', and this was done on purpose by St. Paul. The condemnation by the world is directed against Christ and the Christians, but is accepted by the Christians as their deserved chastisement at the hands of Christ, which will bring them eternal salvation, whereas the world will receive eternal damnation in the judgment of Christ, v. 32b. For this idea we may refer to Wisd.4:16, 'but a righteous man that is dead shall condemn the ungodly that are living'. This parallel shows clearly that the suffering of the Christians is by no means the first step on the road towards damnation, as J. Moffatt, A. Schweitzer, A. Schlatter and other commentators have thought. On the contrary, the unChristian desire to lead a comfortable life is that first step. It is indeed surprising to see that these scholars have overlooked the fact that the logical conclusion of their exegesis can only be a doctrine of purgatory such as no theologian has ventured to contemplate. For, we ask, where else should those who are said to have died because of receiving the Sacrament unworthily have a chance of remedying their mistake and of heeding St. Paul's admonition? As a matter of fact, however, v. 32 confronts man with a clear-cut issue: either to suffer with Christ so as to be justified by Him or to sever himself from Christ together with the world, to be condemned together with the world. Once more we are in a position to mention numerous parallels, beginning with 2.Cor.7:9, 'you were made sorry after a godly sort', and the longer passage Heb.12:6–11, and continuing with the promises in 2.Cor.1:5, 'for as the sufferings of Christ abound unto us even so our comfort also aboundeth through Christ', and in particular 4:17, 'for our light affliction which is for the moment worketh for us more and more exceedingly an eternal weight of glory'. It is a plain fact that the conviction that the sufferings of the Christians are sufferings in Christ finds its expression in all the Epistles of the New Testament and above all in the Paulines, wherever they deal with suffering; and it is therefore certain that St. Paul welcomed the opportunity of expressing this also in his doctrine of the Eucharist.

In this connection it is profitable to cast a glance upon the vocabulary used by St. Paul. First, I would note again the frequency of words derived from the stem κριν- in vv. 31–2, and call to mind that St. Paul was fond of using that particular family of words, as here so also in Rom.2:1f.; 14:22f. In each of these cases the question is of human and Divine judgment and their inter-relation, and it may happen that there are slight variations of meaning, as for instance between κρίνωμεν and κρίνατε, Rom.14:13, or between κρίνειν, κρίνετε, κρινεῖ in 1.Cor.5:12f. and its continuation in chapter six. In our passage too the possibility of these slight variations has to be envisaged. The other observation is concerned with παιδευόμεθα, we are chastened, we are chastised. That is in fact the main meaning of the word, but it has a strong connotation of 'we are educated'. The law was not only the task-master 'to bring us to Christ', but also the 'tutor', παιδαγωγός, Gal.3:24, and the grace of God does not only 'chasten us', but also 'instruct us, to the intent that, denying un-godliness and worldly lusts, we should live soberly and righteously and godly in this present world', Titus 2:12, although it uses suffering for this purpose. Once more the parallel in Jesus' life is expressly stated in Heb. 5:8, 'He learned obedience by the things which He suffered.' The chastisement of God is not only punish-ment for sin but also training in Christianity.

This concludes the instruction given by St. Paul about the theological meaning of the Eucharist. In vv. 33-4 there follow regulations for the transition period, preliminary practical arrange-ments concerning conditions which had become intolerable. These two verses no longer refer to the immediately preceding passage, 27-32, but take up vv. 18-22, the description of the tumultuous meetings of the Corinthian Christians. That much is evident from the parallelism between v. 21, 'for in your eating each one taketh before other his own supper', and v. 33, 'therefore, my brethren, when ye come together to eat, wait one for another'. But St. Paul is not oblivious either of the reason why the poor among the Corinthians found it so hard to take this advice: they were too hungry to wait. Thus he follows up the advice in v. 34, 'if any man is hungry let him eat at a house'. The Revised Version says 'at home' but it seems questionable whether that is correct. For the Greek does not say οἴκοι, which would be normal, but ἐν οἴκῳ, which means 'in a family', and this meaning seems to be borne out by the commandment ἐκδέχεσθε ἀλλήλους which, according to Moulton and Milligan, may mean not only 'wait for one another', but also 'receive one another'. It seems that St. Paul said in this one sentence that the poor should wait for each other, and the rich should receive the poor, so that we would be faced with an inten-tional ambiguity. If this be the case, v. 33 is indeed a milestone on the road towards the separation of the Agape from the Eucharist.

These two rules are then followed by the warning 'that your coming together be not unto judgment', κρίμα, v. 34b. It is this last use of κρίμα which demands our special attention. It would be wrong to exclude it from the list of words derived from the stem κριν- in vv. 27 f., on the strength of Blass-Debrunner[1] having

---

[1] *N.T. Grammatik*, 6th ed., 1931, p.488, 1b.

done so. More to the point is their remark that this accumulation of words belonging to the same family is forced and rather impairs the lucidity of the argument. Having said this, our interpretation of v. 34b has to start from two facts, the one that the word κρίμα there does not refer directly to κρίμα in v. 29, the other that it must not be explained without due recognition of its occurrence in v. 29.

Regarding the first statement, it has to be said that the warning in v. 34 is closely connected with that in v. 27, ἔνοχος, 'guilty of the body and blood of the Lord'. Ἔνοχος as well as κρίμα are legal terms, and he who receives the Sacrament 'unworthily' is judged guilty. The warning also refers to v. 20, 'this is not to eat the Lord's Supper', and v. 32, 'that we should not be condemned with the world'. The English versions of v. 20, do not express that idea of nullity which is contained in the Greek οὐκ ἔστιν. However, this idea is responsible for the warning in v. 34a. If the Sacrament is null and void the communicants so-called are actually on the side of the world to be condemned with the world. These two lines of connection are, I believe, evident. On the other hand, the choice of the word κρίμα makes it clear that St. Paul wished that reference should also be made to v. 29, where the word had been used before. In this respect we have to return to the idea of education. I have stressed before that human suffering, although it may be taken up into the suffering of Christ, is not undeserved. The κρίμα of v. 29 is, according to v. 32a, chastening of the Christians by God for the purpose of their training in Christianity, 'till we all attain . . . unto a fullgrown man, unto the measure of the stature of the fullness of Christ', Eph.4:13. Each one of us has had the experience that God is educating His Church through suffering, and the fact that 'the fire itself shall prove each man's work of what sort it is', 1 Cor.3:13, has just been explained by St. Paul. In this sense, combining v. 29 with v. 32a, the warning of v. 34a is more closely connected with them than with vv. 20–7 on the one hand, and with v. 32b on the other. The condemnation of the world, v. 29, is yet justly ordained by the mercy of God, 'according to what we have done, whether it be good or bad', 2.Cor.5:10.

IV

'And the rest I will set in order whensoever I come', v. 34b.
This sentence might well serve as my conclusion, for there are
many questions yet which had to be left unanswered, concerning
the general problems of the Eucharist. It would be necessary to
connect the exegesis of 1.Cor.11:17f. with the whole doctrine of
the Sacrament; and it would be instructive to know in what way
the additions in v. 29 have come into existence. At least a tentative
answer may be given to the second question. For this purpose it
must first be decided whether we are faced with one interpolation or two, and the answer is: two. That is evident from the fact
that the Latin tradition has accepted the *indigne*, but has on the
whole rejected the *Domini*. In this respect both the *Vetus Latina*
and Jerome even dissociate themselves from the famous Syro-
Latin alliance so well established in other places. Consequently it
has to be assumed that the two additions were made at different
places and, more particularly, that the τοῦ κυρίου is of non-
western origin. This rather ties up with the so-called 'western non-
interpolation' of Luke 22:19b–20, 'which is given for you, etc.' If
it may be assumed that the canonical text of Luke 22:19b–20 is a
later addition, then the τοῦ κυρίου in 1.Cor.11:29 fin. should have
a history going back to the second century and perhaps to an
eastern, Marcionite tradition, as can be derived from Tertullian,
Adv. Marc., 4.40 fin, where the idea behind the interpolation is
clearly defined. For Marcion, as we know, even went so far as to
speak of the 'crucified bread'.

On the other hand, it appears that the Syro-Latin combination
is the strongest witness for the ἀναξίως, and for this reason it
seems unlikely that this addition should have come from the same
source as the other. To be frank, I have not found any specific
ground on which it may have grown, and I have the feeling that
it may have crept in almost by accident from a repetition of v. 27.
It is likely however to have been suggested by the custom of fasting before Holy Communion. It is also evident that it was only
this addition which caused the change in the meaning of 1.Cor.

11:29. The addition of τοῦ κυρίου would have been tolerable, although St. Paul neither made it nor intended to do so. For the communicant is indeed joined in Holy Communion to the 'body of the Lord', the Church. For this reason the Marcionite change was only a slight one, maintaining that in Holy Communion the communicant received in the bread the Church. This idea was well established in the Christian tradition: 'we who are many are one bread', 1.Cor.10:17; 'as this baked bread was scattered upon the hills and, having been gathered, was made one by baking, so also may the Church be gathered from the ends of the world into Thy kingdom', Did.9.4; 'for when the Lord calls His body the bread which has been gathered together by the conflation of many grains . . . He thus signifies our flock', Cyprian, Ep.69.5. Nevertheless, this alteration has befogged Christian minds rather extensively right up to our own time, when it is still held necessary to establish the exact time it takes secular food to vacate the stomach, lest we by 'not discerning the Lord's body' should make our communion unworthily.

SOCIAL PROBLEMS IN THE EARLY CHURCH

THE nineteenth century made enormous progress in that field which may be described as 'major' Church History: the history of the great leaders of the early Church, of the bishops like Cyprian of Carthage or Athanasius of Alexandria who in the war on two fronts, against heresy on the one side and the political power on the other, were called to lead the Church, or of the great theologians like Origen and Augustine who, in attack and defence, partly opposed and partly modified ancient philosophy so as to make it conform with the fundamental Christian truth of the Incarnation of the Logos, and thus to serve the proclamation of the Good News of the salvation of mankind by the death and resurrection of the Son of God. The lesser Church History, however, is still in its beginnings.

By this I mean that we have not so far occupied our minds sufficiently with the social conditions of all the little people who accepted the message. Church historians are all too frequently under the spell of the theory that 'Church' in this expression means above all the worship of the Church. It is for this reason that in the field of lesser Church History the history of the liturgy takes precedence. However, even here social questions are shunned. The question for instance whether the words of institution over the cup, 'do this *as oft as ye shall drink it* in remembrance of me', may indicate that the earliest Christians did not have the money to drink wine daily, is being pushed aside not infrequently as being non-theological. It may be true that the economic historians will be more interested in the fact that the spread of the vine through Europe is directly connected with the spread of Christianity than theologians; but if we are serious in professing that the Church is the congregation of all faithful Christians, not exclusively the priests and theologians, it seems the task of the Church historian to investigate also the changes in the daily life of the newly converted Christians who, by their faithfulness and suffering, have made it possible for subsequent generations to spread the Gospel. They were certainly not like the 'Saints' on the windows in our churches, and a true understanding of their day-to-day necessities and anxieties should give a new aspect to the phrase 'the Church and the world', appearing no longer as two separate entities, but closely intertwined, much more so than the 'major' Church History would allow us to suspect.

It is, therefore, not from insincerity but to underline the 'lesser' character of this approach that I venture to describe the four subjects of this chapter in modern terms as: the Sunday joint of the Christian housewife; Quaker Latin; the Christian schoolmaster; and concubinage and communion.

I

The Sunday joint of the Christian housewife

It can be stated with confidence that there are thousands, even millions of Christian families where 'black pudding' belongs to the regular items of the menu, without them ever considering that they may in this way commit a sin against the Holy Spirit. For it is written, Acts 15:28-9, 'it has pleased the Holy Spirit and us not to lay upon you any other burden than the following necessary ones: That you abstain from meat sacrificed to idols, from blood, from things strangled, and from fornication. If you abstain from those things you do well'. That is the famous decree of the Apostles, issued by the council of Jerusalem in A.D. 50, which was observed by early Christianity, as will be shown, with an almost fanatic determination.[1] Admittedly, the Apostles' decree was received by gentile Christians at the beginning with a certain reserve. Although it is true to say that the Acts of the Apostles try to give

---

[1] The opposite view was held by Hadorn and Bauernfeind, quoted in Hänchen, *Apostelgeschichte*, p.417. The fanaticism may be illustrated by the reply of the martyr Philippa in *Acta Agapes*, etc., 3, *mori malo quam vestris sacrificiis vesci*, Th. Ruinaert, *Acta martyrum*, 1859, p.425.

the impression that the Apostles had bent over backwards to satisfy the Church of the Gentiles, the Apostle of the Gentiles, St. Paul, said something quite different immediately after the event. He wrote to the Galatians, 'those brass-hats have put no strings on me'.[1] It is also true to say that in two respects he was right in asserting this: on the one hand, already in the Noachite food law in Genesis[2] the abstention from blood had been prescribed to all mankind in the person of Noah after the deluge, so that it was obvious even for St. Paul that it had to be observed; and on the other hand, the addressees of the decree were the Christians of Antioch, of whom St. Barnabas in the first instance was in charge, and not St. Paul. It is, however, remarkable that only a short time afterwards, namely after the visit of St. Peter to Corinth,[3] St. Paul greatly changed his tune. In his first epistle addressed to the Corinthians he devoted a longish paragraph under the heading 'About sacrificial meat' to the question.[4] The connection between the two events is to be found in the fact that, according to Acts, it had been St. Peter who had brought about the compromise which is contained in the decree of the Apostles. It is therefore a reasonable guess that it was he also who had insisted upon its general validity, even at Corinth.

The way in which St. Paul now accepted the decree, and in particular the prohibition of the eating of sacrificial meat, is highly significant for the mutual relations between the two Apostles. Not only did he not reject it any longer, but he even supported it strongly as a command of charity in favour of 'the weak'. 'We', so he says, and in this there seems to be a reference to the 'Pauline' party at Corinth,[5] 'we have gnosis', knowledge, 'but gnosis engenders pride, only charity edifies. . . . We know that the idols in this world are nothing, and that there is only One that

---

[1] Galat.2:6.   [2] Gen.9:4.

[3] Hänchen, *N.T. Studies*, VII, 1961, p.192, is pleased to state that Cullmann too assumed with good reason 'that Peter never was in Corinth'. Actually Cullman, *Peter, disciple*, op. cit., p.53f., expresses his conviction that St. Peter did not found the Church at Corinth and his doubt whether he went there at all, but does in no way assert that he was not. I prefer the view of E. Meyer, op. cit., vol.3, p.54, n.55, that he was.

[4] 1.Cor.8:1f.   [5] 1.Cor.1:12f.; 3:4, 22.

is God. . . . But not all have gnosis . . . I would, therefore, rather eat no meat eternally if such food offends my brother.' [1] From this statement by St. Paul two conclusions may be drawn: the first, that St. Paul apparently did eat sacrificial meat at his first stay at Corinth; the second, that without being conscious of any sin against the Holy Spirit, he abandoned this practice at St. Peter's remonstrations 'for conscience sake', which means because of the testimony not only of any pagan scoffers, but even more so because of the 'weak' amongst the Christians,[2] an expression which appears not to be entirely without a certain acerbity directed at the address of St. Peter.

This Pauline advice in 1.Cor. was quoted frequently by subsequent generations of Christians as well as their opponents.[3] That was a fateful practice on account of that unfortunate, fashionable term 'gnosis' which St. Paul used there,[4] a term which had made its way from the mystery religions into Pauline speech.[5] The general distrust against the word had by the end of the first century grown so much that that admirer of St. Paul to whom we are indebted for the Pastoral Epistles, saw cause to warn St. Timothy of the 'falsely so-called gnosis' in order to save St. Paul's reputation from a very real embarrassment.[6] And in this way the eating of sacrificial meat was marked out as one of the enormities in which the Christian intelligentsia indulged. These 'free-thinkers' did not follow the example of the Apostle. Therefore we find in the Revelation of St. John, in the letter to the Church at Pergamum, an accusation of the 'Nicolaitans' because 'they eat meat sacrificed to idols and commit fornication'.[7] It is impossible not to hear the reference to the Apostles' decree in this accusation, and it is important to hear it as a proof for its independent circulation, since there is no obvious sign to show that the

---

[1] 1.Cor.8:4, 7, 13, cf. Rom.14:20f.

[2] 1.Cor.10:28f.

[3] Cf. *Did.*6:3; Ps.Clem., *De virginitate*, II.5.4, Diekamp, *Patres Apostol.*, vol.2, 1913, p.37, 1f., with a literal quotation of 1.Cor.8:12f.

[4] Cf. Knox, *Some Hellenistic Elements*, 1944, p.79, n.2.

[5] Cf. 1.Cor.12:8; 13:2; 14:6, and the remarks by Bauer, *Wörterb. z. N.T.*, 4th ed., 1952, p.296.

[6] 1.Tim.6:20.   [7] Rev.2:14.

author of Revelation used the Book of Acts. On the other hand it has to be emphasised that these Nicolaitans were described as 'Gnostics', certainly in the days of Irenaeus,[1] round about A.D. 180 and probably much earlier. For we see Justin Martyr making the same accusation against all Gnostics, 'that they eat sacrificial meat and say that it does not hurt them', and this statement does indeed appear in a Coptic gnostic writing, the Gospel of Thomas, and in particular in one of the books of Mani, the founder of that world-religion called Manichaeism, which became the inheritor of most of the gnostic sects and doctrines.[2]

But how did it happen that this matter in particular should develop into a sort of shibboleth of the new faith? It is true to say that even today we are surprised to read from the pen of St. Paul,[3] 'but if somebody seeth thee, who hast gnosis, lying at table in the temple of an idol', as if that were the most obvious thing in the world. Let us state it plainly that such was indeed the case: For it has to be realised that it was the temples of the ancient world which had to supply the need for restaurants, particularly in the Greek cities.[4] If a Christian husband for some reason or other wanted to go out for dinner he had, unless he lived in one of the big cities, no other choice. Another equally clear impression of the social problem which existed here we receive when we read a little later in 1.Cor.:[5] 'But if a gentile invites you, and you wish to go, eat anything that is offered you without enquiring for conscience sake. If however someone says to you, this is sacrificial meat, then do not eat it, for the sake of the warner as well as for conscience sake.' Here we have a similar problem, an invitation amongst neighbours at which, apparently without guile, sacrificial meat was offered. The Christian guest was encouraged to eat it without

---

[1] Cf. references in W. Bousset, *Die Offenbarung*, 6th ed., 1906, p.206, enriched by Reicke, *Glaube und Leben d. Urgemeinde*, 1957, p.121, n.10.

[2] Justin, *Dial.*, 35.1f., cf. Thomas' Gospel, log.14. Mani, *Shahpurakan*, frg.1b, A. Adam, *Texte zum Manichäismus*, 1954, pp.7, 51f. This saying is traditional here, since Mani himself preached vegetarianism.

[3] 1.Cor.8:10.

[4] Cf. the collections in Marquardt-Wissowa, *Röm. Staatsverwaltung*, 2nd ed., vol.3, 1885, p.210f.

[5] 1.Cor.10:28-9.

any fear of defilement; but how was he to return the hospitality received? He could not, of course, purchase sacrificial meat; but was there any other than sacrificial meat on offer in ancient Greek and Roman towns? Were there any secular butchers? H. Lietzmann, the only New Testament scholar of whom I know that saw and cared about this question,[1] answered it quite unconditionally, 'that the slaughtering of all animals was seen as a sacrifice' in New Testament times. By and large this answer is correct. The history of words gives an indication how the Jews, who were faced with the same difficulty as the Christians, dealt with the problem: The earliest testimonies for Greek 'butcher' and 'to slaughter' in Hellenistic speech, κρεουργός and κρεουργεῖν, are to be found in the Jewish writers, Philo and Josephus, whilst the earlier Greek term ἄρταμος, which incidentally had the strong connotation of 'murderer', was at this time very much on its way out.[2] At Rome too, the profession had been flourishing once, and even produced a consul, the unhappy C. Terentius Varro, who had been defeated by Hannibal at Cannae;[3] but the contempt with which Livy as well as Valerius Maximus in their account of that disaster treat him shows clearly how, at the time of Our Lord, the profession had suffered an eclipse. As a matter of fact, these *lanii* or *laniones*, as butchers were called at Rome, were, since the first century B.C. under police supervision. Thus the Christian housewife had only the alternative of finding a Jewish butcher—and relations between Christians and Jews were notoriously tense—or to kill a beast privately, a very expensive business, and probably frowned on by the town administration. For the meat that was offered at the *macellum*,[4] the 'halls', was most likely to be sacrificial meat.

Consequently most Christian housewives, especially the poorer ones, would find it almost impossible to return hospitality to their husbands' business friends; and the decree of the Apostles thus

---

[1] Lietzmann, *An die Korinther*, p.49.
[2] Cf. Liddell-Scott, *Greek–English Lexicon*, s.v.
[3] Cf. J. Marquardt-Mau, *Das Privatleben der Römer*, 2nd ed., 1886, p.467.
[4] 1.Cor.10:25, cf. the sketch of the *macellum* of Pompeii in Lietzmann, op. cit., p.52.

caused the Christians to be separated from their neighbours. For on the whole they were poor people, even poorer than the Jews, of whom we know that their Paschal lamb—not a fully grown animal—had to be sufficient for a company of about twelve people. And even if the Christians were not quite so poor, it is to be doubted, as has been mentioned, whether the magistrates would give permission for the private killing of an animal. For on the one hand, the meat prices were strictly controlled in the cities of the Roman Empire; and the political importance of this price control was so great that it was the city prefect, the highest imperial functionary there, who was entrusted with it in the capital.[1] From the point of view of pagan religion it has to be added that it was believed that the killing of an animal polluted not only the person who slaughtered it, but also the place where it was killed.[2] At the altar, in the temple district, however, the gods were reconciled to the killing. The vividness of these convictions may be seen by the fact that it was not only auspicious if the victim shook its head when it was led to the altar, as if it had given its assent to its killing, but that this effect was even artificially produced by various means, e.g. by pouring water into the animal's ear.[3] The civil authorities, on the other hand, had a great interest in the fact that ritual purity also guaranteed a fair amount of secular cleanliness, which from the point of view of social hygiene amounted to a considerable degree of protection for the participants in a sacrificial meal.

It is against this background that the letter of Pliny the Younger to the Emperor Trajan, concerning the Christians in Bithynia, should be read as the first sub-Apostolic document in the case. Pliny reported in this letter on the effects of a persecution of these Christians, which he had staged in his province in the north-western corner of Asia Minor. He writes with noticeable satisfaction: [4] 'It can be said safely that the temples which had been

---

[1] *Dig. Just.*, I.12.1, §11, Ulpian, *sing. de off. praef. urbi.* This text is representative for the legal position already in the second century.

[2] Cf. how in Theocritus, XXIV.86–98, the whole house where young Heracles had killed Hera's dragons had to be purged.

[3] Cf. G. F. Schoemann-Lipsius, *Griech. Altertümer*, 4th ed., vol.2, 1902, p.52.

[4] Plinius Secundus, *Epist.*, X.96, §10.

almost abandoned by the people, are held in veneration once more; that divine services which had ceased since long have been resumed; and that the meat of the victims which for a long time rarely found a purchaser, is being sold again.' Whilst there are several instances in the history of Roman administration in which ancient cults were given a new lease of life by the suppression of new and more fashionable ones,[1] it may be confidently claimed that the interest shown by the proconsul of Bithynia in the renewed prosperity of the meat trade is a novelty. It seems therefore plausible to assume that he intended to make the Christian religion responsible for its previous recession. Unfortunately, he has failed to inform his Emperor—and us—whether the Christians, like the Jews, had given a start to secular rivals for this sacred trade. It can be shown, however, that the observation of the prohibition to eat sacrificial meat by the Christians was regarded as a common practice in various parts of the Empire, and widely discussed in the second century. From Rome, the capital of the Empire, we hear the voice of an African, Minucius Felix, who in his *Octavius* protested vigorously against the well-known slander that the Christians killed little babies and ate them at their services.[2] This slander, he said, had its origin in the pagan myths and human sacrifices: 'For us, on the other hand, it is sin not only to watch a manslaughter (in the circus), but even to hear of it. We abstain from human blood so much that we do not even use the blood of eatable animals in our food.'

More important still are Roman official, or at least semi-official, voices. Pliny's letter shows that the government was concerned about this specially Christian form of abstinence. It did not immediately go to such extremes as Pliny had done in Bithynia, but it used the weapon of propaganda against this practice. A 'philosopher' (every rhetor called himself by that name in the second

---

[1] Cf. W. Warde Fowler, *Social Life at Rome in the age of Cicero*, 1922, p.321f., who gives as an example the report by Valerius Maximus, *Epit.*, III.4, on the suppression of the cult of Isis at Rome in the years B.C. 58 to 48.

[2] Minuc. Fel., *Octavius*, 30.7, quoted incorrectly by Hänchen, *Apostelgeschichte*, p.418, as 37.6.—Cf. the 'antisemite' version of the history of the Maccabees, E. Bickerman, *Der Gott der Makkabäer*, 1937, p.21f., in which the Jews are denounced similarly, because of their *odium generis humani*.

century) called Celsus, produced at that time a pamphlet *A true Word* against the Christians, and in the interest of the Roman government, and probably government inspired.[1] The following passage from it may show that the Roman authorities in Egypt were also worried about the Christian abstinence from sacrificial meat:[2]

If they, [the Christians, writes Celsus], following some ancient custom of their forefathers, abstain from this sort of food, then they should abstain from every kind of animalic food. Such is also the doctrine of Pythagoras, dictated to him by his respect for the soul and its organs. If however they do it in order to avoid any table fellowship with demons, as they say,[3] then I can only congratulate them on their wisdom because they are so slow in understanding that they are nevertheless table fellows with the demons, and protect themselves from it only when they spot a sacrificial victim. For when they eat porridge or drink wine or taste of nuts, yea even water and the air which they breathe, do they not receive all that from one or the other demon who, each for his part, has been entrusted with the care thereof?

Before we admire the 'philosophical' approach made by Celsus, we should take notice of the fact that he does not attack Pythagorean vegetarianism, but only the abstention from sacrificial meat. This shows the political—not to say fiscal—interest of the question, since we have seen that the government had no control over privately killed meat. After these preliminaries I may be allowed to state that Celsus' philosophical smoke-screen seems really somewhat silly. Admittedly this appreciation is not to be found in Origen's reply from which the quotation has been taken. Origen was treading on delicate ground, and knew it. He, therefore, produced the demanded 'ancestral custom', as it were by *legerdemain*, quoting a Pythagorean philosopher of a similar *niveau*, the *Sentences of Sextus*, which support only conditionally the Pythagorean vegetarianism, and thus leave room for the Christian distinction as ordered in the Apostles' decree.[4] What was at stake

---

[1] Cf. my *Polit. Metaphysik*, vol.2, p.184.
[2] Celsus, VIII.28, ed. F. Glöckner, Kl. Texte, 151, 1924, p.9f.
[3] I.Cor.10:20.
[4] Origen, *Adv. Cels.*, VIII.30. Sextus, *Sent.*, 109, ed. H. Chadwick, Texts and

appears rather more clearly from Celsus' brave ally, the paid political agent, for here it can be proved, Lucian of Samosata, in his *Death of Peregrinus*. This clever pamphletist reported there that Peregrinus was expelled by the Christians, 'I believe because he was observed eating some food which is forbidden among them'.[1] The reasons why Lucian invented this story, the reason why Celsus poured his philosophical sauce over the Sunday joint of the Christian housewife, the reason why Pliny was so pleased with the recovery of the trade in sacrificial meat, are all to be sought at the same place, the political importance of the state control of the meat trade.

This will become clearer when one of the most famous documents of the sinking Roman Empire is consulted, the famous maximal tariff decreed by the Emperor Diocletian at the end of the third century. The total number of chapters of this voluminous document is 32, and of these one entire chapter, and one of the first—the fourth—is taken up by the regulation of the prices of the various kinds of meat and game. This was by no means a new invention of the Emperor Diocletian. Blümner, in his commentary on the decree,[2] has shown that the control of the meat prices had been one of the most important concerns of Roman civil administration right from the end of the second century; and it is a well-established fact that such a control presupposes the existence of a public meat market. For it is defeated by black market operations and private killings. Such a public market and controlled killings were provided and safeguarded by the religious convictions which insisted upon the sacrificial slaughter of animals. If the controlling system was relaxed riots amongst the poorer population were inevitable.

From these considerations it becomes understandable why Celsus and Lucian were so busy putting a religious, semi-philo-

---

Studies, new ser., 5, 1959, p.24, cf. ibid., p.107f. To me it appears as evident that in this instance Sextus has to be a 'Pythagorean' (and must not be a Christian) in order to controvert the 'Pythagorean' argument put out by Celsus, and therefore I cannot follow Chadwick maintaining the opposite view.

[1] Lucian, *De morte Peregrini*, 16.

[2] Th. Mommsen–H. Blümner, *Der Maximaltarif des Diokletian*, 1893, p.73f.

sophical veil over this government policy. In this they may not even have been altogether dishonest. It is certain at any rate that the Christians were too naïve to discover the political implications. Not even an educated man like Minucius Felix, whom we have quoted previously, saw them. The defence which he used against the customary slander that the Christians murdered little children and devoured them at their secret celebrations was rather stereotyped, and he did not in this case vary his counter-attack. Apparently he never suspected that the civil authority would be displeased with such a reminder of their trouble because of the Christian refusal to buy sacrificial meat. This situation is illustrated by the utterance of a little French woman, called Biblis, who was tortured to death during the persecution of the Christians at Lyons in A.D. 177. Still dazed by her sufferings, she made exactly the same remark which we find in the *Octavius*.[1]

In fact, the argument seems to have been taken over from the Jewish armoury,[2] and this may account for the Christian Sibyl having no more insight in spite of her renowned clairvoyance. Admittedly, her main task was to warn and to curse; yet we find her a good Christian, refusing any sacrificial meat which those troubled souls who had listened to her prophecies might be moved to offer to her: [3]

> I don't want sacrifice, no more than your sacred offerings,
> Neither the unclean smell, nor blood that is poured out in them.
> For these are offered, as a memorial of kings or tyrants,
> To the demons, the dead, as dwellers in heavenly places,
> A performance of godless and evil-causing worship.

These verses are of a particular interest not only because they clearly refer us back to the 'demons' of 1.Cor.10:20, but also because they add to the demons mentioned there, the 'kings and

---

[1] Euseb., *E.H.*, V.1.26.

[2] Cf. Bickerman, op. cit., 36f., who has proved the importance of the Maccabean martyrdoms for the Christian doctrine of martyrdom, and Josephus, *Adv. Apionem*, II.95f.

[3] Sib., VIII.390f. With regard to 'the dead', cf. *Kerygma Petri*, 2, ed. E. Klostermann, *Apocrypha*, vol.1, 2nd ed., 1921, p.14, taken from Clem. Alex. *Strom.*, VI.5.40, καὶ νεκρὰ νεκροῖς προσφέροντες ὡς θεοῖς.

tyrants'. For, quite apart from the emphasis put on the fact that the contemporary emperors were also mortal,[1] its readers are introduced by it to the conditions of terror which prevailed in the third century. The curtain is raised here for the cruel general persecutions when the firmness of Christian conviction was tested also with regard to their abstention from sacrificial meat.

The prohibition of the consumption of such meat not only separated the Christians from their pagan neighbours, and made them outcasts, but it also made them very conspicuous. All over the world, wherever Jews still observe their ancient food laws, their children in particular are in danger of being forced by their rowdy schoolfellows to eat of their ham sandwiches. How could we expect the early Christians to have fared any better, especially since they were not even 'emancipated' for over a century, as the Jews have been in Europe. It is therefore easily understandable that the imperial edicts of persecution should have made special provision for the compulsory consumption of sacrificial meat by the persecuted Christians. There exists an impressive description of the application of this means of 're-education' already from the first general persecution under Decius (A.D. 249–251) in the Acts of the martyr Pionius. It is said there that this martyr tied a rope round the necks of himself and his companions on the morning of their arrest in order to symbolize that they would not eat sacrificial meat,[2] like so many of the other Christians. Fifty years later, in the persecution under Diocletian, we find this method of confirming the defection of a Christian fully established; and it seems that under the successors of Diocletian, particularly under Licinius, the rival of Constantine, the compulsory consumption of sacrificial meat was expressly commanded as a means of alienating

---

[1] Cf. Ehrhardt, *Polit. Metaphysik*, vol.2, p.22, n.4.

[2] *Acta Pionii*, 2.4, ed. G. Krüger, *Ausgewählte Märtyrerakten*, 2nd ed., 1929, p.46, 'this he did so that no one amongst those who led them away should be able to say that they conducted them to the eating of abomination (μιαροφαγεῖν)'. A similar invitation was made by the governor Marcianus to the martyr Acacius, *ut simul celebrantes dulce convivium numinibus quae sunt digna reddamus*, *Acta Acacii*, 2.7, ibid., p.58. Cf. also the accusation in *Acta Agapes*, etc., 3, ibid., p.96, μὴ βούλεσθαι ἱερόθυτον φαγεῖν, and *Acta Philippi*, 6, ed. Ruinaert, op. cit., p.443, both under Diocletian.

a Christian from his Church. From the Acts of Theodore of Caesarea in Cappadocia, which have been preserved in a reliable form in the Armenian,[1] we learn that Licinius provided for the posting up in every town and village of a decree, 'that they should do homage to stones and to trees fashioned by the hands of men, and that they should offer up holocausts and sacrifices to the so-called gods, and should content themselves with foul food'. This, of course, was the Christian version of the pagan original, which ordered the consumption of sacrificial meat. The Saint, who is said to have held a senior military position in that frontier district, is then said to have been denounced that 'under his influence the people of Caesarea have been perverted by him, along with your army, and have turned away from the worship of idols, and have disobeyed your commands: They no longer keep the mystery festivals of the gods, nor do they taste of their holy sacrifices'.[2] Licinius himself is said to have come for an inspection, which led to the execution of the martyr.

Secular historians in particular are inclined to regard acts of martyrs as suspect witnesses. However, for the harassed Christians of Asia Minor the edict of Licinius brought nothing new. A short time earlier, when Licinius still based his policy upon that short-lived understanding with his brother-in-law, Constantine, in the spring of A.D. 314, shortly after the promulgation of the edict of Milan so-called, a synod of the bishops of Asia Minor had assembled in Ancyra to decide about the necessary re-organization of the Church after ten years of persecution. In the third canon of that synod we read the following:[3]

If people have fled and been arrested, or have been betrayed by their domestics, or have otherwise lost their fortunes, or have endured

---

[1] Cf. C. F. Conybeare, *The Armenian Apology*, 2nd ed., 1896, p.217f., who maintains that the Armenian version reproduces a sermon in honour of the Saint, of the early fourth century, based upon the report of the eye-witness Abgar, whereas the existing Greek and Latin versions have been hopelessly tampered with. The only doubt I have is that the Armenian refers to 'Heraclea' in Cappadocia, which I have not found in the Gazetteer of Kiepert's *Atlas Antiquus*. I have, therefore, emended it to Caesarea, but the damage may go deeper.

[2] *Acta Theodori*, 4.6, ed. Conybeare, op. cit., p.221f.

[3] E. J. Jonkers, *Acta et symbola conciliorum*, *Textus minores*, XIX, 1954, p.29.

torture, or have been jailed, and have shouted loudly that they were Christians, but have been forced either by having incense put into their hands by their persecutors, *or by having been made to swallow some food*, yet constantly protesting that they were Christians, and have always shown their grief at what had happened, in their whole bearing and behaviour, and their humility of life, those people being without sin shall not be turned away from Communion.

When we read that, and consider that the bishop of Caesarea in Cappadocia, the town where Theodore was to suffer martyrdom, was a member of the synod, and also that the method of stuffing sacrificial meat is well supported by other acts of martyrs[1], we may well believe in the truth of his acts, especially with regard to the poor Christians and their wives, whom he encouraged not to buy their Sunday joint at the temples.

There are also traces of these practices in the Western Church. The great persecution of the Christians at the beginning of the fourth century has left its mark in Latin languages down to our own time. In modern English and French the word *traditor*, traitor, traître, has become the contemptuous description of a man betraying his country, and has ousted the classical *proditor*. These *traditores* were the despicable fellows who had surrendered the sacred books of their churches to the pagan police. When considering this development in the modern languages,[2] other linguistic irregularities may assume a special significance. Thus we are interested to find in the canons of the Spanish synod of Elvira, which met in A.D. 306, i.e. immediately after the end of the persecution of Maximian in the West, the word *idolothytum*,[3] the word used by St. Paul for sacrificial meat. Before him the Jews had used it with the same clear denotation, and in the whole New

---

[1] Cf. e.g. *Acta Tarachi*, etc., 8, ed. Ruinaert, *Acta*, op. cit., p.467, *infundite illi vinum et carnes de ara mittite ei in os.*

[2] *Traditor*, with the meaning of traitor, is occasionally found in the silver period of Latin, e.g. Tacitus, *Hist.*, IV.24. It is, however, missing from legal Latinity. Heumann-Seckel, *Handwörterb.*, op. cit., p.588f., s.v. *tradere*, nowhere mentions it. The customary word in pre-Constantinian Latin for 'traitor' is *proditor*. Even Jerome, who in the Vulgate aimed at a classical style, has usually *proditor*, *traditor* only once, Mark 14:44, a slip of the pen, and characteristic as such.

[3] *Conc. Illib.*, can.40, ed. Jonkers, op. cit., p.14.

Testament this meaning of sacrificial *meat* is consistently maintained.[1] In pagan Greek the word is, of course, non-existent; but
its equivalent, *hierothyton*, also means regularly the animal victim
or parts of it.[2] It may even be held that the Greek verb θύω would
have resisted any general enlargement of its meaning beyond the
precincts of animal sacrifice.[3] Yet these Spanish bishops used
idolothytum for any kind of expense on behalf of the pagan idols.
Did they then know more Greek than we? That seems unlikely.
For their general standard of education is characterized by the fact
that another canon of Elvira exhorts them not to go about roving
as traders who put up their stalls at one fair after another;[4] and
such-like business activities may have prevented many of them
from acquiring any knowledge of Greek at all. It is, therefore,
reasonably clear that the word itself had its part during the persecution in Spain, as a symbol of such un-Christian behaviour as
would include the consumption of sacrificial meat. We may
therefore conclude from the appearance of the word in this document that the Christians in Spain too had practised abstinence
from sacrificial meat and had suffered for it during the persecution
under Maximian. For only in this way, it seems to me, was it
possible for the word to become so current that it could—mistakenly—be used as a comprehensive term for all the various dues
to idols, which the Christians refused to pay, the sense it has in
our canon.

The canon is of a special interest in this context, because it
makes it clear that the Spanish Christians in the more peaceful
period before the last persecution abstained from eating sacrificial
meat as much as their brethren in the East;[5] and that the

[1] Cf. F. Büchsel, *Theol. Wörterb.*, vol.2, 1950, p.375f., who for the Jewish
usage refers to 4.Macc.5:2, and ps. Phocylides, verse 31.
[2] G. Schrenk, *Theol. Wörterb.*, vol.3, p.252f.
[3] Cf. Liddell-Scott, s.v.
[4] *Conc. Illib.*, can. 19, Jonkers, op. cit., p.9.
[5] The bishops of Leon and of Merida, who had fallen in the persecution under
Decius, A.D. 250, were *libellatici*, Cyprian, *Epist.* 69, and no eating of sacrificial
meat is mentioned in this connection. I believe, however, that the enlargement
of the meaning of *idolothytum* had its origin in the fact that the Church had
learnt to refuse any distinction between the various classes of the *lapsi*, as
libellatici, thurificati, sacrificati, etc., on occasions like their defection.

persecutors in the West, Maximian and (presumably) Constantius applied the same practices as their colleagues in the East. However, its bearing went far beyond this. It ruled that no Christian squire should reimburse his pagan tenant for any expense incurred on behalf of the idols. It is to be assumed that this was an attempt to prevent those 'Christian' squires from sitting on the fence, so to speak, who would for their persons adhere to the Christian Church, but as a sort of insurance pay the necessary dues to the idols of old through their tenants. Unfortunately, the way in which this goal was reached was not untypical for Spain; It was the tenant, not the master, who was made to suffer. To combine religion with business has not been a monopoly of the Calvinist Church, as certain modern authors are inclined to believe.

II

Quaker Latin

But how, we may ask, did those Spanish bishops ever think of using a Greek term like *idolothytum*, where did they learn of it, if it is true that they knew no Greek? The answer is that we are in this instance faced with what to later generations has become known as 'dog Latin', but might better be described as 'Church Latin'. Our question, therefore, ought to be put in this way: What was the language of the early Christians in the West? The answer to this question is that, thanks to the work of a prominent Roman scholar, Mgr. J. Schrijnen, and his school,[1] we can today state with a fair amount of certainty that these Christians developed a special type of Latin, Church Latin, the rules of which may be found as recognized in all the various literary productions of the Western Church up to the time of Constantine. A certain number of grammatical constructions and a large vocabulary with numerous Greek loan-words can be

[1] Cf. Mohrmann, op. cit., vol.1, p.3f., on the Nijmegen school, and my review in *J.T.S.*, 1959, p.401f.

described today as typically Christian.[1] The impact of this special Christian Latin upon the Latin Christian writers may be shown by the example of one of the greatest fathers of the Church in North Africa, and certainly the greatest bishop of the western Church in the third century, Cyprian of Carthage. He was the scion of a noble and very rich family of the senatorial province of Africa, where literary Latin had taken refuge when Rome itself, in the course of the second century, had succumbed to the Greek language. Prior to his conversion he had occupied a chair of rhetoric, we would say of Latin literary criticism, at the university of Carthage. Who else could be expected more than he, to write faultless Latin in his time. Nevertheless, we learn from Lactantius that the educated pagans found his style, which was specially addressed to the Christians, intolerable;[2] and even Augustine severely reproached Cyprian for his style.[3] To modern readers it is quite evident too that the stylistic art, or rather its opposite, common amongst early Christian Latin writers, and the vocabulary of Church Latin, can be clearly illustrated from his writings, which all originate from the Christian period of his life.

How then is this phenomenon of the rise of a special Christian language in the Western Church to be explained? In the heading of this section I have referred to the related problem of the existence of a special language among the Quakers.[4] We have seen, at the example of the Christians' Sunday joint, how it was that a seemingly small difference in the ordinary conduct of life caused a profound separation of the Christians from their non-Christian fellow-citizens. Not only the civil law, but their own

---

[1] A collection of such words of Greek origin in particular, may be found in Mohrmann's index. Although this list is by no means complete, and does not e.g. contain the words *idolothytum* or *traditor*, it is very useful, and gives a valuable introduction into the character of this special speech of the early western Christians.

[2] 'Ut a solis fidelibus audiantur', Lactant., *Div. Instit.*, V.1.26.

[3] Augustine's remark, *De doctr. Chr.*, 4.14, refers directly to Cyprian, *Ad Donatum*, only, but it plainly echoes a 'communis opinio'.

[4] To gain an impression of this type of speech, G. Locker Lampson, *A Quaker Post-Bag*, 1910, may be consulted. The special Quaker translation of the Bible by A. Purver, 1764, does not seem to have left any lasting impression.

choice, placed the Christians at the margin of contemporary society, if not beyond it. The situation of the 'Friends' and other similar Nonconformist bodies in England from the end of the sixteenth to the middle of the nineteenth century was comparable. Like the early Christians, they refused to do military service,[1] and to swear oaths; and since they were thus ineligible for any public service they found themselves in a situation which may well be compared with that of the early Christians within the Roman Empire, who also refused to accept any public office. Thus they were still more closely joined in their own ranks, and avoided amongst each other all flowery speech for conscience sake, so that they came to adopt more or less closely the language of the English Bible. This special language only disappeared during the nineteenth century, when it was also caricatured good-humouredly by that great observer of English life in early Victorian time, Captain Marryat.[2] The outstanding document of this special language is Bunyan's *Pilgrim's Progress*, which I believe may be characterized as a stylistic curiosity.

In the same way as the English of the Quakers, the Church Latin of the second and third century was built upon the translation of the Bible which, at that time, was common to the Latin West. This has resulted eventually in the undeniable fact that the whole of 'western', European, civilization rose from the acceptance of the Latin Bible as the sacred book of the western Church. Whilst in the East the Syrians, the Armenians, the Arabs, the Ethiopians, yea, even the Visigoths, read their Bible in their respective mother tongues, it was the Latin Bible which was accepted in the West by the Berbers in Africa, the Iberians and Lusitanians in Spain, the Celts in France, the Britons and the Irish, the Franks and the Alamans. The faulty Latin of a number of anonymous Christian writings of the third century,[3] which have

---

[1] v. Campenhausen, op. cit., p.204, has stated quite rightly that 'the earliest Christians did not want the least to do with military service'. Cf. also Ehrhardt, *Polit. Metaphysik*, vol.2, p.287f.

[2] Captain Marryat, *Japhet in search of his father*, chap. 61f.

[3] Practically the whole of the pseudo-Cyprianic corpus, ed. W. Hartel, *S. Thascii Cypriani opera*, vol.3, 1871, may be quoted to support our remark, but cf. in particular *De pascha computus*, and *De montibus Sion et Sina*.

been preserved in the corpus of pseudo-Cyprianic literature, show how hard the struggle was which many of these Westerners had to fight with their sacred language. However, it was by these efforts that Christian Latin became the unifying bond in western Christendom. For it is not to be believed that even in Gaul the masses were brought to the acceptance of the Latin language by a policy of 'Romanization'. I frankly doubt whether the Latin speaking 'Society' in Gaul in the second century even pursued such a policy of Romanization. Already at that time Gaul was organized under a feudal system; and I remember only too well the reply of one of the Baltic barons, one von Engelhardt, in whose province of Livland this system had continued for centuries, to my mother's question whether he spoke German with his Latvian servants. 'Madam,' he said, 'those Letts are such dogs, they do not deserve to be addressed in German; Latvian is the language for them.' [1]

In any case it is true to say that the upper classes in Gaul and Britain, amongst whom Latin had become the current language, were wiped out in that terrible agrarian revolution which swept over those provinces in the course of the third century. Maximian, Constantine, and their successors did their utmost to re-establish the feudal system, but it can be seen from the book by the German historian Strohecker, *The Senatorial Nobility in Gaul under the Christian Emperors*, that not even one of the great Gallic families in the fifth century, who themselves claimed, of course, a descent from Agamemnon, Aeneas, or at least the house of the Scipiones, was even mentioned in our sources before the end of the third century. And where we are able to follow them that far we find very insignificant and even seedy origins of their later splendour. The same may be held with regard to the origins of fourth- and fifth-century nobility at Rome, whilst I have to plead ignorance regarding their contemporary nobility in North Africa.

If then there were Christians amongst these mighty Lords, as for instance Hilary of Poitiers, Ambrose of Milan, or Paulinus of

---

[1] Cf. the snobbish way in which Philostratus, *Vita Apollon.*, VII.4, put on the same level Scythians, Libyans, and Celts, at the beginning of the third century.

Nola, their writings will still show unmistakeable signs of Christian Latin. In some cases it can be shown that this was caused by a conscious decision, as, for example, in the case of Hilary of Poitiers, who was a master of Latin style;[1] but it is at the same time evidence for a complete change in the language policy of the late western Empire, at least in Gaul. Both the feudal system and the imperial administration needed urgently the social rise of talented men from the lower classes,[2] and fluency in Latin was one of the most important conditions of such an ascent. Both Church and state being intent upon the spreading of proficiency in Latin, a somewhat unholy alliance between Church Latin and secular Latin was formed. For the secular Latin received a new and very real impetus from the change of policy which we have mentioned. We see that the population in Southern Gaul and North Italy were seized from the middle of the fourth century by that highly patriotic movement called Romanitas, whether they were Christians or pagans, and it even penetrated the ranks of the lower clergy, as may be seen from the writings of that unknown commentator of the Pauline Epistles, Ambrosiaster.[3]

It remained to be seen which of the two would eventually prove to be the stronger attraction, Church Latin or secular Latin. Perhaps it is true to say that secular Latin started with a small handicap; but at the turn of the fourth century the impulse given to it by the Romanitas movement was so strong that it looked an almost certain winner. How near it was to victory can be seen when we compare the language of the two leading poets of the period, Ausonius and Claudianus. The first was a Christian of sorts, the second a pagan. Admittedly the pagan poet was the far superior talent of the two, but what concerns us here is the fact that their poetic style is curiously similar, and that almost no trace of Church Latin can be detected in Ausonius. Yet the choice of their Latin style was a matter of conscience in those days as

---

[1] Cf. Mohrmann, op. cit., vol.1, p.147f.

[2] Cf. on the linguistic inability of Constantine's chancellery at Trêves, *Zeitschr. d. Savigny Stift.*, rom. Abt., 1955, p.129f.

[3] The valuable study by O. Heggelbacher, *Vom römischen zum christlichen Recht*, 1959, although it does not specially discuss Romanitas, gives the material for doing so on pp.25-32.

much as for Hilary, forty years earlier. That is shown by the famous dream of Jerome. In it Jerome saw himself arrayed before the tribunal of the eternal Judge, and the accusation was: *Ciceronianus es, non Christianus*, you are a Ciceronian, not a Christian. He obtained only a conditional discharge by making that vow, which he discarded immediately, that he would never again read any of the classical authors.

Christian conscience was justly troubled by the demand for classical purity, i.e. imitation of the pagan authors, in the teaching of Latin. For it was thus made evident that the new feudal system which the 'Christian Empire' sought to erect was to be built upon the ideals of the late persecutors of the Church. Many Christians regarded the Empire still with a deep suspicion. This suspicion was fully alive in the outbreak of the Donatist social revolution in North Africa, the influence of which was to be felt also in Italy during the fourth century. *Quid imperatori cum ecclesia* was not just an isolated outcry;[1] 'what business has the emperor with the Church' was the watchword for the entire Donatist schism. And the masses of African Christians followed it.[2] Neither can it be held that the effect of the Donatist schism was limited to the incessant raids of the *circumcelliones* during the fourth and fifth century, for the separation of North Africa from the Mediterranean civilization has continued right down to our own time.

In Gaul and Britain, on the other hand, it was the work of one great Father of the Church in particular, which not only subdued the enthusiasm for the ideal of Romanitas amongst the upper classes, but also knitted together European Christianity by their common use of Church Latin. Martin of Tours won the poor Gallic peasantry not only for the Christian faith, but also for its language.[3] The ideal of Romanitas would hardly have survived in the gales of the peoples' migration which swept over Europe during the subsequent centuries. Himself a semi-illiterate

[1] Optatus Milev., III.3, cf. Ehrhardt, *Polit. Metaphysik*, vol.2, p.281, n.4.
[2] Jerome, *De viris ill.*, 93, 'paene totam Africam decepit', cf. Frend, *The Donatist Church*, 1952, p.164, n.6.
[3] Cf. J. M. Wallace-Hadrill, *Bull. John Rylands Library*, 1961, p.223.

Pannonian soldier, his Latin was that of the Latin Bible and—probably—a military slang of the worst kind. Presumably it was considerably inferior to that which we find in the history of his successor at the see of Tours, Gregory; and this idea may horrify a Latin purist. Nevertheless it was he amongst the great western Fathers of the time who made an advance beyond all others in converting the Gallic peasantry and in setting up monasteries for them; and it was from these monasteries that the great Apostles went out to the other Celtic tribes: Patrick to convert the Irish, Ninian the Apostle of Scotland, Germanus of Auxerre to support and rescue the British Church in its plight. These were then to become the Fathers of those Iro-Scottish monks who proceeded to preach the Gospel and to spread the Bible throughout Europe. And their work resulted in the introduction of Latin, if Church Latin, amongst all the European nations.

III

The Christian Schoolmaster

If the alliance between the Church and the Empire had to be characterized as 'somewhat unholy', it was nevertheless at the beginning of the fourth century an absolute necessity. No doubt, the revolutionary effects of the Christian message showed themselves still in the Donatist rising in North Africa; but that is only one aspect of Christian society at the end of the third century. In the East even the wife and daughter of Diocletian, who became the great persecutor, are said to have been Christians; and in any case he had to begin his persecution with the execution of two of his ministers, Dorotheus and Gorgonius, who would not withdraw from their Christian profession.[1] This situation was not a new one, but had developed gradually. Already at the beginning of the third century we find Hippolytus of Rome having interviews with one of the Syrian Empresses of that time, probably Julia Mammaea, the mother of the Emperor Alexander Severus,

---

[1] Lactant., *De mort.*, 15, about the empress Prisca and her daughter Valeria; Euseb., *E.H.*, VIII.1.4; 6.5, on Dorotheus and Gorgonius.

and Origen corresponding with the same Empress, a fact which, however, did not protect either of these fathers from martyrdom. In the second half of the third century a rumour was even spread that the Emperor Philip (244–8) had become a Christian together with his Empress, but that both had been excommunicated by the Patriarch Babylas of Antioch because they had murdered the son of their predecessor, Gordianus; and we are no longer in a position to disprove this rumour, although there is a strong suspicion that it was a mere invention.[1]

All this, however, is only by the way. What is important is the fact, illustrated by these relations of Christian leaders with the imperial court, that the upper classes began to make their mark in the Church at this time. The revolutionary protest of Donatus in Africa itself was made possible by the financial support given to him by Lucilla, a rich Spanish widow living in Carthage.[2] Her reputation may have been unduly besmirched by those Catholic writers who tell us about her; but an unfavourable light is thrown upon these rich Spanish ladies in the canons of the synod of Elvira, and this is indeed beyond all reasonable suspicion. In its canon 5 it is laid down that a woman who in her fury had beaten her slave girl so cruelly that within three days she died, should do seven years penance, or five years if her intention to kill could not be proved; and that she should not be re-admitted to the Holy Communion before the end of that period. This rule was not limited to the Spanish Church; but it was adopted throughout the Christian West, and Gratian eventually in about 1150 received it in his *Decree*. Thus it remained valid for the whole Roman Church as canon law till 1917.[3] It is a fact, however, that this canon compares unfavourably not only with St. Paul's advice to Philemon concerning his fugitive slave Onesimus, but even with the contemporary Roman imperial legislation. The philanthropic current in the Stoic moral philosophy had caused the Emperors of the second century to issue several edicts in protection of the

---

[1] Cf. Ehrhardt, *Polit. Metaphysik*, vol.2, p.282, n.6, and more detailed in *Zeitschr. der Savigny-Stift.*, op. cit., pp.43, n.23; 54, n.45.

[2] Cf. Frend, op. cit., pp.18, 21, n.1.

[3] Jonkers, op. cit., p.6; *C.J.C.*, can. 43, dist. 50.

slaves. One of these, issued under Hadrian, was actually addressed to the very province of Spain in which Illiberis is situated, and deals with an identical case.[1] In it, however, the time within which the slave must have died in order to qualify his master for criminal prosecution for murder is five days, not three as in canon 5 of Elvira;[2] and it also seems that proof of a special intent to kill was not required by Roman law.[3] Neither can it be held that the bishops at Elvira were ignorant of this regulation by the civil law. If it may not be beyond doubt that they had the words of the imperial decree before them at the council, an almost verbatim quotation in the canon puts it beyond all doubt that they consulted the commentary of the famous Roman lawyer Ulpian on the imperial decree.[4]

If, therefore, the abolition of class distinctions within the primitive Church appears to have belonged to the past in many parts of the Church already by the time of Constantine; if it is true to say that the protection of the slaves—and to some extent even of the poor in general—had been restricted in the pre-Constantinian Church already,[5] it must not be assumed that such a past had never existed at all. It is worth our while to try to cast some light upon the way Christian communities gathered together at that time when the Christian congregations could still be described as 'those who turn the world upside down', Acts 17:6, i.e. had aimed openly at preparing this world for the coming of the Judge of all,

---

[1] *Dig. Just.*, 48.4.1.

[2] Cf. *Dig. Just.*, 1.6.1, §2, 'nam ex constitutione divi Antonini qui sine causa servum suum occiderit non minus puniri iubetur quam qui alienum servum occiderit'; 48.8.14, 'divus Hadrianus in haec verba rescripsit: In maleficiis voluntas spectatur non exitus'.

[3] Cf. *Pauli Sent.*, V.23.3; *Collat.*, I.6.7; 7.1, and G. F. Falchi, *Diritto penale Romano*, 1932, p.152f.

[4] Compare Ulpian in *Collat.*, I.7.1, 'distinctionem casus et voluntatis in homicidio servari rescripto Hadriani confirmatur', with Illib. can. 5, 'eo quod incertum sit voluntate an casu occiderit'. The doubt whether the bishops at Elvira considered Hadrian's decree itself arises from the question whether they would have shortened its five days to three, if they had seen it.

[5] Cf. e.g. how it is said in the *Passio Clementis*, 3.1, ed. F. Diekamp, *Patres Apostolici*, vol.2, 1913, p.55, that the poor Christians had to go begging at the houses of Jews and pagans. This document seems to be fourth century, Diekamp, p.xii.

and had not concerned themselves only with the salvation of their own souls. To answer this question the analogy of modern Communism, which on occasion may provide the historian with a useful pointer, can only teach the direct opposite of the Christian practice. Communist infiltration delights in calling itself non-Communist: 'I am not a Communist, but . . .', or 'I am a Socialist', are remarks which may frequently be heard from emissaries at the meetings of C.N.D. and similar gatherings. The early Christians, however, saw their duty differently. They, like modern Christians, were under the obligation to confess their Master (please, *not* their faith!). 'Whosoever denies me before men, him I will deny also before my heavenly Father.' [1] As the effect of this harsh demand we see, on the one hand, the repeated mass defections under persecution, especially during the third and early fourth century—and earlier, as in Pliny's persecution in Bithynia —but on the other, the rise of the strong conviction that the blood of the martyrs was the seed of the Church.[2]

Who then were those people who accepted the service of the Lord Christ[3] under such conditions? It may seem surprising that they were so numerous that the Church was in the position of selecting suitable ones from the candidates for admission. We hear about this from the Church Order of Hippolytus of Rome, at the beginning of the third century.[4] There it is laid down that certain professions were automatically excluded. A pander was rejected unconditionally. Few people will question the justice of this rule; but it has to be taken into consideration that it affected the whole number of inn-keepers, with only a few exceptions, throughout the Roman Empire, with their damaging influence upon public opinion.[5] Rejected were painters, sculptors, and stone-masons, unless they made a promise that they would never again fashion

---

[1] Matt., 10:33 par.
[2] Tertullian, *Apol.*, 50, cf. E. G. Sihler, *From Augustus to Augustine*, 1923, p.122, n.3.
[3] Bousset, *Kyrios*, pp.240-5, gives an exact analysis of what is meant with this designation here.
[4] Dix, *Treatise*, p.25f., *Ap. Tr.*, XVI.10f.
[5] L. Friedländer-Wissowa, *Darstellungen a. d. Sittengeschichte Roms*, 9th ed., vol.1, p.349.

idols; and this rule, I feel, accounts not only for the rise of a special Christian art from the end of the second century, but also for the adoption of so many pagan symbols in early Christian art.[1] Actors and circus artistes, in short all the people employed in show business, were refused,[2] as were also sorcerers, astrologers and the like who at that time formed a considerable part of the medical faculty. Higher officials were excluded; but the lower grades, i.e. *milites* up to the rank of *centurio*, were admitted on condition:[3] They were forbidden to execute capital punishment and to swear the oath to the Emperor.[4] Amongst all these rules the most consequential for the future history of Europe was the rather pathetic one about the admission of a schoolmaster:[5] 'If a man teaches the children secular wisdom, it would be better if he abstained from it; but if he knows no other skilled trade by which he could live, he may be forgiven.'

It was perhaps the earliest occasion on which the Church deviated on grounds of expediency from a principle which it had laid down for conscience sake, when it made this exception on behalf of the Christian schoolmaster. The reader feels the smile of the Father writing this clause.[6] Yet the rule was of tremendous importance. For the schoolmaster at Rome was not only charged

[1] If I am not mistaken it seems that Th. Klauser in his splendid essays on 'the origins of Christian art', *Jahrb. f. Antike u. Christentum*, vol.1, 1958, p.20f.; vol.2, 1959, p.115f., to which I refer, has by-passed this point.

[2] Hippol., *Ap. Trad.*, XVI.12; 14–15. Legends like the *Passio S. Genesii*, Ruinaert, *Acta*, op. cit., p.312f., were invented in later time in order to account for the revision of this rule.

[3] v. Campenhausen, op. cit., p.207f., in his essay on the military service of the early Christians, has left undiscussed this rule, and given no definition of *miles*, who did not necessarily belong to the fighting forces. Yet both are important for the understanding of Tertullian, *De corona*, in particular.

[4] This apparently meant the actual recitation of the oath, and performing of the sacrifice at the half-yearly celebrations, cf. Nock, *Harv. Theol. Rev.*, 1952, p.185f. Tertullian, *De corona*, shows that the mere presence of a Christian at these solemnities, even if he was garlanded, was not regarded as a defection from the Christian faith.

[5] Hippol., *Ap. Trad.*, XVI.13.

[6] The reason for this remark is that a legend was invented too for the schoolmaster martyr (probably in order to justify the admission of his colleagues to the Christian Church). Cassian of Imola was immortalized by Prudentius, *Peristeph.*, IX, where it is told that he was handed over to his scholars, to be

to teach the three Rs, but also and especially the ancient myths. The text books for this subject were the two great epic poets, Homer in the East, and in the West Vergil, and it is true to say that the Latin West worshipped its Vergil. The rule about the school-master opened the road not only for him to join the Church, but also for the Christian children to acquire Vergil. The result of this deviation may be judged by the title of that fifth-century didactic poem by the Christian Martianus Capella, *On the Marriage of Mercurius with Philologia*, in which Mercurius, Hermes Logios, is the Divine Word. We still possess the handbook of ancient mythology by the bishop Fulgentius of Ruspe, about fifty years later than Martianus, and from the subsequent centuries the three Vatican mythographers, all of them the works of Christian clergy. How times have changed: We poor children of today have to read these mythographers in the bowdlerized edition by Bode[1] because the great librarian of the Vatican 150 years ago, the Cardinal Anglo Mai, regarded them, and in particular the third, which was the most influential, as obscene, and as unsuitable matter for reading. The medieval Church, however, loved and devoured them.[2]

The smallest cause had the most gigantic effect! When the great Church took pity on the poor little schoolmaster, and neglected the warnings of its more serious-minded leaders like Tertullian[3] that no classical authors should be taught to Christian children, it did in fact open the gates for Vergil, by whose greatness it was filled from that time onward for far over a thousand years. From this decision stems Dante's immortal poem; but it was not only Dante who exalted the 'potentially' Christian poet. His opinion of Vergil was in fact the common conviction of all the common people in medieval time. Only one instance may be quoted: On the day of the conversion of St. Paul (Jan. 25), the people of

---

killed by their *stili*, cf. L. Bieler in *Serta philologica Aenipontana*, 1961, p.384. Was that quite serious?

[1] G. H. Bode, *Scriptores rerum mythicarum Latini tres*, Celle, 1834.

[2] Cf. O. Gruppe, *Gesch. d. klass. Mythologie*, 1921, §§3,5,7.

[3] Tertullian, *De idol.*, 10, cf. v. Campenhausen, *Latein. Kirchenväter*, 1960, p.21.

Mantua chanted in the cathedral of Vergil's native town, in honour of St. Paul of course:[1]

> When to Maro's tomb they brought him
> Tender grief and pity wrought him
>   To bedew the stone with tears:
> What a Saint I might have crowned thee
> Had I only living found thee,
>   Poet first and without peers.

In this case it may be said with a real assurance that one stroke of the pen of the legislator has changed the fate of the whole of Europe.[2]

IV

Concubinage and Communion

We have to return once more to the selection of catechumens in the early Church. There was the question also of the admission of slaves. If the candidate was a slave then it had to be found out whether his master was a Christian. For if he was a Christian Hippolytus required a reference from the master without which the applicant was rejected.[3] If he was a pagan such a demand was, of course, impracticable. It seems, however, that in this case, on which no ruling is to be found in Hippolytus' Church Order, admission was granted without any further ado. For already in St. Paul's Epistle to the Philippians we find that the Apostle conveys the greetings of 'those of Caesar's household' to the Church at Philippi.[4]

---

[1] Cf. E. K. Rand, *Founders of the Middle Ages*, Dover Books, 1957, p.36,

> *Ad Maronis mausoleum*
> *Ductus fudit super eum*
>   *Piae rorem lacrimae:*
> *Quem te, inquit, reddidissem*
> *Si te vivum invenissem,*
>   *Poetarum maxime.*

[2] To my mind, E. Fränkel, *Gedanken zu einer deutschen Vergil-Feier*, 1930, is still the unsurpassed introduction to the European significance of Vergil.

[3] Hippol., *Ap. Tr.*, XVI.4.

[4] Phil. 4:22. It is to be regretted that Lohmeyer, *Der Brief an die Philipper*,

When considering the situation of such slaves it has to be remembered that the position of slaves in the first two centuries of the Christian era was vastly different from that in earlier times. For example, there is the strange fact that neither in the so-called war of the federates (B.C. 91–88) nor in the last rebellion of the Samnites (B.C. 81) were the slaves called upon to assist the rebellious peasantry, whilst Spartacus (B.C. 73–71) in his turn neither received nor even seems to have called for the assistance of the free proletariat, although he rose in the very districts where those former rebellions had taken place. This, I believe, has to be explained by the enormous importation of slaves into Italy from abroad at that time, when the Roman legions reduced whole nations to slavery. Farmers and slaves at that time had not even a common language in which to converse.[1] In the Christian period, however, conditions were vastly changed. The unfree population was now part of the resident community; and whilst legislation and administration did their utmost to prevent liaisons between free women and slaves, they looked with comparative ease at their opposite, especially when it was a case of a master and his own slave girl.[2] It was the Church which made the distinction that an unfree concubine should only be received if she reared her own children, and continued 'the wife of one man'.[3] Concubinage between free persons, however, which Roman Law

---

1928, p.191, says no more about this than 'the reason for this mention cannot be stated any more'. For either the stress lies on 'Caesar's', and in that case the Epistle was written in Rome, or it lies on 'household', and then the admission of slaves was at stake—perhaps both.

[1] *Studium Generale*, 1961, p.659f.

[2] It has to be stated, however, that Augustine, *De coniug. adult.*, II.7, quotes from *Cod. Greg.*, XIV, a constitution by Caracalla: 'Periniquum enim mihi videtur esse ut pudicitiam vir ab uxore exigat quam ipse non exhibet', cf. Friedländer-Wissowa, op. cit., vol.I, p.285, n.8, who, following Augustine's interpretation, refer this decree to matrimonial relations of a master with his slave.

[3] Hippol., *Ap. Trad.*, XVI.23. The article is also of legal historical interest: It is well-known that *contubernium*, marriage between slaves, was protected in Roman Law since the beginning of the second century from violent disrupture by the master. Hippolytus, at the beginning of the third century seems to presuppose here that this protection was also given to an unfree mother and her children.

regarded already as a lesser kind of marriage,[1] was not to be tolerated by Christians, but the parties were to be admonished to enter into full matrimony. This disapproval of concubinage by the Church was also used for his own ends in the legislation of Constantine, himself the offspring of such a connection, and father of such a son.[2]

In order to understand the subsequent development we have to start once more with a warning given by Tertullian. He emphasized that the interest shown by the political authority in the raising of the birth-rate was a matter of indifference to the Christians: 'Should we perhaps show an interest in order that the temples should not stand deserted? Or in order that people should be found to shout, "the Christians to the lions"?'[3] This was a thinly veiled threat addressed to the civil authorities, a threat in which Tertullian's writings abound. Its weight has become more evident since the American sociologist, A. E. Boak, has proposed his thesis that the Roman Empire in the West collapsed because of its lack of manpower.[4] I am not one of those who advocate one master solution in cases of political catastrophe like that of the 'Decline and Fall of Rome'. It is nevertheless true to say that the decline in the number of the population of the Empire was one of the chief worries of the Roman authorities of the day; and that its two main causes were the constant decline of the birth-rate, and the plague.[5] This anxiety led to a policy which, with an increasing vigour, made first the agricultural jobs inherit-

---

[1] Cf. the precise summary by P. Bonfante, *Corso di Dir. Rom.*, vol.1, 1925, p.232f.

[2] Hippol., *Ap. Trad.*, XVI.24a.—Constantine, *Cod. Theod.*, IV.6.3, abolished the right of fathers to make a last will in favour of *naturales filii*. H. Dörries, *Das Selbstzeugnis Konstantins*, 1954, p.202, has in his commentary overlooked the fact that this was the technical term for the offspring of a concubinage.

[3] Tertullian, *De exhort. cast.*, 12.

[4] A. E. Boak, *Manpower shortage and the fall of the Roman Empire*, 1955.

[5] Various Christian sources, as Cyprian, *De mortalitate*, testify to this debacle. Most impressive is the story related in the *Life of Gregory Thaumaturge* by Gregory of Nyssa. There we are told how the multitude in the theatre shouts 'Apollo make more space', and immediately afterwards the ranks are emptied by the plague. For Apollo was not only the God of the Muses, but also of the plague.

able,[1] and after that the arts and crafts in the cities as well. Admittedly, this development agreed with the general ideology of that feudalism which was prevalent in Roman ruling circles; and for which we may find parallels in feudal society right up to nineteenth-century Germany.[2] However, it was only the most pressing need which resulted at Rome in the application of this wrong medicine for her ills.

Of the effects of this policy a very sombre picture has been drawn by that great social historian Michael Rostovtzeff, whose hatred for the feudalism of Tsarist Russia made him see things more clearly than other scholars born in more liberal surroundings. His *Social and Economic History of the Roman Empire* was in its first edition (I am not yet sufficiently familiar with the second) one impassioned accusation of that inhuman Emperor Diocletian, who completed the process.[3] The 'ethos'—if it can be so called—of this policy was that every citizen of the Roman Empire must be held responsible for the common weal with all his goods as well as with his whole life. This course was directed too against the middle classes, whose members were held responsible for the local and general revenue in all its forms. Amongst the functions thus supported the pagan cults received, of course, their share. Almost by accident we learn from the canons of the council of Elvira that even the Christians were unable to shake off the inheritable burden of the 'flaminate', one of the public priesthoods,[4] regardless of the fact that their presence at the cult would in the eyes of the heathen pollute the sacrifices.[5]

Far more important, however, was the fact that the positions

[1] How that was organized has been described most learnedly by M. Gelzer, *Studien zur byzantinischen Verwaltung Ägyptens*, 1909, p.69f.

[2] H. A. Oppermann recorded the following interview with the Hannoverian Kabinetts-Rat von Schele under Ernst August, who refused him admittance to the bar: 'What is your father?'—'Bookbinder.'—'In that case you too ought to have become a bookbinder,' cf. Tim Klein, *Der Vorkampf deutscher Einheit und Freiheit*, 1927, p.71.

[3] M. Rostovtzeff, *The Social and Economic History of the Roman Empire*, 2nd ed., 1957, cf. E. Kornemann, *Gestalten und Reiche*, 1943, p.354f.

[4] *Conc. Illib.*, can. 2–4, Jonkers, op. cit., p.5f.

[5] Cf. Lucian, *Alexander*, 25.38, and the *Acta Saturnini*, ed. Ruinaert, op. cit., p.177f.

in the local administration, which were all non-remunerative, were made inheritable in order to safeguard the continuity of the public revenue. The city councillors were in the worst case. These *decuriones*, as they were called, had to guarantee the public revenue of the city district with their own fortune, and to recoup themselves for it from the other inhabitants as best they could. In addition they were responsible for the capital demands of their own city, which they were supposed to meet out of their own pocket. These demands ranged from the heating of the public baths and the repairs of the public buildings to the furnishing of the numerous festivals which were celebrated by all the citizens.[1] The public burden of these unfortunates increased proportionately as the feudal Lords obtained more and more exemptions for their large estates in the later Roman Empire until—at least in the West —the whole monetary system collapsed. There is no need to emphasize specially that the decurionate was inheritable. So also were the craftsmen's guilds. These guilds had proved particularly valuable in those types of business where a considerable capital was required, as mining and shipping,[2] and also where a special risk was involved, as in baking at a time of continuing malnutrition of the bulk of the population. Like the feasts of the *decuriones*, and the sacrifices of the *flamines*, these guilds put the Christian member into a continuing religious stress. For they were on the one hand organized as religious communities, and on the other their membership was compulsorily inheritable. Their—at least—annual meetings assembled around a common sacrifice, and at the subsequent dinner the sacrificial meat was eaten. With the progress of the third century more and more such corporations,[3] usually under government supervision, were formed, and an existence outside them became less and less possible for the towns-people, who contained the bulk of the Christians.

However, the economic pressure was the same for everybody,

[1] Cf. the list in E. Kuhn, *Die städt. und bürgerl. Verwaltung d. röm. Reichs*, vol.1, 1864, p.43f.

[2] Cf. E. Herzog, *Gesch. u. System der röm. Staatsverfassung*, vol.2, 1887, p.1004.

[3] Cf. the list in Marquardt-Wissowa, *Staatsverwaltung*, op. cit., vol.3, p.138, n.5, which only attempts to cover conditions within the city of Rome, and even so is by no means complete.

and there was not a spark of a chance for any resistance by force, although local riots were frequent. The 'modern' armament of the Byzantine soldiers would be just as superior to any chance gatherings of rebels as that of the Roman legions before them. Dr. Spooner's famous German relative, Professor Galetti of Gotha, put the whole matter in a nut-shell when he described Quinctilius Varus as 'the only Roman general who succeeded in letting himself be beaten by the Germans'; and traditions of certain British colonial wars, like the Zulu war, might also help to enlighten the historical scene. I know few historical reports which are more heart-breaking than that about the complete devastation of the Moroccan countryside by the *magister equitum* Theodosius, the father of the Byzantine Emperor of the same name,[1] and those others about the mass suicides of the Donatist *circumcelliones* in all the Roman provinces of North Africa. These people are said to have jumped to their death in their hundreds from the many cliffs in the desert, without any apparent reason apart from their complete despair of life in this world, and the dim hope of a better future.[2]

Where was the way out of such calamities for such a serf, artisan or decurion in the sinking Roman Empire? Where was there any hope for him who, if he himself was unable to escape from his life-long burden, wanted at least to create such an exit for his children? There had been such an opportunity by joining the armed forces at the reorganization of the army under Diocletian and Galerius. In spite of a decreasing population the numerical strength of the army seems to have increased rapidly.

[1] Cf. E. Stein, *Gesch. des spätröm. Reiches*, vol.1, 1927, p.277, and more detailed O. Seeck, *Gesch. des Untergangs d. antik. Welt*, vol.5, 1913, p.28f.

[2] Cf. Th. Büttner-E. Werner, *Circumcellionen u. Adamiten*, 1959, p.46f.—The author does not, it seems, when referring to the hope of martyrdom in these suicides, stress sufficiently the fact that Catholic doctrine regards suicide as murder, which does not lead to the salvation of the 'martyr', and above all that this kind of an eschatological hope will only rise from complete earthly hopelessness. The comparable suicides of gladiators, cf. Friedländer-Wissowa, op. cit., vol.2, p.71, do not show any kind of religious motivation at all; neither seems the unknown artist from Pergamum, whose statue 'The Gaul and his wife' expresses the same situation, to have visualized such a psychological situation.

However, that gap was quickly closed by legislation. Constantine closed with an equal speed the way into the Church's ministry.[1] In the East, particularly in Egypt, such a person might emigrate into the desert, and altogether forego a married life. Already St. Paul had described the celibate life as superior (1.Cor.7:38), and we have seen how Tertullian had changed this advice into an unmistakable threat directed at his contemporary government. There can be no doubt that the immense popularity of monasticism in the East, since the second half of the third century, had its one great cause in the intolerable economic burden which the secular life put on the shoulders of those unfortunate 'villeins' of the early Byzantine Empire. It can be clearly shown how the introduction of *patrocinium*, as the feudal system was called in contemporary laws, in the course of the fourth century powerfully increased the monastic movement in Egypt, which even before had been threateningly popular.[2] Without it Church history might well have taken an entirely different course. For the great Alexandrian Patriarchs of the fourth and fifth centuries became more and more reliant upon the great hosts of monks who gathered under their banners. These monks repeatedly saved great Athanasius from being arrested; these monks defeated at Ephesus the Emperor's protégé Nestorius, and gained the victory for their Patriarch Cyrill, one of the less unambiguous saints of the Church.

In the West, however, this solution, if it was a solution, although it was highly admired in theory, proved far less popular in practice than in the East. Several bishops of the fourth century tried to introduce celibacy among their clergy—and are today highly famed for their attempts. Most famous among them is Pope Damasus (366–384 A.D.). However, his failure may still be read from the tomb-stones of his time. On these there is to be found not only a *presbitera*, the wife of a presbyter in some place in Calabria, which belonged under the ecclesiastical jurisdiction of the bishop of Rome, but even a *venerabilis femina episcopa*

---

[1] The final laws are Constantine's, *Cod. Theod.*, XII.1.13 (soldiers), and XII.2.6 (clerics), both of A.D. 326.
[2] Cf. Gelzer, loc. cit., above, p.305,n.1.

addressed, we would say, by the title of an archdeacon, from
Terni in Umbria, the province of Florence, not very far from
Rome, and the son of a bishop of Narni in Umbria,[1] succeeding
his father in his sacred office.[2] No reproach whatsoever was, therefore, attached to the marriage of the priests or bishops; and we
can understand the bitterness felt by Jerome, the partisan of
Damasus, in his vain and violent struggle about this matter with
men like Vigilantius and Jovinianus.

So much for the clergy; but was there also a chance for a
decurion in the western half of the Empire of marrying without involving his future wife and family in the miseries of his
decurionate? We have to realize that we are here dealing with a
problem which is becoming 'modern' once more. For the same
question is being asked today by many conscientious Anglican
priests in this country, who are compelled to conduct marriage
services during Lent, and even in Holy Week, because the tax
laws of this country grant considerable income-tax reliefs to
couples who marry at that particular period of the year; and the
red-tapeworms answer any, even the most reasonable, sugges-
tions for a change with their dictatorial 'impossible'. And when
the married woman, as is the case, has to pay considerably higher
income tax than her unmarried colleague, the time will come
when the question will be asked whether the official blessing by
the public registrar is worth the expense. I must confess, I do not
feel particularly shocked at the idea of people living in true
marriage, although they lack the rubber stamp of the registrar
of births and deaths.

Unfortunately, Roman Law excluded such a solution, because
at that time there was no solemn form provided by it for the
conclusion of matrimony. Roman marriage was a common law
marriage, i.e. when two persons of different sex had lived together
as man and wife for one year they were legally regarded as a
married couple, without any special formality. However, there
existed a fair number of customs at the solemnization of matrimony, one of which was more pliable than others, the establishing

[1] E. Diehl, *Latein. altchristl. Inschr.*, 1913, nr.62, and 85.
[2] Diehl, op. cit., nr. 65. cf. the footnote on the succession at Narni.

and signing of a document. This was turned into a form for the non-conclusion of marriage. Two persons who wanted to stay unmarried, whilst living together as man and wife, had to sign a written declaration to that effect. It is true that the feudal system, spurning, as it did, all *mésalliances*, had made a marriage between a noble and an ill-famed woman, like Helena, Constantine's mother, illegal already in pre-Christian time; and, as we have seen, the great product of such an alliance had confirmed this ruling.[1] Such couples then lived of necessity in concubinage. Nevertheless, it was the concubinage between commoners—and the decurions were not even regarded as *honestiores*, and thus exempt from corporal punishment—which became so frequent as to constitute not only a social but also a religious problem.[2] It seems that this form of inferior marriage was even adopted by the 'barbarian laws' of the immigrants of the fifth and subsequent centuries, resulting in the fact that right down to the twelfth century there were two forms of matrimony at the disposal of the people of western Europe; so that for instance Siegfried and Kriemhild lived together in 'Friedel-Ehe', the type arisen out of the late Roman concubinage.

It has been shown that in the pre-Constantinian period the Church had expressly opposed this type of matrimony, just as she does today; but it is worth our while to have a look at the legislation of the 'Christian' Emperors, which took its stand upon this tradition. The earliest is a law which has been mentioned already, produced by Constantine. It lays it down that in the case of a *mésalliance* between a nobleman and an actress not only the last will of the father, if it had been erected in favour of the children of such an alliance, should be null and void, but even all the gifts which he might have made them should lie open to being claimed by the imperial treasury. Constantine used this pretext for the moral and material annihilition of Licinianus, the son of his former rival's concubine.[3] Later Emperors who boasted

---

[1] *Cod. Theod.*, IV.6.3, cf. the not fully satisfactory discussion by M. Kaser, *Das röm. Privatrecht*, vol.2, 1959, p.126, n.3.

[2] Cf. my references in Pauly-Wiss., vol.17.2, 1937, p.1481f., s.v. *nuptiae*, III.

[3] Cf. Seeck, op. cit., vol.1, 1910, p.140.

about their leniency allowed such provision to be made for the 'natural children', as the offspring of such an alliance were called, up to one-fifth of the paternal fortune. It seems to be a widespread custom to call this legislation 'Christian'; but I defy anybody to make this claim in good faith! To prevent a father from providing for his children may be seen as a political necessity. In the same sense it may be true that the destruction of Licinianus was for Constantine a 'cruel necessity'; but to describe such an action as 'Christian' is sheer hypocrisy.

It is, therefore, a pleasure to record that at least one Christian Church, and, perhaps rather unexpectedly, the Spanish Church, saw through this camouflage of conceit and bigotry. At the first council of Toledo in A.D. 400, she protested quite unequivocally. The seventeenth canon of this council, a clause which has been glossed over rather shamefacedly by the late bishop of Rottenburg, and most learned authority on all the councils of the Church, C. J. Hefele, decided:[1] 'He who has no wife, but in her stead a concubine, as he considers it right, is not to be excluded from Holy Communion, if only he is satisfied to live with one wife or concubine.' Imagination may well conjure up phantasms of social pressure brought to bear upon the bishops who formulated this canon, and why should not a Spanish grandee have supported a just cause. The moral principle *ut ei placuerit*, 'as he considers it right', is yet of perpetual importance. These Spanish bishops do not deserve criticism for 'laxity' because they came to the conclusion that it was morally wrong to allow the bullies in the public 'service' to make use of their spiritual authority for very worldly aims.

I have offered a number of anecdotes, and the reader may well ask, 'what does this all add up to'? The answer is that there exists for the historian a great material for a social history of the

---

[1] *Conc. Tolet.*, I, can. 17, cf. C. J. Hefele, *Conciliengeschichte*, vol.2, 2nd ed., 1875, p.75. Some caution may be used when dealing with Hefele's remark there in note 3.—On the other hand it may be added that the *Acta Bonifatii*, ed. Ruinaert, op. cit., p.325f., presumably of the end of the third century, were probably invented in order to characterize even the concubinage of a *femina nobilis* with her unfree *procurator* as a venial sin—in direct opposition to the old-established civil law.

Christian Church, which is as yet almost untouched, and of which these anecdotes may be regarded as samples. The material is, however, well worth collecting and working upon. On the one hand, I feel that those great scholars Ernst Troeltsch and Max Weber in Germany, or Tawney in this country, may have built their conclusions upon too circumscribed a basis, and deserve a continuation of their researches, which at the moment seems sadly lacking. On the other, and this makes this a theological task, it is true to say that those who are convinced that a Christian is not proved by his attendance at Sunday worship but by his whole working life, of which the Sunday worship ought to be the culmination, have no right to neglect that 'lesser' Church History in which lie all the roots of Christian theology and liturgy.

BIBLIOGRAPHY

AKLAND, K., 'Der Montanismus und die kleinasiatische Theologie', *Zeitschrift für die Neutestamentliche Wissenschaft*, 46, 1955.

AMBROSE, *St.*, *see* Connolly.

ARISTOTLE, *Aristoteles Werke*, tr. and ed. C. Prantl, *et al.*, 7 vols., W. Engelmann, Leipzig, 1854–79.

ARNIM, H. F. A. VON (ed.), *Stoicorum Veterum Fragmenta*, 4 vols., Teubner, Leipzig, 1903–24.

BADCOCK, F. J., *The History of the Creeds*, S.P.C.K., 2nd ed., 1938.

BALL, W. E., *St. Paul and the Roman Law*, T. and T. Clark, Edinburgh, 1901.

BARDY, G., *La Question des Langues dans l'Église ancienne* (Études de théologie historique), Beauchesne, Paris, 1948.

BARNARD, L. W., 'St. Stephen and Early Alexandrian Christianity', *New Testament Studies*, vii, 1960.

BARNES, E. W., *The Rise of Christianity*, Longmans, London, 1947.

BARRETT, C. K., *The Holy Spirit and the Gospel Tradition*, S.P.C.K., 1947.

BARTH, K., *Römerbrief*, Kaiser, Munich, 5th ed., 1926.

BAUER, W., *Johannes-Evangelium*, Handbuch zum N.T., vol. 6, J.C.B. Mohr, Tübingen, 3rd ed., 1933.

—— 'Rechtgläubichkeit und Ketzerei', *Beitrag z. historischen Theologie*, Mohr, 1934.

—— *Wörterbuch zum Neuen Testament*, 4th ed., Töpelmann, 1952.

BAUMEISTER, A., *Denkmäler des Klassischen Altertums*, R. Oldenburg, Munich, Leipzig, 1888f.

BECK, A., *Römisches Recht bei Tertullian und Cyprian*, Niemeyer, Halle (Saale), 1930.

BELSER, J. E., *Die Apostelgeschichte*, 1905.

BERNAYS, J., 'Über die unter Philons Werken stehende Schrift über die Unzerstörbarkeit des Weltalls', *Abhandlungen der K. Preussischen Akademie der Wissenschaften* (Philosophisch-Historische Klasse), Berlin, 1883.

BEURLIER, E., *Le Culte Impérial*, E. Thoria, 1891.

Bible, A New and Literal Translation of all the books of the Old and New Testament, 2 vols., by A. Purver, W. Richardson and W. Johnston, 1764.

—— *Apocalypses Apocryphae, Mosis, Esdrae, etc.*, ed. C. Tischendorf, H. Mendelsohn, Leipzig, 1866.

—— *Apocrypha of John*, ed. W. Till, Die Gnostischen Schriften, Texte und Untersuchung, 60, 1955.

—— *Die Apokryphen und Pseudepigraphen des Alten Testaments*, 2 vols., trans. and ed. E. Kautsch, Mohr, Tübingen, 1900.

—— *Die Weisheit des Jesus Sirach*, ed., R. Smend, P. Reimer, Berlin, 1906.

—— *The Apocrypha and Pseudepigrapha of the Old Testament*, 2 vols., ed. R. H. Charles, Oxford University Press, 1913.

Bible, The Apocryphal New Testament, trans. M. R. James, Oxford University Press, 1924.

—— Old Testament Apocrypha, Ecclus, Die Sprüche Jesus des Sohnes Sirachs, ed. H. L. Strack (Institutum Judaicum, Schriften 31) Leipzig, 1903.

—— Novum Testamentum Graece, ed. Nestle, Würtembergische Bibelgesellschaft, 22nd ed. 1956.

—— The Book of Job, trans. with commentary by E. J. Kissane.

BICKERMAN, E., Der Gott der Makkabäer, Schocken, 1937.

BIELER, L., 'Beiträge Zur Geschichte eines Motivs' in Serta philologica Aenipontana, Innsbrucker Beiträge zur Kultur Wissenschaft, Sprachwissenschaftliche Institut der Leopold-Franzens-Universität, 7–8, Innsbruck, 1961.

BILLERBECK, P., Kommentar zum Neuen Testament aus Talmud und Midrasch, Beck, Munich, 1922f.

BINGHAM, J., Antiquities of the Christian Church, Chatto and Windus, London, 1875.

BLACK, M., An Aramaic Approach to the Gospels and Acts, Oxford University Press, 1946.

BLACKMAN, E. C., Marcion and his Influence, S.P.C.K., 1948.

BLAIR, H. A., A Creed before the Creeds, Longmans, 1955.

BOAK, A. E. R., Manpower Shortage and the Fall of the Roman Empire in the West, University of Michigan Press, 1955.

BODE, G. H. (ed.), Scriptores rerum mythicarum Latini tres, Schulze, Celle, 1834.

BOEHLIG, H., 'Geisteskultur von Tarsos', Forschungen zur Religion und Literatur des Alten und Neuen Testaments, N.F.2, Vandenhoeck und Ruprecht, Göttingen, 1913.

BOLL, F., Aus der Apokalypse (ETOIXEIA, 1), Teubner, 1914.

BONFANTE, P., Corso di Diritto Romano, I, Attilio Sampaolesi, 1925.

BONNET, M., see Lipsius.

BONWETSCH, N. (ed.), Texte zur Geschichte des Montanismus, Kleine Texte für Vorlesungen und Übungen, 129, Marcus und Weber, Bonn, 1914.

BOUSSET, W., Die Offenbarung des Johannes, Kritisch-exegetischer Kommentar über das Neue Testament, 6th ed., Vandenhoeck und Ruprecht, Göttingen, 1906.

—— 'Kyrios Christos', Forschungen zur Religion und Literatur des Alten und Neuen Testaments, N.F.4., 4th ed., Vandenhoeck und Ruprecht, Göttingen, 1935.

BOUSSET AND GRESSMANN, W., Die Religion des Judentums, Handbuch zum Neuen Testament, 21, Mohr, Tübingen, 3rd ed., 1926.

BRANDON, S. G. F., The Fall of Jerusalem, S.P.C.K., 1951.

BREHIER, E., Les Idées philosophiques et religieuses de Philon, Etudes de Philosophie médiévale, Vrin, Paris, 1925.

BREMER, F. P., Die Rechtslehrer und Rechtsschulen im Römischen Kaiserreich, I. Guttentag, Berlin, 1867.

BRISSONIUS, B., De Verborum Significatione, ed., J. G. Heineccius and J. H. Böhmer, Waisenhaus, Halle, Magdeburg, 1743.

—— De Formulis, ed., F. C. Conradi and J. U. Bach, Weidmann, Frankfurt a.O., Leipzig, 1755.

BROWNE, R. E. C., 'Schizophrenia' in *The Ministry of the Word*, S.C.M., 1958.
BRUCE, F. F., *The Acts of the Apostles*, Tyndale Press, 2nd ed., 1952.
BRUNS, C. G., AND GRADENWITZ, O., *Fontes Iuris Romani*, Mohr, Tübingen, 7th ed., 1909.
BÜCHLER, A., *Das Synedrion in Jerusalem*, A. Hölder, Vienna, 1902.
BULTMANN, R., *Geschichte der Synoptischen Tradition*, Vandenhoeck und Ruprecht, Göttingen, 2nd ed., 1931.
—— *Johannes Evangelium*, Kritisch-exegetischer Kommentar, Vandenhoeck und Ruprecht, Göttingen, 1937/41.
—— *Das Urchristentum*, Forschungen zur Religion, Artemis, Zürich, 1949.
BURKITT, F. C., *Early Eastern Christianity*, Murray, 1904.
BÜTTNER, T., AND WERNER, E., *Circumcellionen und Adamiten*, Akademie Verlag, 1959.

CADBURY, H. J., *The Book of Acts in History*, Adam and Charles Black, 1955.
CAIRD, G. B., *The Apostolic Age*, Duckworth, 1955.
CAMPENHAUSEN, H., VON, *Tradition und Leben*, Mohr, Tübingen, 1960.
—— *Lateinische Kirchenväter*, Kohlhammer, Stuttgart, 1960.
CASEY, R. P., *see also* Foakes-Jackson.
—— *The Excerpta ex Theodoto of Clement of Alex.*, Studies and Documents, Christopher, 1934.
CASPAR, E., *Die älteste römische Bischofsliste*, Schriften der Königsberger Gelehrten Gesellschaft, 2, 4, Berlin, 1926.
—— *Geschichte des Papstums*, Mohr, Tübingen, 1930.
CASPARI, C. P., *Ungedruckte, unbeachtete und wenig beachtete Quellen zur Geschichte des Taufsymbols*, 3 vols, Videnskabs-Selskabet, Christiania, Oslo, 1866–75.
—— *Alte und neue Quellen zur Geschichte des Taufsymbols und der Glaubensregel*, Videnskabs-Selskabet, Christiania, Oslo, 1879.
CHARLES, R. H. (trans. and ed.,) *The Ascension of Isaiah*, A. and C. Black, 1900.
CLARKE, W. K. L. (ed.), *The First Epistle of Clement to the Corinthians*, Macmillan, 1937.
CLEMENT *of Alexandria*, *see* Stählin.
CLEMENT, I., *St., Pope., see* Clarke and Lightfoot.
COHN, L., AND WENDLAND, P. (eds.), *see* Philo.
CONNOLLY, R. H. (trans. and ed.), *Explanatio symboli ad initiandos*, Texts and Studies Series, No. 10, Cambridge University Press, 1952.
CONYBEARE, F. C. (ed.), *The Apology and Acts of Apollonius*, Swan, Sonnenschein & Co., 2nd ed., 1896.
CORSSEN, P., 'Monarchianische Prologe zu den 4 Evangelien', *Texte und Untersuchungen*, 15, 1, Leipzig, 1896.
Councils of the Church, *see* Jonkers
CREMER, A. H., *Bibl-theol. Wörterbuch der neutestamentlichen Gräcität*, ed. J. Koegel, Gotha, Perthes, 11th ed., 1923.
CROSS, F. L. (ed. and trans.), *The Jung Codex*, Mowbray, 1955.
CULLMANN, O., *St. Peter, Disciple, Apostle, Martyr*, trans. F. L. Filson, S.C.M., 1953.
CUMONT, F., *Lux Perpetua*, Geuthner, 1949.
CYPRIAN, *St., of Carthage, see* Hartel.

DANZ, H. A. A., *Der Sakrale Schutz*, Mauke, Jena, 1857.
DARMSTETER, J., see Zend-Avesta.
DAVIES, J. G., *He ascended into Heaven*, Lutterworth, 1958.
DAVIES, W. D., AND DAUBE, D. (eds.), *The Background of the New Testament and its Eschatology*, Cambridge University Press, 1956.
DEUBNER, L., 'Mundus', *Hermes*, 1933.
DIBELIUS, M., 'Die Pastoralbriefe', *Handbuch zum Neuen Testament*, 13, Mohr, Tübingen, 2nd ed., 1931.
—— *From Tradition to Gospel*, trans. B. L. Woolf, Ivor Nicholson and Watson, 1934.
—— *Studies in the Acts of the Apostles*, ed. H. Greeven, S.C.M., 1956.
DIEHL, E., 'Lateinische altchristliche Inschriften', *Kleine Texte*, 26-28, Marcus und Weber, Bonn, 1913.
DIELS, H., *Fragmente der Vorsokratiker*, 5th ed., by W. Kranz, Weidmann, 1934.
DINDORF, L. (ed.), *Diodori Bibliotheca Historica*, 2 vols., Didot, 1842-4.
DIX, G., AND EASTON, B. S., *The Apostolic Tradition*, S.P.C.K., 1934.
Treatise on the Apostolic Tradition, Cambridge University Press, 1937.
DODD, C. H., *The Apostolic Preaching and its Developments*, Hodder and Stoughton, 1936.
—— *The Johannine Epistles* (Moffat, N.T. Commentary), Hodder and Stoughton, 1946.
—— *New Testament Studies*, Manchester University Press, 1953.
DOERRIES, H., *Das Selbstzeugnis Konstantins* (Abhandlungen der Akademie d. Wiss.), Vandenhoeck und Ruprecht, Göttingen, 1954.
DOMASZEWSKI, A. VON., *Die Religion des Romischen Heeres*, Fr. Lintz, Trier, 1895.
DRUMMOND, J., *Philo Judaeus on the Jewish Alexandrian Philosophy*, 2 vols, Williams and Norgate, 1888.
DUENSING, H. (ed.), *Epistola Apostolorum*, Kleine Texte für Vorlesungen und Übungen, 152, Marcus and Weber, Bonn, 1925.

EDMUNDSON, G., *The Church in Rome in the First Century*, Longmans, 1913.
EHRHARD, A., *Die Kirche der Martyrer*, Kösel and Pustet, Munich, 1932.
EHRHARDT, A. A. T., 'The Beginnings of Mon-Episcopacy', *Church Quarterly Review*, 140, 1945.
—— *The Apostolic Succession*, Lutterworth, 1953.
—— *Politische Metaphysik*, Mohr, Tübingen, 1959.
—— 'Constantine, Rome and the Rabbis', *Bulletin of the John Rylands Library*, 42, 1960.
—— 'Imperium und Humanitas', *Studium Generale*, 14, 1961.
ELBOGEN, J., *Der Jüdische Gottesdienst*, Gesellschaft zur Forderung der Wissenschaft des Judentums, Schriften, etc., Berlin, 1924.
EVANS, E., *Tertullian's Treatise against Praxeas*, S.P.C.K., 1948.

FALCHI, G. F., *Diritto penale Romano*, Zannoni, Padua, 1932.
FERET, H. M., *Pierre et Paul à Antioche et à Jérusalem*, Editions du Cerf, Paris, 1955.
FINKELSTEIN, L., *Akiba*, Friede, Covici, 1936.
FLEMINGTON, W. F., *The New Testament Doctrine of Baptism*, S.P.C.K., 1948.

FOAKES-JACKSON, F. J., *The Acts of the Apostles* (Moffat New Testament Commentary), Hodder and Stoughton, 1931.
—— AND LAKE, K. (eds.), *The Beginnings of Christianity*, 5 vols., Macmillan, 1920–33.
FOWLER, W. W., *Social Life at Rome in the Age of Cicero*, Macmillan, London, 1908.
FRÄNKEL, E., *Gedanken zu einer deutschen Vergil-Feier*, Weidmann, 1930.
FRAZER, J. G., *Pausanias' Description of Greece*, Macmillan, London, 1898.
FREND, W. H. C., *The Donatist Church*, Oxford University Press, 1952.
FREY, J. B., *Corpus Inscriptionum Judaicarum*, Citta del Vaticano, 1936f.
FRIEDLÄNDER, L., *Darstellungen aus der Sittengeschichte Roms*, I, 9th ed., ed. G. Wissowa, Hirzel, Leipzig, 1919.

GAVIN, F., *The Jewish Antecedents of the Christian Sacraments*, S.P.C.K., 1928.
GEBHARDT, O., HARNACK, A., AND ZAHN, T., (eds.), *Patr. Apost.* Opera, editio minor, Hinrichs, Lepizig, 6th ed., 1920.
GELZER, M., *Studien zur byzantinische Verwaltung Ägyptens*, Diss. Phil., Leipzig, 1909.
GHELLINCK, J. DE, et al. *Pour l'histoire du mot 'Sacramentum'* (Spicilegium Sacrum lovaniense, Études, etc., 3), E. Champion, 1924.
GILBERT, O., *Griechische Religionsphilosophie*, Engelmann, Leipzig, 1911.
GOPPELT, L., *Christentum und Judentum*, Beiträge zur Förderung Christlicher Theologie, Bertelsmann, Gutersloh, 1954.
GREENSLADE, S. L., *Schism in the Early Church*, S.C.M., 1953.
Griechische Christliche Schriftsteller, see Stählin.
GRIMM, J. AND W., *Irische Elfen-Märchen*, Fleischer, Leipzig, 1826.
GROBEL, K. (trans.), *The Gospel of Truth: a Valentinian meditation on the Gospel*, Adam & Charles Black, 1960.
GRUPPE, O., *Geschichte der klassischen Mythologie*, Teubner, Leipzig, 1921.
GUNDEL, W., *Hermes Trismegistus*, Neue astrologische Texte von W. Gundel (Abhandlung der bayrischen Akademie der Wissenschaften, Phil.-Hist. Abt. N.F. 12), Munich, 1936.

HAHN, A., *Bibliothek der Symbole*, 3rd ed., by G. L. Hahn, E. Morgenstern, Breslau, 1897.
HÄNCHEN, E., *Die Apostelgeschichte*, Kritisch-exegetischer Kommentar über das Neue Testament, 3, H. A. W. Meyer, Vandenhoeck und Ruprecht, Göttingen, 1956.
—— 'Petrus Probleme', *New Testament Studies*, vii, 1961.
Handbuch zum Neuen Testament, vol. 1, by Wendland, ed. Lietzmann, Mohr, Tübingen, 1912; vols.3, 4, 5, by Klostermann; vols.8, 9, ed. Lietzmann; vol.16, ed. Lohmeyer.
HARDY, E. R., *Christian Egypt*, Oxford University Press, New York, 1952.
HARNACK, A., *Das neue Testament um das Jahr 200*, Mohr, Freiburg, 1889.
—— *Geschichte der alt-christlichen Literaturs*, 2 vols., Hinrichs, Leipzig, 1893–1904.
—— *Militia Christi*, Mohr, Tübingen, 1905.
—— *Lukas, der Arzt*, Hinrichs, Leipzig, 1906.

HARNACK, A., *Die Apostelgeschichte*, Hinrichs, Leipzig, 1908.
—— *Mission und Ausbreitung*, 2 vols., Hinrichs, Leipzig, 4th edition, 1924.
—— *Einführung in die alte Kirchengeschichte*, Hinrichs, Leipzig, 1929.
—— *see also* Schmidt.
HARTEL, W., S. *Thascii Cypriani opera*, C.S.E.L., I–III, Gerold & Sohn, Vienna, 1871.
HARVEY, W. W. (ed.), *Sancti Irenaei . . . libros quinque adversus Haereses . . . 2* vols., Deighton Bell, Cambridge, 1857.
HASTINGS, J. (ed.), *Encyclopaedia of Religion and Ethics*, 13 vols., T. and T. Clark, Edinburgh, 1908–26.
HEFELE, C. J., *Conciliengeschichte*, II, Herder, Freiburg i Br., Augsburg, 2nd ed., 1875.
HEGGELBACHER, O., *Vom Römischen zum christlichen Recht*, Universitätsverlag, Freiburg (Schweiz), 1959.
HEINEMANN, I., 'Synkrisis oder äussere Analogie in der Weisheit Salomonis', *Theologische Zeitschrift*, 4, 1948.
HEITMULLER, W., 'Im Namen Jesu', *Forschungen zur Religion und Literatur des Alten und Neuen Testaments*, 1, 27, Vandenhoeck und Ruprecht, 1903.
HENNEKE, E., AND SCHNEEMELCHER, W., *Neutestamentliche Apokrophen*, I, Mohr (Siebeck), 3rd ed., 1959.
HEPDING, H., *Attis*, Religionsgeschichtliche Versuchet Vorarbeiten, I, Ricker, Giessen, 1903.
HERZOG, E., *Geschichte und System der Röm-Staatsverfassung*, vol. 2, Teubner, Leipzig, 1887.
HEUMANN, H. G., *Handlexikon zur Quellen des römischen Rechts*, 2 vols., Fischer, Jena, 9th ed., by E. Seckel, 1907.
HIPPOLYTUS, *St.*, *see* Dix and Easton.
HIRZEL, R., *Der Eid*, Hirzel, Leipzig, 1902.
HITZIG-BLÜMNER, *Pausanias*, O. R. Riesland, Leipzig, 1891–1907.
HOBART, W. K., *The Medical Language of St. Luke*, Dublin University Press, 1882.
HOLL, K., *Gesammelte Aufsätze zur Kirchengeschichte*, 3 vols., Mohr, Tübingen, 1927–8.
HOLLAND, R., 'Zur Typik der Himmelfahrt', *Archiv Relig. Wissenschaft*, 1925.
HOPFNER, T. (ed.), *Fontes hist. rel. Aegypt*, 5 parts, Marcus und Weber, Bonn, 1922–5.
HOW, W. W., AND WELLS, J., *A Commentary on Herodotus*, Oxford University Press, 2nd ed., 1928.

IRENAEUS, *see* Harvey
ISAIAH, *see* Charles

JANZON, R., *Svensk Exegetisk Arsbok*, 21, 1956.
JEREMIAS, J., *Jerusalem zur Zeit Jesu*, Pfeiffer, Leipzig, 1937.
—— *Die Abendmahlsworte Jesu*, Vandenhoeck und Ruprecht, Göttingen, 2nd ed., 1949.
—— *The Eucharistic Words of Jesus*, Blackwell, Oxford, 1955.
JEROME, *St.*, *De Viris Illustribus*, ed. Bernoulle, Mohr, Freiburg, 1895.

JONKERS, E. J., *Acta et symbola conciliorum*. Textus minores 19, Brill, Leiden, 1954.

JUSTER, J., *Les Juifs dans l'Empire Romain*, 2 vols., Genthner, Paris, 1914.

KÄSEMANN, E., *Die Legitimität des Apostels*. Wissenschaftliche Buchgesellschaft, Darmstadt, 1956.

KASER, M., *Das Römische Privatrecht*, II, C. H. Beck, Munich, 1955.

KATTENBUSCH, F., *Das Apostolische Symbol*, 2 vols., Hinrichs, Leipzig, 1894–1900.

KELLY, J. N. D., *Early Christian Creeds*, Longmans, 1950.

KERN, O. (compiler) *Orphicorum fragmenta*, Weidmann, Berlin, 1922.

KIDD, B. J., *The Roman Primacy*, S.P.C.K., 1936.

KIDDLE, M., *The Revelation of St. John* (Moffat N.T. Commentary), Hodder and Stoughton, 1940.

KILPATRICK, G. D., *The Origins of the Gospel according to St. Matthew*, Oxford University Press, 1946.

KITTEL, G., *Theologisches Wörterbuch zum Neuen Testament*, Kohlhammer, Stuttgart, 1935ff.

KLAUSER, T., *Miscellanea Mercati*, I, Vatican, 1946.

—— 'The Origins of Christian Art', *Jahrbuch für Antike und Christentum*, I, 1958.

KLEIN, T., *Der Vorkampf deutscher Einheit und Freiheit*, Langewiesche, Ebenhausen, 1927.

KLOSTERMANN, E., *Apocrypha*, III, (Kleine Texte 33), Cambridge, 1905. *see also Handbuch zum Neuen Testament*.

KNOPF, R., *Einführung in das Neue Testament*, 3rd ed., edited by H. Lietzmann and H. Weinel, Töpelmann, Giessen, 1930.

KNOX, W. L., *St. Paul and the Church of Jerusalem*, Cambridge University Press, 1925.

—— *St. Paul and the Church of the Gentiles*. Cambridge University Press, 1939.

—— *Some Hellenistic Elements*, Oxford University Press, 1944.

—— *The Acts of the Apostles*, Cambridge University Press, 1948.

KOCH, H., 'Zu Harnacks Beweis für den . . . Ursprung des Muratorischen Fragments', *Z.N.W.*, 25, 1926.

KORNEMANN, E., *Gestalten und Reiche*, Dietzrich, Leipzig, 1943.

KROLL, W., *Festschrift für Kretschmar*, Innsbruck, 1926.

KUHN, E., *Die städtische und bürgerliche Verwaltung des römischen Reichs*, I, Teubner, Leipzig, 1864.

LAKE, K., *see* Foakes-Jackson.

LA PIANA, G., 'The Roman Church at the end of the second century', *Harvard Theological Review*, 1925.

LAWSON, J., *The Biblical Theology of Irenaeus*, Epworth Press, 1948.

LEBRETON, J., AND ZEILLER, J., *De la fin du 2me siècle à la paix constantinienne*, Blond et Gay, Paris, 1945.

LEIPOLDT, J., *Geschichte des neutestamentlichen Kanons*, 2 vols., Hinrichs, Leipzig, 1907–8.

LEUTSCH, E. L. VON, AND SCHNEIDEWIN, F. W., *Corpus Paroemigraphorum Graecorum*, 2 vols., Vandenhoeck und Ruprecht, Göttingen, 1839–51.

320   *Bibliography*

LICHTENSTEIN, E., 'Das älteste christliche Bekenntnis', *Zeitschrift für Kirchengeschichte*, LXI, 1950.

LIDDELL, H. G., AND SCOTT, R., *Greek-English Lexicon*, Oxford University Press, 1925, new ed. 1940.

LIEBERMAN, S., *Greek in Jewish Palestine*, Jewish Theological Seminary of America, New York, 1942.

LIETZMANN, H., *Geschichte der alten Kirche*, I, de Gruyter, Berlin, Leipzig, 1932–44.
    see also, *Handbuch zum Neuen Testament.*

LIGHTFOOT, J. B., *The Apostolic Fathers, part I: Clement of Rome*, Macmillan, 1890.

LIPSIUS, R., AND BONNET, M., (eds.), *Acta apostolorum apocrypha*, Wissenschaftliche Buchgesellschaft, Darmstadt, reprinted 1959.

LOBECK, C. A. (ed.), *Phrynici Eclogae Nominum et Verborum Atticorum*, Leipzig, 1820.

LOCKER LAMPSON, S. F. (ed.), *A Quaker Post-bag*, Longmans, 1910.

LOHMEYER, E., *Die Briefe an die Philipper, an die Kolosser und an Philemon*, Vandenhoeck und Ruprecht, Göttingen, 8th ed., 1930.
    see also, *Handbuch zum Neuen Testament.*

LOHSE, E., *Die Ordination im Spät-Judentum und im Neuen Testament*, Vandenhoeck und Ruprecht, Göttingen, 1951.

—— 'Die Bedeutung des Pfingstberichts', *Evangelische Theologie*, 1953.

LOOFS, F., *Leitfachen zum Studium der Dogmengeschichte*, Niemeyer, Halle (Saale), 4th ed., 1906.

LORIMER-KÖNIG, E. (ed.), *Pseudo-Aristotle: de Mundo*, Sociéte d'édition 'Les belles lettres', Paris, 1933.

LOWE, J., *St. Peter*, Oxford University Press, 1956.

MADVIG, J. N., *Die Verfassung und Verwaltung des römischen Staates*, 2 vols., Teubner, Leipzig, 1881-2.

MARQUARDT, J., 'Römische Staatsverwaltung', *Handbuch der römischen Altertumer*, 4–6, Hirzel, Leipzig, 2nd ed., 1881-5.

—— 'Das Privatleben der Römer', *Handbuch der römischen Altertumer*, 2nd ed., 1886.

MENOUD, P. H., 'Le plan des actes des apôtres', *New Testament Studies*, 1954.

MEYER, E., *Ursprung und Anfänge des Christentums*, Cotta, Stuttgart, 1924.

MEYER, K., *Prolog des Johannes Evangeliums*, Lippert, Naumburg, 1902.

MILBURN, R. L. P., *Early Christian Interpretations of History*, A. and C. Black, London, 1954.

MINGANA, A. (ed.), 'East-Syrian Acts of Clement', *Bulletin of the John Rylands Library*, 1917.

—— 'Apocalypse of Peter in Syriac', *Woodbrooke Studies*, Heffer, Cambridge, 1933.

MITTEIS, L., *Reichsrecht und Volksrecht in den östlichen Provinzen des römischen Keiserreichs*, Teubner, Leipzig, 1891.

—— 'Römisches Privatrecht', *Systematisches Handbuch der deutschen Rechtswissenschaft*, Ducker und Humblot, Leipzig, 1908.

MOHRMANN, C., *Études sur le latin des Chrétiens*, Edizioni di Storia e Letteratura, Rome, 1958.

MOMMSEN, T. AND BLÜMNER, H., (ed.), *Edictum Diocletiani de pretiis venalium*, Reimer, 1893.

MÜLLER, F. W. F., *Anhang z.d. Abhandlung der Preussischen Akademie der Wissenschaft*, 1904.

MÜLLER, K., AND CAMPENHAUSEN, H. VON, *Kirchengeschichte*, I, (Grundriss der theologischen Wissenschaften), Mohr, 3rd ed., 1938.

MUNRO, H. A. J., *Lucreti Cari de rerum natura libri sex.*, Deighton Bell, Cambridge, 3rd ed., 1863.

MUSURILLO, H. A., *The Acts of the Pagan Martyrs*, Oxford University Press, 1954.

NESTLE, E., *Einführung in den Griechischen Neuen Testament*, 4th ed., edited by E. von Dobschutz, Vandenhoeck und Ruprecht, Göttingen, 1923.

NEWMAN, J., *Semikhah*, Manchester University Press, 1950.

NINEHAM, D. (ed.), *Studies in the Gospels*, Blackwell, Oxford, 1955.

NOCK, A. D., 'The Apocryphal Gospels', *Journal of Theological Studies*, 1960.

NORDEN, E., *Agnostos Theos*, Teubner, Leipzig, 1913.

—— *Die Geburt des Kindes*, Teubner, Leipzig, 1924.

Novum Testamentum Graece, see Bible.

OESTERLEY, W. O. E., *An Introduction to the Books of the Apocrypha*, Macmillan, 1935.

OTTO, A., *Die Sprichwörter und sprichwörtlichen Redensarten der Römer*, Teubner, Leipzig, 1890.

OVERBECK, see Wette.

PAULY, A. F., *Real-encyclopädie der klassischen Altertumswissenschaft*, new edition, ed. G. Wissowa, Metzler, Stuttgart, 1894–19—.

PAUSANIAS, see Frazer.

PETERS, N., *Der jüngst wiederaufgefundene hebräische Text des Buches Ecclesiasticus*, Herder, Freiburg, 1902.

PETERSON, E., *Heis Theos*, Vandenhoeck und Ruprecht, Göttingen, 1926.

—— *Frühkirche, Judentum und Gnosis*, Herder, Rome, Freiburg and Vienna, 1959.

PETSCHENIG (ed.), 'Explanatio in XII Psalm', C.S.E.L., Hölder and Tempsky, Vienna, 1919.

PHILO, *Opera*, ed. L. Cohn, P. Wendland, and S. Reiter, Teubner, 7 vols., 1896–1930.

PHRYNICHUS, see Lobeck *and also* Rutherford.

PICKMAN, E. M., *The Mind of Latin Christendom*, Oxford University Press, New York, 1935.

PREUSCHEN, E., *Palladius and Rufinus*, J. Ricker, Giessen, 1897.

QUISPEL, G., 'Philo und die alterchristliche Häresie', *Theologische Zeitschrift*, 1949.

RAND, E. K., *Founders of the Middle Ages*, Dover Books, 1957.

REICKE, BO, *The Disobedient Spirits and Holy Baptism*, Munksgaard, Copenhagen, 1946.

REICKE, Bo, *Glaube und Leben der Urgemeinde*, Abhandlungen zur Theologie des Alten und Neuen Testaments, 32, Zwingli Verlag, Zürich, 1957.

REITZENSTEIN, R., *Poimandres*, Teubner, Leipzig, 1904.

—— *Die Hellenistischen Mysterienreligionen*, Teubner, Leipzig, 3rd ed., 1927.

RENGSTORF, K. H., *Apostolat und Predigtamt*, Kohlhammer, Stuttgart, 1934.

RIESSLER, P. (ed. and trans.), *Altjüdisches Schrifttum ausserhalb der Bibel*, Filsen, Augsburg, 1928.

ROBINSON, J. A. T., *In the end, God...* (Theology for modern man), J. Clarke, S.C.M., 1950.

ROSCHER, W. H. (ed.), *Ausführliches Lexikon der griechischen und römischen Mythologie*, Teubner, Leipzig, 1884f.

ROSTOVTZEV, M., *The Social and Economic History of the Roman Empire*, 2 vols., Oxford University Press, 2nd ed., 1957.

RUINAERT, T., *Acta Martyrum*, C. J. Manz, Ratisbonae, 1859.

RUTHERFORD, W. G. (ed.), *The new Phrynicus*, Macmillan, 1881.

SANDERS, J. N., *The Fourth Gospel in the early Church*, Cambridge University Press, 1943.

SCHEPELERN, V. E., *Der Montanismus und die phrygischen Kulte*, Mohr (Siebeck), Tübingen, 1929.

SCHLATTER, A., *Der Evangelist Matthaeus*, Calwervereinsbuchhandlung, Stuttgart, 1929, 2nd ed., 1933.

SCHLEUSNER, J. F., *Novus Thesaurus*, Weidmann, Leipzig, 1820–1.

SCHLINK, E., *Die Theologie der Lutherischen Bekenntnis-Schriften*, Kaiser, Munich, 2nd ed., 1947.

SCHMIDT, C., *Gespräche Jesu*, Texte und Untersuchung zur Geschichte der altchristlichen Literatur, 43, ed. Harnack, *et al.*, Hinrichs, 1919.

SCHNIEWIND, J., *Evangelion*, C. Bertelsmann, Gutersloh, 1927–31.

SCHOEMANN, G. F., *Griechische Altertumer*, II, Weidmann, Berlin, 4th ed., by J. H. Lipsius, 1897–1902.

SCHÖPS, H.-J., *Paulus*, J. C. B. Mohr (Siebeck), Tübingen, 1959. see also Davies and Daube.

SCHÜRER, E., *Geschichte des Jüdischen Volkes*, 3 vols., Hinrichs, Leipzig, 4th ed., 1909.

SCHWARTZ, E., 'Aporien', *Nachrichten Geschichte der Wissenschaft*, Vandenhoeck und Ruprecht, Göttingen, 1907.

SCHWEIZER, E., 'Die Bekehrung des Apollos', *Evangelische Theologie*, 1955.

SCOTT, S. HERBERT, *The Eastern Church and the Papacy*, Sheed and Ward, 1928.

SEECK, O., *Geschichte des Untergangs der antiken Welt*, 6 vols., Siemennoth and Troschel, 1897–1920.

SEIDL, E., *Der Eid im Ptolemäischen Recht*, (Ph.D. thesis), Akademischen Buchdrückerei F. Straub, Munich, 1929.

—— *Der Eid im röm-agypt. Provinzialrecht*, 2 vols., Beck, Munich, 1933–5.

SELWYN, E. G. (ed.) *The First Epistle of St. Peter*, Macmillan, 1946.

SIHLER, E. G., *From Augustus to Augustine*, Cambridge University Press, 1923.

SODEN, H. VON, 'Mysterion und Sacramentum in der alten Kirche', *Z.N.W.* 1911.

SPENCE-JONES, H. D. M., *The Early Christians in Rome*, Lane, 1910.

STÄHLIN, O., *Clement of Alexandria*, G.C.S., Hinrichs, 1905f.

STEIN, E., *Geschichte des spätrömischen Reiches*, vol. I, Seidel, Vienna, 1927.

STEINACKER, H., *Die antiken Grundlagen der frühmittelalterlichen Privaturkunde*, Teubner, Leipzig, 1927.

STEVENSON, J. (ed.), *A new Eusebius*, S.P.C.K., 1957.

STEVENSON, W. B., *Critical Notes on the Hebrew Text of the Poem of Job*, Aberdeen University Press, 1951.

STRECKER, G., 'Christentum und Judentum in den beiden ersten Jahrhunderten', *Evangelische Theologie*, 1956.

STREETER, B. H., *The Primitive Church*, Macmillan, 1929.

SUKENIK, L., *Jüdische Gräber Jerusalem um Christi Geburt*, 1931.

SYMONDS, H. E., *The Church Universal and the See of Rome*, S.P.C.K., 1939.

TERTULLIAN, *see* Evans.

THOMAS, J., *Le Mouvement Baptiste*, J. Duculot, Gembloux, 1935.

THOMPSON, SIR D'ARCY W., *A Glossary of Greek Birds*, Oxford, 2nd ed., 1936.

TROJE, L., 'The Platonic and Manichean Conception of Matter', *Museum Helveticum*, 5, 1948.

TURNER, H. E. W., *The Pattern of Christian Truth*, Mowbray, 1954.

USENER, H., 'Milch und Honig', *Kleine Schriften*, Teubner, Leipzig, 1912.

VIELHAUER, P., 'Zum Paulinismus der Apostelgeschichte', *Evangelische Theologie*, 1950.

VÖLKER, W. (ed.), *Quellen zur Geschichte des Gnosis*, Mohr, Tübingen, 1932.

WALLACE-HADRILL, J. M., 'Gothia and Romania', *Bulletin of the John Rylands Library*, 1961.

WEBER, W., *Der Prophet und sein Gott*, Hinrichs, Leipzig, 1925.

WEISS, B., *Die Quellen des Lukas-Evangeliums*, J. G. Cotta, Tübingen, 1907.

WENGER, L., *Institutionen des römischen Zivilprozesses*, Hueber, Munich, 1925.

WEST, E. W. (ed. and trans.), *Pahlavi Texts*, 5 vols., Oxford University Press, 1880–97.

WETTE, W. M. L., DE, *Kurze Erklärung der Apostelgeschichte* (Kurzgefasstes exegetisches Handbuch zum Neuen Testament 4), 4th ed., by Overbeck, Weidman, Leipzig, 1870.

WILDBERGER, H., 'Manual of Discipline', *Evangelische Theologie*, 1953.

WILLIAMS, C. S. C., *Alterations to the Text of the Synoptic Gospels and Acts*, Blackwell, Oxford, 1951.

WILSON, R. McL., *The Gnostic Problem*, Mowbray, 1958.

WINDISCH, H., *Taufe und Sünde*, Mohr, Tübingen, 1908.

—— *Die katholischen Briefe*, Handbuch zum neuen Testament, 15, Mohr, Tübingen, 2nd ed., 1930.

—— *Der Hebräer-Brief*, Mohr, Tübingen, 2nd ed. 1931.

ZAHN, T., *Geschichte des neutestamentlichen Kanons*, 2 vols., Deichert, Erlangen, 1888–92.

—— *Evangelium der Matthaeus*, Deichert, Erlangen, 1903.

Zeitschrift der Savigny Stift, rom. Abt., 1955.

ZEND-AVESTA, *The Zend-Avesta*, trans. J. Darmsteter (Sacred Books of the East), Oxford, 1883.

ZUCKER, H., *Geschichte der Jüdischen Selbstverwaltung in Ägypten*, C. H. Beck, Munich, 1934.

INDEX

OLD TESTAMENT

NEW TESTAMENT

325

GENERAL